Charles Macklin and
the Theatres of London

Eighteenth-Century Worlds

Series Editors:
Professor Eve Rosenhaft (Liverpool) and Dr Mark Towsey (Liverpool)

Eighteenth-Century Worlds promotes innovative new research in the political, social, economic, intellectual and cultural life of the 'long' eighteenth century (c. 1650–c. 1850), from a variety of historical, theoretical and critical perspectives. Monographs published in the series adopt international, comparative and/or interdisciplinary approaches to the global eighteenth century, in volumes that make the results of specialist research accessible to an informed, but not discipline-specific, audience.

Charles Macklin and the Theatres of London

Edited by
Ian Newman and David O'Shaughnessy

LIVERPOOL UNIVERSITY PRESS

First published 2022 by
Liverpool University Press
4 Cambridge Street
Liverpool
L69 7ZU

Copyright © 2022 Liverpool University Press

Ian Newman and David O'Shaughnessy have asserted the right to be identified as the editors of this book in accordance with the Copyright, Designs and Patents Act 1988.

All rights reserved. No part of this book may be reproduced, stored in a retrieval system, or transmitted, in any form or by any means, electronic, mechanical, photocopying, recording, or otherwise, without the prior written permission of the publisher.

British Library Cataloguing-in-Publication data
A British Library CIP record is available

ISBN 978-1-80085-598-4 cased
ISBN 978-1-80085-691-2 limp

Typeset by Carnegie Book Production, Lancaster
Printed and bound by CPI Group (UK) Ltd, Croydon CR0 4YY

Contents

List of Illustrations   vii

List of Plates   x

List of Tables   xi

List of Abbreviations   xii

List of Contributors   xiii

Acknowledgements   xvii

Introduction: Macklin and the Performance of Enlightenment   1
   Ian Newman and David O'Shaughnessy

Representing Macklin

1 Macklin's Look   23
   David Francis Taylor

2 Macklin's Books   55
   Paul Goring

3 Macklin in the Theatre, the Courts, and the News   73
   Manushag Powell

4 'Strong Case': Macklin and the Law   91
   David Worrall

5 Macklin and the Novel   111
    Ros Ballaster

Theatre

6 Macklin as Theatre Manager   131
    Matthew Kinservik

7 Macklin and Song   149
    Ian Newman

8 Ethnic Jokes and Polite Language: Soft Othering and
    Macklin's British Comedies   173
    Michael Brown

9 Macklin and Censorship   193
    David O'Shaughnessy

Sociability

10 Macklin's Coffeehouse: Public Sociability in
     Mid-Eighteenth-Century London   215
     Markman Ellis

11 Macklin's Talking 'Wrongheads': The British Inquisition and
     the Public Sphere   243
     Helen Burke

Restaging Macklin

12 Restaging Macklin   265
     Nicholas Johnson

13 *Love à la Mode* in Performance: A Dialogue   281
     Colm Summers and Nicholas Johnson

Bibliography   295

Index   313

Illustrations

1.1 John Lodge, *Mr Macklin in the Character of Shylock, in Shakespeare's Merchant of Venice* (London: T. Wright, 1 November 1775). Metropolitan Museum of Art, New York.   26

1.2 Henry Cook, after Johann Heinrich Ramberg, *Mr Macklin in Shylock* (London: John Cawthorn, 20 January 1806). By permission of the Folger Shakespeare Library, Washington, DC.   29

1.3 *Mr Macklin in the Character of Shylock* (London: J. Wenman, 1 June 1777). By permission of the Folger Shakespeare Library, Washington, DC.   32

1.4 James Newton, after John Kitchingman, *Mr Macklin as Shylock* (London: W. Lewis and J. Russell, 27 February 1784). By permission of the Folger Shakespeare Library, Washington, DC.   33

1.5 *An Infallible Recipe to Make a Wicked Manager of a Theatre* (Chester, 20 August 1750). © Victoria and Albert Museum, London.   35

1.6 Frontispiece to *An Apology for the Conduct of Mr Charles Macklin, Comedian* (London: T. Axtell, 1773). By permission of the Folger Shakespeare Library, Washington, DC.   38

1.7 *Mr Macklin, In the Character of Macbeth, Act II^d Scene 3^d* (n.d.). By permission of the Folger Shakespeare Library, Washington, DC.   40

1.8 *Roscius in Triumph, or the downfall of Shylock alias Mackbeth* (*Macaroni, Savoir Vivre and Magazine*, 1 December 1773). © The Trustees of the British Museum.   41

1.9 Inigo Barlow, *Monument to the Memory of David Garrick, Esq.ʳ* (London: W. Bent, 3 August 1797). By permission of the Folger Shakespeare Library, Washington, DC.   43

1.10 *Shylock turnd Macbeth* (London: M. Darby, 5 November 1773). © Victoria and Albert Museum, London.   44

1.11 James Hook, *The Trial* (London: S.W. Fores, 17 May 1788). Courtesy of The Lewis Walpole Library, Yale University.   46

1.12 John Boyne, *Mr Macklin & Mrs Pope in the Characters of Shylock and Portia* (London: J. Boyne, 1 April 1789). © Victoria and Albert Museum, London.   48

1.13 Detail of John Boyne, *Sir Zealous Godfrey* (London: H. Humphrey, 7 April 1784). Courtesy of The Lewis Walpole Library, Yale University.   50

1.14 John Boyne, *The Adventure of Prince Pretty Man* (London: J. Boyne, [1783]). Courtesy of The Lewis Walpole Library, Yale University.   51

7.1 Thomas Arne, 'Serenade', in *The Songs and Duetto, in the Blind Beggar of Bethnal Green … with the Favourite Songs Sung by Mr Lowe in the Merchant of Venice* (London, 1740). © The British Library Board (Music Collections G.320.f).   157

7.2 Thomas Arne, 'To Keep my Gentle Jesse', *The Songs and Duetto, in the Blind Beggar of Bethnal Green … with the Favourite Songs Sung by Mr Lowe in the Merchant of Venice* (London, 1740). © The British Library Board (Music Collections G.320.f).   159

7.3a–c 'You Never Did Hear of an Irishman's Fear', *Crosby's Irish Musical Repository* (London, 1813), 119–21. Reproduced from the original held by the Department of Special Collections of the Hesburgh Libraries of the University of Notre Dame, Indiana.   164–65

7.4a–c 'Let Other Men Sing of their Goddesses Bright', *Crosby's Irish Musical Repository* (London, 1813), 129–31. Reproduced from the original held by the Department of Special Collections of the Hesburgh Libraries of the University of Notre Dame, Indiana.   170–71

9.1 Charles Macklin, *A Will and No Will*, LA 58, f. 20v, John Larpent Collection, The Huntington Library, San Marino, California. 200

9.2 Charles Macklin, *Covent Garden Theatre*, LA 96, f. 19v, John Larpent Collection, The Huntington Library, San Marino, California. 204

9.3 'Iphigenia' (Elizabeth Pierrepont [née Chudleigh, later Hervey], Duchess of Kingston), by unknown artist. Attributed to Charles Mosley. © National Portrait Gallery, London. 206

10.1 *The Robin Hood* (1 June 1752), Lewis Walpole Library, 752.06.01.01+. Courtesy of the Lewis Walpole Library, Yale University. 235

11.1 'The British Inquisition or Common Sence in Danger/Oh Thou Head of the Wrongheads', British Museum, London (Ref. 1868,0808.3977). 245

Plates

1 Mordecai (Colm Gleeson) courts a sceptical Charlotte (Caitlin Scott). [Smock Alley, 2017]. Photograph by Colm Summers.

2 Clutching only his script and a balloon sword, Sir Callaghan O'Brallaghan (Fionn Foley) prepares to defend himself from Sir Archy Macsarcasm (Leonard Buckley). [Smock Alley, 2017]. Photograph by Colm Summers.

3 Squire Groom (Norma Howard) re-enacts his Newmarket escapades, helped by Mordecai (Colm Gleeson) and Sir Archy (Leonard Buckley), as the Harlequin (Honi Cooke) eggs him on. [Smock Alley, 2017]. Photograph by Colm Summers.

4 The ensemble cast sing themselves out as the play comes to an end. [Smock Alley, 2017]. Photograph by Colm Summers.

5 An amorous Sir Archy (Colm Lennon) applies the Scottish method to a bemused Charlotte (Caitlin Scott). [Smock Alley, 2018]. Photograph by John Cooney.

6 Mordecai (Fionnuala Gygax) woos Charlotte (Caitlin Scott) with some deft dance moves. [Smock Alley, 2018]. Photograph by John Cooney.

7 Johan Zoffany, unfinished theatrical conversation piece, with Charles Macklin as Shylock (*c.*1768). © Tate.

8 Johan Zoffany, *Charles Macklin as Shylock in The Merchant of Venice*. The Holburne Museum, Bath/Bridgeman Images.

Tables

10.1 British Inquisition lecture topics   234
10.2 British Inquisition debate questions   236
10.3 Macklin's model of 'polyhedonic sociability'   240

Abbreviations

Appleton William W. Appleton, *Charles Macklin: An Actor's Life* (Cambridge, MA: Harvard University Press, 1960)
Congreve Francis Aspry Congreve, *Authentic Memoirs of the Late Mr Charles Macklin, Comedian* (London, 1798)
Cooke William Cooke, *Memoirs of Charles Macklin, Comedian* (London, 1804)
Kirkman James Thomas Kirkman, *Memoirs of the life of Charles Macklin, Esq. principally compiled from his own papers and memorandums*, 2 vols (London, 1799)

Contributors

Ros Ballaster is Professor of Eighteenth-Century Studies in the Faculty of English, Oxford University at Mansfield College. Her particular research interests are in oriental fiction, women's writing, drama, and performance. She is author of three monographs: *Seductive Forms: Women's Amatory Fiction, 1684–1740* (1992); *Fabulous Orients: Fictions of the East in England, 1662–1785* (2005); and, most recently, *Fictions of Presence: Theatre and Novel in Eighteenth-Century England* (2020).

Michael Brown holds a Chair of Irish, Scottish and Enlightenment History at the University of Aberdeen, where he is also co-director of the Research Institute of Irish and Scottish Studies. He is the author of *Francis Hutcheson in Dublin* (2002); *A Political Biography of John Toland* (2012); and *The Irish Enlightenment* (2016). He is a commissioning editor of the Routledge book series 'Poetry and Song in the Age of Revolution' (7 volumes to date). He is currently writing a textbook entitled *A Cultural History of Europe, 1688–1914* and a collection of interlocking essays, *Making Up Britain in the Eighteenth Century*.

Helen Burke is Professor Emerita of English at Florida State University. She is the author of *Riotous Performances: The Struggle for Hegemony in the Irish Theatre, 1712–1784* (2003) and numerous articles on eighteenth-century theatre. Recent publications include 'The Catholic Question, Print Media, and John O'Keeffe's *The Poor Soldier* (1783)', *Eighteenth-Century Fiction* (2015); 'The Irish Joke, Migrant Networks, and the London Irish in the 1680s', *Eighteenth-Century Life* (2015); and 'Samuel Whyte and the Irish Private Theatrical Movement of the 1760 and 1770s', in *Irish Literature in Transition, 1700–1780* (2020).

Markman Ellis is Professor of Eighteenth-Century Studies at Queen Mary University of London. He is the author of *The Politics of Sensibility: Race, Gender and Commerce in the Sentimental Novel* (1996); *The History of Gothic Fiction* (2000); *The Coffee-House: A Cultural History* (2004); and co-author of *Empire of Tea* (2015). He edited *Eighteenth-Century Coffee-House Culture* (2006) and co-edited *Tea and the Tea-Table in Eighteenth-Century England* (2010). He is currently working on sociability and intellectual culture in London in the mid-eighteenth century, focusing in particular on the Hardwicke and Bluestocking circles.

Paul Goring is Professor of British Literature and Culture at the Norwegian University of Science and Technology in Trondheim. He has published essays on Charles Macklin in *Representations*, *Review of English Studies*, and elsewhere and is the editor of a volume of texts pertaining to Macklin in the Pickering & Chatto series *Lives of Shakespearian Actors*. He has in addition published many essays on Laurence Sterne and is the author of *The Rhetoric of Sensibility in Eighteenth-Century Culture* (2005) and *British Literature and Culture* (2008). He has edited fiction by Sterne and Samuel Johnson for Penguin Classics and, more recently, has edited a collection of essays on the history of news and newspapers (2018).

Nicholas Johnson is Associate Professor of Drama at Trinity College Dublin, where he directs the Trinity Centre for Beckett Studies and convenes the college-wide Creative Arts Practice research theme. Monographs include *Experimental Beckett* (2020) and *Bertolt Brecht and the David Fragments* (2020), and he co-edited the collections *Beckett's Voices / Voicing Beckett* (2021) and *Influencing Beckett / Beckett Influencing* (2020). With Jonathan Heron (Warwick), he co-founded the Samuel Beckett Laboratory and co-edited special issues on performance (23.1, 2014) and pedagogy (29.1, 2020) for the *Journal of Beckett Studies*. He works as a dramaturg with Pan Pan and Dead Centre. Directing credits include *Virtual Play* after Samuel Beckett (1st prize, New European Media awards).

Matthew J. Kinservik is Professor of English and Vice Provost for Faculty Affairs at the University of Delaware. He holds degrees from the University of Wisconsin–Madison (BA & MA) and the Pennsylvania State University (PhD). He has taught at Delaware since 1997, primarily offering courses in literature and theatre, with an emphasis on eighteenth-century Britain. His books include *Disciplining Satire: The Censorship of Satiric Comedy on the Eighteenth-Century London Stage* (2002) and *Sex, Scandal, and Celebrity in Late Eighteenth-Century England* (2007). He has published articles on drama, literature, and theatre history in *Theatre Survey*, *PQ*, *The British Journal of Eighteenth-Century Studies*, *Huntington Library Quarterly*, *Harvard Library Bulletin*, and elsewhere.

Ian Newman is Associate Professor of English at the University of Notre Dame and a fellow of the Keough-Naughton Institute for Irish Studies. He specializes in eighteenth- and nineteenth-century British and Irish literature. He is the author of *The Romantic Tavern: Literature and Conviviality in the Age of Revolution* (2019); co-editor of *Charles Dibdin and Late Georgian Culture* (2018); and he edited a Special Issue of *Studies in Romanticism* on 'Song and the City'. He is also responsible for a digital project tracing the meeting places of the London Corresponding Society and is a contributing editor to the Keats Letters Project.

David O'Shaughnessy is Professor of Eighteenth-Century Studies at the National University of Ireland, Galway. He is the author of *William Godwin and the Theatre* (2010) and editor of *The Plays of William Godwin* (2010). Most recently, he edited *Ireland, Enlightenment and the English Stage, 1740–1820* (2019) and co-edited *The Letters of Oliver Goldsmith* (2018). His website on eighteenth- and nineteenth-century theatre censorship is available at https://tobeomitted.tcd.ie. With Michael Griffin, he is a general editor of a new 8-volume edition of *The Collected Works of Oliver Goldsmith* for Cambridge University Press.

Manushag N. Powell is Professor of English at Purdue University. She is the author of *Performing Authorship in Eighteenth-Century English Periodicals*, co-author with Fred Burwick of *British Pirates in Print and Performance*, editor with Jennie Batchelor of the Edinburgh *Women's Periodicals and Print Culture in Britain, 1690–1820*, and the editor of the Broadview edition of Daniel Defoe's *Captain Singleton*. Research interests include eighteenth-century periodicals, theatricals, piraticals, and dragon musicals.

Colm Summers is an artist–scholar and theatre director. Recent credits include *Pseudaria* (Live Collision, 2017–2018), *Papini* (Dublin Fringe, 2017), *Love à la Mode* (Smock Alley, 2017–2018), *Gays Against the Free State!* (Dublin Fringe, 2016), and *God's Ear* (Samuel Beckett Theatre, 2015). He co-directed *Enemy of the Stars* after Wyndham Lewis (Dublin and Morocco, 2015, winner of Best Experimental Theatre award at Fez International Theatre Festival) and published on the project in *BLAST at 100* (2017). He co-founded Felicity, a collective making work in Dublin and New York, and has worked with Dead Centre, Pan Pan, and the Wooster Group. He is currently training for an MFA in directing at Columbia University.

David Francis Taylor is Associate Professor of Eighteenth-Century Literature at the University of Oxford, where he is a Fellow of St Hugh's College. He is co-editor of *The Oxford Handbook of the Georgian Theatre, 1737–1832* (2014) and author of *Theatres of Opposition: Empire, Revolution, and Richard Brinsley Sheridan* (2012) and *The Politics of Parody: A Literary History of Caricature, 1760–1830* (2018).

David Worrall is Emeritus Professor in English Literature at Nottingham Trent University. He is the author of *Theatric Revolution: Drama Censorship and Romantic Period Subcultures* (2006); *Harlequin Empire: Harlequin Empire: Race, Ethnicity and the Drama of the Popular Enlightenment* (2007); *The Politics of Romantic Theatricality, 1787–1832: The Road to the Stage* (2007); and *Celebrity, Performance, Reception: British Georgian Drama as Social Assemblage* (2013). Other publications include essays in *A Cultural History of Theatre*, ed. Mechele Leon, Tracy C. Davis, and Christopher B. Balme (2018); *Oxford Handbook to British Romanticism*, ed. David Duff (2019); and *Teaching Laboring-Class British Literature of the Eighteenth and Nineteenth Centuries*, ed. Kevin Binfield and William Christmas (2019). In 2018, he abridged Horace Walpole's *The Mysterious Mother* for a staged reading at Yale University.

Acknowledgements

THIS VOLUME EMERGES from a symposium on Charles Macklin held at the University of Notre Dame's London Global Gateway in July 2018. We would like to thank all the speakers and respondents at the conference, especially Amanda Weldy Boyd, Oskar Cox Jensen, Georgina Lock, and Joshua Wright.

Generous funding for this event was kindly provided by Notre Dame Research, the Institute for Scholarship in the Liberal Arts, College of Arts and Letters, and the Keough-Naughton Institute for Irish Studies at the University of Notre Dame; and the Long Room Hub, Arts and Humanities Research Institute and the School of English at Trinity College Dublin. We are very grateful to all these bodies for their support. We would also like to express our tremendous gratitude to Joanna Byrne, Charlotte Parkyn, Lauri Roberts, and the wonderful staff of the London Global Gateway for their warm hospitality and exemplary professionalism, which ensured the smooth running of the symposium.

The event was greatly enriched by a performance of *Love à la Mode* by Felicity Theatre, after a demanding two-week run at Smock Alley Theatre. We are extremely grateful to the director and cast who travelled over from Dublin to illuminate the conference: Honi Cooke, Morgan Cooke, Colm Gleeson, Fionnuala Gygax, Stephen O'Leary, Caitlin Scott, and Colm Summers. Thanks are also due to producer Michael Stone who was instrumental in the planning of the performance.

This volume has received generous subvention from the Institute for Scholarship in the Liberal Arts, College of Arts and Letters Notre Dame, and the Trinity College Dublin Association & Trust. We gratefully acknowledge this vital support which allowed the reproduction of the colour plates. Thanks to Alison Rice for her support of this project from its inception, and to Peter Holland for his moral and bibliographic support.

Finally, we would like to thank Liverpool University Press for their adroit shepherding of the book from inception through to publication. In particular, we are grateful to Alison Welsby for commissioning the volume, Emma Burridge for seeing it through the process, and to Sarah Warren at Carnegie for assistance with production. Thanks also to the anonymous readers whose suggestions and advice were helpful and constructive.

Introduction
Macklin and the Performance of Enlightenment

Ian Newman and David O'Shaughnessy

In *Retrospections of the Stage*, the actor John Bernard told the story of an encounter between Charles Macklin and Samuel Johnson:

> The Ursa Major of literature paid the Ursa Major of theatricals a visit, to ascertain the extent of his pretensions. Macklin showed him his library, and seemed to have a sufficient knowledge of every work it contained. They then sat down to converse, and rambled over a variety of subjects, upon all of which Macklin kept his legs, to the Doctor's satisfaction. When grappling on a level ground of an equally well understood question, their strength seemed to be equal. The Doctor, nevertheless, was desirous of overthrowing him before they parted, and touched on the score of his classic attainments. Greek and Latin the actor knew as intimately as French and Italian, and defended himself grammatically and colloquially, from every thrust of the lexicographer. Johnson, growing more determined from the failure of his attempts, at length addressed him with a string of sounds perfectly unintelligible. 'What's that, Sir?' inquired Macklin. 'Hebrew!' answered Johnson. 'And what do I know of Hebrew?'—'But a man of your understanding, Mr. Macklin, ought to be acquainted with every language!' The Doctor's face glowed with a smile of triumph.—'Och neil end eigen vonsht hom boge vaureen!' exclaimed Macklin. Johnson was now dumb-founded, and inquired the name of the lingua? 'Irish, Sir!'—'Irish!' exclaimed the Doctor. 'Do you think I ever studied that?'—'But a man of your understanding, Doctor Johnson, ought to be acquainted with every language!'[1]

The anecdote gets to the heart of several of the preoccupations of this volume—Macklin's claims to learning, his sociability, and his Irishness.

---

1 John Bernard, *Retrospections of the Stage*, 2 vols (London, 1830), II.125–26.

We'll discuss each in more detail in what follows, but for now what matters is what might appear to us a questionable bit of hyperbole, concerning the equivalent status of Johnson and Macklin—'the Ursa Major of literature' and 'the Ursa Major of theatricals', as Bernard would have it. Part of the ambition of this volume is to assert the validity of this claim. As James Robert Wood has recently noted, anecdotes are 'little Enlightenments' that tend to 'unsettle conventional notions of what was central and what was peripheral in human life'.[2] Clearly, John Bernard—a theatrical practitioner himself, and a well-known teller of tall tales—is biased in his narrative towards Macklin's part, and inevitably the pugnacious Macklin gets one better over his learned disputant, suggesting perhaps the glee of the victory of the underdog, and an attempt to unsettle literary hierarchies. Certainly, the story suggests the greater cultural capital of the literary over the theatrical, not to mention the English over the Irish, but, with those qualifications acknowledged, the claim that if Johnson was the accepted sovereign of the literary domain Macklin was the equivalent in the theatre is worth investigating.

It is true that we don't speak of the Age of Macklin in the same way that we speak of the Age of Johnson. Indeed, if eras are to be measured out in exemplary male names (something we should be wary of for many reasons), we are more likely to speak of the Age of Garrick than that of Macklin, not least, as Leslie Ritchie has shown, because of Garrick's powerful grip on Georgian media.[3] Garrick's canny management of his public persona has skewed our view of the mid-century theatrical world so it is worthwhile pointing out that when Garrick and Macklin trod the boards together—which they did frequently in the early 1740s—Macklin was the senior partner. While Garrick is acknowledged as the great promotor of Shakespeare, helping 'The Bard' achieve his insurmountable position at the pinnacle of the literary totem, Macklin's restaging of *The Merchant of Venice* in 1741, a production that pointedly left behind George Granville's *The Jew of Venice* and reinstated much of Shakespeare's original text, significantly paved the way for many of Garrick's innovations. And while Garrick is frequently credited with a revolution in acting style, abandoning the more declamatory manners of the early eighteenth century in favour of a more 'naturalistic' acting style, Macklin too championed a less bombastic mode of delivery, and had indeed served as Garrick's acting teacher, notably coaching him for his breakthrough role as *Richard III* at Drury Lane in 1741.

---

2 James Robert Wood, *Anecdotes of Enlightenment: Human Nature from Locke to Wordsworth* (Charlottesville: University of Virginia Press, 2020), 3, 8.

3 Leslie Ritchie, *David Garrick and the Mediation of Celebrity* (Cambridge: Cambridge University Press, 2019).

The reasons why we don't talk of the Age of Macklin are doubtlessly numerous, but among them is surely because we'd be hard-pressed to identify which Age we were talking about, a point that can be illustrated by another anecdote concerning Macklin and a man well known to both Johnson and Garrick: Edmund Burke.

In 1752, Henry Fielding and John 'the Inspector' Hill were firing printed barbs at each other over the truth of Elizabeth Canning's claim that she had been abducted for the purposes of prostitution. Fielding believed the young woman whereas Hill did not. Edmund Burke, who had been in London for just two years after departing from Ireland, took the part of Fielding in support of Canning's veracity and penned a brief and unpublished satire at Hill's expense: 'A funeral oration on the Inspector to be pronounced in the Bedford Coffee House by Mr. Macklin'. It has been speculated that Burke and Macklin may have collaborated on this and it was certainly possible that they did.[4] The pair would have been known to each other from Robin Hood Society meetings and it has even been said that Burke first tried his oratory at Macklin's British Inquisition in 1754.[5] Collaboration or not, it is not surprising that the fresh-faced Burke looked to Macklin to give one of his very earliest works some cultural heft. For while the young legal student was then only about twenty-two, Macklin had a quarter-century of experience acting on London's main theatres. More than twice Burke's age in 1752, Macklin had fame and infamy in equal measure behind him and was one of London's best known cultural figures. But although he conceived of the British Inquisition as a retirement plan, he had plenty more left in the tank: despite being at the point of retirement when Burke started his lengthy career, Macklin outlived Burke by two days when they both died in July 1797.

Macklin's professional longevity is truly astounding, even by twenty-first-century standards. Much of his early life is clouded in mystery and speculation, and there is some controversy about when he was born, hence we have been cautious throughout this volume in providing his exact age at various moments. Some accounts suggest Macklin was born as early as 1690 while others indicate he was born in 1699 in Donegal, the latter date being the more usually accepted figure. Macklin moved to Dublin as a young child, then moved to England in around 1710. At some point around the early 1720s Macklin established himself as a working actor, first as a strolling player having joined a travelling troupe headed by Charles Fleetwood. We can say

---

4 Macklin lectured on the Canning case at the British Inquisition. *Appleton*, 104.
5 George W. Cooke, *The History of Party; From the Rise of the Whig and Tory Factions, in the Reign of Charles II, to the Passing of the Reform Bill*, 3 vols (London, 1836–1837), III.66.

with some certainty that his professional acting career in London began in 1725 when he was engaged by John Rich to perform Alcander in Dryden and Lee's *Oedipus* at Lincoln's Inn Theatre.[6]

It seems likely that Macklin continued to perform in provincial theatres in the late 1720s and early 1730s but there were sporadic appearances at Lincoln's Inn and Goodman's Fields theatres. When Theophilus Cibber led a walkout of actors from Drury Lane in May 1733, this presented an opportunity for Macklin to establish himself at the patent theatre. He took on many of the comic roles that Cibber had previously performed, such as Whisper in *The Busy Body*, Clodio in *Love Makes a Man*, and Teague in *The Committee*. Matthew Kinservik shows Macklin became established in Drury Lane in this decade to the point that he became *consigliere* to manager Charles Fleetwood—despite the small matter of a murder charge in 1735 (which only interrupted his career for six weeks). He continued to add role after role to his repertoire and grew sufficiently confident to have a physical altercation with James Quin, Drury Lane's alpha male star, after Quin threw a piece of apple at Macklin's head.

The watershed moment in his career was of course the 1740–41 season when he played Shylock. After that success, he added other Shakespearean roles to his list, notably Malvolio in *Twelfth Night* and Touchstone in *As You Like It*. Before they fell out, in 1743, Macklin and Garrick acted beside each other in *The Old Bachelor* (Noll Bluff and Fondlewife), *The Wedding Day* (Stedfast and Millamour), and *Jane Shore* (Duke of Gloucester and Hastings). Thomas Sheridan lured Macklin and his wife Ann to Dublin for the 1748–49 and 1749–50 seasons with an offer of £800 a season, but this did not end well (Macklin did not get paid and had to sue Sheridan). The Macklins returned to London and signed for John Rich's Covent Garden in 1750 where they would regularly act alongside each other. In 1751, Macklin supervised Sir Francis Delaval and other aristocrats in a performance of *Othello* at Drury Lane: such was the level of public interest that the House of Commons adjourned two hours early to allow members to attend.

Macklin seems to have tired somewhat of the theatre in the early 1750s. He added very few new roles to his *curriculum vitae* and retired for the first time on 20 December 1753 when he played Sir Gilbert Wrangle in Colley Cibber's *The Refusal* alongside his wife and his daughter Maria. After stepping back from the stage he opened a coffeehouse in the Piazza of Covent Garden,

---

6 *Appleton*, 18. This engagement is listed in both *Congreve* (12) and *Cooke* (12–13), but Appleton points out that there is no mention of Macklin's name in the Lincoln's Inn Fields MS list of performances, and indeed it hasn't been verified outside of these sources.

but, as Helen Burke and Markman Ellis document in this volume, Macklin's commercial venture was a failure and he had to return to theatrical matters. Records of his activities in the late 1750s are patchy but we can record that Ann Macklin died in December 1758 and that Macklin found love again very shortly afterwards with Elizabeth, a young servant in his house, although they did not formally marry until 1778.

When he offered *Love à la Mode* to Garrick's Drury Lane in 1759, Macklin was astute enough to insist on his playing the part of Sir Archy Macsarcasm as a condition. As David Worrall discusses in this volume, he guarded the copyright of this, his greatest success, with ferocity but we perhaps don't always remember that it was the means by which he got himself reinstated to the stage. In 1760–61, he and Maria moved to Covent Garden but he sailed for Dublin again in 1761 where he had tremendous success at Crow Street Theatre. He shuttled between Dublin and London, and various theatres in those cities for the rest of the 1760s and early 1770s. In his early seventies at this point, he also spent time coaching young actors in Dublin. And of course he had added the part of Sir Pertinax Macsycophant from *The Man of the World* to his roles. The *Macbeth* performance in 1773 and subsequent court case were followed by periodic illness, which restricted his stage performances (7 appearances in 1779–80; 14 in 1780–81, 12 in 1781–82). He had brief engagements in Manchester and Dublin in the 1780s as well as London. He was now being very well rewarded: in February 1784, he was paid £126 for four nights' work. But age did begin to wither him: deafness and forgetfulness were increasingly a problem.

His career ended on Thursday evening, 7 May 1789, when he played Shylock for his benefit night at Covent Garden. After a remarkable forty-eight years of playing the role, his memory finally failed him and at about eighty-nine years of age he shuffled off the stage after delivering a few early speeches. The *Gazetteer and New Daily Advertiser* noted poignantly:

> Poor old Macklin may be said to have taken his final leave of the stage last Thursday night. He came forward weighed down with these infirmities natural to a man entering on the last ten years of a century in this world, and, addressing himself to the audience, prayed their indulgence to accept a substitute in the character of Shylock, for he found himself at last unequal to the task ... There was something so affecting in what may be called his Farewell Speech, that the audience looked with reverence at the Father of the Stage, and giving the old man an universal hand of applause, he retired.[7]

A near half-century playing a major Shakespearean role in London's patent theatres is an astonishing achievement; playing the part in his eighties in

---

7 *Gazetteer and New Daily Advertiser*, 9 May 1789.

a period when the average life span was around forty for urban London is remarkable.[8] Shylock is undoubtedly the part that we remember him best for today but this volume adumbrates the many other aspects of his varied career. It is, we think, uncontentious to situate Macklin as one of the great theatrical personalities of the century. After getting his start with Rich, he worked with (and occasionally against) figures such as Charles Fleetwood, Peg Woffington, David Garrick, Tate Wilkinson, and Thomas Sheridan to name a few. As well as Shylock (purported to have given George II nightmares) he was well known for his roles as Sir Archy Macsarcasm and Sir Hector MacCrafty, satirical Scottish types that he both wrote and played to audiences who were tickled and scandalized by these outrageous stereotypes. He wrote the only eighteenth-century play twice refused a performance licence by the Examiner of Plays. He gave public lectures on matters theatrical, as well as acting classes—even, as we have seen, to a young David Garrick. Quite right then that he was referred to reverentially in the press as the 'Father of the Stage'. But to make a claim for him as a figure of Enlightenment is a rather bolder assertion, requiring more careful substantiation.

The encounter between Macklin and Johnson related by Bernard offers a helpful starting point, as it illustrates quite pointedly that Macklin was keen to be seen as a man of learning, one who could and would directly engage major Enlightenment figures of the day. As Paul Goring points out in his discussion of Macklin's library in this volume, one effect of considering the books that Macklin owned is 'the solidification of the idea of him as a serious, engaged thinker' who was 'a participant in the intellectual culture of his time'.[9] How many of the 3,000 or so books that were auctioned off after his death Macklin had in fact read is impossible to know, but at the very least the library (Macklin's second book collection, after the first was lost at sea) suggests someone with intellectual aspirations, who wanted to be seen and understood as a figure of learning.[10] The library example and the uncertainty as to how many of those books were actually read by him is a useful way to approach the idea of Macklin as performing Enlightenment. This is not to suggest a lack of substance, an insincerity on his part nor indeed a dismissiveness to his contributions to Georgian culture; rather, thinking of Macklin's life as a

---

8 The figures for life expectancy are skewed considerably by high infant mortality rates. Nevertheless, surviving until 1797 demonstrates no little resilience on Macklin's part. For details about life expectancy, see E.A. Wrigley, et al. *English Population History from Family Reconstitution, 1580–1837* (Cambridge: Cambridge University Press, 1997).
9 Paul Goring, 'Macklin's Books', 69, in this volume.
10 Paul Goring, 'The Sinking of Charles Macklin's Scholarship', *Notes and Queries* 66.4 (2019), 577–81.

performance of Enlightenment allow us an unusually appropriate metaphor for considering the many facets to this theatrical practitioner's career while retaining an appropriate degree of critical scepticism as to the magnitude of his *intellectual* achievement. Macklin was not Samuel Johnson or Edmund Burke but the significance of his socio-cultural contribution to London over many decades and the drive towards self-improvement demand, we argue, consideration within the category of Enlightenment. The various contributors to this volume each have their own take on the importance of Macklin, and each reflects the particular prism by which Macklin is viewed, as is perhaps appropriate for such a varied and multifaceted career. Macklin performed many parts on the many stages of London's cultural life during his career: even though he never produced a truly great piece of literary writing, his lived experience and his theatrical influence affected generations of London's population. Overall though, the evidence of his various contributions suggests the importance of a capacious and more inclusive understanding of Enlightenment while insisting that Macklin retains true to its traditional core values of self-improvement and daring to know.

There is every reason to think that Macklin's intellectual ambition was sincere and was pursued with some considerable conviction. Markman Ellis delineates in careful detail the focused intellectual curiosity revealed by Macklin's Commonplace Book: 'a practice of note-taking, memory, and information control, but [he] also repurposed and transformed that practice, so as to a create an idiosyncratic but flexible system for creative composition, in which information retrieval allowed Macklin to establish synchronic connection between topics and ideas'.[11] In his contribution to this volume David O'Shaughnessy argues that Macklin's plays exhibit an unacknowledged coherence. Collectively, they constitute a consistent intellectual project that aims beyond party politics to expose hypocrisy in all its shapes. With these various plays, Macklin strives to reform society as a whole.[12]

Throughout the chapters that appear in this volume (the chapters by Burke, Goring, O'Shaughnessy, and David Worrall most notable among them), Macklin emerges as a man with strong intellectual aspirations. Whether this qualifies him as a figure of the Enlightenment, however, requires a more considered rationale. By considering Macklin as 'an Enlightenment figure' our ambitions are multiple. First, we want to address Ian McBride's suggestions that the theatre is one of the unexamined 'institutional structures of the

---

11 Markman Ellis, 'Macklin's Coffeehouse', 218, in this volume.
12 See David O'Shaughnessy, 'Macklin and Censorship' in this volume and '"Bit, by some mad whig": Charles Macklin and the Theater of Irish Enlightenment', *Huntington Library Quarterly* 80.4 (2017), 560, 567.

Irish Enlightenment'.[13] This claim is itself part of a larger body of work that reconsiders Ireland's place in the Enlightenment, expressed most clearly in Michael Brown's ground-breaking *The Irish Enlightenment*. 'Ireland was not in a moribund catatonic state in the eighteenth century', Brown asserts, 'Rather it was a vigorous and controversial participant in the transcontinental experiment of creating a modern world'.[14] Following McBride, this volume takes the theatre seriously as one of the most powerful means of experimenting with notions that lay the foundations for modernity, both shaping and disseminating the ideas that would create the modern world. It offers Macklin, one of the best-known figures of the eighteenth-century stage as one of the Irish Enlightenment's central figures. When we remind ourselves that he was born before the 1707 Union of Scotland and England and died very shortly before the 1801 Act of Union between Britain and Ireland, that he lived through virtually the whole century—through the lives of Swift, Burke, Goldsmith, and Sheridan, and through those of Hume, Smollett, Lennox, and Burns—we may start to feel the urgency of considering Macklin's unique perspective on the cultural and political interplay of Anglo-Hiberno-Scottish affairs. Macklin's Irishness, then, is central to our conception of his significance, but it is not treated as determining. Recent work on the Irish Enlightenment, allows us to unpack a more fully fleshed out Macklin, a complicated figure who held multiple allegiances that waxed and waned across his lengthy life. Macklin was certainly a proud Irishman but he was also committed to the British state and its institutions and should be understood as working at the interstices of both the Irish and British Enlightenments: he is a crucial figure for working through the symbiotic elements of their interplay. He was a patriotic Irishman but equally he was a staunch Briton and he represented for many the importance of the free flow of ideas and people across borders at a time of frosty political negotiation on trade between Ireland and Britain. But it is also important to recognize that these negotiations between Britain and Ireland were both influencing and were influenced by wider European experiments. Previous important studies of Macklin have underlined Macklin's status as a dissident ethnic figure, aggressively keen to subvert Irish stereotypes.[15] This

---

13 Ian McBride, 'The Edge of Enlightenment: Ireland and Scotland in the Eighteenth Century', *Modern Intellectual History* 10.1 (2013), 147–48.

14 Michael Brown, *The Irish Enlightenment* (Cambridge, MA: Harvard University Press, 2016), 7. See also David O'Shaughnessy (ed.), *Ireland, Enlightenment and the English Stage, 1740–1820* (Cambridge: Cambridge University Press, 2019).

15 See, for example, Emily Hodgson Anderson, 'Celebrity Shylock', *PMLA* 126.4 (2011), 935–49; Michael Ragussis, 'Jews and Other "Outlandish Englishmen": Ethnic Performance and the Invention of British Identity under the Georges', *Critical Inquiry* 26.4 (2000), 773–97; and Paul Goring, '"John Bull, pit, box, and gallery, said No!":

volume helps place this dissidence within broader European patterns, in which the theatre took on new significance as the relations between politics, society, and selfhood were reimagined.

Though not determining, Macklin's Irishness was central to both his identity and his legacy, but it was an identity that was shaped and given force by his presence in London, where he enjoyed many of his greatest theatrical triumphs. It was in the metropolis, and in the theatres of London—both on stage and in other venues of performance, like the courts, coffeehouses, and debating societies—that he could most robustly challenge Irish stereotypes and actively promote new forms of dissident behaviour in line with broader European trends.

At issue in understanding Macklin as a figure of the Enlightenment, then, is the definition of the term 'Enlightenment' and how capacious we understand that term to be. Most literally it is a term meaning 'letting in light' where light is a symbol for 'thought' broadly conceived. For Immanuel Kant, the term indicated overcoming indecision and lack of courage in order to assert one's own understanding without depending on others. It is '*daring to know*' and exists by the motto 'have the courage to use your understanding'.[16] This is notably a position that does not doubt the capacity for thought but acknowledges the systems of power that prevent the articulation of that thought. The Enlightenment then is a process by which individuals might overcome the social order through courage. It is the assertion of individuality over structures of power, and it requires individual bravery.

By this measure, Macklin would have to be seen as an exemplary figure of the Enlightenment, as fortitude was not a quality that he lacked. Even the sketchiest of outlines of Macklin's biography illustrates that he had ample capacity for courageous assertion of self over systems of power. Most obviously in terms of his professional career as an actor on the London stage, Macklin overcame considerable obstacles to become accepted, not least of which was his outsider status as an Irish immigrant with a strong Irish brogue and a face James Quin once described as nothing but 'a d⸺n'd deal of *cordage*'.[17] In order to overcome what were widely understood to be disadvantages, Macklin again and again asserted himself, doing battle

---

Charles Macklin and the Limits of Ethnic Resistance on the Eighteenth-Century London Stage', *Representations* 79.1 (2002), 61–81.

16 Immanuel Kant, 'An Answer to the Question: What is Enlightenment?' in *Practical Philosophy*, trans. and ed. Mary J. Gregor (Cambridge: Cambridge University Press, 1996), 11.

17 For more on Macklin's accent and voice, see Ian Newman, 'Macklin and Song' in this volume; for more on Macklin's face as '*cordage*', see Ros Ballaster, 'Macklin and the Novel', 118–19, in this volume.

with the most powerful figures of the eighteenth-century theatre. Indeed, Macklin's posthumous reputation has been one in which his obduracy has been consistently emphasized, his capacity for turning friends into enemies (including George Colman, Samuel Foote, Garrick, and Thomas Holcroft, to mention just four of the better known from the first third of the alphabet) a notable feature. But outside of the theatre Macklin's determination enabled him to record a number of important victories against a social order that frequently must have seemed intent on keeping him in a position of subjugation. David Worrall shows in this volume how Macklin achieved considerable success in the courts, not only defending himself against a murder charge, but also protecting his right to earn a living by the stage after the Macbeth riots of 1773, and by asserting the copyright to his plays, which were being mercilessly pirated. So what has been portrayed as Macklin's belligerence might in fact qualify him as an exemplary Enlightenment figure, standing up for himself, and speaking back to those in power who attempted to keep him in fear.

This is, it should be acknowledged, an unfashionable way to think of the Enlightenment, and our histories of the eighteenth century have tended to move away from the individual heroism of Kant's account, emphasizing instead the more sociable and collective features of the Enlightenment project. In recent decades this has most obviously taken the form of an interest in sociability, and the role of clubs and societies—people working together, in concert—to advance knowledge and encourage thought.[18] Here, once again, Macklin played a pivotal role, through his participation in societies such as the Benevolent Society of St Patrick's, a society formed in 1783 to provide relief to the Irish poor in London and help forge closer ties between Ireland and Britain. Macklin was made a lifetime governor in 1784, was a member of the select committee in 1786, and, as Craig Bailey has observed, 'was a fixture at the anniversary meetings and in some ways, a curiosity on display'.[19] Newspaper reports emphasized that Macklin was still able to toast, drink, and sing with the other 'Sons of St Patrick' into the early hours of the morning, even after his retirement from the stage in 1789.[20]

Macklin's involvement with the societies of the associational world, however, was longstanding, dating back at least as far as his attendance at

---

18 The definitive study of this phenomenon is Peter Clark, *British Clubs and Societies, 1580–1800: The Origins of an Associational World* (Oxford: Oxford University Press 2000).

19 Craig Bailey, 'From Innovation to Emulation: London's Benevolent Society of St Patrick, 1783–1800', *Eighteenth-Century Ireland* 27 (2012), 176.

20 See, for example, *Morning Post*, 19 March 1789 and *E. Johnson's British Gazette and Sunday Monitor*, 20 March 1791.

the Robin Hood Society, the debating society which provided a venue for the oratorical aspirations of artisans and the middling sorts in the mid-century.[21] Most notable among his commitments to sociability was his opening of his own coffeehouse and multi-purpose entertainment venue—a site for 'polyhedonic sociability', as Markman Ellis calls it—in the Piazza of Covent Garden in 1754. Among the pleasures these rooms offered were a coffeehouse and tavern, two of the usual venues of the associational world, but it also hosted frequent debates and offered the spectacle of Macklin performing oratory. Whether we understand the value of this venue in terms of its capacity for entertaining performance, or as serious attempts at improving Enlightenment discourse, depends a little on the research agenda (Macklin's Coffeehouse is read differently by various authors in this volume), but what seems clear is Macklin's commitment to sociability as one important strand of his larger intellectual project.

By focusing less on heroic individualism in the Kantian model, and more on the collective efforts of the associational world (correlating perhaps better with Habermasian models of the Enlightenment), it becomes immediately clear that an important aspect of the Enlightenment is a commitment to enjoyment as much as to improvement. That is, if the coffeehouse and tavern societies of the eighteenth century were the engine rooms of Enlightenment thought and the advancement of knowledge, the things that made people return to meeting after meeting were not simply intellectual pursuits but other forms of concomitant pleasure—the drinking, singing, and toasting and other forms of shared bonhomie described in the newspaper reports of the Benevolent Society of St Patrick. And this is where this collection of essays distinguishes itself from other considerations of Macklin, which, as we have suggested, tend to focus on his abrasiveness. Scholars have described his altercation with Thomas Hallam, his battles in the courts, and his frequent fallings-out with his fellow actors. This image of irritability is seemingly confirmed by John Opie's portrait, on the cover of this volume, which shows Macklin wielding his papers with truculent gravity, his bold features staring out humourlessly from under a powdered wig. The image of the irascible Macklin was promoted by his early biographers, of which there was a considerable number in the years after his death, eclipsing even the number of memoirs of Garrick.[22] So it is worth remembering that in his day

---

21 Mary Thale, 'The Robin Hood Society: Debating in Eighteenth-Century London', *London Journal* 22.1 (1997), 33–50.
22 For an account of Macklin's early biographies, see Amanda Weldy Boyd, *Staging Memory and Materiality in Eighteenth-Century Theatrical Biography* (London: Anthem Press, 2017), 61–102.

Macklin was known primarily as a comic actor, who often played humorous roles, and who wrote comic afterpieces and Christmas entertainments.[23]

This volume contends then that one significant heretofore underappreciated aspect of Macklin is his commitment to entertainment and enjoyment, his sense of humour and of fun. As Helen Burke discusses in her chapter, in his two-act afterpiece *The Covent Garden Theatre; or, Pasquin Turn'd Drawcansir* (1752), Pasquin is asked to hear a 'Presentiment against one Charles Macklin, Comedian' on the charge that he has written 'a strange hotch-potch Farce, and puff'd it on the Town as written after the manner of Aristophanes and the Pasquinades of the Italian Theatre'.[24] This carnivalesque self-referentiality nicely exhibits the forms of pomposity-puncturing irony at which Macklin excelled, but we should also be alert to the way Macklin describes himself as 'Charles Macklin, Comedian', using an epithet that adheres to his name with frustrating persistence. After the success of *Love à la Mode*, Macklin offered his services to Covent Garden, 'but not as a Comedian', which, as Matthew Kinservik points out, suggests Macklin's frustration with being pigeonholed merely as a comic actor when he was capable of so much more—possessing experience as a stage manager, as Kinservik emphasizes, but including also some noteworthy talent as a writer and a capacity for a wider variety of roles.[25] Still, his reputation as a comedian stuck, so that even in 1804, several years after his death, William Cooke's anecdotal biography was entitled *Memoirs of Charles Macklin, Comedian*.[26]

Several of the essays in this volume emphasize this more rambunctious side to Macklin's character. O'Shaughnessy's discussion of the censorship of Macklin's plays highlights what he calls the 'Rabelaisian streak' of bawdy humour that runs throughout Macklin's writing and that frequently ran afoul of the censor's pen. Michael Brown meanwhile focuses squarely on the question of what made audiences laugh in the eighteenth century, considering how and why the humour of ethnic difference worked in the theatre. Needless to say, this can sometimes make for uncomfortable reading, as Brown

---

23 Macklin produced a play (now lost) called *The Whim; or A Christmas Gambol* which was performed on 26 December 1764 at the Crow Street Theatre in Dublin. See *Appleton*, 236.
24 Charles Macklin, *The Covent Garden Theatre; or, Pasquin Turn'd Drawcansir* (1752), Augustan Reprint Society, no. 116, ed. Jean B. Kern (Los Angeles: Clark Memorial Library, University of California, 1965), 62–63.
25 Macklin's characterization of a December 1772 letter to Colman, offered in his 'Answer to the Mgrs. Original Bill of Complaint, 13 March 1778'. Preserved in the National Archives, Kew, C 12/1667/30. Kinservik, 'Macklin as Theatre Manager', 138 and 144, in this volume.
26 For a discussion of Cooke's biography, see Boyd, *Staging Memory*, 85–91.

examines the use of Scotophobia and anti-Semitism in Macklin's plays. As Colm Summers notes, these are aspects of Macklin's comic art that do not translate easily to the modern theatre, yet they are aspects that should not be ignored or dismissed. They are complex reactions to complex situations that demand analysis and examination, but they also reveal that a focus on comedy by no means precludes the pursuit of more serious concerns. Indeed, this focus on comedy may help leaven our image of Macklin's austerity. O'Shaughnessy's essay reveals that comedy is often inextricably entwined with the pursuit of deeply serious intellectual and political agendas— Macklin's comedy, he suggests, uses entertainment to publicly interrogate the hypocrisy of the ruling classes.

It is in this broad sense that we might consider Macklin as a figure of the Enlightenment. As Ian McBride has pointed out, the theatre was itself a crucial engine of Enlightenment thought, not only for disseminating more widely ideas that were elsewhere available only in (possibly unread) books, but for experimenting with and showcasing behaviours that were laid before the public, inviting evaluation.[27] Not for nothing were the words 'School for' featured in so many titles across the century, a trope that Macklin's *The School for Husbands* (Covent Garden, 1761) both participated in and helped to create.[28] The point of the 'School for' trope was to suggest that behaviours could be learned, and characters could be reformed, but it was also to suggest that certain behaviours were in need of reformation, and that audiences could be trained in the art of recognizing aberrant behaviour. The pedagogical implications of 'School for' plays, however playfully the trope was used, were underwritten by an understanding of the theatre as a vehicle for social reform, not only for the characters within the play, but for the audience who were invited to evaluate forms of behaviour that were or were not appropriate, and which they could chose to uphold or reject.

Unlike the novel, which Nancy Armstrong famously argued modelled forms of interiority, the theatre as an embodied art modelled forms of physical behaviour, as well as speech.[29] It was in the latter category of speech that

---

27 McBride, 'The Edge of Enlightenment', 147–48.
28 In addition to Sheridan's famous *The School for Scandal* (Drury Lane, 1777), other plays include *The School for Guardians* (Arthur Murphy, Covent Garden, 1766), *The School of Eloquence* (Hannah Cowley, Drury Lane, 1780), *A School for Grey Beards, or The Mourning Bride* (Hannah Cowley, Drury Lane, 1786), *The School for Widows* (Richard Cumberland, Covent Garden, 1789), *The School for Arrogance* (Thomas Holcroft, Covent Garden, 1791), *The School of Reform; or, How to Rule a Husband* (Thomas Morton, Covent Garden, 1805), and *The School for Authors* (John Tobin, Haymarket, 1808).
29 Nancy Armstrong, *Desire and Domestic Fiction: A Political History of the Novel* (Oxford: Oxford University Press, 1987).

Macklin proves a decisive figure, not only because, as Ian Newman discusses, Macklin had to discipline his own voice in order to conform to the tastes and expectations of London audiences, but also because of the way dialect functions in his plays. As Michael Brown argues, Macklin's Scotophobia is exposed through the way the speech of Archy Macsarcasm—the arrogant Scot of *Love à la Mode*, played to some considerable acclaim by Macklin himself— is reproduced as a series of almost incomprehensible phonetic renderings on the page (for example, 'I hai had letters fai the duke, the marquis and aw the deegnearies of the family remonstrating—nay axpressly proheebeting my contaminant the blood of Macsarcasm wi' ainy thing sprung frai a higsheed, or a counting hoose').[30] To state the case mildly, the audience member is not encouraged to aspire to Macsarcasm's absurdly caricatured behaviours nor to imitate his form of speech, but there are other characters in the play—the Irishman Sir Callaghan O'Brallaghan, and possibly the female love interest Charlotte—whose attitudes and speech patterns are far less cruelly caricatured and are ultimately held up by the play as admirable and worthy of emulation.

This is the version of the Enlightenment that Macklin reveals. The Enlightenment not simply as the pursuit of thought as an end in itself, but the pursuit of understanding as mediated by the practical business of day-to-day interactions and embodied action; the Enlightenment, that is to say, as doing not just thinking. Macklin helps us to see the theatre as an agent of Enlightenment ideas and principles, and can provide a sense of the broad range of ideas and principles that were up for grabs as the light was let in. But Macklin can also help us to understand some of the varied methods by which these principles were promulgated, including both aggressive 'manly' claims to truth-telling and lighter uses of playful comedy. And here we might return to the discussion of Macklin's confrontation with Johnson, mindful that while there is a serious battle of wits there is also an important spirit of playfulness.

Most obviously, the encounter with Johnson reveals the martial qualities of Enlightenment conversation, it emphasizes conversation as a battle, with two combatants fighting *mano-a-mano* to gain the upper hand in the competitive business of sociability. The conversation provides further evidence of Jon Mee's description of Johnson's conversation as 'talking for victory', a point illustrated by Joshua Reynolds's account of Johnson's conversational habits: 'In mixed company he fought on every occasion as if his whole reputation depended upon the victory of the minute, and he fought with all the weapons'.[31] Enlightenment conversation is conceived as a kind

---

30 Charles Macklin, *Love à La Mode, a Farce* (London, 1793), 73.
31 Jon Mee, *Conversable Worlds: Literature, Contention, and Community, 1762–1830* (Oxford: Oxford University Press, 2011), 90–95; Charles Leslie and Tom Taylor, *The*

of game in which there are victors and losers, that could certainly become at times cruel and even bloodthirsty, but which was ultimately a form of play. Not play in any frivolous sense, but a deeply earnest play, a form of testing, which was at the same time capable of spirited lightness. Here the opposition of humour and seriousness are collapsed into a single form that was frequently understood in the eighteenth century as 'wit'.

But Macklin's verbal battle with Johnson might also call to mind Horkheimer and Adorno's critique of Enlightenment thinking as 'a process of establishing a unified scientific order and of deriving factual knowledge from principles, whether these principles are interpreted as arbitrarily posited axioms, innate ideas, or the highest abstractions'. According to Horkheimer and Adorno, what matters, for Enlightenment thinking, is not so much being right, but having the best argument, where the quality of the argument is judged by its internal consistency. 'The laws of logic establish the most universal relationships within the order and refine them. Unity lies in self consistency'.[32] The zinger of the Johnson–Macklin anecdote is the moment when Macklin uses Johnson's own logic to defeat him: 'But a man of your understanding, Doctor Johnson, ought to be acquainted with every language!' The satisfaction of the anecdote lies in its application of consistent logic; Irish (or what passes for Irish in Bernard's mangled, untranslatable phonetic rendering) is clearly within the category of 'every language' that Johnson had previously invoked.[33] It does not matter that neither man is in fact acquainted with every language, nor that knowledge of languages is not directly correlated to 'understanding'. Macklin has in no way 'proven' his superior understanding to Johnson and is in no way 'right'. What matters (at least within Bernard's anecdote, however proximate to a real life event it might be) is that he has used consistent logic, and so wins the conversational battle.

For Horkheimer and Adorno, the internal consistency of logic was the destructive fallacy of Enlightenment thought because it divorced 'science' from practical life, but the case of Macklin demonstrates that thought and embodied action were never as separable as Kant's formulation of the Enlightenment as principally related to the understanding (to which Horkheimer and Adorno were responding) suggests. After all, for all his pretentions to Enlightenment

---

Life and Times of Sir Joshua Reynolds, with Some Notices of His Contemporaries, 2 vols (London, 1865), II.462.

32 Max Horkheimer and Theodor W. Adorno, *Dialectic of Enlightenment: Philosophical Fragments*, ed. Gunzelin Schmid Noerr, trans. Edmund Jephcott (Stanford, CA: Stanford University Press, 2002), 63.

33 Thanks are owed to Barry McCrea, Lesa Ní Mhungaile, and Diarmuid Ó Giolláin for their valiant, if ultimately unsuccessful attempts to make sense of this phonetic gibberish.

learning, Macklin was a man of action not just of words. He *did* things: he emigrated to a new country, he took on the legal system, he built and ran his own coffeehouse, and (as Matthew Kinservik discusses in this volume) he was a theatre manager who was at various times responsible for the day-to-day running of several theatres. But, above all, he was a physical presence, a body on the stage, who you could go to see and experience night after night in the theatre, in all his fleshy corporeality. His body was not just a housing for ideas and principles, but an essential part of his identity; its many and varied London performances took place both on and offstage.

This point is made clear by Craig Bailey's discussion of Macklin's attendance in his nineties at meetings of the Benevolent Society of St Patrick, referred to earlier. Bailey describes the way newspapers treated Macklin's presence as a kind of spectacle and comments that 'it would have been worth attending the dinner to see if Macklin had survived long enough to be there, and to get a chance of witnessing one of his last performances'.[34] John Opie's portrait provides further evidence that Macklin remained a spectacle, a sight to behold, even after his retirement from the stage. Indeed, Paul Goring has recently suggested that Macklin may have exerted some control over the portrait and was ambitious to be viewed not merely as an actor on the stage but as an author.[35] Regardless, Opie's portrait still foregrounds the idea of Macklin's exceptional, and exceptionally old, body as something to be viewed. But the 'Nestor of the Stage' was a spectacle long before his eventual retirement. As David Taylor remarks in this volume, he featured in countless prints, drawings, and paintings, most frequently as Shylock. Macklin's career spanned the years in which portraits of actors (often in character) became increasingly popular, echoing a broader shift in the phenomenology of the theatre, as plays became less something audiences listened to and more something they went to see (although, as Ian Newman points out, this transition may have been over-emphasized and aurality remained a central component of the theatrical experience).

Macklin's exceptional body, with its brutal ungainly strength, was on display night after night in the theatres of London, Dublin, and on tour throughout Britain. It was something that could be viewed, and indeed gained its power from being repeatedly viewed in the act of modelling behaviours that could be judged by audience members as appropriate (or not) to the Age of Enlightenment. The performance of Enlightenment might also be considered as the practice of Enlightenment—an idea of the

---

34 Bailey, 'From Innovation to Emulation', 176.
35 Paul Goring, 'John Opie's Portrait of Charles Macklin and the Shakespeare Gallery', *Source: Notes in the History of Art* 39.3 (2020), 184–93.

Enlightenment as not just thought, reason, and rationality, but a praxis of embodied being. This idea of Enlightenment suggests not only an event in the history of mediation (as proposed by Siskin and Warner) but an event that also celebrated the immediacy of physical presence and the possibilities of improvised responses to the immediate moment as exemplified by theatrical performance.[36] Our investment in performing Enlightenment inspires an interest in this volume with practice as research, or research beyond simply academic discussion—with learning from doing. The volume closes with two substantial discussions concerning the staging of Macklin's *Love à la Mode* in our time (see also the colour plates) against the backdrop of our contemporary concerns.

It is perhaps surprising to the *dix-huitièmiste* to see Macklin in the same company as Vorticist drama and Brechtian fragments but the parallels drawn by Colm Summers and Nicholas Johnson give us some sense of the difficulty involved in reviving Georgian farce, to make it something more than museum theatre. Summers's firm rejection of the divisions between academic and artistic practice offers a productive way of thinking through the possibilities of practice-as-research and indeed research-as-practice. Moreover, his neat observation of how the 'weight of scholarship' can retard the capacity of academics to appreciate artistic performance on its own terms is a useful tenet for those of us engaged in this kind of work.[37] Johnson's chapter encourages us to embrace a more radical notion of adaptation, one which privileges the director over the writer, the new over the old. *Kinesis* must be prized above *mimesis* 'even if this gesture might entail distortion of outright rejection of the original'.[38] If eighteenth-century drama is to sustain itself on the boards of modern-day theatres, the reflections offered by Summers and Johnson must be heeded.

This investment in theatrical practice returns us to Kant's essay 'What is Enlightenment?' which draws an important distinction between private and public uses of reason: 'by the public use of one's own reason I mean that use which anyone may make of it as a man of learning addressing the entire reading public. What I term the private use of reason is that which a person may make of it in a particular civil post or office with which he is entrusted'. Kant goes on to explain that any individual might at different times operate either in a civic role or as a 'man of learning'. Thus, an officer on duty cannot

---

36 Clifford Siskin and William Warner, 'This is Enlightenment: An Invitation in the Form of an Argument', Introduction to Clifford Siskin and William Warner (eds), *This is Enlightenment* (Chicago: Chicago University Press, 2010), 1.
37 Johnson and Summers, '*Love à la Mode* in Performance: A Dialogue', 287, in this volume.
38 Johnson, 'Restaging Macklin', 273, in this volume.

argue with his superiors or question an order, but neither can he be stopped, when off duty, from making observations about military service and making them available for the judgement of the public. To translate this to the world of the eighteenth-century theatre, an actor has a civic duty to perform a role they have been assigned, or indeed that they earned and made their own. She must say the lines written and stand in the appropriate place on stage and generally fulfil the expectations of the theatre manager as outlined in her contract. Moreover, she must fulfil, to some extent at least, the expectations of an audience primed by the ghosts of actors past. This is her civic duty as an actor. But, occasionally—and the example of Macklin's Shylock is perhaps the most well-known of the century—actors can re-imagine a role in an extraordinary and iconoclastic fashion, and channel their learning in an embodied fashion that recalibrates the parameters of the possible on the stage. Macklin shows us how acting can be a praxis of Enlightenment, straddling both the public and private uses of reason brought before mass audiences. And, as Manushag Powell outlines in this volume, the Georgian mediascape then mediated accounts of performance to even bigger audiences in London and beyond. In addition, an actor might also write plays, informed by their theatrical experiences, which test out behaviours and modes of speech and lay them before the public for their judgement. Macklin had considerable success in both endeavours, showcasing the extraordinary dialectic of Enlightenment possible between acting and writing. In Kant's terms he performed his civic duty by acting in preassigned roles and he performed his public duty by writing plays which had an agenda of social reform as well as calling into question ideas of ethnicity, the law, and gender relations, amongst others. Macklin's theatrical activities were a civic duty that he took on with such powerfully independent freedom that he obliterates the idea that an actor playing a role might somehow be constrained into a subaltern position. He was most certainly, to adopt Nicholas Johnson's terms, a man of *kinesis*, rather than *mimesis*.

Macklin's Shylock demonstrates that when executed with sufficient courage, or indeed obstinate-minded originality, civic duty might become public duty, and provide a contribution to furthering understanding. The contingent nature of this 'understanding', however, is illustrated by the fact that this signal contribution to the theatre, and, on balance, his most lasting legacy, was also a study in anti-Semitism. This doubleness—contributing to understanding in a way that is always partial and compromised, might similarly characterize Macklin's Macbeth or his Stage Irishman. Given his longevity and his success, Macklin's career is thus a telling example of acting as an Enlightenment activity, an art and a practice in which the public and private functions of reason might coalesce in the nightly ritual of an intellectually kinetic actor performing for a public audience. While some recent accounts of the Enlightenment privilege the printed word above all else, this volume's reflections on Macklin's life and career, tracing the links between his reading, commonplacing, acting, activism, and writing, reminds us that Enlightenment can be embodied in a set of mutually interconnected diurnal activities linked by the idea of performance.[39]

These are some of the contradictions and complications of thinking about the career of Macklin, an actor and playwright, whose stubborn insistence on truth-telling was both an embodiment of Enlightenment principles and a measure of their inadequacy; he was the cause of much agony, pain, and even death, but also the source of laughter; he was responsible for a revolution in the way the Irish were portrayed on the English stage, and made use of Scotophobic and anti-Semitic stereotypes; he was one of the most admired performers of the eighteenth century, while being reviled and even feared by many of his fellow actors. It is ultimately in this complex, multifaceted sense, operating across the many theatres of London's eighteenth-century life, that we propose Macklin should be regarded as an exemplary if unorthodox figure of the Enlightenment.

---

39 Siskin and Warner, 'This is Enlightenment', 22.

Representing Macklin

1
Macklin's Look

David Francis Taylor

Rightly to *seem*, is transiently, to be.

Aaron Hill, *The Art of Acting*[1]

To consider Macklin's look is not only to ask how he managed his own stage presence and persona but also to think about how his body was read—*in* performance and *through* performance—by his contemporaries. It is to parse the ways in which images of that body circulated visually and textually, acquired particular resonance, and were put to specific use within eighteenth-century culture. As Samuel Johnson tells us, 'look' in this context means 'To have a particular appearance' and 'To have any air, mien, or manner', but also 'To seem'. It is worth registering the constitutive tension between these different senses of the word. Where Johnson's first two definitions refer to the particular embodiedness of an individual, the third instead denotes how that same individual's comportment and actions are seen from the vantage point of another. This last sense concerns the exercise of judgement, as is readily suggested by the quotation from Thomas Burnet's *Sacred Theory of the Earth* with which Johnson glosses it: 'To complain of want yet refuse all offers of a supply, *looks* very sullen'.[2] This difference of agency, of 'look' meaning the body as style, as the vehicle of self-expression, and of 'look' meaning the body as constituted by and for the gaze of the other is of

---
1 Aaron Hill, *The Art of Acting* (London, 1746), 9.
2 Samuel Johnson, *A Dictionary of the English Language*, 2 vols (London, 1755–56), II.1222, q.v. 'To look'.

course imminent to the phenomenology of the theatrical event. The labour of the actor is to seem to be someone (else), but it is ultimately the audience—and, more broadly, the public culture to which the actor necessarily bequeaths her or his body—that determines what that actor seems to be, both in the dramatic moment and for posterity. Macklin, as we know, struggled throughout his career with this fundamental asymmetry of interpretative power; his determination legally to oppose those responsible for the Macbeth riots of 1773, as discussed by David Worrall in this volume, discloses just how uncomfortable he was with the abjection that public performance implicitly (and at that violent moment, explicitly) involved. And it is for this very reason that the question of Macklin's look, of the nature of his seeming, is so important, because in terms of his playing of Shylock it takes us from the rigorous methods through which he newly defined the part to the cultural procedures through which that part came always to define him.

This line of thought brings me close to Emily Hodgson Anderson's fascinating reading of Macklin's Shylock as a case study in the shifting of celebrity from actor to character. But where, for Anderson, Macklin came to be effaced by the very role that brought him such fame, I rather regard the figures of Irish actor and Shakespeare's Jew as so intricately meshed in contemporary paintings, engravings, and testimony as to be almost indivisible. In other words, Anderson's analysis rests on a secure ontological distinction between player and part, the real and the mimetic, that just doesn't hold in the instance of Macklin's Shylock. In particular, this distinction enables Anderson to locate celebrity outside of and away from the body; for her, Shylock is 'a celebrity who transcends embodiment—a celebrity who does not depend on the physical body in the traditional sense'.[3] Yet the many images and descriptions I negotiate here suggest that neither Shylock nor Macklin were or could be culturally legible other than through the protocols of embodiment. As an Irishman and as a Jew, and in their splicing of what one observer termed an 'Irish Jew',[4] they were *of* the body in powerful and highly problematic ways that point to the extent to which the prevailing aesthetic and pictorial codes that informed the image of the eighteenth-century actor were themselves imbricated in pressing ethical, ethnic, and ideological considerations.[5]

In taking *look* rather than *celebrity* as my heuristic here I thus signal not only my attention to visual sources but also my specific interest in what and

---

3 Emily Hodgson Anderson, 'Celebrity Shylock', *PMLA* 126.4 (2011), 946.
4 'Impromptu's, On seeing Mr Macklin in *Macbeth*', *St James's Chronicle*, 23–26 October 1773. Signed 'Bob Short'.
5 See Shearer West, *The Image of Actor: Verbal and Visual Representation in the Age of Garrick and Kemble* (London: Pinter, 1991).

how an actor's body is made to mean in the period. Heather McPherson has convincingly shown both the visual constitution of theatrical celebrity at the end of the eighteenth century and the cultural role that the arts of painting, engraving, and caricature played in resurrecting the ephemeral bodies of performer and performance.[6] But where the concept of celebrity concerns the construction, presence, and visibility of a personality (matters of course centred on the body), to think in terms of a look is rather to insist on how far, as a mediated object, an actor's body was—and still is—made to stand for something else, something other than itself: style, ethnicity, age, morality, sexuality.

Of course, the story of Macklin's first performance as Shylock at Drury Lane in 1741 has been much rehearsed but it bears briefly repeating at the outset here for what it tells us about how far Macklin and his later interlocutors understood this crucial moment in his stage career in terms of the entwined imperatives of authenticity (of character), restoration (of Shakespeare's text), and professional reputation (of the actor). In the first decades of the eighteenth century, it was George Granville's Shakespearean adaptation *The Jew of Venice* (1701) that held the stage, with Shylock played as a comic part by the likes of Thomas Doggett, himself an Irishman. Macklin not only returned audiences to *The Merchant of Venice* but also strove to offer a new and far darker depiction of Shylock. Anecdotal evidence suggests that he undertook considerable research in preparing for the role. He studied Josephus's *History of the Jews* and reflected upon it in his Commonplace Book;[7] he took pains to ensure his costume—'red hat … piqued beard … loose black gown'—exactly represented that of a Venetian Jew, reportedly telling Alexander Pope that, having 'staked [his] reputation on the character, [he] was determined to spare no trouble in getting at the best information';[8] and, according to *The Connoisseur*, 'he made daily visits to the center of business, the '*Change* and the adjacent coffee-houses; that by a frequent intercourse and conversation with "the unforeskinn'd race," he might habituate himself to their air and deportment'.[9] Macklin thus sought first to recognize and then to embody as precisely as possible a particular Jewish look.

This portrayal, which he had concealed from the rest of the company until the night of performance, was a huge success. 'In *Shylock* his merit was such', writes Macklin's 1804 biographer William Cooke, 'that, whilst ever

---

6 Heather McPherson, *Art and Celebrity in the Age of Reynolds and Siddons* (University Park: Pennsylvania State University Press, 2017).
7 Frank Felsenstein, *Anti-Semitic Stereotypes: A Paradigm of Otherness in English Popular Culture, 1660–1830* (Baltimore, MD: Johns Hopkins University Press, 1999), 168–69.
8 *Cooke*, 92, 94–95.
9 *The Connoisseur*, 1 (31 January 1754), 1.

Figure 1.1: John Lodge, *Mr Macklin in the Character of Shylock, in Shakespeare's Merchant of Venice* (London: T. Wright, 1 November 1775). Metropolitan Museum of Art, New York.

the English Stage preserves its character, his name will be remembered, as the *original*, in its fullest extent of praise'.[10] As the doggerel, apocryphally attributed to Pope and invariably quoted in images and descriptions of Macklin, puts it: 'This is the Jew | That Shakespeare drew' (see Figure 1.1). These accounts posit a relationship between recovered authenticity and signal innovation, the shock of the new: Macklin ascends to the status of an 'original'—of the prototypical Shylock—by 'reviving the original of Shakespeare'.[11] Of his debut in the role, Francis Aspry Congreve, Macklin's first biographer, notes that 'his reputation as an actor was established, by his masterly performance of Shylock, which then for the first time was restored to its native lustre, as written by our immortal Bard'.[12] And James Thomas Kirkman, whose own biography of Macklin followed a year later in 1799, similarly observes that the 'sudden, unexpected, and happy catastrophe of that night's representation, conferred on *Mr. Macklin* immortal fame, as an actor, and transmitted to posterity another proof of the amazing genius and wonderful talents of unrivalled Shakspeare'.[13] In both instances, Macklin's Shylock serves to restore the hitherto imperilled or occluded cultural prestige of Shakespeare. Yet such a formulation perforce raises the question of how far Macklin's body—the body of an Irishman playing a Jew who wishes to carve open the body of a Christian—could properly perform this act of cultural, and national, surrogation. Implicit to these avowals that Macklin's virtuosity secures and newly embodies a pre-eminent Shakespeare is an equivalence that would seem radically to compromise the ideological coherence of the very ideas of canonicity and English cultural hegemony they announce. It is this equivalence, which I take to be nothing less than the expression of a cultural impossibility, that I explore in this essay.

Looking the part

MACKLIN'S BODY WAS ALWAYS MARKED as static, solid, and abrasive. Cooke tells us that 'his figure "even from his boyish days," must have been coarse and clumsy' and that 'he was above the middle size, rather stout than well proportioned, with a marked eye, an aquiline nose, and a face altogether that expressed more acumen than grace'.[14] Rival James Quin

---

10 *Cooke*, 413.
11 *Cooke*, 90.
12 *Congreve*, 17–18.
13 *Kirkman*, I.259–60.
14 *Cooke*, 346, 400. See also *Congreve*, 58–59 and *Kirkman*, II.429.

was less kind, bluntly observing that he saw 'nothing in the fellow's face, but a d--n'd deal of *cordage*'.[15] In part, such testimony reminds us that, whatever the natural contours of Macklin's body and face, he was already in his early forties when he first played Shylock. Living into his late nineties and acting professionally well into his eighties, Macklin's was one of the most publicly visible aged bodies of the latter half of the century. And this increasing infirmity was essential to the efficacy of his Shylock. Francis Gentleman, who regarded the character as 'a most disgraceful picture of human nature', wrote that 'there is no doubt but Mr. Macklin looks the part as much better than any other person as he plays it' due to his 'sententious gloominess of expression' and 'sullen solemnity of deportment'.[16] Hazlitt, meanwhile, recalled seeing 'a decrepit old man, bent with age and ugly with mental deformity, grinning with deadly malice, with the venom of his heart congealed in the expression of his countenance, sullen, morose, gloomy, inflexible, brooding over one idea, that of his hatred, and fixed on one unalterable purpose, that of revenge'.[17] Note here that Hazlitt deploys the familiar trope of ugliness as an ethical category, a trope renewed and given new pseudo-scientific credence by the work of Johann Kaspar Lavater, for whom physiognomy indexed personality. Macklin's tense and awkward body-shape as Shylock—the soreness of hip joints and lower back implied by the splayed-legged, slightly crouched posture common to the many engravings of his figure in Act 4 Scene 1—at once bespeaks decrepitude and turpitude (see Figure 1.2). Macklin's oft-noted ponderousness *is* Shylock's perverse obstinacy; the inelegance and age of the actor's body signals the pathology of hatred.

My point here is that observers of Macklin's Shylock invoke a notion of style only to negate it. Joseph Roach notes of theatrical performance that 'the higher the level of stylization, the greater the perceived distance of the substitute from the original it represents', yet for the likes of Gentleman and Hazlitt what initially seems to be style, in the sense of *mimesis*, gives way entirely to the actor's body as something that is manifestly not transformed and that performs only itself.[18] So in Maria Edgeworth's 1817 novel *Harrington*, a friend of the protagonist promises to introduce him to 'the most celebrated Jew that ever appeared in England' and then promptly delivers him

---

15 *Cooke*, 19.
16 Francis Gentleman, *The Dramatic Censor; or, Critical Companion*, 2 vols (London, 1770), II.291–92.
17 William Hazlitt, *Characters of Shakespear's Plays* (London, 1817), 276.
18 Joseph R. Roach, 'The Inscription of Morality as Style', in Thomas Postlewait and Bruce A. McConachie (eds), *Interpreting the Theatrical Past: Essays in the Historiography of Performance* (Iowa City: University of Iowa Press, 1989), 107.

Figure 1.2: Henry Cook, after Johann Heinrich Ramberg, *Mr Macklin in Shylock* (London: John Cawthorn, 20 January 1806). By permission of the Folger Shakespeare Library, Washington, DC.

to the door of Macklin, 'the real, original Jew of Venice'.[19] Once more the word 'original' indicates and enacts the ontological slippage from seeming to being that underlies the success of Macklin's Shylock; in the repeated insistence that Macklin is the 'original' we register the cultural logic of a substitution that takes place in the very disavowal of substitution. It is not that Macklin *acts* naturally but rather that Macklin does not act at all. The very facts of his body are enough. He is the first and only genuine Shylock; he is always already Shylock.

And these facts of the body encompassed not only physique and age but also, inevitably, ethnicity. When he first appeared on stage, Macklin was supposedly known as the 'Mad Irishman',[20] and, as Paul Goring discerns, the man born Cathal McLaughlin in County Donegal may have changed his 'tongue, name, and religion' but his public persona was one of 'acceptable Irishness' rather than 'a simulated image of Englishness'.[21] So far as this Irishness was ever truly accommodated by London audiences it was required to signify—or not signify, as we'll see—in particular ways. It could be and was commuted into Jewishness with troubling ease. The actor and theatre manager John Bernard recalled that Macklin 'possessed by nature certain physical advantages, which qualified him to embody Shylock', not least that there were 'certain complexional resemblances between the two'.[22] Macklin's Irishness renders him especially fit to play—to be—Shylock because the Irishman and the Jew are ethnically commensurate not only in being other than English but because this difference is, supposedly, immediately legible at the level of the body.[23] Thus, Johan Zoffany's unfinished painting of *Merchant*'s trial scene (*c*.1768; see Plate 7) spins around the opposing figures of Macklin's Shylock and Portia, played by his own daughter Maria. Portia here is erect, youthful, and strikingly pale, the almost spectral whiteness of her face matched only by that of Antonio's bare—and imminently threatened—chest. Her body serves as a visual counterpoint both to the awkwardness of Macklin's characteristic wide-legged posture and, more

---

19 Maria Edgeworth, *Harrington* (Peterborough, ON: Broadview Press, 2004), 114.
20 *Cooke*, 412.
21 Paul Goring, '"John Bull, pit, box, and gallery, said No!": Charles Macklin and the Limits of Ethnic Resistance on the Eighteenth-Century London Stage', *Representations* 79.1 (2002), 67.
22 John Bernard, *Retrospections of the Stage*, 2 vols (London, 1830), I.88.
23 See Michael Ragussis, *Theatrical Nation: Jews and Other Outlandish Englishmen in Georgian Britain* (Philadelphia: University of Pennsylvania Press, 2010). Ragussis notes: 'In Georgian England, Jewish identity typically functioned at a highly symbolic level to set the farthest limits of the question of the internal other within Britain, both entirely opposite to, and yet increasingly a double of, the English' (29).

crucially, to the discernibly darker tone of his skin. This is the drama of a racial encounter.

At the same time, Zoffany's conversation piece, in which Shylock seems poised to strike with the knife clasped in his right hand, reminds us that what Macklin brought to the role—what made him both original and *the* original—was a palpable sense of menace. Kirkman applauded Macklin's Shylock for exhibiting 'the malevolence, the villainy, and the diabolical atrocity of the character', while Elizabeth Inchbald wrote that 'no fiend-like malice, no outrageous cruelty, no diabolical joy in human misery, seemed too excessive for the nature of mankind, when he [Macklin] depicted those extraordinary crimes'.[24] Macklin's Shylock was the bogeyman of Georgian culture; he was its theatre's most emphatic embodiment of monstrosity.

Admittedly, Zoffany's other portrait of Macklin in the part (*c.*1767–68; see Plate 8) offers perhaps the one exception to this reading of his Shylock. Shown alone and without the otherwise ubiquitous knife and scales, Macklin's pose in this picture suggests an anger tempered by abiding sorrow. But the pathos of this painting only helps us more clearly register its absence in other images of Macklin's Shylock. In an engraving published by Joseph Wenman in 1777 (Figure 1.3), he whets his blade on the ground, a gesture that in one performance reportedly caused a young man sat in the pit to faint and which in this image is rendered as a pose of extreme contortion, of a body bent double.[25] But it is a stipple half-length portrait of 1784, engraved by James Newton after a now lost painting by John Kitchingman, that most completely captures the terrifying, demonic alterity that so many spectators observed in Macklin's Shylock (Figure 1.4). There is no need of the familiar props in this image, for Macklin's now eighty-something-year-old face does all the necessary symbolic work: his large ears, rotten-toothed mouth, and huge forehead, marked by deep furrows and warts, all signal his physio-ethical deformity. The striking disjunction between, on the one hand, the decorousness of the stipple technique, the oval frame, and the calligraphic lettering, and, on the other, the almost caricature grotesqueness of Macklin's features only enhances the discomfiting effect of the image; it offers ugliness in a visual register customarily associated with beauty. According to Bernard, so terrified was George II upon seeing Macklin's Shylock that he was unable to sleep the night of the performance and when asked by Robert Walpole the following morning for a means of 'frightening' the House of Commons into submission the King advised his prime minister to dispatch MPs to Drury

---

24 *Kirkman*, I.259; Elizabeth Inchbald, preface to *The Merchant of Venice*, in *The British Theatre; or, A Collection of Plays*, 25 vols (London, 1808), II.4–5.
25 *Morning Post*, 9 November 1781. Cited in Felsenstein, *Anti-Semitic Stereotypes*, 171.

Figure 1.3: *Mr Macklin in the Character of Shylock* (London: J. Wenman, 1 June 1777). By permission of the Folger Shakespeare Library, Washington, DC.

Figure 1.4: James Newton, after John Kitchingman, *Mr Macklin as Shylock* (London: W. Lewis and J. Russell, 27 February 1784). By permission of the Folger Shakespeare Library, Washington, DC.

Lane 'to see that Irishman play Shylock'.[26] Whether or not there is any truth to this anecdote, it renders explicit the relationship between doubly suspect ethnicity and terror that gave Macklin's Shylock such remarkable cultural valency.

That Macklin's public persona was freighted by two histories of violence must have reinforced this profound—and for many spectators, compellingly terrifying—sense that he 'looked the part'. The first of these histories was national, for the English view of the Irish was powerfully informed by the distorted memory of the Ulster Rebellion of 1641, as sustained by regular reprintings of Sir John Temple's *History of the Irish Rebellion* (1646), a lurid and propagandistic report of Irish Catholic brutality. Issued in a new London edition in 1746 and largely retold in David Hume's *History of England* (1754), the continued circulation of Temple's account ensured that the spectre of innate Irish savagery remained deeply impressed upon the English consciousness. It is an image that descriptions of the 'diabolical atrocity' and 'outrageous cruelty' as Macklin's Shylock ('that Irishman') surely, if quietly, mobilize.[27]

The second history was very much personal. In 1735, six years before he first played Shylock, Macklin stood trial for murder after a greenroom altercation ended with him fatally thrusting his cane through the eye of fellow actor Thomas Hallam. The jury accepted Macklin's claim that Hallam's death was an accident, returned a verdict of manslaughter, and sentenced the actor to be branded. Though this punishment was likely carried out with a cold iron, as Frank Felsenstein notes it nonetheless signals the manner in which Macklin's body came to be marked as criminal, culturally if not literally.[28] In *An Infallible Recipe to Make a Wicked Manager of a Theatre* of 1750, a caustic broadside ostensibly by a disgruntled member of the company Macklin had managed at Chester, Hallam is shown clutching the black wig that was the cause of the disagreement, while a hand from the right wields a stick that is about to penetrate his left eye (Figure 1.5). Macklin himself isn't graphically represented, but he doesn't need to be. Rather he is made powerfully present through the body of his victim, through the mortal injury he inflicts. In turn, the accompanying verses to which the figure of Hallam directs the reader's attention, and which likewise do not name Macklin, unfold their satire through a series of racial slurs—Macklin is accused of having 'the Heart of a Pharaoh, the Kiss of a Judas [...] The Bowels of a Herod'—that posits his

---

26 Bernard, *Retrospections of the Stage*, II.121–22.
27 See David Berman, 'David Hume on the 1641 Rebellion in Ireland', *Studies: An Irish Quarterly Review* 65.258 (1976), 101–12.
28 Felsenstein, *Anti-Semitic Stereotypes*, 175.

Figure 1.5: *An Infallible Recipe to Make a Wicked Manager of a Theatre* (Chester, 20 August 1750). © Victoria and Albert Museum, London.

violent past as a symptom of his otherness, and vice versa. Less overtly but more disquietingly, George Lichtenberg vividly described Macklin's Shylock in 1778 as 'a fairly sturdy man, with a coarse yellow face, a nose which is large in all three dimensions, a long double chin, and a mouth which appeared to me to have been slit by the knife of nature, on one side at least, right up to the ears'.[29] Anderson rightly reads the striking troping of lacerated skin here as 'invoking the character's most famous prop', but where she regards this conceit as implying the violence that the role does to the performer I would instead argue that, like *An Infallible Recipe*, this passage discloses the visceral ways in which in the signature menace of Macklin's Shylock could be seen to make present the very punctured flesh of an adversary that marked the actor's past and the character's most desperate wish. Such testimony suggests that at moments Macklin's Shylock, ghosted by the figure of Hallam, terrified spectators because he gave to the notional wound at the centre of Shakespeare's play an embodied reality.

Looking apart

WHAT WE APPROACH HERE is one key reason why—despite the success with which Macklin returned Shakespeare's *Merchant* to the stage—it was David Garrick and not Macklin who came to be credited with, and to figure, the mid-century cultural elevation of Shakespeare. Unlike the unwieldy Macklin, Garrick was praised for his grace and mobility; he brought a balletic energy (a Harlequin energy, we might say, for he likely played the part at Goodman's Fields in spring 1741) to serious Shakespearean roles.[30] Macklin, for one, considered Garrick's style as consisting 'in incessantly pawing and hawling' his fellow actors and 'stalk[ing] between them and the Audience' in ways that ensured he was always the centre of attention.[31] This dynamism, the spectacle of a body ever poised to transition from one emotion to the next, is what defines Garrick's look (think of the many images of his signature start). But, just as crucially, Garrick, the son of an officer and an Anglican clergyman's daughter, was a provincial middle-class Englishman.

---

29 George C. Lichtenberg, 'Schlus des dritten Briefes aus England an Boie' (1778), trans. Paul Goring and Tone Midtgård, with assistance from Julia Krankenhagen and Stefan Krankenhagen, in Paul Goring, 'Volume 2: Charles Macklin', in Michael Caines, et al. (eds), *Lives of Shakespearian Actors I: David Garrick, Charles Macklin and Margaret Woffington by their Contemporaries* (London: Pickering, 2008), 206.
30 See Denise S. Sechelski, 'Garrick's Body and the Labor of Art in Eighteenth-Century Theater', *Eighteenth-Century Studies* 29.4 (1996), 369–89.
31 *Kirkman*, II.265.

His respectable, bourgeois body was an unthreateningly normative and therefore culturally fit vehicle for the canonization of the national poet, and, as the likes of Michael Dobson and Heather McPherson have shown, he strove relentlessly and successfully to fashion himself as the living embodiment of Shakespeare.[32] Garrick, too, made his name in the theatre at the beginning of the 1740s in the performance of a Shakespearean anti-hero, but for all that Richard III was a tyrant and villain he was a regal and an unquestionably English one.

By contrast, as we've seen, in becoming Shylock so completely, not only on stage but in the cultural imaginary, Macklin's body was always doubly racialized, his 'stout' and 'coarse' physique seen to indicate the alarming intransigence and self-reinforcing otherness of a vicious mind. So 'sublimely infernal' was Macklin's 'blood-thirsty Shylock', wrote the poet John Williams (aka 'Anthony Pasquin'), that 'Could Shakespeare behold him, e'en Shakespeare would tremble'.[33] The very terms of such praise mark the radical separateness of Macklin and Shakespeare; the more completely the Irish actor is Shylock, the further he stands from the great poet. Shakespeare is here peculiarly removed from his own play. We have many images that bring the bodies of Garrick and Shakespeare into an intimate proximity that actively pushes towards a conflation of their identities: the double-sided enamel pendant, created to celebrate Garrick's Shakespeare Jubilee of 1769, that shows the actor on one side and the poet on the other; Thomas Gainsborough's now lost painting of Garrick casually cuddling-up to a bust of Shakespeare (*c.*1769), which was displayed for centuries in Stratford-upon-Avon Town Hall; and Louis-François Roubiliac's life-size marble statue of Shakespeare (1758), made for Garrick's Shakespeare Temple at his home at Hampton, for which the actor himself allegedly modelled. But the only image in which Macklin and Shakespeare share the same pictorial space is one that emphatically articulates their difference. The frontispiece to *An Apology for the Conduct of Mr Charles Macklin*, a pamphlet attack published in the heat of the 1773 *Macbeth* debacle, shows Macklin's Shylock carrying a triumphant, irradiated Shakespeare on his shoulders (Figure 1.6). The accompanying verses make the point in the bluntest of terms: 'Immortal Shakspear! Child of Heaven & fire, | The more we sink

---

32 See Michael Dobson, *The Making of the National Poet: Shakespeare, Adaptation and Authorship, 1660–1769* (Oxford: Clarendon Press, 1992), 176–84 and Heather McPherson, 'Garrickomania: Garrick's Image', on *Folgerpedia* (2015): https://folgerpedia.folger.edu/Garrickomania:_Garrick%27s_Image (accessed 10 August 2021).

33 Anthony Pasquin [John Williams], *The Children of Thespis. A Poem. Part the Second* (London, 1767), 23.

*Immortal Shakespear! Child of Heaven & fire,
The more we sink him rises still the higher:
E'en thro' THIS Vehicle the Bard can pass
Like Mecca's Prophet — mounted on an ASS.*

Figure 1.6: Frontispiece to *An Apology for the Conduct of Mr Charles Macklin, Comedian* (London: T. Axtell, 1773). By permission of the Folger Shakespeare Library, Washington, DC.

him rises still the higher: | E'en through this Vehicle the Bard can pass | Like Mecca's Prophet—mounted on an Ass'. Hinged on the juxtaposition of art and labour, this satire regards Macklin as not merely—and in this case, literally—any 'vehicle' for Shakespeare. Rather, Macklin's very abjectness proves the acid test of Shakespeare's cultural worth, because if such worth can not only withstand but even flourish through the aberrant body of an Irishman playing a Jew then its durability cannot be in doubt. Shakespeare is all that Macklin isn't.

Garrick never played Shylock and so never invited audiences directly to compare—or worse, equate—his performing body with that Macklin's. But, as we know, at Covent Garden in 1773 Macklin had the audacity to play Macbeth, a role that Garrick had in many ways made his own since the 1740s. The sequence of events that swiftly followed this late-career move—the rioting, humiliation, and trial of Macklin's adversaries—has been thoroughly charted by Paul Goring and Kristina Straub.[34] What concerns me here is the extent to which this moment discloses with far greater clarity than any other in Macklin's career the cultural logic of bodily seeming that I've been tracing, precisely because that logic found itself so flagrantly violated. When Macklin played Macbeth, that is, he sought publicly to shift his orientation towards and within the Shakespearean repertory. Outrageously, he endeavoured not to look like Shylock.

Macklin famously played the role in Scottish highland dress, once more laying claim to an authenticity that his rivals had bypassed. Yet contemporaries nonetheless regarded his performance as an attempt not only to compete with or replace but actively to *be* David Garrick. In this way, the blatant, perhaps even intentional, inaccuracies of the print, *Mr Macklin, In the Character of Macbeth, Act II^d Scene 3^d* (Figure 1.7) only make sense if we regard this image as a depiction of Macklin *as* Garrick's Macbeth, for the modern military costume and startled gesture are unmistakably the latter's. Of course, as the astringent satire of the *Apology*'s frontispiece suggests, to be Garrick was by extension to stand as the very embodiment of Shakespeare and therefore, in Macklin's case, to be guilty of a gross, albeit necessarily failed act of ethnic confusion and cultural desecration (the two are one and the same here). *Roscius in Triumph, or the downfall of Shylock alias Mackbeth* (Figure 1.8), an etching published in the *Macaroni Magazine* in 1773, vividly imagines

---

34 Paul Goring, 'Theatrical Riots and Conspiracies in London and Edinburgh: Charles Macklin, James Fennell and the Rights of Actors and Audiences', *Review of English Studies* 67.278 (2016), 122–45; Kristina Straub, 'The Newspaper "Trial" of Charles Macklin's *Macbeth* and the Theatre as Juridical Public Sphere', *Eighteenth-Century Fiction* 27.3–4 (2015), 395–418.

Figure 1.7: *Mr Macklin, In the Character of Macbeth, Act II^d Scene 3^d* (n.d.). By permission of the Folger Shakespeare Library, Washington, DC.

Figure 1.8: *Roscius in Triumph, or the downfall of Shylock alias Mackbeth* (*Macaroni, Savoir Vivre and Magazine*, 1 December 1773). © The Trustees of the British Museum.

Macklin's punishment for such a transgression, with his Shylock tormented and hauled into the pit of hell by two devils while a resplendent Garrick, held aloft by the figures of Tragedy and Comedy, looks on.[35] The contrast is between decorous and indecorous bodies, between Macklin's dishevelled, shaggy-haired, sprawling Shylock and the statuesque, clean-shaven, smartly dressed Garrick, who figures as both the epitome of cultural hygiene and—in his Elizabethan shirt and doublet—the effigy of Shakespeare. The print evidently draws on Joshua Reynolds's 1761 portrait, *Garrick between Tragedy and Comedy*, but in its staging of simultaneous apotheosis and damnation, of a rise and fall that are inversely proportional, it more precisely replays and adapts the climactic spectacle of Garrick's own play *Harlequin's Invasion* (1759), in which 'Shakespeare rises' and 'Harlequin sinks'.[36] Like the speaking, habitually violent Harlequin of Garrick's pantomime, Macklin as would-be Macbeth is the cultural trespasser, the embodied inversion of the native canon.

This satire makes no attempt to capture either actor's likeness. Garrick, as the English Roscius, is made known through his interaction with the classical genres in a scene that strikingly presages the design of his memorial in Westminster Abbey (1797; Figure 1.9), where he stands tall with the figures of Tragedy and Comedy at his feet. Macklin, however, isn't an actor; he is identifiable only as Shylock. No distinction is to be made between the two: he doesn't play Shakespeare's Jew, he *is* Shakespeare's Jew. And another caricature of the same year, *Shylock turnd Macbeth* (Figure 1.10), points with still greater clarity to this deep, irrevocable conjoining of Macklin's and Shylock's bodies in the cultural memory. Here Macklin, shown in profile, plays the medieval Scot and is decked out in a feathered bonnet, plaid, kilt, thistle badge, claymore, and tartan socks. For Michael Ragussis, this image's overlaying of Irish, Jewish, and Scottish identities posits Macklin 'as a kind of ethnic shape-changer', but the joke is surely that Macklin hasn't really shifted shape at all: Macklin as Macbeth is always, impossibly, Shylock as Macbeth.[37] The caricature's epigraph—'I see thee yet, in form as palpable | As that which now I draw'—would seem to indicate that we here view Macklin reciting Macbeth's 'Is this a dagger which I see before me' soliloquy (2.1.33–64),

---

35 Felsenstein notes that assumptions that Jews conversed with devils 'were also commonplace in the iconographical representation of Jews' (*Anti-Semitic Stereotypes*, 173). See, for instance, the satirical print *A Prospect of the New Jerusalem* (BM 3204), which attacks the ministry for its passing of the Jewish Naturalization Act of 1753.

36 David Garrick, *Harlequin's Invasion*, in Harry William Pedicord and Fredrick Louis Bergmann (eds), *The Plays of David Garrick*, vol. 1, *Garrick's Own Plays, 1740–1766* (Carbondale: Southern Illinois University Press, 1980), 224.

37 Ragussis, *Theatrical Nation*, 45.

Figure 1.9: Inigo Barlow, *Monument to the Memory of David Garrick, Esq.ʳ* (London: W. Bent, 3 August 1797). By permission of the Folger Shakespeare Library, Washington, DC.

Figure 1.10: *Shylock turnd Macbeth* (London: M. Darby, 5 November 1773). © Victoria and Albert Museum, London.

except that the weapon in question is no 'dagger of the mind'; it pertains, like the actor, to the wrong play.[38] Clutching a real blade, Macklin continues to be Shylock even as he strives to embody Macbeth. It is the performer, not Shakespeare's character, who is shown to be in the sway of a powerful delusion. So the words of the quotation function doubly and also give voice to the satirist who in this etching undertakes to 'draw' the Shylock that he and others 'see yet', despite Macklin's manifest efforts to be someone else. 'I learn'd To-night what ne'er before I knew', went one impromptu of the day, 'That a *Scotch Monarch*'s like an *Irish Jew*'.[39]

In the look of his relentlessly vindictive Shylock, and in so forcefully exploiting and renewing anti-Semitic stereotypes, Macklin thus paradoxically put his body at the furthest possible remove from the ideological construct of 'Shakespeare' in the very act of restoring one of Shakespeare's plays to the London stage. In many ways, Macklin's and Garrick's bodies were commensurately powerful as cultural and racial signifiers. Both were 'originals', the first and truest of their kind, but where Garrick came to function as a surrogate for the Shakespearean nation, for the very essence and achievement of English culture itself, the abject body of Macklin (read Macklin's Shylock) conversely provided the late eighteenth century with a convenient, immediately legible shorthand for that which stood outside of and challenged the boundaries of Englishness. 'Take of every thing Odious that's under the Sun, | By which Social Order is Chiefly Undone', begins *An Infallible Recipe*'s satirical portrait of him. If Garrick gave the public someone with whom they could identify or stand in close relation to, then Macklin's look was equally important in the evolving project of English cultural definition in that it gave compelling corporeal form to a particular kind of monstrous alterity—an alterity deserving of praise so long as it performed only itself—against which the public might readily define themselves. Roach notes that the actor 'is not there *for* us, but *instead* of us', yet Macklin reminds us how far the efficacy of theatre's fantasies also depend on the presence on stage of performers who are there precisely because they are *not* us.[40]

So, where the bodies of Garrick and Shakespeare tightly overlay one another in eighteenth-century visual culture, we contrastingly find Macklin—if only for a brief moment in the late 1780s—serving as a curious body double for the period's most prominent and suspect figure of political opposition, the Whig parliamentarian Charles James Fox. As Don Herzog

---

38 All references to Shakespeare's plays are taken from *The Complete Works*, ed. Stanley Wells and Gary Taylor, 2nd edn. (Oxford: Clarendon Press, 2005).
39 ['Bob Short'], 'Impromptu's, On seeing Mr Macklin in *Macbeth*'.
40 Roach, 'Morality as Style', 107.

Figure 1.11: James Hook, *The Trial* (London: S.W. Fores, 17 May 1788). Courtesy of The Lewis Walpole Library, Yale University.

notes, the Whigs were often derided as 'Jews' in the years immediately following 1753, when they had backed the controversial Jewish Naturalization Bill, and Fox's notorious reliance on Jewish financiers to manage his huge debts made the same disturbing racialization of party politics an all too easy manoeuvre for opponents and satirists some thirty years later.[41] Richard Newton's *Cries of London* (May 1797), for instance, caricatures Fox as a corrupt Jewish moneychanger who traffics in fake currency, while James Hook's 1788 satirical print, *The Trial*, casts him as Shylock (Figure 1.11). This latter image specifically responds to Fox's role as one of the managers of the impeachment of Warren Hastings, the former governor general of the East India Company. Hook parodies *Merchant*'s courtroom drama in order satirically to parse the Foxite agenda in prosecuting Hastings, here shown (in oriental dress) as Antonio and protected from the bloodlust of Fox's Shylock by the Portia of Edward Law, the defence counsel. As Daniel O'Quinn rightly observes, this 'image of Fox the Jew depicts him and, by extension, the managers as agents of vengeance, not justice', with Fox shown to use the law

---

41 Don Herzog, *Poisoning the Minds of the Lower Orders* (Princeton, NJ: Princeton University Press, 1998), 377–78.

as a pretext for undermining the Pitt ministry and moving against the King, who had engineered his expulsion from office in 1783. But, as O'Quinn goes on to note, 'the invocation of Shylock' also signals Fox's vociferous opposition to the prerogative of the Crown—here the embodiment of the mercy for which Portia calls—to be 'contrary to the interests of an ethnically defined Christian Britain'.[42] Fox others himself at the impeachment by so resolutely opposing not only against Hastings but, more fundamentally, the spirit of the English law and the sovereignty of George III.

At first glance, Fox's Shylock is not Macklin's: Hook's satire gives the Whig leader a sense of potential energy, of the body as a coiled spring that is rather redolent of Garrick's look. Yet, as we've established, in this period it was not possible to think of Macklin without conjuring Shylock or of Shylock without conjuring Macklin and given how far the parodic thrust of *The Trial* depends on a reading of Shylock's character as terrifyingly vengeful—a reading Macklin instituted—the shadow of Macklin certainly hangs over this print. Indeed, the two men's bodies at moments seem to stand in for one another. Fox, too, was said physically to resemble a Jew, while, in his 1798 biography of Macklin, Francis Aspry Congreve wrote that the actor's 'complexion was cadaverous, and much resembling that of the Right Hon. Charles James Fox'.[43] And just a year after Hook's caricature, John Boyne published a stipple engraving of *Merchant* Act 4 Scene 1 in which Macklin's Shylock seems almost to have become Fox (Figure 1.12). The thick, black, languid eyebrows, the girth of frame and protruding belly that strains the buttoned waistcoat, and most especially the five o'clock shadow that here even a stage beard and moustache don't conceal—none of these features is present in any other image of Macklin and all are entirely common to those of Fox. Would we, in honesty, recognize this as Macklin were it not for the print's title?

As in Zoffany's painterly rendering of the same dramatic moment, Boyne stages this courtroom exchange as one of racial difference, with Shylock visibly as well as figuratively darker than the bodies that surround and oppose him. At the same time, the engraving so closely replays the compositional arrangement of Hooke's *Trial* that we might ask whether that caricature provided a template for Boyne's far more costly print. However, in stark contrast both to all other visual representations of Macklin's Shylock and also to the Fox of Hook's satire, Boyne's Shylock is a conspicuously morose

---

42 Daniel O'Quinn, *Staging Governance: Theatrical Imperialism in London, 1770–1800* (Baltimore, MD: Johns Hopkins University Press, 2005), 224–26.
43 Karl Philipp Moritz, *Journeys of a German in England in 1782*, trans. Reginald Nettel (London: Jonathan Cape, 1965), 52; *Congreve*, 58–59.

Figure 1.12: John Boyne, *Mr Macklin & Mrs Pope in the Characters of Shylock and Portia* (London: J. Boyne, 1 April 1789). © Victoria and Albert Museum, London.

figure. There is a manifest discordance here between the character's downcast expression as he looks directly out at us and the specific point in the scene that is depicted. Where the quotation at the foot of the print offers a Shylock still thrilled by the prospect of revenge—'Por. *Have by some surgeon, Shylock, on your charge, to stop his wounds lest he should bleed to death.* Shy. *Is it so nominated in the bond?*' (4.1.254–56)—the image instead gives us something closer to the defeated, thoroughly humiliated Shylock who departs the scene ('give me leave to go from hence; | I am not well' [4.1.393–94]). Boyne published this engraving on 1 April 1789, just a few weeks after George III's recovery had brought an abrupt end to the Foxites' hopes of establishing a regency under the Prince of Wales, who would then have returned Fox and his Whig associates to government. I'd go so far as to suggest that Boyne's representation of a sullen Shylock, of a character who finds his opportunity for vengeance frustrated and himself humbled, offers an encoded satirical portrait of Fox's despair at the collapse of the proposed regency.

Boyne was himself a caricaturist who between 1783 and 1787 had repeatedly excoriated Fox for his ambition and cynical opportunism. Indeed, all but three of the twenty-one satirical prints attributed to Boyne in the British Museum catalogue feature Fox and the vast majority of this number take the Whig statesman as their central subject. Boyne obsessively etched Fox's body (see Figure 1.13). What is more, his caricatures evidence a particular delight in parody: of history painting (Fox as Benjamin West's dying Wolfe), of Hogarthian satire (Fox as a Methodist preacher), and, most especially, of Shakespeare, for three of Boyne's caricatures cast Fox as Falstaff and a further one imagines him as Bottom (Figure 1.14). The correspondences between these earlier satires and the engraving of Shylock in terms of their treatment of physiognomy of difference is striking—note, again, the paunch, the slumped eyebrows, the stubble—but it is equally significant that so many of Boyne's caricatures marshal the Shakespearean canon as a diagnostic tool for understanding Fox's political persona. In their occasional use of a stipple technique to render faces, Boyne's satirical prints trouble generic distinctions between the topical etching and the fine engraving, and *Mr Macklin & Mrs Pope in the Characters of Shylock and Portia* takes this a step further by quietly smuggling political satire under the guise of the supposed sincerity and verisimilitude of an expensive stipple engraving of a Shakespearean scene.

A host of questions arise from this reading of what is, in fact, the last image of Macklin as Shylock published in the actor's own lifetime. What, for instance, is the relationship between the theatre print and the satirical print at this time? How far should we attend to the differences between one image of a particular actor and another or seek to understand why some theatrical portraits barely resemble their subjects at all? And, most especially, when is

Figure 1.13: Detail of John Boyne, *Sir Zealous Godfrey* (London: H. Humphrey, 7 April 1784). Courtesy of The Lewis Walpole Library, Yale University.

Figure 1.14: John Boyne, *The Adventure of Prince Pretty Man* (London: J. Boyne, [1783]). Courtesy of The Lewis Walpole Library, Yale University. Fox, bottom right, is shown as Falstaff.

an image of an actor not an image of an actor? Together, the many pictures of Macklin, spanning the hierarchy of visual genres in the eighteenth century, confront us with the vexed issues of likeness, irony, and the cultural and ethnic valencies of the performing body. The work these images undertake is to both mark and enact the transformation of seeming into being, not transiently, as in Aaron Hill's formulation, but rather irrevocably. Boyne's depiction of a Macklin who doesn't much resemble Macklin only makes sense, and can be read properly, once we understand this history of Macklin's look—of how his body so entirely became that of Shylock and, concomitantly, of the Other that all concern with pictorial verisimilitude might put in abeyance. Put simply, Macklin's look displaced what Macklin looked like. As in *An Infallible Recipe*, Boyne's engraving physically invokes Macklin (because Macklin's body is the sign) without actually representing it. His rendering of Macklin's Shylock as Fox-as-Shylock—or, at the very least, as a discernibly Fox-like Shylock—suggests how far an actor's look might circulate and signify well beyond the boundaries of theatrical media, and indeed might come to function within an expressly political discourse.

As other chapters in this book suggest, Macklin's sustained and interlocking interests in literature, theatre, oratory, law, and education mark him as a figure who compellingly realizes—and complicates—scholarship's recent reconceptualization of the Enlightenment as a repertoire of embodied practices as much as a history of ideas. But this understanding of the Enlightenment also opens on to a media theory approach to the period that ultimately vexes any sense of Macklin's agency or exemplariness. If, as Clifford Siskin and William Warner insist, the Enlightenment was 'an event in the history of mediation', then Macklin seems to be its victim and not its instantiation.[44] On the one hand, the many images of Macklin I've considered here certainly corroborate Leslie Ritchie's definition of celebrity—one which allows us to push back against Siskin and Warner's privileging of the technology of print—as 'an iterative form of public recognition that is the product of repeated media exposures across multiple media platforms'.[45] On the other hand, what we see across Macklin's long career is that this process, through which the significance of his labour and body were recursively determined, is one over which he had precious little control. In the game of seeming, you'll remember, someone's 'look' runs both ways. To speak of 'Garrick's look' is

---

[44] Clifford Siskin and William Warner, 'This is Enlightenment: An Invitation in the Form of an Argument', Introduction to Clifford Siskin and William Warner (eds), *This is Enlightenment* (Chicago: Chicago University Press, 2010), 22.

[45] Leslie Ritchie, *David Garrick and the Mediation of Celebrity* (Cambridge: Cambridge University Press, 2019), 10.

to locate the self as style, to encounter a man who was, as Ritchie shows, the consummate self-publicist even in his marshalling of negative press. But to speak of 'Macklin's look', as we have seen, is rather to confront an actor whose body was relentlessly represented and judged by others—and whose standout success resided in the completeness of that abjection.[46]

---

46 A useful point of comparison here is offered by Oskar Cox Jensen, 'The Diminution of "Irish" Johnstone', in David O'Shaughnessy (ed.), *Ireland, Enlightenment, and the English Stage, 1740–1820* (Cambridge: Cambridge University Press, 2019), 79–97. Jensen argues the Irish comic actor John Johnstone was 'complicit' in the process that 'enshrined the Stage Irishman as crude stereotype' (95). On this account, and for all their differences as performers, the stage successes of both Johnstone and Macklin depended on their otherness as Irishmen.

2

Macklin's Books

Paul Goring

Macklin showed [Samuel Johnson] his library, and seemed to have a sufficient knowledge of every work it contained.

John Bernard, *Retrospections of the Stage* (1830), II.125

We might be the owners or purveyors of books [...] but we are not always their readers.

Christina Lupton, *Reading and the Making of Time in the Eighteenth Century* (2018), 20

MACKLIN WAS UNDOUBTEDLY one of the most bookish figures of the eighteenth-century theatrical world. This was noted by his contemporaries and we see traces of it in his plays and correspondence, but the fullest evidence lies in the records of his personal library. These records suggest, in fact, that Macklin was an almost compulsive bibliophile. At the time of his death he was in possession of a library of more than 3,000 volumes. That figure does not place it among the truly monumental personal libraries of the period, such as Topham Beauclerk's, which ran to more than 30,000 volumes and took fifty days to be auctioned off.[1] But Macklin's was still a very large collection and, given his relatively limited means, the building up

---

1 See *Bibliotheca Beauclerkiana: A Catalogue of the Large and Valuable Library of the late Honourable Topham Beauclerk* (London, 1781).

of it may be taken as a sign of his priorities, his interests, and, arguably, his self-image.[2] What might Macklin's book collection, this essay asks, tell us about its owner?

In terms of scale, Macklin's library was comparable with Garrick's, which included a general collection of over 3,000 volumes plus a corpus of early English printed plays. Garrick's collection was renowned and has been closely scrutinized—most recently in Nicholas D. Smith's *An Actor's Library: David Garrick, Book Collecting and Literary Friendships* (2017).[3] By contrast, Macklin's library has yet to receive more than incidental scholarly attention, despite rich evidence provided by two catalogues. As a first step towards rectifying the neglect, the aim here is to consider the general contours of the collection as well as the significance of the books as a gathered mass. What did the accumulation and possession of an extensive library mean to Macklin, and how may the collection have been used both personally and socially? What can Macklin's books tell us about his status not only as an actor and playwright but also as a figure within eighteenth-century networks of learning? Macklin has a walk-on part in Michael Brown's far-reaching recent study *The Irish Enlightenment* (2016), and this is due to his authorship of *Love à la Mode*; can a more extensive role be afforded to Macklin when his intellectual leanings are fleshed out through consideration of his books?[4]

The posthumous auction and the catalogues of Macklin's books

MACKLIN'S LIBRARY was dispersed a few months after his death in 1797. It was sold at auction to raise funds for his widow, Elizabeth Jones, and the catalogues that were drawn up for the sale provide almost all the evidence that we have of the collection. The auction took place at the Macklins' home at 6 Tavistock Row, Covent Garden, overseen by the auctioneer Thomas King, who had premises nearby.[5] Since King did not have

---

2 Regarding Macklin's disposable income, it may be said that during his successful working years he was well paid, but he suffered serious financial difficulties later; see *Appleton*, 230–32.

3 Nicholas D. Smith, *An Actor's Library: David Garrick, Book Collecting and Literary Friendships* (New Castle, DE: Oak Knoll Press, 2017).

4 Michael Brown, *The Irish Enlightenment* (Cambridge, MA: Harvard University Press, 2016), 337–39.

5 King took premises in King Street in Covent Garden in 1789. See 'King Street and Floral Street Area: King Street', in F.H.W. Sheppard (ed.), *Survey of London*, vol. 36,

the books moved from the house prior to the sale, we can be fairly sure that this was an auction purely of works that actually belonged to Macklin; in other words, the practice of adding extra stock to collections which were sold as private libraries probably did not occur. The sale lasted for five days starting at noon on Tuesday, 21 November. On the Monday before the auction, the public could go and inspect the collection and, for sixpence, could buy a printed *Catalogue of the Library of the Late Mr Charles Macklin*.[6]

There are two known extant copies of this printed catalogue (according to the *ESTC*). One is at the New York Public Library and the other is at the Folger Shakespeare Library (the latter appearing to be the copy of the auctioneer's clerk since it is annotated with buyers' names and purchase prices).[7] It is a fairly standard auction catalogue. It promotes Macklin's collection as 'A General Assemblage of Books in the Various Languages', while also drawing attention, through its title page, to some particular treasures: 'Nuict's de Straparole, 5 vol. on vellum; Harding's Shakspeare; Wood's Athenæ [...] Chronicle History of King Lear and Richard II. by Shakspeare [...] several excellent French Books' and others. It then presents the day-by-day schedule for the auction, with the collection divided into 1,117 lots, with many lots including multi-volume works, bundles of titles, and also unnamed 'others'. The first three lots, for example, are:

1 Comenius Janua Linguarum, or Gate of Languages Unlocked, 1650, and 11 others
2 Ainsworth's Latin Dictionary, by Thomas, vol. 1st, 1758, and 18 others
3 Latine Primitives, wants title, Gradus. Mair's Tyra's Dictionary, *Edin*. 1760. Caninii's Gr. Grammar, *Lond*. 1624, and 1 other[8]

There are signs that it was a challenge to organize the 'General Assemblage' that Macklin had accumulated. At the start of the catalogue keen taxonomic intentions are in evidence, with a heading for a section of 'Dictionaries and Grammars *Octavo et Infra*', but the content is not entirely true to the heading and the categorizations remain loose as the catalogue progresses. The few

---

Covent Garden (London: London County Council, 1970), 151–78: *British History Online*: www.british-history.ac.uk/survey-london/vol36/pp151-178 (accessed 25 April 2019). The auction catalogue, cited below, indicates that King also had premises at 369 Oxford Street—one of several addresses where the catalogue was available.

6 *A Catalogue of the Library of the Late Mr Charles Macklin, Comedian, Deceased* (London, 1797).

7 There is potential for further research in these annotations: they may illuminate the spectrum of buyers that the auction attracted, the monetary value of the collection, and also its afterlife following dispersal.

8 *Catalogue of the Library of the Late Mr Charles Macklin*, 3.

further headings that are included—'*Octavo & 12mo. French*', '*Histories, Miscellanies, &c. Octavo and 12mo*', '*Mathematical and Medical. 8vo. and 12mo*', '*Poetry and Plays. 8vo and 12mo*', and the like—provide little true systemization of the mass. Potential bidders were presented with a partially organized list, and because of the unspecified 'others', they must have consulted the books themselves in order to see all that was on offer.[9]

In addition to the printed catalogue, there is a manuscript catalogue, held by the Houghton Library, and it is this that forms the main foundation for the discussion here. Running to over 150 pages, this document must have been produced as part of the preparatory work for the auction, and there is much that it illuminates that is not disclosed by the subsequent print catalogue. The manuscript provides a more complete list of titles—with none obscured as 'others'—and it also reveals how Macklin's books were arranged in his home. It actually includes two inventories. There is an initial listing, of around a hundred pages, which records the titles as they were shelved. It begins by listing the volumes in the 'Front Room' on the 'Shelves on left hand beginning at the bottom'. It moves through the various shelves in this room and then on to the 'Middle Room', where most of the books were kept, starting with the 'Shelves on the Right hand begin^g at the bottom', and then onwards across dozens of shelves and through many hundreds of titles.[10] It then presents a second list of around fifty pages—a neater, more systematic revision of the first—which again indicates shelf positions but which reveals, when compared with the first, that some rearrangement of the library had been undertaken between the drawing up of the lists.[11] The rearrangement was presumably a part of the process of organizing the books into auction lots, and side by side the two lists afford a glimpse of the work that lay behind an eighteenth-century book auction. For scholars of Macklin, though, it is the

---

9 The difficulties of navigating the catalogue faced by those at the auction are, of course, shared by anyone attempting a scholarly investigation of the collection. To make the catalogue data more amenable to analysis—for the current essay and future research—the titles listed in the printed catalogue have been entered into a digital catalogue, using the online application *Librarything*. This catalogue is a *Librarything* 'Legacy Library' and is publicly available here: www.librarything.com/profile/CharlesMacklin. I am grateful to Rebecca Vollan who undertook the data entry and classification of the works.

10 James Thomas Kirkman, *Memoirs of the life of Charles Macklin, Esq. principally compiled from his own papers and memorandums*, 2 vols (London, 1799), extra-illustrated, Houghton Library, Harvard Theatre Collection TS 943.2 (I: pt. 2).

11 The second list also omits many titles given in the first—hence its shorter length—but it may be that the manuscript is missing parts or that sections in the first list were deemed adequate for the division of the collection into bundled lots and the production of the print catalogue.

first list that is the more useful: it gives the fuller inventory, while the shelving notes offer both a vivid impression of the imposing physical presence of the collection and clues as to how Macklin may have used his library.

We must, of course, be cautious about treating these catalogues as keys to Macklin's reading. '[P]ossessing books', as Abigail Williams warns in her recent *The Social Life of Books*, 'was not the same as reading them. [...] A catalogue on its own will never really enable us to understand the correlation between the listing of a book as a possession and its significance for its owner'.[12] We will never truly establish what Macklin read, ignored, admired, yawned over, scorned, and so on, and, in fact, we cannot be sure that he controlled everything that ended up in the collection. Book gifts may have been imposed upon him and we should remember that Macklin did not live alone; to what extent was 'the Library of the Late Mr. Charles Macklin' also the library of his wife? She had, according to James Kirkman, 'many polite accomplishments' and may have been a keen reader, despite her decision to sell the collection.[13] It is impossible, in short, to use the catalogue as a watertight index of Macklin's interests and to conclude, for example, that since the library contained Thomas Chatterton's *Miscellanies in Prose and Verse* he had any relationship with Chatterton's work. But it is reasonable to be somewhat less suspicious of trends and tendencies within the whole, and it is worth searching the catalogues for patterns from which inferences about Macklin might guardedly be drawn. Before beginning such an examination, though, it should be observed that the collection which was listed in 1797 was, remarkably, not the result of a lifetime of acquisition but was actually a type of *replacement* library—a fact which has implications for how we interpret the catalogues and which also points to the depths of Macklin's bibliophilia.

Macklin's lost library

'Crossing the Irish Sea', Craig Bailey observes in his study of eighteenth-century migration from Ireland to London, could be a 'dangerous undertaking'.[14] Macklin was fortunate to sail those treacherous waters unscathed numerous times—unlike several theatre colleagues, such as Theophilus Cibber, who died alongside many others when the *Dublin Trader*

---

12 Abigail Williams, *The Social Life of Books: Reading Together in the Eighteenth-Century Home* (New Haven, CT: Yale University Press, 2017), 108.
13 *Kirkman*, I.405.
14 Craig Bailey, *Irish London: Middle-Class Migration in the Global Eighteenth Century* (Liverpool: Liverpool University Press, 2013), 43.

went down in 1758. Macklin did, though, lose much of his personal property in a 1772 accident and this included an extensive book collection. Little is known about this earlier library, except that Macklin valued it very highly and that it was shipped after him when he moved from London to start an engagement at Dublin's Crow Street Theatre.[15] Kirkman describes the loss:

> When Mr. Macklin left London, in 1771, he shipped all his furniture, plate, pictures, and a very choice and valuable library of books, worth upwards of five thousand pounds, on board a Dublin trader, then lying in the River Thames, but, unfortunately, this ship was stranded on the Coast of Ireland, off Arklow, and almost the whole of Mr. Macklin's property was lost. What he had to regret most was the destruction of his books and manuscripts, the labour of many years close study and application.[16]

Sources suggest that Macklin visited the wreck himself to salvage what he could, for it was reported that, as the *Leinster Journal* put it, 'the greatest part of the cargo will be saved', but there was little of his property that survived.[17] He fell ill that spring—perhaps because of his foray into the sea—and when news reached his daughter Maria in London, she wrote with concern: 'I sincerely lament the loss of your most valuable Library, it was indeed a dreadful Stroke. Yet I had rather all the Books in the World had been lost sooner than you shou'd have suffer'd such an Illness or have ventur'd down to the Wreck in such Weather'.[18] Her singling out of the library—with no mention of the other possessions—is suggestive of her awareness that Macklin valued his books above all other chattels. She wrote a further letter that day and offered her ailing father the type of medicine a bibliophile would most appreciate: 'pray let me know if there are any Books of any kind that you want that I can send you'.[19]

It was a loss which could partly be translated into monetary terms, and Macklin became involved in a drawn-out insurance claim involving a London broker. In December 1772, Maria wrote to him to report a lack of progress: 'The affair remains just as it did, & will do so till you send over more Proofs to satisfy the Insurers that you had Goods on board to the Value of the sum

---

15 For a fuller discussion of the shipwreck and Macklin's loss, see Paul Goring, 'The Sinking of Charles Macklin's Scholarship', *Notes & Queries* 66.4 (2019), 577–81.
16 *Kirkman*, II.46.
17 *Finn's Leinster Journal*, 22–25 January 1772.
18 6 May 1772, in Kirkman, *Memoirs*, extra-illustrated, Houghton Library, Harvard Theatre Collection TS 943.2 (II: pt. 1), 54.
19 6 May 1772. This letter was auctioned by International Autograph Auctions Ltd on 5 July 2018, with an image that was consulted on 10 April 2019. The site is no longer live. The other letter of 6 May cited above states that she will write him a further letter.

insured'.[20] As Kirkman's report suggests, though, not all that was gone could have a price put upon it. Macklin's library was a truly personal collection in that he had not only assembled it but had used it as a basis for his studies—perhaps annotating the books as he read—and his own writings, in manuscript form, had grown out of his intellectual engagement with the collection and, without having reached a printing press, were gathered with the books. Macklin lived a further quarter of a century after the shipwreck, but he never managed to publish a work of theatrical scholarship. In Kirkman's account, the shipwreck was the main reason for this gap in his output and legacy:

> It was not Mr. Macklin alone that had to lament this loss; the Stage, and the whole of the dramatic world, suffered very materially by the shipwreck; the merciless waves destroyed his Treatises on the *Science of Acting*, on the *Works of Shakespeare*, on *Comedy*, *Tragedy*, and many other subjects, together with several manuscripts of infinite value and importance to the British Theatre.[21]

Much of Kirkman's biography was based on late conversations with Macklin, and so what we probably have here is a rendering of Macklin's own version of the significance of the 1772 disaster. The state of completion and quality of the lost treatises is not known, but what is clear—if Macklin was indeed the source—is that Macklin saw himself as having been cheated by the waves of the intellectual status he deserved as a scholarly author. And this may partly explain why, after the shipwreck, he zealously embarked upon a process of re-establishing a rich and imposing library—a personal resource, but also an outward sign of his learning which he never came to prove through scholarly publications bearing his name.

Exactly how much of the new library Macklin acquired after 1772 is unclear because we do not know what survived the shipwreck—and also what might have been stored in London and never been put on board. In line with Kirkman's account of some materials having survived, the printed auction catalogue lists a number of items that are suggestive of Macklin having not lost everything. For example, it concludes with eleven lots of manuscripts and among the named items are 'Mr. Macklin's Case' and 'a Will and no Will, or a Bone for the Lawyers'.[22] There is no good reason for manuscript versions of either of these works to have been produced after 1772—*The Case of Charles Macklin* had been published in 1743; *A Will and No Will* was not played after the 1750s—and so we can probably deem them survivors or non-travellers. The catalogue also includes a sequence of lots (817–23) presenting works

---

20 9 December 1772, Folger Shakespeare Library, Y.c.5381 (2).
21 *Kirkman*, II.46–47.
22 *Catalogue of the Library of the Late Mr Charles Macklin*, 41.

published before 1772, described as 'stained'; were these volumes perhaps salvaged from the Arklow waters yet left with marks of their misadventure? Whatever survived, Macklin was clearly deeply bereft and despite his age—more than three score years and ten by that time—his response was to set about gathering the new library that would come to pack the home he made in London following his return from Dublin in 1773.

A tour across Macklin's shelves using the manuscript catalogue

WHILE MACKLIN VALUED BOOKS he was relatively casual when it came to their arrangement. Examining his library via the manuscript catalogue, it soon becomes apparent that a large proportion of the collection was shelved in a largely unsystematic way. The list begins with a heading 'Folio Quarto' (suggesting that the cataloguer may have been learning about book sizes on the job) and what follows is a long and largely miscellaneous collection of titles running to some forty pages—getting on for half the library. The shelf locations are noted but within this sequence there is no heading indicative of subject area, and, in fact, despite the promise of 'Folio Quarto', format turns out not to be an organizing principle as folio and octavo volumes are found rubbing shoulders with the quartos.[23] The listing shows some thematic groupings—seven works of grammar are gathered together, for example—but much is randomly ordered, with sequences such as 'Rusden on Bees' (1679), 'The Civil Wars of England' (1680), 'The High German Doctor' (1720), 'Montagu's Letters' (1777), and 'The Historian's Guide' (1688).[24] Macklin may have been able to navigate this assortment of volumes—and it should be noted that there are many multi-volume works in this section which probably stood out visually—but the lack of order (plus further evidence later in the catalogue) suggests that this part of the collection, filling the 'Front Room' and reaching into the 'Middle Room', was the less regularly used part of the library. Thereafter, the catalogue shows the care of organization at work and thematic groupings begin to appear in the list, but the whole library was not trawled to gather the volumes which 'should' have been placed within

---

23 Some headings in the manuscript may have been lost through cropping, since the leaves have been mounted and bound. The titles in this section, though, suggest no thematic or generic arrangement.

24 Titles are presented here as given in the manuscript, which uses many shortened forms. To retain a sense of the catalogue's register, many other titles are presented in this way. In some cases, where clarity is lost by retaining the manuscript form, italics are used and the titles are given as generally recognized.

particular sections. The miscellaneous section and another such section at the end of the catalogue both contain many works which would have been appropriate within the generically defined gatherings.

The first generically headed section is 'Divinity', filling six pages of the list. It is, of course, quite normal to find a substantial gathering of religious and theological works in an eighteenth-century book collection, but it is noteworthy that this should appear as an organized section in Macklin's library, given that he was not known for great devotion. Brought up with a Catholic mother and a Presbyterian father, Macklin, according to his early biographer William Cooke, 'inclined to her religion' but only 'as much as a man may be said to belong to any religion, who was so careless as he was about its ceremonies and injunctions'. Aged around forty, Macklin converted to Protestantism—and notable here is a story that it was a book that brought about his change. Cooke writes that Macklin picked up 'a little book upon a stall called "The Funeral of the Mass"' while strolling through Lincoln's Inn Fields. Struck by the title, Macklin bought it and 'read it two or three times over very attentively, the consequence of which was, that he deserted his mother church, and became a convert to the Protestant religion'.[25] The paucity of references to his religion in early accounts, though, suggests that he gave little attention to matters of faith, and it is significant that the Divinity section contains mostly older publications. There are many seventeenth-century titles and just four dated later than 1772, the year of the shipwreck, from which the most concrete conclusion to be drawn is that post-1772 Macklin was not, at least through book purchases, keeping up with the very latest sermons and currents of thought within divinity. Indeed, two of the four more recent publications—'Keach's Scripture Metaphors' (1779) and 'Bunyan's Holy War' (1775)—were not new as such but reprints of seventeenth-century works. However, one cannot definitively equate a scarcity of new titles in a library with a lack of interest in a subject on the part of the owner—something which the next section of the catalogue eloquently demonstrates.

That section is headed 'Law', a topic which preoccupied Macklin more than most matters, aside from the theatre. Through his trial for the killing of Thomas Hallam in 1735, Macklin developed a keen interest in the law and he can be said to have had an amateur legal career as he pursued later cases, fighting in the courts for the rights of performers (in the 1740s and 1770s) and fiercely defending his authorial rights to *Love à la Mode*. It is almost inevitable that his library should have had a designated 'Law' section, and yet it is more modest than might be expected, running to only two and a half pages in the catalogue, and containing just seventy-one titles. As in the

---

25 *Cooke*, 75.

'Divinity' section, many of the books were timeworn—there are twenty-one seventeenth-century titles and one work, 'Commonwealth of England', from 1583 (presumably *De Republica Anglorum* by Sir Thomas Smith). All but a handful of publications pre-date the shipwreck, but among the later works are titles that do point to Macklin's engagement with contemporary legal matters. From 1772, Macklin had two copies of Henry Dagge's *Considerations of Criminal Law*, a substantial and important critique of English penal law.[26] He also had three volumes of George Wilson's *Reports of the cases argued and adjudged in the King's Courts at Westminster* (1784) and five volumes of Sir James Burrow's *Reports of Cases Adjudged in the Court of King's Bench* (1785). Macklin knew the legal institutions of London well—it was in the Court of King's Bench that his own case in the long controversy surrounding his 1773 production of *Macbeth* had been heard and judged by William Murray, the Lord Chief Justice and Earl of Mansfield.[27] These volumes in his library suggest that, well into his eighties, Macklin liked to remain in touch with the proceedings of the courts. He also had a modern edition of a fifteenth-century legal work, 'Fortescue on the Laws of England', published in 1775, the year of his own victory in the Court of King's Bench; perhaps this work by Sir John Fortescue, an early Chief Justice of that same court, was acquired in 1775 in recognition of his triumph at the end of a drawn-out and taxing dispute. Alternatively, it may be a sign of Macklin's interest in the history of the law alongside his personal engagement with contemporary legal matters. If Macklin did lose all or most of his legal library in 1772, he built up its replacement primarily through the acquisition of older volumes, and the catalogue suggests that antiquarian or historical interest dictated many of the choices rather than an ambition to build up a comprehensive modern collection. The library includes, for example, 'Blount's Law Dictionary' from 1670, but, surprisingly, there is no volume of William Blackstone's celebrated *Commentaries on the Laws of England* (1765–69).

Following 'Law', there is a small collection of medical books,[28] and then follows the largest headed section in the library, running to twenty pages

---

26 Dagge's work was expanded for a 1774 edition in three volumes; Macklin's library appears to have two copies of the one-volume 1772 version. For a brief account of Dagge's position within the philosophy of the law, see Lindsay Farmer, 'Of Treatises and Textbooks: The Literature of Criminal Law in Nineteenth-Century Britain', in Angela Fernandez and Markus D. Dubber (eds), *Law Books in Action: Essays on the Anglo-American Legal Treatise* (Oxford: Hart Publishing, 2012), 149.
27 For more on Macklin and Mansfield, see David Worrall, '"Strong Case": Macklin and the Law', in this volume.
28 A title in the manuscript here has been cropped but it can be deciphered as 'Physick'; the section is headed thus in the second list.

of the manuscript list: 'French Books'. With language being the ordering principle, this section has a wide generic reach and includes dictionaries, grammars, histories, sermons, prose fiction, and more. There are also many volumes of French drama and works on the theatre and acting, such as two editions of 'Observations sur l'art du Comedien' (1774 and 1775) by Jean Nicolas Servandoni D'Hannetaire. Here the catalogue confirms what is clear from other sources: that Macklin was very attentive to what was happening in the world of the theatre across the Channel. Gaining access to the developments that were occurring within his profession on the continent was doubtless one of the greatest benefits of developing his French proficiency, which he apparently did late in life: 'at sixty', according to John Bernard's *Retrospections of the Stage*, 'he was versed in [the grammar] of the Latin, Greek, French, and Italian languages'.[29] But French was also crucial to participation in European intellectual life and the library shows that Macklin was also interested in following the currents of French Enlightenment thought: the catalogue presents many philosophical and scientific works by such luminaries as Rousseau, Voltaire, Diderot, Fontenelle, and Montesquieu. French appears to have been Macklin's preferred language for prose fiction too. The library contains relatively little prose fiction: a tally of titles in the print catalogue presents around seventy titles that may be categorized as such, but it is notable that over half of those are French-language works. Overall, the section of French books constitutes around a fifth of the library, and many of the titles are more recent publications, including many published after the year of the shipwreck; there are also older volumes but the bulk of the French works have publication dates from the middle decades of the eighteenth century. This part of the library points conclusively to French thought and culture having become a very particular interest for Macklin in his later years.

Thereafter six headed sections of the catalogue present what is entirely expected in the library of a busy actor and playwright whose career had spanned many dozens of roles. They present Macklin's drama collection, subdivided according to genre and print format: 'Quarto Plays Comedies'; 'Tragedies. Quarto'; 'Quarto. Operas, Pastorals'; 'Comedies. Octavo'; 'Tragedies Octavo'; and 'Operas, Farces, Pastorals etc. Octavo'. Together these sections fill nine pages of the catalogue (five of them half pages) and they present altogether around 180 titles. Reflecting a significant shift in the printing of dramatic works during Macklin's lifetime, the quartos are, with just a few exceptions, earlier publications, dating from the late seventeenth century and early years of George I's reign. Then the collection reflects the later preference for the octavo format, and most of these smaller volumes date

---

29 John Bernard, *Retrospections of the Stage*, 2 vols (London, 1830), II.120.

from the period of Macklin's career as an actor.[30] Many of the titles, though, were published long before the shipwreck, so if Macklin was gathering them post-1772 then he was acquiring them largely as used books. This part of the library was clearly a professional resource, but the catalogue shows that Macklin continued to add dramatic works to his library as he neared his final performance in 1789 and during his retirement. He maintained an interest in what the very latest authors for the stage were writing in the 1780s and 1790s. He had two works by the soldier-turned-dramatist John Burgoyne: *The Heiress* (1786) and *The Maid of the Oaks* (1794). He had *Julia, Or, The Italian Lover* (1787) by his fellow countryman, Robert Jephson, and *Zorinski* (1795) by the up-and coming Thomas Morton. By the largely unknown John Macaulay he had *The Genius of Ireland: A Masque* (1785), a title which probably appealed to him. The drama section provides confirmation of what was obviously a true passion, and it shows that that passion never left him. It should be noted also that his collection of plays was considerably larger than that shown in these six designated sections in the catalogue. The less-organized part of the library (listed in the catalogue's first forty pages) includes numerous dramatic works: 'Beaumont and Fletcher's Plays in 10 Vols' (1750), 'Johnson's Shakespeare 8 Vols' (1765), 'Johnson's Shakespeare 12 Vols' (1771), 'Massinger's Works 4 Vols' (1759), six volumes of 'Anonymous Comedies' (1760), and many others. If there was a policy determining the arrangement, multi-volume runs of drama were shelved in the front room, while individually published plays were gathered in the drama section in the middle room, but it was not strictly applied.

In the final twelve pages of the manuscript catalogue (that is, of the first of the two manuscript inventories) there is a return to a mixing of genres, but when compared with the earlier miscellaneous section there is a much higher proportion of newer publications, with many works published in the 1770s and 1780s. It seems that this was the place for 'latest acquisitions' and contemporary material; alongside the dated titles, a small number of summary entries, such as 'Magazines & Reviews 39 numbers', are indicative of such a profile. Again, we cannot point to a strict policy since the first miscellaneous section includes some later publications, but the catalogue is suggestive of such a leaning. Most importantly, we may presume that this later section, with the large number of post-1772 titles, lists considered purchases and that

---

30 On changes in the typical book format for the publication of plays, see Judith Milhous and Robert D. Hume, *The Publication of Plays in London, 1660–1800: Playwrights, Publishers, and the Market* (London: The British Library, 2015). Milhous and Hume divide the period into 'The Age of the Quarto, 1660–1715' and 'The Era of Octavo and Duodecimo, 1715–1800'.

the titles found on these final twelve pages are reflective of Macklin's actual interests; the same cannot be said of the earlier miscellaneous section, which, with its many older titles, could well include some job-lot purchases.

There are further plays here and works of dramatic criticism and theatre history—for example, three volumes of 'Dramatic Miscellanies' (1784), 'The Faithful Shepherd' (1782), 'Remarks on Shakespeare' (1783), and a life of the actor John Henderson (1777). There are also French works (more Voltaire, for example) and some works, such as 'Divinity Lectures' (1775), which might have found a place in the 'Divinity' section, although these are very few, suggesting again that Macklin did not devote great energies to religious matters in his later years. He did, though, take a keen interest in the politico-theological controversies surrounding the Dissenter and scientist Joseph Priestley in 1787: 'Letters to Priestley by the rev[d] Mr Madan' (1787), 'Remarks on David Levi's Letters to Dr Priestly' (1787), and 'A Letter to D[r] Priestley' (1787) all appear in his library. There are also further medical works and a good many additions to the collection of law books. Macklin followed closely the legal work of Lord Mansfield, to whose rulings he was personally indebted. He owned, for example, 'Judgment of the Earl of Mansfield on a Cause' (1784) and 'A Letter to the Jurors of Great Britain occasioned by an Opinion of the Court of King's Bench, read by Lord Chief Justice Mansfield in the Case of the King v Woodfall' (1785). Unsurprisingly, we also find matter relating to his own past legal actions: 'Arguments of the Council in the Cause of the conspiracy against Macklin' (1774).

These final pages also list a substantial poetry collection—around three dozen volumes, largely from the 1770s, which appear as a grouping within the other miscellaneously arranged material. But what is most striking here are the catalogue's indications of Macklin's interest in contemporary politics and of his attention to ongoing events and debates, both local and international. He appears to have kept a close eye on the American Revolution, through reports of the most important developments—for example, 'Votes & proceedings of the American Congress' (1774)—and works of opinion such as 'Reflections upon the present state of England, and the Independence of America' (1782) by Thomas Day, a supporter of the American colonists. Military matters were of ongoing interest to him, as suggested by copies of 'Advice to the Officers of the British Army' (1782) and 'History of the Campaigne of 1794' (1794). He had works examining the British political system, such as 'Thoughts on equal representation' (1783) by Francis Basset, and also works conveying what was going on at the heart of that system, including a 1780 'Speech of Edmund Burke' and 'Fox & Pit's Speeches in the House of Commons on June 8th '84' (1784). His library contained both conservative and liberal opinion; Burke is there but so too is Thomas Paine's *Rights of Man* (dated 1791, so presumably the first part). Macklin supported the Whigs; he exercised his franchise, and we know that in a Westminster election in 1796 he gave his vote to Charles James Fox.[31] But his library was no echo chamber of his own views, and the catalogue suggests that he informed himself of the various sides of the debates in the heated political climate of his last years.

He particularly followed Irish news and the politics of Anglo-Irish relations. He retained a passionate interest in his native country and it is known that he remained involved in London's Irish social and intellectual networks until his final years. His library reflects this strand of his sociability, with many works concerning Ireland, and notably a clutch of titles published in the wake of the establishment of the Irish Parliament in 1782. The catalogue lists 'Tucker on England and Ireland', 'Reflections on the Trade between England & Ireland', and 'Plan for settling the Government of Ireland', all from 1785. He had two copies of John Magee's 'An Irishman's reception in London' (1787), which was doubtless of personal interest to him, and he also followed Irish theatrical news, notably the passage of the Irish Stage Bill in the 1780s. He had, for example, 'Candid remarks on the Stage Bill now defending' (1785) and two copies of 'Case of the Stage in Ireland' (1786). These titles were doubtless of great personal interest but they would also have rendered him a knowledgeable participant in the intellectual circles in which he moved. They were published while Macklin, for example, was a governor and select committee member of the Benevolent Society of St Patrick, founded in 1783. He was a loyal attender of this charitable society's anniversary dinners, and his library suggests that at such events he would have been a well-informed conversationalist and disputant on a wide range of contemporary Irish topics.[32]

Overall, the titles in this final section show Macklin to be a serious reader who, in his later years, was deeply engaged in what was happening in the world and in the ongoing debates which surrounded a whole spectrum of issues. Collectively, the titles also, of course, display Macklin's fundamental bibliophilia, and it is worth noting that his own library included two copies of the vast 'Catalogue of the Library of Topham Beauclerk' (1781). Had Macklin been one of the buyers at the fifty-day auction of Beauclerk's books? Perhaps Beauclerk's 30,000 volume library was something to aspire to—even for an octogenarian.

---

31 See the database within 'London Electoral History 1700–1850': http://leh.ncl.ac.uk/ (accessed 10 August 2021).
32 Craig Bailey, 'From Innovation to Emulation: London's Benevolent Society of St Patrick, 1783–1800', *Eighteenth-Century Ireland* 27 (2012), 176.

Macklin and Enlightenment learning

ONE BASIC EFFECT of conducting an overview of Macklin's library is the solidification of the idea of him as a serious, engaged thinker. It allows us to recognize better the intellectual leanings of a figure who published plays and pamphlets concerning controversies he was involved in but was frustrated—perhaps because of a shipwreck, perhaps for other reasons—in his ambitions to produce scholarly works on the art of acting, drama, the history of the stage, and more, and so has rarely been remembered as a figure within the eighteenth-century world of learning. David O'Shaughnessy has described how 'Macklin's Enlightenment credentials have been lost in plain sight to modern critics', despite being recognized in his time, and O'Shaughnessy has worked to rehabilitate Macklin 'as a writer with a coherent intellectual and political vision'.[33] By considering the traces of Macklin's library—the toolbox of the intellectual—we are able, in a very general sense, to advance that rehabilitation, whilst the pursuit of particular threads within the library's wide-ranging content may afford a refinement of our knowledge of Macklin as a participant in the intellectual culture of his time.

The long story of Macklin's life offers more than a few opportunities to dwell upon non-achievement as an intellectual: the ridicule that his British Inquisition prompted in the 1750s, the rioting that followed his historically researched production of *Macbeth* in the 1770s, as well as the treatises that never appeared. The library may act as a counterweight here, providing an indication of Macklin's role as a node within contemporary networks of learned life. In this respect, it important to recall the place the library had in Macklin's home and that it had a social function as well as serving as a personal resource. At Tavistock Row, in the heart of London's theatre district, Macklin not only read and studied but also entertained numerous guests: friends and acquaintances, established colleagues from the theatre world, aspiring actors seeking the advice of the 'Nestor of the Stage', students of elocution, and more. The manuscript catalogue, with its shelving notes, shows that Macklin surrounded himself with a mass of books and that visitors to his 'Front Room' and 'Middle Room' would have encountered him against a powerful and eloquent backdrop—walls of spines, asserting with heavy presence the scholarly inclinations of the host and creating an environment which would foster erudite exchange. The actor John Bernard was one of those who experienced Macklin as a conversational partner. In his *Retrospections of the Stage*, he described how Macklin spent his last decades

---

33 David O'Shaughnessy, '"Bit, by some mad whig": Charles Macklin and the Theater of Irish Enlightenment', *Huntington Library Quarterly* 80.4 (2017), 560, 567.

'laying up his knowledge'; he was not uncritical of how Macklin handled this knowledge, suggesting that 'prejudice spoiled it, as heat mostly does grain', but importantly he recalled Macklin as someone keen to engage in learned discussion: 'he had two of the qualities of an instructive companion,—his information was extensive, and his ideas were specific and practical'.[34] In an age which revered the art of conversation, such contributions to intellectual culture, whilst they left little residue when compared with the work of Enlightenment authors, should not be discounted. We know also that Macklin was prepared to lend his books to those around him. In a note to a Mr Grignion we find him sending compliments and politely asking for the return of a volume: 'if he has done with the French book he sent him with Lord Bacon's Tracts he should be obliged to him if he would send it by the bearer'.[35] Macklin, in short, both absorbed knowledge and played an active part in its circulation.

As we consider Macklin's 'Enlightenment credentials', though, we should not overlook his well-known pugnaciousness and his apparent desire not only to *be* a man of learning but also to assert that identity and gain recognition for it. Edward Abbott Parry, a nineteenth-century biographer, described Macklin as 'a self-willed and self-educated man, who [...] full of knowledge and conceit, burned to impart to the universe some crumbs of the information he had acquired with such difficulty, and to receive in return the homage due to a philosopher and a man of learning'.[36] This is harshly put, but accounts of Macklin suggest there to be truth in the depiction of him as a man with much to prove, and there is strong evidence to suggest that Macklin's library played a part in his self-representation. Bernard's memoir includes a vivid depiction of Macklin asserting his scholarly prowess in a scene which sees him receiving Samuel Johnson into his book-lined home. A line from the passage has already been quoted as an epigraph to this chapter; it gains resonance when it is placed in the broader context of Bernard's account of the two famously combative personalities engaging in a tense battle of brains:

> When Macklin grew into notice as a man of letters [...] the Ursa Major of literature paid the Ursa Major of theatricals a visit, to ascertain the extent of his pretensions. Macklin showed him his library, and seemed to have a sufficient knowledge of every work it contained. Then they sat down to

---

34 Bernard, *Retrospections of the Stage*, II.76.
35 Private Collection, PC1/6/31 NAD540, by permission of the owner and Julian Pooley, The Nichols Archive Project. The addressee is very probably the watchmaker Thomas Grignion, who was based in Covent Garden.
36 Edward Abbott Parry, *Charles Macklin* (London: Kegan Paul, Trench, Trübner & Co., 1891), 127.

converse, and rambled over a variety of subjects, upon all of which Macklin kept his legs, to the Doctor's satisfaction. [...] their strength seemed to be equal. The Doctor, nevertheless, was desirous of overthrowing him before they parted, and touched on the score of his classic attainments. Greek and Latin the actor knew as intimately as French and Italian, and defended himself grammatically and colloquially, from every thrust of the lexicographer. Johnson, growing more determined from the failure of his attempts, at length addressed him with a string of sounds perfectly unintelligible. 'What's that, Sir?' inquired Macklin. 'Hebrew!' answered Johnson. 'And what do I know of Hebrew?'—'But a man of your understanding, Mr. Macklin, ought to be acquainted with every language!' The Doctor's face glowed with a smile of triumph.—'Och neil end eigen vonsht hom boge vaureen!' exclaimed Macklin. Johnson was now dumb-founded, and inquired the name of the lingua? 'Irish, Sir!'—'Irish!' exclaimed the Doctor. 'Do you think I ever studied that?'—'But a man of your understanding, Doctor Johnson, ought to be acquainted with every language!'[37]

In this telling, Johnson's visit is a deliberate testing of Macklin—of his 'pretensions': there is an underlying idea that his intellectualism may be a pose and that he is an imposter in the world of letters. The library performs a key function in Macklin's passing of the test: it is something initially to be *shown*, but possession alone is not enough, and Macklin must also demonstrate his intimacy with his own collection. And as the scene develops we come to see Macklin triumphant: the autodidact from rural Donegal standing up to and ultimately overthrowing 'the greatest Genius of the present age', as Charlotte Lennox had dubbed Johnson.[38] Heightening Macklin's victory, of course, is the fact that he uses the language of his native Ireland to trounce his supercilious English guest: this is a colonial encounter as well as an intellectual one—a strike not only for Macklin but also for Ireland, with Johnson's baffled response to hearing Irish providing a reminder of the ongoing oppression, in terms of both attitudes and power, of Ireland and its people. It is, of course, a preposterously pro-Macklin account and, in fact, it is likely that it was Macklin himself who provided the story.[39] This may explain the narrative bias, yet, while some veracity may slip away when we consider Macklin as the source, the episode loses none of its suggestiveness regarding Macklin's character. Indeed, the idea that he told this tale about himself brings into even sharper focus the sense of him as profoundly driven both by scholarly passion and by a desire for respect and recognition as a man of letters.

Macklin's books, then, can be said to have performed a declarative function. That should not be taken to imply that Macklin—the brilliant actor—was ever

---

37 Bernard, *Retrospections of the Stage*, II.125–26.
38 Charlotte Lennox, *The Female Quixote*, 2 vols (London, 1752), II.314.
39 *Appleton*, 198.

a man of masks and that offstage he was merely playing the part of the scholar, with his books providing the setting and props for his performances within the theatre of his home. Acknowledging the force of the library as a domestic spectacle does not undermine the idea of Macklin as a sincerely scholarly figure, but it opens up for an understanding of Macklin's intellectual 'project', if we may call it that, as one involving a thread of assertive image building of which his imposing library may be treated as both a part and a sign.

There are some entries in the manuscript catalogue that might actually be used to support an argument that Macklin's acquisition of books was sometimes driven by vanity. At the start of the listing of French books there is a series of titles of French intellectual works and included in the cataloguer's description of them is a notable detail: the pages are uncut. The list includes, for example, '1775 Encyclopdie 42 Vols in boards uncut 4to', '1770 Questions sur l'encyclopedie 9 Vols 8° boards uncut', and also from 1770 'L'Esprit de l'encyclopedie 5 Vols 8° boards uncut'. Macklin, we discover here, had acquired numerous volumes—among them key works of French Enlightenment thought—and had never actually used them. How we interpret that information is, though, open to question. We might well want to use it to cast doubt upon, to use O'Shaughnessy's phrase again, the 'Enlightenment credentials' that Macklin seemed to be so keen to establish, and thus see Macklin as, in part, a poseur in the world of letters. Is there indeed a better emblem of eighteenth-century intellectual posturing than a copy of the *Encyclopédie* standing in full view on a shelf and yet untouched?

We do not, though, have to treat these pointers to unread material with such cynicism. An owner of an unread book is not necessarily without intentions to read it or refer to it, plus a large collection is not necessarily assembled purely for the individual collector's use. As Christina Lupton makes clear in her *Reading and the Making of Time in the Eighteenth Century* (quoted earlier in the second epigraph), the activity of reading cannot be separated from questions of time—and eighteenth-century reading, like modern reading, was often conducted in fits and starts in the time snatched between other activities.[40] Many books lie dormant awaiting their moment of activation, and however tempting it is to find performance in the off-stage activities of a great actor, Macklin's uncut *Encyclopédie* may be seen as an untapped resource with future potential—either for Macklin, when he could find the time, or for his acquaintances. When we consider Macklin's library as a whole, we certainly find enough evidence of genuine bookishness to allow for such a reading.

---

40 Christina Lupton, *Reading and the Making of Time in the Eighteenth Century* (Baltimore, MD: Johns Hopkins University Press, 2018).

3

Macklin in the Theatre, the Courts, and the News

Manushag Powell

THIS ARGUMENT WILL, IN SOME SMALL WAY, BRING TOGETHER news writing, public trials, and stage entertainment as exercises less of public truths than of how an audience is taught to develop criteria for perceiving right (and rights) in eighteenth-century public discourse. We begin with a frequent theme for periodical commentary on the last third of Macklin's career: Macklin's physicality drew attention throughout his life (occasionally because of his capacity for physical violence); as he aged, his public admired the durability of his aged body but watched avidly for its inevitable failure. On Friday, 2 July 1784, the London daily newspaper *Parker's General Advertiser and Morning Intelligencer* exclaimed, 'A few days since that worthy theatrical veteran, Charles Macklin, who was born in the last century, gave five guineas to a gentleman, to receive 100, if he (Macklin) should be alive on New Year's day 1800! This is a fact, and the proper documents were drawn up on the occasion'.[1] Whether the documents really were drawn up it has not been possible to ascertain, but if the bet existed, the long-lived Macklin nearly won it; he lived to July 1797 (which puts his death at somewhere between the ages of 97 and 107), and his death did not harm his fame. Macklin had murdered and escaped punishment, won over audiences and judges alike, but in the eighteenth century, two forces were inescapable: death and the newspapers.

The connection between eighteenth-century periodical media and public celebrity culture is well established, and the peculiar case study of Charles Macklin has recently been treated with luminous scholarship from readers

---

1 *Parker's General Advertiser and Morning Intelligencer*, 2 July 1784.

such as Emily Hodgson Anderson, Kristina Straub, and Paul Goring.[2] It is uncontroversial to suggest, then, that Macklin was not above using the periodical platforms that fed off his celebrity, without mercy or compunction, to his own advantage whenever he could. His most consistent attitude towards newspapers seems primarily to have been cynicism: 'A *Newspaper* may be compared to a Sophist', he wrote; 'it can take any side of the question. There never was a character so pure white that it cannot blacken, nor one so black that it cannot whiten'.[3] This pronouncement was not so much a call for correction as it was a factual blanket assessment. (There is some amusing affinity between Macklin's early-career successes and the coffeehouse haunts of periodical culture: in 1737, James Miller's satirical play *The Coffee-House* featured Charles Macklin playing, ostensibly, a general stereotype of a poet, but while pointedly dressed as the infamous, and at the time itinerant, street-haunting poet Richard Savage.[4]) There is, of course, an underlying irony (one Macklin was surely sharp enough to see) in an actor's declaiming against a mode of entertainment because it manipulates its audience's perception of truth, when that was exactly Macklin's own profession as well. But since the eighteenth-century periodical press originated not only the obituary genre but the theatrical review as well, that tension between actor and periodicalist was probably inevitable.

We need not dwell on using Macklin as a case study to show that a connection between newspaper writing and acting exists—how obvious—but rather to assert that this connection is, in Macklin's case, peculiar, because the driving forces behind Macklin's appeal were themselves so peculiar; Macklin's personal quarrels had a habit of turning into public discussions with wide cultural implications. Having been a recurring subject for periodical writing during his life, Charles Macklin's character experienced a renewal of fame fanned by some provocative retrospective writing after his death, prompted in part by the longer-than-normal period of anticipation that preceded his demise. Lisa Freeman and Joseph Roach have established how actors in the eighteenth century are haunted by the roles they played in the past, arguing that every new performance carries with it the haunting of other stagings and

---

2 Emily Hodgson Anderson, *Shakespeare and the Legacy of Loss* (Ann Arbor: University of Michigan Press, 2018), 111–37; Kristina Straub, 'The Newspaper "Trial" of Charles Macklin's *Macbeth* and the Theatre as Juridical Public Sphere', *Eighteenth-Century Fiction* 27.3–4 (2015), 395–418; Paul Goring, 'Theatrical Riots and Conspiracies in London and Edinburgh: Charles Macklin, James Fennell and the Rights of Actors and Audiences', *Review of English Studies* 67.278 (2016), 122–45.
3 Macklin, 'On Newspapers', in *Kirkman*, I.366.
4 Andrew Benjamin Bricker, 'Libel and Satire: The Problem with Naming', *ELH* 81.3 (2014), 903.

other bodies.[5] For Macklin, at least, his later career performances had begun to carry with them the ghosts of papers past, as well: not only his most famous role as Shylock, but the newssheets, paragraphs, pamphlets, and poems that dogged his days and hissed him through the nights.

When he finally died, the newspapers that opined about him in his life obligingly ran a wide variety of memoirs and biographies whose judgements of Macklin's achievements covered, shall we say, a wide spectrum of assessments; in this they were consistent with the way they'd covered him in life. Taken as a whole, however, the coverage of Macklin's death is strong evidence of the stature of his fame, and the fact that his fame often rested equally upon his long career of controversial choices anchored to his version of verisimilitude in acting—and explosions of violence, both physical and legalistic.

Periodical writing in the eighteenth century had developed a particular affinity for the intersections of death and the artist's voice; Macklin's final departure from a long life pockmarked with episodes of violence and public declamation was inevitably attractive to the genre.[6] Amanda Weldy Boyd points out that Macklin was the subject of six full-length biographies immediately following his death; by way of comparison the quondam-incomparable David Garrick, who was the great rival actor–manager of Macklin's lifetime, only got two.[7] Indeed, Macklin had been a figure much in the public eye at least since his 1735 murder trial for killing another actor over a stock wig that they had each claimed. His acquittal, which owed much to his performative abilities; his persistent litigiousness; and his famous portrayal of Shylock (1741 onwards), which arguably rivalled in stature Garrick's enduring portrayals of Hamlet and Richard III, all made sure he was frequently the subject of the periodical press from then on. The *Parker's General Advertiser* notice that is quoted above, then, only stands out because the titbit it reports on Macklin is more-or-less neutral, calling him a 'worthy theatrical veteran' and engaging in no gestures towards the many public and printed controversies that had long dotted his curious career. The fact that it portrays him as making a jest of fate is perfectly in line with the larger body of Macklin coverage. That the anecdote of the bet is plausible but unverifiable, whose

---

5 Cf. Lisa A. Freeman, *Character's Theater: Genre and Identity on the Eighteenth-Century English Stage* (Philadelphia: University of Pennsylvania Press, 2001) and Joseph R. Roach, *Cities of the Dead: Circum-Atlantic Performance* (New York: Columbia University Press, 1996).

6 Manushag N. Powell, *Performing Authorship in Eighteenth-Century English Periodicals* (Lewisburg, PA: Bucknell University Press, 2012), 193–210.

7 Amanda Weldy Boyd, *Staging Memory and Materiality in Eighteenth-Century Theatrical Biography* (London: Anthem Press, 2017), 61.

truth must ultimately be decided by the reader, is also in keeping with many of the most important episodes of Macklin's career.

Acting manuals in the eighteenth century were divided on the relationship between truth and performance: some held that only a body constitutionally prone to feelings such as joy or anger could convincingly portray them, while others suggested that a truly malleable body could produce internal emotional effects—in actor and audience alike—when it assumed their outward sign. Macklin, meanwhile, discovered that, to some extent, through reviews, news reports, pamphlets, and indeed legal writings and court proceedings, the theatrical world could be reshaped, sometimes in his favour, and sometimes the opposite. If the human body could create performative truths in its audience, the textual body might do the same for performance conventions. To an extent—but the human body is never quite as changeable as a textual one, and Macklin worked in a world where much about his identity, and identity formation in general, would mark him as a man apart. The obvious case study here is the 1773–74 scandal over Macklin's *Macbeth* and its portrayal in the press, also discussed by David Worrall in this volume, which morphed into a legal–cultural question about audience rights and responsibilities that exceeded Macklin's own interest in the matter. In what follows, we will survey Macklin's relationship with periodical and print forms of identity, consider the case of the hissed *Macbeth*, and then conclude with another, less-sensational, but, I think, more formally interesting example of how a theatrical periodical used Macklin's archived public writing to serve its own agenda. The view sketched out by these complex intersections of issues reveals at least one thing: that periodical writing was less bounded than theatrical or legal pieces and could overwhelm both.

The player in the periodicals: newsprint, national identity, and Macklin's acting

The actor–playwright Macklin is not among the substantial cohort of eighteenth-century dramatists who were also journalists (such as his fellow Hibernians Arthur Murphy and Oliver Goldsmith). Still, his long life was, at least from middle age forward, profoundly affected by the newspapers and their peculiar Enlightenment-era volatility. Recently, for example, Kristina Straub has written about the London newspapers' role in the explosive controversy touched off by his 1773 staging of *Macbeth*;[8]

---

8 Straub, 'Newspaper "Trial"', 395–418.

other modern scholars, including Elaine McGirr, Betsy Bolton, and, in this volume, Helen Burke, are interested by his opaque decision to intervene in the mid-century Fielding–Hill paper war by writing and staging *Covent Garden Theatre; or, Pasquin Turn'd Drawcansir*, a bizarre farcical send-up of a diverse gang of periodical writers, for his own benefit night in 1752.[9] Notably, Macklin had worked as an acting tutor to the periodicalist, [failed] actor, and performance writer John Hill, which sheds some—but not enough—light on his decision to intervene in the paper war. Macklin was also friendly with Arthur Murphy, who, like Fielding, was not a fan of Hill's. Although he was not a periodicalist in any strict sense, Macklin's time spent as a feature of periodicals inflected his stage career, helping him, over the years, to hone his sense of public response to spectacle.

We may trace a suggestive connection between the newspapers and the naturalistic mode of acting Macklin developed and taught in contradistinction to popular heroic modes of declamation, the performative legerdemain that convinced audiences that his deliberately alienating creation, a distortion of Macklin's intercourse with Jewish men he met in coffee shops and in the 'Change, was 'the Jew/That Shakespeare drew'. Macklin connected his first-hand experience of human beings reading periodicals in the coffee shops with a thrilling stage monster that awed thousands with his alienating menace. This was no passing moment; Shylock remained a popular vehicle for Macklin when the periodicals had begun to suggest that he had lost the power to charm in many other guises. The *Gazetteer and New Daily Advertiser* said of Macklin as late as 1780 that his Shylock still had the power to fascinate audiences, it being a 'wonder, as it must ever be considered in theatrical history, that a man born in the last century should [...] continue with full vigour of mind, and strength of memory', and yet 'Mr. Macklin never played better, if so well, as on Thursday evening', evincing 'A thousand minute strokes of natural passions, and almost imperceptible traces of the workings of the human mind'. (Remarkably, Macklin is even explicitly called the 'Michael Angelo' of acting by our enamoured theatre critic—Michael-angelo being famous for having blended nonpareil professional ability with striking imaginative originality.[10]) This careful dissection of the 'natural

---

9 See Elaine McGirr, *Heroic Mode and Political Crisis, 1660–1745* (Newark: University of Delaware Press, 2009), 10–12; Betsy Bolton, 'Theorizing Audience and Spectatorial Agency', in Julia Swindells and David Francis Taylor (eds), *The Oxford Handbook of the Georgian Theatre, 1737–1832* (Oxford: Oxford University Press, 2014), 38–39, 45–46. See also Powell, *Performing Authorship*, 85–87. Esther M. Raushenbush suggests that Fielding may have collaborated with Macklin on the piece in 'Charles Macklin's Lost Play about Henry Fielding', *Modern Language Notes* 51.8 (1936), 507–8.

10 *Gazetteer and New Daily Advertiser*, 4 November 1780.

passions', the laying bare of the 'workings of the human mind', may sound like pursuits from the realm of natural philosophy as much as popular theatre.

In fact, the *Gazetteer* is praising Macklin for doing the same thing for which authors perennially praised Joseph Addison and Richard Steele in their essays: breaking down for the reader or the audience truths about human behaviour. The heights of the *Spectator* were seldom reached by later writers, if indeed they had ever really been reached by Addison, who often used both didacticism and sensationalism as cudgels to drive circulation. A parallel, then, runs between Macklin's career and the weekly reviews and news dailies read by theatregoers, which were literally as quotidian as could be, and yet (as Macklin himself complained) they often deliberately roiled seas of passion in their audiences, but seldom did so for the best of motives beyond the perpetuity of their own print careers.

Macklin was depicted as a powerful actor, one who could both convey and raise the passions, but not to an infinite extent. He was limited in old age by his body, and even in youth by his material character: reviewers found for good and ill that there were pieces of his identity the actor could not act away. Opined *Lloyd's Evening Post*, in a good example from his earlier career in 1758, 'Mr. Macklin, however skilful in his execution of many characters, was not by nature fitted for Marplot [in Centlivre's popular comedy, *The Busy Body*]: his features are too strong, and his looks too busy: every cast of his eye denoted too much thought, and the florid, free, and vacant, were not sufficiently in his mien and countenance'.[11] While the language in this review could be taken as praising Macklin for evincing an admirable masculinity that causes him to fail as a fop, still the tendency is to argue that what is inborn cannot be overcome. In effect, there is a newspaper investment in finding something immutable about the mercurial Macklin. An acting career of seven decades—and one that was not without method—implies an internal continuity, but journalists did not agree on the origins of his talents, and 'Macklin's personality assured that he would never be without enemies', as a modern biographer ably puts it, so any critic's position on Macklin was bound to court dissent.[12]

Importantly, Macklin could not be a full part of the periodical discourse invested in delineating an English national character. He was known to be Irish, of course, and, said *Bell's Weekly Messenger*, 'though somewhat warm in argument', he was also, not coincidentally, 'fond of his country, and vain of

---

11 *Lloyd's Evening Post*, 11–13 December 1758.
12 'Macklin, Charles, 1699–1797, actor, dancer, singer, manager, playwright', Philip H. Highfill, Jr., Kalman A. Burnim, and Edward A. Langhans, *A Biographical Dictionary of Actors, Actresses, Musicians, Dancers, Managers & Other Stage Personnel in London, 1660–1800*, 16 vols (Carbondale: Southern Illinois University Press, 1984), X.10.

being an Irishman'.¹³ *Lloyd's* had damned Macklin with faint praise for his inability to excel in a comic role in which Garrick had succeeded very well due to an indefinable but immutable quality in Macklin's person—too much energy, too much thought in his eyes. *Bell's* makes a thematically similar claim about Macklin's Irishness, stating in a posthumous 1797 note that without actually having an Irish accent Macklin's speech nonetheless suggested an Irish accent: 'Though a native of the *humblest* description, he had not the least of the Irish *patois*, but a *tone* was observable like the Scotch accent'. But Macklin fooled himself and, 'Conceiving that he had a pure and correct delivery, with the accent of genuine Anglicanism, he gave lectures in a great room' in Covent Garden of the 1750s.¹⁴ The theatrical world of the eighteenth century, Paul Goring reminds us, 'had an immense capacity for counterresistance' when it came to improving ethnic stereotyping.¹⁵ 'Ambitious, resilient, and dedicated to his craft', Macklin 'learnt early on that more secure and illustrious positions in England would be contingent upon personal metamorphosis'.¹⁶ An actor who, the papers noted, 'made acting a science',¹⁷ with considerable creative powers, and yet, these same papers held, was in key ways perpetually bound by his body and background, Macklin did not so much resist the inevitable as determine to make much of the power of stereotype across his career. In an extended conceit that unpacks the ambiguity of Macklin's reputation, a 1770 column gossiping about new and forthcoming stage plays, called Macklin a privateer:

> Theatrical Ship-News: On Friday last arrived at Gravesend, *The Lame Lover*, Capt. *Foote* (being her twelfth voyage) in sound condition, and well man'd. Expected this tide at the *Hope*, the *king John*, Capt. *Sheridan*, from the land of *Nod*, in a shattered condition, from the malevolence of the *Dog-Star*. Still hovering on the coast, the *Macklin* privateer (with several piratical prizes in tow.) This vessel (like the Kentish small craft) is rather calculated to prey on shipwrecks, than do the Government any *real* service.¹⁸

A privateer was a figure poised between the possibilities of national hero and villain, conceivably a man who could win acclaim but did not precisely

---

13 *Bell's Weekly Messenger* 65 (23 July 1797), 518.
14 *Bell's Weekly Messenger* 65 (23 July 1797), 518.
15 Paul Goring, '"John Bull, pit, box, and gallery, said No!": Charles Macklin and the Limits of Ethnic Resistance on the Eighteenth-Century London Stage', *Representations* 79.1 (2002), 61–62.
16 Goring, '"John Bull, pit, box, and gallery, said No!"', 62.
17 *Morning Chronicle*, 2 August 1781.
18 *Gazetteer and New Daily Advertiser*, 13 August 1770. This notice is discussed in Matthew Kinservik, 'New Light on the Censorship of Macklin's *Man of the World*', *Huntington Library Quarterly* 62.1–2 (1999), 48; the 'Macklin privateer' is his *Man of the World*, being delayed by problems with the Lord Chamberlain's office.

belong to a defined rank—and, upon reflection, the squib hints that Macklin is maybe more of a disreputable wrecker anyway ('Kentish small craft'). Pirates were men of no nation, but the barely legal privateers depended upon national divisions for their livelihood and legitimacy. So did the newspapers attempting to write an English middling class consciousness into reality.

And so did Macklin. Shylock was not Macklin's only racialist invention, nor was his Macbeth in highland drag (about which more in a moment) an isolated outlier. Much of Macklin's theatrical life was driven by ethnic stereotypes—not any single stereotype in particular as much as the Enlightenment preoccupation with such things in general.[19] Macklin's Irishness, and his extensive time on the Dublin stage, complicated his appeal, but did not, it should be clear, at all disqualify him from audience attention (arguably, the reverse; Susan Canon Harris says there are 'three things that eighteenth-century British theatre couldn't do without: marriage, plagiarism, and Irish men').[20] Macklin's productions were reviewed by the same papers advertising and often praising Macpherson's hoax epic *Fingal*, while also watching the heated divisions within Ireland's parliament. It was a good moment, in other words, for experimenting with friendly essentialist inquiries that did little to unseat colonial hierarchies. The late-century fading of anti-Jacobite, anti-Scots sentiment registers particularly in the reviewers' reception of *Love à la Mode* (1759), which would become, arguably, Macklin's greatest hit as an author. *Love à la Mode*, performed while Macklin was still playing Shylock, is stocked with ethnic caricatures. It championed its Irish character at the expense of the others, irritating Scottish sympathizers who thought 'Sir Archy Macsarcasm' (Macklin's role) went too far, although others appreciated Macklin's 'satirical talents in ridiculing the follies of our northern neighbours'.[21] Rather than conclude from the reviewers' reactions that he ought to draw back from stereotypes, Macklin seemed to take the lesson that they were culturally powerful devices; Kinservik thinks in particular that the critics' resistance to Macklin's anti-Scottish behaviour in

---

19 That considerable Enlightenment thought engaged ethnic and racialized categorizations is an established commonplace. See, for example, Emmanuel Chukwudi Eze (ed.), *Race and the Enlightenment: A Reader* (Cambridge, MA: Blackwell, 1997). On specific connections among the British eighteenth-century theatre and marking out of ethnic minorities, see Michael Ragussis, 'Jews and Other "Outlandish Englishmen": Ethnic Performance and the Invention of British Identity under the Georges', *Critical Inquiry* 26.4 (2000), 773–97.
20 Susan Canon Harris, 'Mixed Marriage: Sheridan, Macklin, and the Hybrid Audience', in Michael Cordner and Peter Holland (eds), *Players, Playwrights, Playhouses: Investigating Performance, 1660–1800* (Basingstoke: Palgrave Macmillan, 2007), 189.
21 *Gazetteer and New Daily Advertiser*, 25 July 1764.

Love à la Mode 'hardened his resolve to satirize them again' in his controversial later work *The Man of the World* (formerly entitled *The True-Born Scotchman*).[22] And, as a whole, that decision paid off for him; despite substantial initial resistance to its staging, the work was at last performed, and it came to be acclaimed.[23]

My point is not to dismiss Macklin as a performer who excelled by playing to the prejudices of his audience; certainly, his career was a great deal more complicated than that. Instead, I want to underscore how Macklin was in a good position to develop a canny awareness of what might play successfully because of the time, much of it negative, that he spent as a public subject. Some of this time was spent in a court of law, attempting to find remedies for damage being done to his career by periodicals. In an example that underscores how small the London print world could be, Samuel Richardson, of *Pamela* fame, has also the distinction of having been sued by Macklin for publishing a pirated version of half of *Love à la Mode* in his periodical *The Court Miscellany* (April 1766). *Love à la Mode*, which Macklin had never published, was then running at Drury Lane. Macklin won easily, establishing an important right for playwrights who wished to control the fruits of their labour.[24] Somewhat similarly, the legal remedy that the litigious but astute Macklin would later advocate for during his *Macbeth* debacle helped to establish some regulations for the implied 'contract between audience and performer' that would come to the aid of later actors.[25] What Straub has characterized as

> Uppity actors and unruly audiences asserting their control over theatrical space, throughout the century so often the object of the newspapers' reportage, came to epitomize the potential for social disorder implicit in a British public arena that valued liberty and individual rights. The newspapers recast the heterogeneous, performative power of the theatre as a dangerous force that confused identity categories and disrupted class and gender hierarchies.[26]

This might seem to contradict my earlier characterization of Macklin as preying upon ethnic categories of identity. Yet the addition of performance always had

---

22 Kinservik, 'New Light on the Censorship', 50.
23 Matthew Kinservik refers to Macklin's *The Man of the World*, denied a licence not once but twice, as 'the most heavily censored play of the eighteenth century'. 'New Light on the Censorship', 43.
24 For an excellent discussion of the circumstances around the case, see Oliver Gerland, 'The Haymarket Theatre and Literary Property: Constructing the Common Law Playwright, 1770–1833', *Theatre Notebook* 69.2 (2015), 78–81. See also David Worrall's essay in this volume.
25 Goring, 'Theatrical Riots and Conspiracies in London and Edinburgh', 125.
26 Straub, 'Newspaper "Trial"', 398.

at least the potential to destabilize any characterization, in part because there was no widespread agreement as to just how much of a convincing performance was artifice and how much was the performer's nature.

The Scot that Macklin begot: *Macbeth* and the rights of the audience in law and opinion

Much earlier in his career, Macklin had participated in *Macbeth* as one of the three wyrd sisters, apparently without any controversy—for example, in 1738 a column in the *London Daily Post and General Advertiser* notes Drury Lane's plans for *Macbeth*, warning that since at the previous performance a number of persons had crowded the stage, interrupting the performances, and 'very much' disgusting the audience, no further admissions behind the scenes shall be allowed—but this same notice had been running all week, attached to a number of different stagings. The problem of the unruly audience was a general one, and does not seem, here, to have been caused by Macklin's choices.[27] This would not always be true.

In 1773, Macklin debuted a deliberately disruptive staging of *Macbeth*. Echoing in preparation his painstaking creation of what he felt was a realistic ethnic other figure in Shylock, Macklin depicted his *Macbeth* not in London but in Scotland, and in highland dress, on a stage crowded with broadswords and backed up by bagpipe music—tapping into contemporary interest in Scottish identity and its post-'45 modes of expression. Moreover, Macklin rejected Thomas Davenant's then-dominant staging, which meant eliminating Lady Macduff and putting far more focus on the centrality of the Macbeth duo.[28] He particularly reinterpreted the title character as his own: this was, importantly, a role that had once belonged clearly to David Garrick; Macklin nursed an old grudge against Garrick and hoped to outdo and perhaps embarrass him.[29] There was quite a bit of lead up and public interest in the play before it was even staged, in part due to Macklin's active encouragement of press interest and the publication in daily papers of reports

---

27 *London Daily Post and General Advertiser*, 20 October 1738.
28 For more details on Macklin's staging and its considerable reach and influence, see Gay Smith, *Lady Macbeth in America: From the Stage to the White House* (New York: Palgrave Macmillan, 2010), 35–37.
29 Straub is helpful here: 'The dominance of Garrick's adaptation, his almost godlike status on the London theatre scene, and the fact that Garrick had not performed the role since 1768 made acting techniques for this role a favourite topic in the newspapers, and Macklin knew quite well what he was getting into'. See 'Newspaper "Trial"', 396.

on its rehearsals. Indeed, the staging both made an initial splash and would become highly significant to subsequent versions of 'the Scottish play'. But it was not greeted with universal approval—like the era in which he lived, and the newspapers he battled, Macklin was always creating contradictions.

Some critics disliked his radical reinterpretation, while others thought that Macklin had conceived some meritorious plans but was trying to do more than his seventy-plus-year-old body could bear, and that his staging thus fell short of what he'd wished to realize, for he had lost both teeth and strength as the years wore on. Said one critic, more bluntly, 'Hard Macklin late guilt's feelings strove to speak/While sweats infernal drench'd his iron cheek'.[30] For others, however, the problem was not age but something more essentially Macklin: some critics claimed that, at bottom, Macklin had always lectured rather than performed, invoking a darker version of the claim that when Macklin acted 'every cast of his eye denoted too much thought'. The *Whitehall Evening Post*, for example, called him a hard worker rather than a naturally gifted actor, interested in systems but not the finer passions.

Macklin, in such views, is really something like a newssheet, conveying a form of truth but not an aesthetic, and he is a newssheet with some problems of punctuation at that. Macklin on stage was supposedly given to a curious affectation of speech. In both teaching and practising, according to another 1797 digest of his career, he 'had his *simple pause*, his *middle pause*, and his *grand pause*'.[31] The modern reader will begin to think here that his enemies would have Charles Macklin made out to be the William Shatner of the eighteenth century.[32] *The Evening Post* continues that, 'The last *pause* was his favourite; and he sometimes indulged himself so long in it, that the Prompter [...] made him quit the stage with indignation, and complain of being interrupted in the midst of his *grand pause*'.[33] Macklin of course disputed such stories angrily. Rejecting the attempt to render him merely a newssheet creation, Macklin rebelled by literally bringing the papers to the stage, collapsing the distinction between performance and writing in his attempt to establish his own version of the truth behind both worldly events and his own abilities.

---

30 This bit, taken from a short anonymous poem chronicling the stagings of *Macbeth* from Quinn to Macklin, was among the more quotable reviews and appears in many venues; the origin seems to be the *St. James's Chronicle* for 23–26 October 1773.
31 *Whitehall Evening Post*, 27–29 July 1797.
32 The actor William Shatner's propensity for elongated pauses has earned the 'Shatner Pause' an entry in the *Urban Dictionary*: www.urbandictionary.com/define.php?term=Shatner%20Pause (accessed 10 August 2021).
33 *Whitehall Evening Post*, 27–29 July 1797.

The mixed reviews, and their volume, infuriated him, and he took the unusual step of greeting his audience during a subsequent performance with a pile of them in hand in a truly boundary-melting *Gestus*. According to Arthur Murphy, '*Mr. Macklin*, finding all the Newspapers, day after day, morning and evening, pouring out the most virulent abuse upon him, calling him murderer, villain, and the most opprobrious names of every sort [...] he went upon the Stage with a large bundle of Papers, the Papers of a week', pointing to them sarcastically as his reward for his long years 'in their service'.[34] Macklin, in other words, had a problem with controlling his audience, and he understood it to be partly the fault of the news, to such an extent that the offending papers were introduced onto the stage as a prologue prop. He was correct insofar that the paper coverage hardly restricted itself to the aesthetic discussion of the play; rather, the public ledgers were encouraging the public to sort themselves into Macklinite and anti-Macklinite camps driven by personality and old grievances; and Macklin and his adherents suspected that rival stage personality and author David Garrick was encouraging the controversy, either tacitly or directly.[35]

But the controversy had another dimension as well. The lines of opposition could not be drawn cleanly between the papers and their readers versus the stage audience, because the reactions of the audience shortly developed a print life of their own. The first night of *Macbeth*'s performance had had to overcome some scattered hissing. Macklin's wife, who was in the audience, accused two men of being behind the uncivil noises, with what truth we will never know: these were James Sparks, the son of the deceased but well-known actor Luke Sparks; and the actor Samuel Reddish, who at the time was the presiding Macbeth at Drury Lane Theatre.[36] Macklin made the accusation public and the men denied it just as publicly, retaliating with further interruptions of *Macbeth*. The dispute launched a massive entanglement that shortly became

---

34 Quotation from the proceedings of Macklin's 11 June 1774 trial, in which Murphy was a witness, printed in *Kirkman*, II.135. Kirkman states 'the whole of the proceedings *which have never before been published*' 'were taken in short hand by *Mr. Gurney* [who was a note-taker used in court trials], exclusively for the Prosecutor' and corrected by Macklin. *Kirkman*, II.64. This passage appears verbatim in a pamphlet contemporary to the trial: *The genuine arguments of the council, with the opinion of the Court of King's Bench, on cause shewn, why an information should not be exhibited against John Stephen James ... By a citizen of the world* (London, 1774), 71.

35 On Macklinitism, see Edward Abbot Parry's biography in particular: *Charles Macklin* (London: Kegan Paul, Trench, Trubner & Co., 1891), 163–64.

36 Reddish had taken over the role on 25 April 1772; prior to this time he had been well received for his portrayal of Macduff. Interestingly, after Macklin's *Macbeth*, Reddish was returned to Macduff (23 March 1775), and William Smith, recently hired from Covent Garden—whence he had been dismissed for quarrelling with Macklin—took over as Macbeth.

less concerned with what had actually happened that first night than with larger questions entirely: who had the right to hiss, and who had the right to accuse, and who was supposed to be in charge of the theatrical world at all.

Because of the press coverage of this leg of the controversy, rioters continued to attack Macklin, even when he attempted to appease his public by setting aside Macbeth in favour of the still-darling role of Shylock—he was, even as Shylock, pelted with apples, according to the *Gazetteer*, the fact that his age had long passed the 'grand climacteric' offering him no protection at all.[37] Finally, his manager, George Colman the elder, fired him via a chalkboard message (he could not make himself heard over the raucous crowd), in an attempt to end the disruption. That attempt failed: Macklin sued a group of concerted hissers, and in a closely watched result Lord Mansfield—he of the 'Mansfield Judgment' in *Somerset* v. *Stewart* (1772) that had outlawed chattel slavery in England and Wales—eventually ruled in his favour, forcing the malefactors to pay restitution.[38] The public was hotly divided throughout this contest, with newspapers running letters both pro- and con-, including one in the *Middlesex Journal*, highly critical of Macklin, that went so far as to sign itself, 'The Ghost of Shakespear'.[39]

The legal question mutated in public coverage far beyond Macklin's own sense of grievance; it became a question of freedom of speech. It was widely reported how Lord Mansfield explained,

> that the right to hissing and applauding in a theatre was an unalterable right, but there was a wide distinction between expressing the natural sensations of the mind as they arose on what was seen and heard, and executing a pre-concerted design not only to hiss an actor when he was playing a part in which he was universally allowed to be excellent [Shylock], but also to drive him from the theatre, and promote his utter ruin. (*Morning Chronicle*, 12 May 1775)

There is an analogy in this judgment to Macklin's having long ago escaped the charge of murder in favour of manslaughter when he killed poor Thomas Hallam in 1735: Macklin had been able to persuade a jury that he acted out of passion and without premeditation, and was therefore returned for the lesser charge of manslaughter. The point in both cases is that spontaneous physical violence is one thing; planned physical violence is another, and a disciplined performance is held as a virtue over all. Further, across his career Macklin unwittingly put himself in situations where his personal imbroglios had wide-reaching implications for cultural expectations.

---

37 *Gazetteer and New Daily Advertiser*, 19 November 1773.
38 On Macklin and Lord Mansfield, see David Worrall's chapter in this volume.
39 *Middlesex Journal*, 28–30 October 1773.

Green room legacies: Macklin in the news and some critical implications

Macklin's career was understood, both in its own moment and in posthumous retrospect, as having a great deal to do with the power of theatre managers, and the results of his own litigation with the theatrical managers was repeatedly re-litigated in print. In helping to disarm the ability of hissers and rioters to force managers to accede to their demands, had Macklin unwittingly empowered the same managers against whose abuses he had railed for so long? The *Whitehall Evening Post* went so far as to blame the deceased Macklin for empowering the theatre managers with his litigious triumphs: 'Before this event there was a kind of *popular justice* that was always able to control the power of a Manager' but now 'The Town' dare not appear 'lest The LAW should inflict its vengeance'.[40] The meta-treatments of the battle in newspapers presents it as one between the managers and their public; at some point, the actor becomes only the medium—but that was not Macklin's understanding at all; he persisted in thinking the issue was personal, and that Garrick was somehow involved in plotting against him.

I want now to go back a few years and look at a very different example of a periodical treating something that was very personal to Macklin as evidence of the broader problems of the remuneration of theatre workers. The *Theatrical Monitor, Or, The Green Room Laid Open* (October 1767–April 1768), a singularly cranky, tri-weekly, threepenny periodical published by William Bingley, was obsessed with what it saw as the malfeasance of the London theatre managers Colman and Garrick, and especially suspicious of the relationship between David Garrick and the journalist Hugh Kelly.[41] While on balance the work spends more energy decrying Garrick's relationship with the press than Colman's, the fourth issue of the *Theatrical Monitor* spends its time attacking Colman through reviving the long-simmering brouhaha going on between Garrick and Macklin.[42] The essay begins,

---

40 *Whitehall Evening Post*, 27–29 July 1797.
41 See Robert Bataille, *The Writing Life of Hugh Kelly: Politics, Journalism, and Theater in Late Eighteenth-Century London* (Carbondale: Southern Illinois University Press, 2000), 38–45 for full discussion.
42 Garrick led an actors' strike against Fleetwood, the manager at Drury Lane, in May 1743, but was unable to establish an independent company. The troupe returned to Drury Lane—Garrick at better pay—but Fleetwood refused to take back Macklin. Macklin blamed Garrick, and their breach was both public and permanent (though James Lacy took over Drury Lane in 1744 and hired Macklin back). Macklin had joined Covent Garden under Colman's controversial leadership in 1767.

I have in my former numbers partly taken notice of the ill behaviour of managers to the players, and that from the enormous produce of the nightly accounts, they ought to be better paid, especially when they are considered in the same light as managers are, the *servants* of the *public*. Play-house pay is inadequate to the profits, to a shameful degree. *Theatrical Monitor* 4 (14 November 1767), 2.[43]

The essay then changes the subject to lament the falling off in stature of theatricals and acting from the halcyon days of Homer. But, 'Herein, again the managers are beyond dispute to blame; they have in the choice of stock plays, made it too much their designs to familiarize the audience to the impression of malignant and diabolical tempers, such as pride, perfidy, pleasure, lewdness, delusion, and treachery', and so forth (1). 'Managers, of so powerful and consequential a trust, ought to be the best sort of men, nay better than men in general are, or how are they fit to mend others?' (2). That is, the managers are mismanaging the repertory, staging too much Wycherley and Congreve, and not enough Addison and Steele, and when they attempt a new play matters are even worse, because they can choose to stage only the work of their friends, or, even shoddier, their own productions. Colman's recent comedy, *The Oxonian in Town*, is held up as an example: 'This piece having glaring defects, and being the work of a manager, who thereby eats the bread of men of genius who want it, deserves the less countenance; the business of managers is to attend the conduct of the theatre, where there is visible room for great amendment' (4).[44] And the business of periodical culture, as the self-appointed guardians of urbane English character, is to point this out in an endless attempt to govern that which must remain ungovernable if it is to maintain its interest.

From this observation, the periodical segues, with no introduction or explanation, to reprinting in its entirety the decades-old 'CASE of *Charles Macklin*, Comedian', turning from the attack against Colman to one against Garrick, but in a strangely asynchronous manner; this is actually its way of returning to that pay issue that had started the number.[45] 'The Case of Charles Macklin' savaged Garrick for his role in getting Macklin fired from Drury Lane by its manager, Fleetwood, in 1743. The essay had formerly touched off a sensational pamphlet war between Macklin and Garrick. In other words, then,

---

43 Subsequent citations of this number appear parenthetically in the text.
44 'P.S. As *Green-room puffs* in servile news-papers, cannot be depended upon, I therefore must observe, that the *Oxonian in town*, [which was a new piece composed by George Colman the Elder] is *very well cast* and acted, and it has very good ideal morals, but they are not sufficiently digested' (3). After explaining this moral indigestion, we are treated to a Nota Bene to the postscript: 'N.B. …'
45 Charles Macklin, *The Case of Charles Macklin, Comedian* (London, 1743). Macklin was suspected of being the author; Garrick replied *in propria persona*.

this partially anti-Garrick periodical is using a nearly twenty-five-year-old grievance to stir up sentiment against him, since in the piece Macklin, using the same terms of the *Monitor*'s opening paragraph, decries the inadequacy of 'Playhouse pay' to compensate him and his wife for their services, and begs the public to adjudicate his cause (6). He is oddly careful to lay blame at the feet of Garrick and not Fleetwood: not management per se but outsized actor personalities are shown as ultimately at fault (5). And then it concludes with a letter from a correspondent calling himself 'Candid', who complains that a friend had tried sending a letter to the rival *Public Ledger* that contained 'some strictures upon Mr. Garrick's conduct, and it was conceived that, as the servant of the public pleasures, he cannot but be amenable to the public reprehension: notwithstanding the delicacy with which these observations were guarded, they were not allowed a place in that paper'. This is even though it 'professes itself to be *open to all parties and influenced by none*'—proof positive, says Candid, 'of the almost absolute subjection to which the present race of writers are reduced by our arbitrary and triumphant managers', warning those managers that 'they had much better receive the correction of the public in a newspaper essay, than within the doors of their own theatres' (6). Candid, in other words, threatens the same audience correction that Lord Mansfield would try to decree was beyond the pale, but implies that it is the newspapers, not the judiciary, who should have the final say in the matter.

The *Theatrical Monitor*'s zany editorial decisions are fascinating in their own right, but also significant here is that while the *Monitor* is sympathetic to Macklin's cause, or, at a minimum, is the enemy of his enemy, it also transforms the still-vital Macklin from a person to a type, a well-known example, perhaps, but not a current subject. The *Theatrical Monitor* says that stage managers are causing public depravity, even quoting Macklin in its cause, while elsewhere Macklin himself was writing that, 'As Doctors live by diseases, so newspapers are supported by the idle, universal curiosity, and universal depravity of the times' (368). Just who is really depraved here, and whose fault is it? 'Depravity', from the Latin *pravus*, carries the sense not only of being immoral but specifically of being crooked, turned around— obstinately unreasonable and against the rules. The problem was that there was no universal agreement about the rules for whom and how the theatrical world should be run, and so depravity was indeed by default a universal plight.

If Macklin was not precisely depraved, he was often perverse. Macklin's appeal, and his weakness, tended to come from the same sources: his capacity for violence,[46] his inability to take a joke or let go of a grudge, his appetite for

---

46 Quite aside from his wig-murdering days, Macklin once 'gave [the actor James] Quin such a drubbing in the Green Room, that the latter could not proceed in his part of

suing people, his Celtic outsider status, and, finally, his interest in material details over classical theory in setting up a character study. Emily Anderson has shown how, having made Shylock his own, Shylock also came to own Macklin; my sense is that something analogous to this is going on with his print identity. Macklin knew he could often persuade audiences over to his side when the stakes were higher than mere theatrical applause. He did this repeatedly in court, and he at least held his own in multiple paper wars whose legacies long outlasted the events that touched them off. But there is no security in a periodical triumph, because any paper, opinion, review, or memoriam can easily be swallowed and repurposed by another. In the end, periodicals themselves should be understood as actors hoping not to be hissed off their own unpatented stage, and therefore they are at once allied to and locked in combat with the other actors, and other theatres, too.

Manly, in *The Plain Dealer*, without making an apology to the audience'. See 'Old Macklin', in *True Briton*, 13 July 1797. Quin himself had already called two other men out at the time of this alteration, of course—the realm of the Green Room was no safe haven in the eighteenth century.

4

'Strong Case': Macklin and the Law

David Worrall

THIS ESSAY EXAMINES THE LEGAL ACUMEN of Charles Macklin. It sets out the crucial role played by the Irish playwright and lawyer, Arthur Murphy (1727–1805), in acting as Macklin's legal adviser.[1] Their association, connecting the upper echelons of London's theatrical and legal professions in the early 1770s, amounts to the identification of a specific London Irish diaspora consistent with the findings of Craig Bailey's influential book, *Irish London: Middle-Class Migration in the Global Eighteenth Century* (2013).[2] Macklin's connections with London's legal profession provides evidence of highly effective Irish social networks operating at an accomplished technical level managing evolving case history, a cornerstone of the progress and reliability of the Enlightenment project.

The essay discusses the ways in which English law impacted Macklin's life and career, tracing significant moments in his encounter with the legal system. The first such incident concerns his extraordinary trial for murder in 1735; the second, his antagonism with the actor–manager David Garrick in 1743; the next, two sets of legal cases in 1769 and 1770, which, by their setting of legal precedents, allowed Macklin to protect the performance copyright

---

1 An earlier version of this essay appeared as 'Charles Macklin and Arthur Murphy: Theatre, Law and an Eighteenth-Century London Irish Diaspora', *Law and Humanities* 14.1 (2020), 113–30.

2 Craig Bailey, *Irish London: Middle-Class Migration in the Global Eighteenth Century* (Liverpool: Liverpool University Press, 2013). See also 'Networks of Aspiration: The London Irish of the Eighteenth Century', a special issue of *Eighteenth-Century Life* 39.1 (2015).

title to his successful farce, *Love à la Mode*. Finally, the essay examines his litigation, encouraged by the Scottish-born lord chief justice, William Murray, Earl of Mansfield (1705–1793), against a riotous Covent Garden audience faction in 1774, a high-water mark in Macklin's recurrent anxieties over threats posed by auditorium disorder. The essay aims to trace both the development of this litigation and his degree of sophistication in bringing the cases to court. Despite enterprises such as the British Inquisition, discussed by Helen Burke and Markman Ellis in this volume, Macklin's principal livelihood ('his Bread', as the Covent Garden trial put it) was derived from money earned either writing for, or performing in, theatres. Protecting these sources of income from copyright theft and riot was the principal motivation of his litigation activity.

New forms of commercial activity (from merchant sailors demanding extra money during storms to new rules governing stock market disclosure) had resulted in rapid developments to contract law. Common law, the fundamental basis of the English legal system, had developed to settle relatively simple cases such as murder, theft, or the misappropriation of goods or property (jewellery or land, for example). It functioned much less well in the adjudication of assets linked to contracts. Changes in contract law were particularly relevant to actors because they required reliable guarantees for a season's work but any playwriting they undertook might also require copyright protection, another area of common law that sought to treat copyright as a type of property felony.[3] During Macklin's working lifetime both contract and copyright law were fraught with attempts to determine the degree to which older English common law ideas of legal 'equity' (rational principles of justice) could be said to already reside in contracts and copyright agreements without resort to creating new branches of the existing legal system.[4] Macklin also encountered, at first hand, the concomitant rise in the importance of precedent (case history) in deciding legal judgments. The interpretation of law in the copyright case of *Millar v. Taylor* (1769), on which Macklin quickly based his successful suit, *Macklin v. Richardson* (1770), is exemplary in this respect because it (possibly erroneously) founded the legal basis for interpreting Parliamentary legislation as developing from subsequent case history rather than from its original legislative intention.[5]

---

3 Warren Swain, *The Law of Contract, 1670–1870* (Cambridge: Cambridge University Press, 2015), 107–25; Ronan Deazley, 'Commentary on Dramatic Literary Property Act 1833' (2008), in L. Bently and M. Kretschmer (eds), *Primary Sources on Copyright (1450–1900)* (2008): www.copyrighthistory.org/ (accessed 10 August 2021).

4 Swain, *Law of Contract*, 107–25.

5 For the paradox of historic legal error in interpreting *Millar v. Taylor* (1769), see John J. Magyar, 'Millar v Taylor as a Precedent for Statutory Interpretation', *Common Law World Review* 47.3 (2018), 217–21.

In short, challenged by increased trade and empire, English law muddled through to create efficient and reliable professional practices consistent with principles of justice.

Macklin's legal activities largely fell within the spheres of contract law, copyright protection, or else specific public order concerns arising from theatre auditorium riots and disturbances impacting on his employment. Law was never far away from theatre. In England, theatres and theatre workers were already highly regulated through processes of state censorship, restrictions on literary genre imposed by royal patent theatre monopolies, and licensing interventions by local magistrates, not to mention sporadic extrajudicial influences exerted by religiously motivated anti-theatricalism.

As Paul Goring's essay in this volume shows, Macklin had a considerable private library to draw on, including around ninety titles devoted to law. By using printed commentaries and abridgements, although they developed at an uneven pace, Macklin could observe the increasing role played by precedent in modifying common law.[6] Although some books may have been lost in the 1772 shipwreck, his library shows he could access legal information at a technical level adequate to follow developing case history. His owning a copy of *The Question Concerning Literary Property, Determined by the Court of King's Bench on 20th April, 1769, in the Cause Between Andrew Millar and Robert Taylor* (1773) confirms that the *Millar* v. *Taylor* case provided the route to *Macklin* v. *Richardson* (1770), although, consistent with the evidence presented here, its outcome would have come to his attention through his network of legal friends. Noticeably absent from the library is William Blackstone's *Commentaries on the Laws of England* (1766–69), possibly because it was less technically helpful. However, typical amongst his legal books are Timothy Cunningham's *A New and Complete Law-dictionary. Or, General Abridgment of the Law* (Dublin, 1764) and William Peere Williams's *Reports of Cases Argued and Determined in the High Court of Chancery and ... King's Bench* (1740). Although Macklin's library included some works on jurisprudence, his collection largely reflected very pragmatic interests about legal process. Perhaps the best indicator of this practicality is his copy of William Addington's *An Abridgment of Penal Statutes* (1775). Addington's book, printed in an oblong octavo format, 'exhibits at one view' tabulated details of offences, relevant statutes, penalties, the numbers of witnesses required, and other information, all gathered to enable an at-a-glance appraisal of the possibilities of prosecution.

---

6 Julia Rudolph, *Common Law and Enlightenment in England, 1689–1750* (Woodbridge: Boydell & Brewer, 2013), chap. 2.

Macklin's early encounters with the law

MACKLIN'S LONG CAREER as playwright, performer, and theatre employee, together with a conspicuous public profile, almost inevitably meant he would encounter legal problems associated with his expanding profession. Probably his first encounter with the English legal system, however, was his prosecution for the manslaughter of the actor Thomas Hallam (d.1735). The tragic event was the result of a fracas in the Drury Lane retiring room about the ownership of a wig when costuming for a performance of Robert Fabian's farce, *Trick for Trick* (1735). Whether by accident or irascible impulse, Hallam's eye was punctured by Macklin's crab tree stick cane in a moment of temper. He died the next day. The legal procedures would have introduced him to progression from the coroner's verdict in May (*'Wilful Murder'*), to an Old Bailey trial in December 1735 (where he was found guilty of manslaughter). The trial transcript suggests he already possessed impressive forensic skill at cross-examining witnesses before a jury. Faced with the box-keeper (and composer) Thomas Arne's courtroom evidence ('he gave a full Longe [*sic*] at the Deceased, and thrust the stick into his left Eye'), Macklin steered him towards testifying to his visible remorse ('Did I shew any Concern afterwards[?]'). With another witness, the singer Thomas Salway, Macklin structured his questions, first of all, to explain the presence of the cane ('Was … a Stick necessary for my part, as a Spanish servant?') but also to ensure the jury understood it was a face-to-face confrontation ('Which side of him was towards me when I pushed?').[7]

Having survived this brush with the law, indications of an early willingness to use the language of litigation are apparent in his falling-out with David Garrick in 1743. The dispute arose because Macklin thought they had entered into an informal agreement about boycotting Drury Lane while it was under Charles Fleetwood's management. When, as Macklin construed it, Garrick broke ranks, his *Case of Charles Macklin, Comedian* (1743) and *Mr Macklin's Reply to Mr Garrick's Answer* (1743) alleged his treatment to be 'a Crime', requiring a *'Dernier Resort'*, a court of last appeal.[8] Although Garrick replied in full and reprinted key correspondence from other players, his evident reluctance to be drawn into public statements makes it difficult to entirely

---

7 *The Country Journal: or, The Craftsman*, 17 May 1735; Charles Mechlin, 10 December 1735, *Old Bailey Online*, Ref. T17351210-40. The manslaughter verdict probably arose because Hallam died the next day.

8 Charles Macklin, *The Case of Charles Macklin, Comedian* (London, 1743), 1; *Mr Macklin's Reply to Mr Garrick's Answer* (London, 1743), 4; and cf. Robert Whatley, *The Dernier Resort: Or, An Appeal to the King, in the Cause Between the Right Honourable Sir Robert Walpole and Mr Whatley* (London, 1741).

verify Macklin's version, although the episode seems to mark a turning point. Rightly or wrongly, Macklin expected an informal agreement to have the force of contract. Garrick seems to have thought otherwise. It was not a mistake Macklin would repeat.

MACKLIN AND COPYRIGHT PROTECTION FOR *LOVE À LA MODE*

IN THE LATE 1760S AND EARLY 1770S, Macklin thought carefully about how to preserve the earnings deriving from his successful farce, *Love à la Mode*, by establishing an effective property title to protect its text but, more importantly, his rights over its performance. The outcome was his suit *Macklin v. Richardson* (1770), specific litigation aimed at protecting these rights. The first act of the farce had been taken down 'from the mouths of the actors' in shorthand in a theatre, and then printed by Richardson in the *Court Miscellany, or Gentleman and Lady's Magazine*. In 1766, Macklin had been granted a 'common injunction' against Richardson and his then partner Urquhart to stop them publishing act two in the next issue. Although there is no evidence to suggest Macklin was advised by Arthur Murphy in 1766, as the plaintiff he had the good sense to request a declaration of the profits arising from their selling 3,400 copies of the *Court Miscellany* if the case was granted a rehearing.[9] Macklin's motives in pursuing this claim, and others, requires an understanding of the contingency of his position as a post-bankrupt, semi-retired actor and playwright.

For reasons which were ultimately financial, Macklin needed to conserve what he described as 'the novelty' of *Love à la Mode* by restricting its performance. Being able to perform in a successful farce he had written himself, and to which he controlled rights of access, was extremely attractive. Over time, his needs were becoming more imperative as advancing age made it less plausible for him to play other principal repertoire roles. This strategy is apparent in his initial correspondence with Covent Garden manager, George Colman the Elder, in February 1773:

> Love a la mode is my favorite Feather,—the best in my cap.—and, without a metaphor, like every other Production[,] would by too much use, lose its

---

9 The decision on *Macklin v. Richardson* (1770), ruled on 5 December 1770, is in Charles Ambler, *Reports of Cases Argued and Determined in the High Court of Chancery, with some few in other Courts* (London, 1790), 694–97; W. Matthews, 'The Piracies of Macklin's *Love à-la-Mode*', *Review of English Studies* 10.39 (1934), 311–18. Urquhart was not involved in the 1770 trial, possibly because he was deceased.

attraction. Should that be its Case while I live the consequence respecting my Income would be bad indeed. Therefore common prudence dictates that I ought to preserve its strength, within the Rule of Equity, as much as I can.[10]

The letter unequivocally sets out the 'consequences respecting my Income', if he failed to conserve *Love à la Mode* by protecting his title (and, quite noticeably, he refers to the 'Rule of Equity', the principles of justice residing in English common law).

It is likely that Macklin's initial method of copyright protection was simply, after every production or performance (in which, of course, he would have been playing), to gather up the individual manuscript 'parts' at the end of the show.[11] And while *Love à la Mode* was first performed in 1759, and there were pirated editions by 1779, Macklin did not authorize an edition until 1793, long after the time he was physically able to perform in it. Writing in 1790, offering flimsy excuses, Yorkshire circuit manager Tate Wilkinson recalled how he had 'obtained the parts' of *Love à la Mode* which 'promised much credit and cash'.[12] Although they must have been aware of Macklin's interdiction, Garrick, Edward Shuter, and several other performers forwarded Wilkinson copies of 'parts' they had illicitly retained. Macklin had little option but to pursue them through the courts. As Jane Wessel has noted, in his own professional dealings, seen most clearly in his correspondence with Colman, Macklin respected the informal titles of other actors to occupy 'parts'.[13] Ironically, it was his inadvertent infringement of this custom which allegedly precipitated William 'Gentleman' Smith's grievance against him at Covent Garden in 1773.[14]

In short, where Tate Wilkinson saw 'much credit and cash' from pirating *Love à la Mode*, Macklin felt 'the consequence respecting my Income'. He decided to seek a remedy in law. In pursuing this claim, *Macklin* v. *Richardson* (1770) developed from significant copyright precedents established in *Millar* v. *Taylor* (1769), a case concerned with Robert Taylor, a printer, whom the

---

10 Charles Macklin to George Colman the Elder, 17 February 1773, Folger Shakespeare Library, Y.c.5380 (1–15).
11 For an example of a 'Part for the role of Shylock', Doncaster, Yorkshire, 1772, see Folger Shakespeare Library, Y.d.42.
12 Tate Wilkinson, *Memoirs of His Own Life*, 4 vols (York, 1790), IV.9.
13 Jane Wessel, 'Possessing Parts and Owning Plays: Charles Macklin and the Prehistory of Dramatic Literary Property', *Theatre Survey* 56.3 (2015), 268–90.
14 Smith had left Drury Lane to set up a theatre venture with Mary Ann Yates, which collapsed before the start of the 1773–74 season, leaving him unemployed. Macklin, with Colman's agreement, had taken over some of Smith's roles, principally Macbeth. Macklin's view of this background is given in his pretrial briefing notes. Folger Shakespeare Library, T.b.23.

bookseller Andrew Millar alleged had appropriated his copyright to James Thomson's successful poem, *The Seasons*. How did he keep himself abreast of changes in case history?

Lord Mansfield, *Millar* v. *Taylor* (1769), and *Macklin* v. *Richardson* (1770)

Macklin seems to have quickly realized that *Millar* v. *Taylor* (1769) could facilitate the success of *Macklin* v. *Richardson* (1770). Although he was not involved in *Millar* v. *Taylor* (1769), which was presided over by Lord Mansfield, its implications meant Macklin could pursue a claim against Richardson beyond the limits set out in the Statute of Anne, 1710 (8 Ann. c. 19), the eighteenth-century's originating legislation giving limited copyright protection for printed books. Macklin would have noted that in *Millar* v. *Taylor* (1769) Mansfield had made a remarkable courtroom intervention, interrupting its proceedings to iterate a much wider, almost transcendent, principle of copyright for intellectual property.[15] He argued that 'The property in the copy ... is *equally* an incorporeal right ... detached from the manuscript, or any other *physical* existence whatsoever'. If a right of property could exist without requiring, as Mansfield put it, a '*physical* existence' (that is, because it existed as 'an incorporeal right', its 'intellectual' content 'communicated by letters'), then any appropriation of 'The property in the copy' of *Love à la Mode* without the creator's consent would be criminal, an issue capable of being dealt with under common law. Mansfield had insisted in *Millar* v. *Taylor* (1769) that 'We are considering the *common* law', potentially simplifying processes of litigation by widening the range of courts available to deliberate on such cases.[16]

From Macklin's point of view, an 'incorporeal right' 'detached from [...] any other *physical* existence' (such as an associated manuscript), also happened to be a good description of how the law might recognize the copyright of theatrical performance. In the eighteenth century, 'The property in the copy' of theatrical performance immediately became 'incorporeal' as soon as the curtain came down. In Mansfield's judgment, the author or publishers retained a 'right' to that 'property in the copy' even when that 'property' had changed its state of being into something 'incorporeal'. Such considerations may have informed Macklin's decision in his case against Richardson to testify that 'two of the actors applied to him, to have it performed at their benefits; and that he made them pay, once 20 guineas, and at another time

---

15 References are to *Millar* v. *Taylor* (1769), sections 2395, 2396, 2398.
16 See Deazley, 'Commentary on Dramatic Literary Property Act 1833'.

30 guineas, for one night's performance'.[17] This would have been sufficient to prove *Love à la Mode* existed as an 'incorporeal' 'property', even though it was 'detached from the manuscript, or any other *physical* existence whatsoever', because a contract of sale and purchase had been recognized by both parties, even if its performance no longer materially existed. Certainly, at some time in 1770, no doubt emboldened by *Millar* v. *Taylor* (1769), Macklin had written to Tate Wilkinson, asking him to desist performing *Love à la Mode*: 'I am sensible that several Companies act it; and the reason why they have hitherto done it with impunity is, because I was in Ireland: but now I am returned, and shall settle here, depend upon it, I shall put the law against every offender of it, respecting my property, in full force'.[18]

Despite having had his case confirmed by the courts, some theatre managers, including Wilkinson, were tardy in observing its import. That *Macklin* v. *Richardson* (1770) had limited immediate effect is clear from his threat in May 1771 to prosecute James Whitley, a provincial manager in Leicester, who had performed *Love à la Mode* without either permission or, of course, payment. Macklin was well aware that his possession of a playbill advertising his farce for performance by Whitley's company was good evidence but he also recommended to his solicitor (identified below) that the entire cast should be named in the indictment ('that would deter them, and the like of them').[19] The comment is significant in indicating Macklin's willingness to conceive of his legal opponents as multiple parties, a forerunner of the more ambitious indictments he pressed in 1774.

Macklin's barrister: Arthur Murphy

How did Macklin reach this level of legal acumen? There were profound incentives. By the 1770s, he was a semi-retired, once-bankrupted performer still jobbing for work. In the background, however, lay another crucial factor. This was his access to a circle of legally trained friends, some with theatrical sympathies, in London's Irish community. No later than 1781, he was friendly with the solicitor, editor, and avid theatregoer, Isaac Reed (1742–1807), and had known the barrister and playwright, Leonard Macnally (1752–1820) since 1774–75, and hosted both for dinner.[20] However,

---

17 Ambler, *Reports of Cases*, 694.
18 *Kirkman*, II.33.
19 *Kirkman*, II.35.
20 David O'Shaughnessy, '"Rip'ning buds in Freedom's field": Staging Irish Improvement in the 1780s', *Journal for Eighteenth-Century Studies* 38.4 (2015) 541–54; Diary of Isaac Reed, 29 November 1781, Folger Shakespeare Library, M.a.125.

perhaps his most significant professional friendship was with the lawyer and playwright, Arthur Murphy, the person who eventually saw the authorized *Love à la Mode* through the press.

Born in Clooniquin, Co. Roscommon, Ireland, Murphy moved to London at the end of 1751 and, after several attempts, was admitted to Lincoln's Inn in 1757 and called to the bar in 1762. His successful tragedy, *The Orphan of China* (Drury Lane, 1759) had starred Garrick and Mary Ann Yates. His comedy, *The Way to Keep Him* (Drury Lane, 1760), a repertoire staple, was eventually followed, in the midst of the events related here, by *The Grecian Daughter* (Drury Lane, 1772), a tragedy, and later a notable vehicle for Sarah Siddons. Murphy's stature as a barrister has been underestimated. The Shakespeare scholar Richard W. Schoch writes that Murphy 'failed in the law', a finding contrary to the evidence presented here.[21] On account of being his executor, Murphy's second biographer, the surgeon Jesse Foot (1780–1850), was able to provide an extensive 'general sketch of his [legal] practice [...] taken from his note books'. Although the notebooks remain untraced, Foot's synopsis reveals a remarkable series of cases where he had variously acted as prosecutor, defence counsel, or had simply been 'retained' for advice, earning him £3,863 15s. 0d. between 1771 and 1773.[22] By the time Macklin was considering how to protect his title to *Love à la Mode*, Murphy had acquired recent copyright law experience as the defence counsel in *Millar* v. *Taylor* (1769), acting for the printer Robert Taylor.[23] Murphy's defendant lost but, paradoxically, it made him perfectly placed to advise Macklin on how to test the courts. Ironically, Murphy's unsuccessful argument on behalf of his client in *Millar* v. *Taylor* (1769) had 'denied that any [...] right remained in the author, after the publication of his work: and [...] treated the pretension of a common law right to it, as mere fancy and imagination, void of any ground or foundation' (4 Burr. 2304). However, both he and Macklin, independently or together, must have realized the significance of the new precedent, implicit in Mansfield's judgment, that an 'incorporeal right [...] detached from the manuscript, or any other *physical* existence whatsoever' still resided with the author. Whether they conferred directly, or not, Murphy's collapsed defence in *Millar* v. *Taylor* (1769) had important implications for protecting *Love à la Mode* in *Macklin* v. *Richardson* (1770). Mansfield's innovative notion of an 'incorporeal right' perfectly suited the circumstances of eighteenth-century performance.

---

21 Richard W. Schoch, '"A Supplement to Public Laws": Arthur Murphy, David Garrick, and *Hamlet, with Alterations*', *Theatre Journal* 57.1 (2005), 21–32.
22 Jesse Foot, *The life of Arthur Murphy, esq.* (London, 1811), 354.
23 Murphy's role in *Millar* v. *Taylor* (1769) seems to have been first noted by Schoch, '"A Supplement to Public Laws"', 22 n. 5.

Although it is not known whether Murphy was directly involved in *Macklin v. Richardson* (1770), their acquaintance may have been long-standing. As Helen Burke notes elsewhere in this volume, they could have met as early as 1754 when Murphy began acting at Covent Garden but, subsequent to *Macklin v. Richardson* (1770), Macklin pursued the Leicester theatre pirate James Whitley in 1771 for continuing to perform *Love à la Mode*, employing Murphy as his counsel.[24] Macklin's 1799 biographer, Thomas Kirkman, only mentions that Macklin was advised 'by his Solicitor', but Jesse Foot, writing in 1811, identifies this 'Solicitor' as Murphy.[25] Despite Kirkman not clarifying the outcome, Foot records that Murphy acted for Macklin against Whitley in Chancery in 1771.[26] Although he lost *Millar* v. *Taylor* (1769), with copyright case history evolving quite swiftly at this time, his expertise seems to have been quickly recognized because he was employed again in *Donaldson* v. *Beckett* (1774), another landmark case (again, about Thomson's *Seasons*), which established that publishers could not hold copyright title in perpetuity.[27] When preparing this case, one of the precedents cited by Murphy was 'Macklin against Richardson, for printing Love A-la-Mode'.[28]

Macklin, Murphy, and the Covent Garden Riots

THE EVIDENCE FOR A CLOSE RELATIONSHIP between Murphy and Macklin is substantial in this early 1770s period. Macklin's procession through the courts was, as noted above, motivated by the need to protect his livelihood through copyright protection but he had long been anxious about problems arising from auditorium disorder. These anxieties began with a personally traumatic riot at Drury Lane in 1740 but reached their height at Covent Garden at the beginning of the 1773–74 season and quite evidently still worried him as late as 1788, when he republished, within the Scottish legal jurisdiction, a précis of the Covent Garden trial outcome.[29]

---

24 *Appleton*, 114.
25 *Kirkman*, II.36, 42; Foot, *Life of Arthur Murphy*, 354.
26 Foot, *Life of Arthur Murphy*, 354; *Macklin* v. *Whitley* (1771), Court of Chancery: Six Clerks Office: Pleadings 1758–1800, National Archives, Kew, C 12/1327/5.
27 The correct legal citations are: 2 Brown's Parl. Cases (2d ed.) 129, 1 Eng. Rep. 837; 4 Burr. 2408, 98 Eng. Rep. 257; 17 Cobbett's Parl. Hist. 953.
28 Arthur Murphy, et al., *Case of the Appellants: Alexander Donaldson, and John Donaldson, Booksellers (1774) to be heard at house of Lords 4th Feb 1774* (London, 1774), 6.
29 Paul Goring, 'Theatrical Riots and Conspiracies in London and Edinburgh: Charles Macklin, James Fennell and the Rights of Actors and Audiences', *Review of English Studies* 67.278 (2016), 122–45.

Murphy was one of the prosecution counsel at Macklin's 1774–75 trial against the Covent Garden rioters. Foot simply notes that Murphy 'was retained by Macklin' against the defendants 'for a riot at Covent Garden Theatre'.[30] In this case, however, his appointment was more than simply advisory. He made an important, if not quite decisive, intervention by steering Mansfield away from exploring the supposition that (in Mansfield's words), Macklin might be 'in the wrong'. Murphy's testimony also fixes him with Macklin in October 1773, personally advising him in the middle of the riots. Murphy got Macklin to agree ('he readily concurred with me') that it would not be a good idea for him to appeal directly to the audience from the stage on account of the conspirators being in the auditorium.[31]

Once one connects Murphy to Macklin, there unfolds a series of London Irish networks closely linked to money, credit finance, and the English judicial system. Craig Bailey's study of Irish lawyers in eighteenth-century London particularly discusses the social networks revealed at the 1777 trial of the lawyer Joseph Stacpoole, an exasperated creditor who fired a gun at another Irishman, John Parker, inside the Bull Inn, Southwark, on 17 August 1775.[32] A complex mix of bonds, sureties, mortgages, Irish real estate, legal tutelage, lawyer's fees, and tardy debtors all surfaced at the trial. Foot records that Murphy was 'retained for the Defendant, at the suit of the King against Joseph Stackpoole [*sic*]'.[33] Placing Murphy in the midst of this important case, advising Stacpoole in the capacity of the crown's appointed solicitor, tells us much about the circles Macklin also moved in. Not least, as Bailey argues, since the wealth of Irish estates could only be fully realized in London's financial markets, immense sums of money were involved. A banker character witness, George Clive, testified Stacpoole had raised over £150,000 for Irish mortgages. Ironically, in 1767, Murphy was awarded (through the Lord Chancellor) the lucrative sinecure of Commissioner of Bankrupts, an appointment which may itself have arisen through his familiarity with English credit and Irish debt.[34]

---

30 Foot, *Life of Arthur Murphy*, 357.
31 Charles Macklin, *The genuine arguments of the council, with the opinion of the Court of King's Bench, on cause shewn, why an information should not be exhibited against John Stephen James … By a citizen of the world* (London, 1774), 26, 55, 69–71.
32 Bailey, *Irish London*, 89–98; *The Trial (At Large) of Joseph Stacpoole, Esq, William Gapper, Attorney at Law, And James Lagier; for Wilfully and Maliciously Shooting at John Parker Esq … Thursday, March 20, 1777* (London, 1777).
33 Foot, *Life of Arthur Murphy*, 357.
34 His start date is given in J.C. Sainty, 'Commissioners of Bankrupts *c*.1720–1831: A Provisional List': https://web.archive.org/web/20180929194740/https://www.history.ac.uk/publications/office/comms-bankrupts (accessed 10 August 2021).

By c.1773, no doubt advised by Murphy acting as a friend or in a professional capacity, Macklin had developed a good working knowledge of case law. With his 1735 trial demonstrating his calmness under stress, and with a substantial copyright ruling already under his belt, he was a formidable legal adversary. While the 1773 Covent Garden conspirators may have seen him as someone they could intimidate, they might have paused if they had checked more carefully his legal dealings, doubly so if they were aware he was supported by Murphy's counsel.

As it was, Macklin's litigation had already received the support of the highest echelons of the English judiciary. In *Macklin v. Richardson* (1770), the sole verbal contribution of Henry, 2nd Earl Bathurst (1714–94), one of the two trial judges, was to provide a decisively worded, unequivocally supportive, declaration: 'The printing it before the author has, is doing him a great injury. Strong case'.[35] Similarly, the transcript of the 1774 Covent Garden trial reveals Mansfield's personal backing, the judge telling the court, 'I hinted and recommended to him to have brought an Action'.[36]

The Covent Garden trial, ruled in King's Bench in May 1775 and finding in Macklin's favour, was significant in that it offered protection to actors' careers by ensuring that lost earnings caused by broken contracts could be recovered, and gaol sentences imposed, if audience members (either as factions or as individuals) conspired to prevent them working.[37] The case has attracted growing critical attention.[38] The most authoritative account remains William W. Appleton's 1963 biography of Macklin. Understandably, Appleton looks at the episode as part of his narrative of a life in progress, faithfully précising sources but without particularly commenting on its implications.[39] The most dramatic narrative of the bare events is Macklin's manuscript, 'The Cause, Rise, Progress & Summary of the Riot 18th November [1773]', a document probably prepared by him for the trial with its disjointed format conveying some sense of the rush of incident.[40]

---

35 Ambler, *Reports of Cases*, 696.
36 Macklin, *Genuine arguments*, 42–43.
37 Macklin, *Genuine arguments*; Kirkman, II.240.
38 Heather McPherson, 'Theatrical Riots and Cultural Politics in Eighteenth-Century London', *The Eighteenth Century: Theory and Interpretation* 43.3 (2002), 236–52; David Worrall, 'Quiet Theatres, the Rise of Celebrity and the *Case [of] Mr Macklin, Late of Covent-Garden Theatre* (1775)', *Arrêt sur scene/Scene Focus* 3 (2014), 207–17; Kristina Straub, 'The Newspaper "Trial" of Charles Macklin's *Macbeth* and the Theatre as Juridical Public Sphere', *Eighteenth-Century Fiction* 27.3–4 (2015), 395–418; Goring, 'Theatrical Riots and Conspiracies in London and Edinburgh', 122–45.
39 *Appleton*, 168–94.
40 Charles Macklin, 'Covent Garden Riot', Folger Shakespeare Library, T.b.23.

The criminal background can be easily stated. The rioting was targeted at Macklin in order to stop him acting. Within a few nights, the disturbances provoked the manager, George Colman, to discharge Macklin from his contract. In court, Mansfield ruled that John Stephen James, Joseph Clarke, Ralph Aldys [or Aldus], Thomas Lee [or Leigh], James Sparks, and William Augustus Miles had formed a conspiracy, 'to advise the Managers [of Covent Garden theatre] to discharge him, and take his Bread from him'.[41] He was unequivocal: 'They are convicted of a Conspiracy; they all joined in the Riot'.[42]

In Macklin's later iteration of Mansfield's judgment, apparently aimed at alerting the precedent of the English court to the Scottish legal jurisdiction in 1788, his summary of the case described it as 'a riotous conspiracy, founded on premeditated malice, to deprive Mr. Macklin of his livelihood [and] the loss of his bread, by causing him to be expelled the [sic] Theatre'.[43] Crucially, the crime was deemed a 'capital Felony', able to be prosecuted as an 'action at Common Law'.[44] This meant that the offences against Macklin were equivalent to 'tak[ing] his Bread', that is, a straightforward felony suitable for hearing in a criminal court, with King's Bench one of the most senior courts of that type. Although he had been dismissed by Colman, his employer, the 'Felony' classification meant he could avoid the civil courts, the courts of Chancery, the default jurisdiction for matters unable to be settled under common law.[45]

By 1774, Mansfield may similarly have thought it was time for the courts to intervene. Towards the end of the first trial hearing, reminding the court that the disturbances targeting Macklin had been aimed 'to deprive him of his Bread', Mansfield remarked that, if there was a 'Conspiracy against the Person who is the Actor, to strip him of the Means of Living, that is a strong Ground of Action, which may be brought by him'.[46] Murphy may also have acted as a powerful advocate, bringing Macklin to the attention of Mansfield. He had been something of a protégé of Mansfield, with the judge intervening in 1757

---

41 Macklin, *Genuine arguments*, 68.
42 *Kirkman*, II.241.
43 Charles Macklin, *Case, Mr. Macklin late of Covent-Garden Theatre, against Mess. Clarke, Aldys, Lee, James, and Miles* (Edinburgh, [1775]), 8. For a discussion of its publication date, see Goring, 'Theatrical Riots and Conspiracies in London and Edinburgh'.
44 Macklin, *Genuine arguments*, preface; Macklin, *Case*, 7.
45 The problems of Chancery are famous from Charles Dickens's novel *Bleak House* (1852). For Chancery's reform, see Michael Lobban, 'Preparing for Fusion: Reforming the Nineteenth-Century Court of Chancery, Part I', *Law and History Review* 22.2 (2004), 389–427.
46 Macklin, *Genuine arguments*, 42–43.

to get him admitted as a student of Lincoln's Inn.[47] Of course, Mansfield may not have been thinking exclusively about Macklin's personal predicament. One of the indicted was Ralph Aldus, an 'Attorney at Law'. Cleaning up the law may have been as much a motive for Mansfield as ensuring public order. Commenting after the trial, the *Gentleman's Magazine* reported that Mansfield's view was that the entire episode was 'a national disgrace'.[48]

MACKLIN'S ANXIETY ABOUT THE THEATRE RIOTS

MACKLIN'S COMMONPLACE BOOK AND NOTES for the trial also add to our knowledge of Macklin's decision-making process. His experience of theatre riots can be traced as least as far back as 1740. Macklin's recollection of those episodes reveal how deeply anxiety about the precariousness of his career had become embedded. The Commonplace Book, thought to be in use *c*.1778–90, describes his involvement in a Drury Lane riot on 23 January 1740 caused by a misunderstanding arising from the non-appearance (although billed) of the dancers Philip Denoyer (*c*.1700–88) and Marie Chateauneuf (1721–?).[49] In an entry headed 'Theatre', Macklin referred to 'the Case of Denoyer' alongside 'Macklin's Case', the latter allusion helping date its post-1775 inscription. However, the entry not only suggests Macklin conceptualized these incidents as 'Case' histories, consciously referencing legal discourse, but it also shows that he was carefully recording his experiences of theatre disturbances. The 1740 riot had a significant impact on him. While simply following his profession as an actor, Macklin had become caught up in an unpredictable mix of politics and ethnic violence.

On the night of the 1740 riot, the main piece had been *Hamlet*, with James Quin as the Ghost and Kitty Clive as Ophelia. Macklin played 'Ostrick'. The set must have been cleared before the 'Pantomime', which was *The Fortune Tellers*, with Henry Woodward as Harlequin. According to the Commonplace Book, although not billed in the newspapers, Macklin was 'the Clown' (much less of a role than it became in Grimaldi's day). The pantomime was to

---

47 Foot, *Life of Arthur Murphy*, 14, 108.
48 *Gentleman's Magazine*, 44 (1775), 265.
49 The date of its earliest use derives from an inscription of 29 May 1778 (f. 15v), Folger Shakespeare Library, M.a.9. Denoyer is also known as 'G. Desnoyer'; see Philip H. Highfill, Kalman A. Burnim, and Edward A. Langhans, *A Biographical Dictionary of Actors, Actresses, Musicians, Dancers, Managers & Other Stage Personnel in London, 1660–1800*, 16 vols (Carbondale: Southern Illinois University Press, 1973–1993), III.181–82; IV.332–34. This episode was reprinted in instalments in *The Monthly Mirror* 7 (May 1799) under the heading, 'Mackliana'.

conclude with 'a New Grand Entertainment of Dancing' called *A Voyage to the Island of Cytherea*. Unfortunately, the newspapers had billed Denoyer and Chateauneuf to dance in it, inadvertently precipitating the riot.[50] Although it is sometimes difficult to disentangle the detail of Macklin's account, he wrote that the rioters assaulted someone 'very ill five or six of them', identifying the victim as 'a natural son of a Lord a Scotch Lord—who suffered for Rebelling in 1716'. The theatre auditorium was a cauldron of different factions, both real and imagined. Not only can one glimpse a possible ethnic, anti-Jacobite, motive for the attack on the Scottish lord's son but Macklin also adds, 'they thought he was an Actor'. This comment, perhaps more than anything else in the narrative, captures Macklin's anxieties about being an actor with an ethnically marked accent who was potentially an audience target for violence.

Presumably just before *The Fortune Tellers* began, no doubt already dressed as the Clown, Macklin 'made an apology—for Denoyer—was hissed'. Macklin's address (he would have stood alone at the front of the stage) seems to have sparked off the disturbances. According to his account, the audience were already 'in a great rage created by the Calveshead Club', a reference to blasphemous gatherings allegedly convened to travesty the execution of King Charles I by drinking wine from calves' skulls.[51] Leading the riotous faction of (what one assumes to have been) reactive loyalist Protestants, were people he named as 'Lord Boyn' and his 'Brother Captain Hamilton', the former identifiable as the thirty-year-old Irish-born, Gustavus Hamilton, 2nd Viscount Boyne (1710–46). His role as ringleader provides a glimpse of the several overlapping layers of rank and ethnicity in the auditorium that night, not least implying Macklin's own place amongst these enmities. Even by 1740 was Macklin overwhelmingly aware of auditorium riots as a theatre public order issue.

It is not difficult to appreciate Macklin's perception of his precarious position as an Irish actor on the London stage. Considerations such as these no doubt motivated him to seek protection for his professional practice in law. The 1740 riots revealed the audience's jumble of sectarian anxieties about phantom Calves' Head Clubs, disruptive Irish and Scottish aristocrats (some with government sinecures), accusations of Jacobitism, and all concurrent with George II's sensitivities about loyalty. That Macklin was aware of widespread, unpredictable perceptions of national identity, even about the monarchy, is manifest in a section of the Commonplace Book headed 'Hanoverians', evidently written after George II's death: 'The People while

---

50 *London Daily Post and General Advertiser*, 23 January 1740.
51 Michelle Orihel, '"Treacherous Memories" of Regicide: The Calves-Head Club in the Age of Anne', *Historian* 73.3 (2011), 435–62.

the two Georges lived they impressed the weak & malicious mind with the Idea of being governed by Foreigners, & Foreign hanover [sic] Influence'. Macklin was also one of London's 'Foreigners'. Perhaps also with a foreigner's perspective (some of his relatives had been Jacobites), Mansfield may have shared similar anxieties when he 'hinted and recommended to him to have brought an Action'.

That Mansfield would have been aware of the violent nature of the 1773 rioting is probable from another Macklin narrative, probably also written preparatory to the trial, 'The Cause, Rise, Progress & Summary of the Riot 18th November [1773]'. The Covent Garden incident was certainly every bit as violent as the 1740 riot:

> the Actors were hooted & pelted off the Stage [...] Apples thrown, Sticks held up [...] Benches torn up.—Chandeliers broke—Ladies ordered to leave the Boxes [...] [Joseph] Clark[e] got a Piece of Wood in his hand [...]—this he waved about & when Macklin approached him to speak to him, with that Piece of Wood Clark menaced Macklin by shaking it at him, in the Manner of striking.[52]

It is plausible that knowledge of this narrative, put to him by Murphy, may have provoked Mansfield's comment that he 'recommended to him to have brought an Action'.

Given Macklin's facility with dramatic writing, it is not surprising many of the notes provide fascinating evidence of his desire to shape the case. Unfortunately, although Macklin understood copyright law, he had only a legal amateur's idea about how to pursue a successful conviction in a case of rioting. The backing and assistance of Murphy and Mansfield were crucial.

A typical example is his copying of a letter he sent to Colman from Dublin on 17 February 1773, at the beginning of his negotiations for the following season. Macklin attached a note, 'This Letter contains the Foundation of Macklin's intended agreement with Colman—and the principles on which I should agree conduct myself [sic] and be conducted. Therefore it should be, in every part, made clear to the Counsel, the Court, and particularly to the Jury'.[53] Although Macklin obviously thought the document important, the trial ignored this type of evidence as proof of contract. Possibly of more importance were details contained elsewhere in the 'Cause, Rise, Progress & Summary' narrative, where Macklin describes how

> Colman goes on the Stage says,—'At the Command of the Public, Macklin is discharged.' then [sic] sends on a Piece of a Board painted black, with Large

---

52 Folger Shakespeare Library, T.b.23.
53 17 February 1773, Folger Shakespeare Library, Y.c.5380 (14–15) (1); Kirkman, II.56.

Capital Letters written in Chalk, with the Inscription on it, 'At the Command of the Public Mr. Macklin is discharged.' This is presented to the Eyes of the Audience by one of the Actors.

This declared, in front of witnesses, Colman's breaking of the contract. However, in the event, the trial simply confirmed the existence of a contract by subpoenaing Jonathan Garton, Covent Garden's Treasurer, who stated under oath, 'The Witness says that *Macklin was in the list* at 400l. for the season'. This was sufficient to confirm the contract had been documented at the theatre with a specified duration and rate of pay. Garton also confirmed that 'The last payment was on the 20th of November [1773], and that was 34l. 14s. which was to the 17th *of that month*'.[54] This demonstrated that the contract had ended prematurely and the balance of salary was outstanding.

The Folger Macklin documents reveal the actor's understandable consternation at his treatment, but his notes were not always of use to the prosecution. His attempts to subpoena David Garrick ('I have sent to you Several times in order to have you served with the enclosed Subpaena [*sic*]') were futile, driven by an unfounded rumour that the Drury Lane manager was behind the conspiracy. He had tried to deliver to Garrick a letter to 'desire your Presence and Evidence tomorrow morning at nine oClock Westminster Hall'. The subpoena could not formally be served (which required it to be physically handed over) apparently because Garrick or his servants did not answer the door ('I have called myself for the same purpose but ineffectually').[55] Macklin had even formulated phrasing to cover this eventuality, writing, 'you have a legal & a moral option to attend or not', correctly stating attendance was an 'option' (because the subpoena had not been properly served).[56] Since no one had testified to seeing Garrick at any of the performances, Macklin would have found it almost impossible to implicate him. However, the incident tells us much about Macklin's misplaced zeal. This final attempt to serve the subpoena was made on 23 February 1775, the day before the start of the hearings under Sir Richard Aston (1717–78).[57]

Macklin's willingness to act proactively, possibly with a degree of malice, is discernible in his copying of a letter endorsed, 'No. 16 March 14—1774 from Macklin to his daughter [Maria]'. Macklin noted that Maria 'sent [it] to Colman for his Perusal which he detains [*sic*] as part of his defence for breaking the agreement'. The letter is dated to the latter part of the 1773–74

---

54 *Kirkman*, II.182.
55 It had to be 'personally served'; see Cornelius Wendell, *The Young Clerk's Magazine: or English Law-Repository, Fourth Edition* (1763), 203.
56 23 February 1775, Folger Shakespeare Library, Y.c.5380 (6–9).
57 *Kirkman*, II.138.

season, around the time when Maria Macklin—then engaged by Covent Garden—would normally have requested confirmation of a benefit night date (usually taken in April or May). The issue at hand was Colman's tardiness in assigning her a date because he knew that, if she played a benefit, she would also have invited her more famous father to act in it.

In the letter, Macklin wrote that 'if I play at your Benefit I shall as I am informed, be insulted again by my Enemies', 'I shall be pursued with greater Resentment than before'. The implication is that the November 1773 rioters, or their friends, not only firmly existed as conspirators (something the courts had yet conclusively to prove), but that they had conspired once again. Macklin was attempting to demonstrate that Colman's refusal to designate his daughter with a benefit date was an acknowledgement such a conspiracy existed and that he was contributing to it effects. Predictably, Macklin took care to provide an estimate for Maria's loss of earnings: 'The loss my not playing will no doubt be considerable—near two hundred pounds—a great Sum in a players Revenue'.[58]

Crucially, by sending this letter to Maria to forward to Colman, and by retaining a copy himself for possible production in court, knowing that Colman 'detains' (*retains*) a copy, Macklin must have hoped its retention would prove Colman a party to this, a second conspiracy, on account of his having acknowledged its contents by having received it (much like serving a subpoena on Garrick). It was a manoeuvre of entrapment, almost amounting to planting evidence. Of course, Colman had not been indicted and in any case the alleged financial injury was against Maria, not her father.

Conclusion: Macklin and Murphy as members of a London Irish professional diaspora

THE EVIDENCE PRESENTED demonstrates Macklin's deep immersion in English law. To Macklin's own determination and resilience must now be added his crucial association with Arthur Murphy. Far from being a failed lawyer, Murphy's legal career was high-profile. In late 1772, according to Foot, he was 'retained' by Garrick in his action against the newspaper, the *Public Ledger*, for printing an anonymous libel against him (he won).[59] Theirs was a remarkable conjunction, not only because Macklin was involved in significant litigation but also because their connection occurred amidst Murphy's growing reputation as a playwright, culminating in his 1772

---

58 14 March 1774, Folger Shakespeare Library, Y.c.5380 (6–9).
59 Kirkman, II.36, 42; Foot, *Life of Arthur Murphy*, 354.

tragedy, *The Grecian Daughter*, a year before the Covent Garden riots where he had counselled Macklin apparently at the height of the disturbances. With *Macklin* v. *Richardson* (1770) almost certainly developed from a realignment of Murphy's unsuccessful tactics in *Millar* v. *Taylor* (1769), this was a close relationship. Even if not counselled by Murphy directly for *Macklin* v. *Richardson* (1770), Macklin must have rapidly assimilated recent case history and acquired the confidence, with Murphy acting as his barrister, to proceed against the Covent Garden conspirators. The endorsements he received from Bathurst and Mansfield confirmed the correctness of his judgements. Contrarily, his attempts to subpoena Garrick and incriminate Colman betray a zealotry indicative of personal animosities whose motives are no longer fully recoverable. However, with Arthur Murphy fast becoming a significant barrister on the legal circuit, and Charles Macklin a high-profile, if controversial, figure in the acting world as both performer and playwright, their conjunction in the early 1770s uncovers, as predicted by Craig Bailey, the existence of a fully functioning London Irish diaspora operating across two high-profile professions located at the heart of Britain's capital city. Insofar as law, its reliability, ease of access, impartiality, and ability to meet new social conditions are concerned, then Charles Macklin's career of litigation, running in parallel with his life as a playwright and performer, is a powerful illustration of Enlightenment progress.

Plate 1: Mordecai (Colm Gleeson) courts a sceptical Charlotte (Caitlin Scott). [Smock Alley, 2017]. Photograph by Colm Summers.

The first four plate images are from the initial 'work in progress' production of *Love à la Mode after Macklin* at the Scene & Heard Festival, Smock Alley Theatre, 2017.

Plate 2: Clutching only his script and a balloon sword, Sir Callaghan O'Brallaghan (Fionn Foley) prepares to defend himself from Sir Archy Macsarcasm (Leonard Buckley). [Smock Alley, 2017]. Photograph by Colm Summers.

Plate 3: Squire Groom (Norma Howard) re-enacts his Newmarket escapades, helped by Mordecai (Colm Gleeson) and Sir Archy (Leonard Buckley), as the Harlequin (Honi Cooke) eggs him on. [Smock Alley, 2017]. Photograph by Colm Summers.

Plate 4:
The ensemble cast sing themselves out as the play comes to an end. [Smock Alley, 2017]. Photograph by Colm Summers.

Plate 5: An amorous Sir Archy (Colm Lennon) applies the Scottish method to a bemused Charlotte (Caitlin Scott). [Smock Alley, 2018]. Photograph by John Cooney.

The fifth and sixth plate images are from the next iteration of the production, *Love à la Mode* at Smock Alley Theatre, 2018.

Plate 6: Mordecai (Fionnuala Gygax) woos Charlotte (Caitlin Scott) with some deft dance moves. [Smock Alley, 2018]. Photograph by John Cooney.

Plate 7: Johan Zoffany, unfinished theatrical conversation piece, with Charles Macklin as Shylock (c.1768). © Tate.

Plate 8: Johan Zoffany, *Charles Macklin as Shylock in The Merchant of Venice*. The Holburne Museum, Bath/Bridgeman Images.

5
Macklin and the Novel
Ros Ballaster

> Character is a Thing, mark or Letter, which, by its ^Form^ or temper is distinguished from every other Thing, mark, Letter, or Temper.
>
> Every human mind has a peculiar manner by which it is distinguished ^by nice observers^ from every other in Society. This Peculiarity of mind is what is called <u>Character</u>.

CHARLES MACKLIN MAKES THIS OBSERVATION in his Commonplace Book.[1] That this was Macklin's settled opinion is confirmed by his biographer James Kirkman, who reports that Macklin responded to the question, 'what is character?' with the answer: 'the alphabet will tell you. It is that which is distinguished by its own marks from every other thing of its kind'.[2] The Greek *kharakter* (Χαρακτηρ) refers to an instrument for marking or stamping a distinctive mark: its denotation swiftly moves, however, from tool to the mark itself.[3] Marks constitute the characters of the alphabet; these serve the purpose of distinguishing one element from another in a graphic or verbal system. Put together in different combinations they form different meanings. Stage character clearly worked this way. The 'dramatis personae' of each play consisted of a familiar set of types—the blustering father, the witty daughter, rakish suitor of comedy, or the tyrant, the virgin, the sexual

---

1 Charles Macklin, 'Commonplace Book, 1778–1790' [manuscript], Folger Shakespeare Library, M.a.9, f. 54v.
2 *Kirkman*, I.66.
3 See John Frow, *Character and Person* (Oxford: Oxford University Press, 2014), 7.

predator of tragedy—put together to deliver a plot with some variation through combination and complexity. This was a requisite of a repertory theatre where each actor has his or her own 'lines of business', kept even when the performer's physical appearance had changed so that he or she spoke visibly against type: heavily pregnant women played virgins, elderly men played young rakes. A customary 'right' of the repertory actor was his or her personal repertory of parts. When actors played against their 'type' they were criticized for 'stepping out of line'. They could also step out of character when they 'pointed', directing a speech with gesture directly to the audience. These repertory conventions suggest that audiences did not come to the theatre to be surprised by what characters did but to be impressed by the quality of the actors' technique in delivering their business.[4]

Note, though, that Macklin figures the alphabet here as itself a kind of 'actor': 'the alphabet will tell you'. Like an actor stepping on the stage to deliver a prologue, the alphabet will 'tell' its audience how the system works. When a male actor presents a prologue or a female actor an epilogue (and this was the common distribution of labour on the eighteenth-century stage), she or he steps out of the characters they take in the plays performed that night. And sometimes the actor does not have a part in any of the performances and rather speaks in his or her 'own' public character. He or she stands as surrogate or alphabetical 'sign', most commonly of the author, but sometimes the theatre manager, sometimes another actor for whose benefit the performance was given. A litigious, ambitious man who relied on the stage and theatrical performances of many kinds to keep afloat his career, Macklin was especially proprietorial about his parts. He took steps, both through the law and through the withholding of his own manuscripts from print, to protect his property over the parts he wrote for himself in his own plays. The actor's customary right of possession of his or her parts in the repertory was in decline through the eighteenth century. In that context, 'Macklin was determined to possess his dramatic parts permanently as a form of job security, for both his personality and happenstance often left him in a precarious professional state'.[5] He won a form of cultural property in the part of Shylock after his debut in the role in 1741 at Drury Lane through his secret working up of a naturalistic performance that instantly associated the performance with the actor and retained his hold on the role for forty years. And he intentionally withheld his very successful 1759 farce, *Love à la Mode*, from print and fiercely protected

---

4 See Lisa Freeman, *Character's Theater: Genre and Identity on the Eighteenth-Century English Stage* (Philadelphia: University of Pennsylvania Press, 2001), 28, 31.

5 Jane Wessel, 'Possessing Parts and Owning Plays: Charles Macklin and the Prehistory of Dramatic Literary Property', *Theatre Survey* 56.3 (2015), 268–90.

the manuscript and copies from circulation in order to maintain his property over the (lucrative) part he played in it of the Scotsman Archy Macsarcasm.

In this essay, Macklin serves as a case study to think about what it means—what happens—when the actor steps 'out' or 'off' the stage into the pages of a printed and fictional narrative, and particularly when he (or she) appears in a novel. What is the role of the actor in the business of novelistic character? And is the representation of a well-known actor in a novel different from the representation of other non-acting celebrities? There are a number of ways we can come at this question. First and foremost is Gillian Russell's insight that visits to the theatre and encounters with actors are important sites (and sights) in the eighteenth-century novel: the theatre visit adds to the novel's claims to naturalism and to realism, adds thickness to the rendering of fictional character by placing its imagined protagonists in a cultural event that did in fact happen.[6] These experiences are formulaic: an ingénue comes to the theatre and what happens in watching the play is a significant moment of public exposure as well as setting up a potential romantic attachment. Narrative fictional moments of transition such as these are tagged to specific performances, as is Evelina's visit in Frances Burney's novel to see Garrick as Ranger in a retirement performance of 1776 of *The Suspicious Husband* at Drury Lane.[7] And those performances often have a direct relevance to the hero's or heroine's future unfolding story: Evelina must evade a cad to find a true-hearted lover as must the female protagonists of the play she watches. Russell concludes that the theatre visit proves the moral virtue of the genre of the novel by comparison with the theatre whilst also adding density to its realism: 'an art form and cultural institution that was regarded with suspicion on account of its shameless reliance on presence was often used to enhance the reality effect of these narratives'.[8] We might say that the contrast of theatre and novel proves the 'character' of the novel: its tendency to promote morality rather than peddle the cheap entertainment tricks that are being (lightly) satirized in the theatre experience described *in* the novel.

Second, drawing the character of the actor was not largely or primarily the business of the novel as a form. The very popular form of the biography of the actor, or memoir, was the primary vehicle for this work. However, the boundaries did blur: actors wrote fictionalized forms of autobiography, such as Thomas Holcroft's *Alwyn: or the Gentleman Comedian* (1780), which presents

---

6 Gillian Russell, 'The Novel and the Stage', in Peter Garside and Karen O'Brien (eds), *The Oxford History of the Novel in English*, vol. 2, *English and British Fiction, 1750–1820* (Oxford: Oxford University Press, 2015), 513–28.
7 Frances Burney, *Evelina, or a Young Lady's Entrance into the World* (1778), ed. Susan Kubica Howard (Peterborough, ON: Broadview Press, 2000) (Letter X), 116–17.
8 Russell, 'The Novel and the Stage', 515.

his own experience as a young strolling player in fictional form.⁹ However, the fortunes of the actor's memoir were closely tied to the attractions of the fictional first person of the novel. Colley Cibber's *Apology for the Life of Mr Colley Cibber* was published on 7 April 1740 and Samuel Richardson's *Pamela; or, Virtue Rewarded* on 6 November of the same year.¹⁰ David Garrick and Charles Macklin both saw their debuts in plays that made their names in the season of the following year: Garrick as Richard III at Goodman's Fields and Macklin as Shylock at Drury Lane.

Both Cibber's *Apology* and Richardson's *Pamela* sought to prove the virtue, integrity, and cultural sway of relatively low-born characters and both innovated in terms of form and style. Cibber, coauthor of *The Provok'd Husband*, introduced the genre of actor's memoir, the account of theatre history intermingled with a single life. Richardson invented the dramatic rendering of experience close to the moment in Pamela's letter–journal technique. Sterne's *Tristram Shandy* alluded to Cibber's memoir in its title, parodied and played with its style and sentiment in its pages. When Laurence Sterne wrote to a friend after the publication of the first two volumes of *Tristram Shandy* 'I wrote not [to] be *fed*, but to be *famous*', he inverted Cibber's defence of his *Apology for the Life of Colley Cibber* in a pamphlet of 1742: 'I wrote more to be Fed, than to be Famous'.¹¹

Third, stage plays from the 1740s onward—with the huge success of *Pamela* and the growing symbolic capital of the novel—made reference to the novel as a rival form and mode. They also put novel-reading women on stage; the best-known examples are Polly in George Colman's *Polly Honeycombe* (1760) and Lydia Languish in Richard Sheridan's *The Rivals* (1775). And these comic heroines are mocked for their inability to 'read' true character. Authors such as Oliver Goldsmith cast the novel as a villain in the degrading of the authenticity of original kinds of stage comedy. The association of the 'sentimental' with the 'novel' is most apparent in the play

---

9 Thomas Holcroft, *Alwyn: or the Gentleman Comedian* (London, 1780).
10 Samuel Richardson, *Pamela, or, Virtue Rewarded*, *The Cambridge Edition of the Works and Correspondence of Samuel Richardson*, vol. 2, ed. Albert Rivero (Cambridge: Cambridge University Press, 2011); Colley Cibber, *An Apology for the Life of Colley Cibber: With an Historical View of the Stage during his Own Time*, ed. B.R.S. Fone (Ann Arbor: University of Michigan Press, 1968).
11 See Julia H. Fawcett, 'The Canon of Print: Laurence Sterne and the Overexpression of Character', *Spectacular Disappearances: Celebrity and Privacy, 1696–1801* (Ann Arbor: University of Michigan Press, 2016), 98–99. The references are to 'Laurence Sterne, letter to an unknown gentleman, Wednesday, 30 January 1760', in Lewis Perry Curtis (ed.), *Letters of Laurence Sterne* (Oxford: Oxford University Press, 1935), 88–91 (Letter 47) and Colley Cibber, *A Letter from Mr Cibber to Mr Pope* (Dublin, 1742), 5.

that is now perhaps the best known from the Georgian repertory: Oliver Goldsmith's *She Stoops to Conquer* opened on 15 March 1773 at George Colman's Covent Garden theatre and was a huge overnight success. Only a few months earlier, Goldsmith had published an 'Essay on the Theatre: Or, A Comparison between Sentimental and Laughing Comedy' in which he had yoked the sentimental with the novelistic. He complains of the lack of comedic skill required of authors who sought success through writing sentimental comedies, the only apprenticeship required being that of hack novel-writing. 'Those abilities that can hammer out a Novel are fully sufficient for the production of a Sentimental Comedy'.[12] Yet, Goldsmith was one of the most celebrated practitioners of the sentimental novel, his 1766 *The Vicar of Wakefield* one of the most widely read sentimental comic works of the century. Goldsmith is not so much attacking the novel itself as the undue influence of fiction-writing techniques in the formation of a new humane stage comedy which toned down a customarily satirical and rakish manner.[13]

In what follows, I evaluate Macklin's appearances in each of these three roles: first, as a walk-on part adding to the realism of a novel in Maria Edgeworth's *Harrington*; second, as the subject of (fictionalized) and novelistic pseudo-biography in Edward Kimber's *Juvenile adventures of David Ranger* (1757); and third, as an author–actor very aware of the rise of the novel as a challenge to the (classical) authority of stage drama and especially stage satire. Here I concentrate on two mid-century dramatic works, *The New Play Criticiz'd* (1747) and *The Covent Garden Theatre; or, Pasquin Turn'd Drawcansir* (1752).

Macklin became the subject of theatre biography very soon after his death; Francis Aspry Congreve's pamphlet-length summary, *Authentic Memoirs of the Late Mr Charles Macklin, Comedian* (1798), James Kirkman's two volume, digressive and anecdotal *Memoirs of the Life of Charles Macklin* (1799), and William Cooke's attempt at synthesis, *Memoirs of Charles Macklin, Comedian* (1804).[14] Macklin apparently had embarked on an autobiography of his own

---

12 Arthur Friedman (ed.), *The Collected Works of Oliver Goldsmith*, 5 vols (Oxford: Clarendon Press, 1966), III.213.
13 The reader searching for *She Stoops* among the John Larpent Plays held at the Huntington Library Manuscript Collections, then, might be slightly less surprised than expected to discover it submitted to the licenser under the title *The Novel; or Mistakes of a Night*. Also available from Adam Matthew Digital, *Eighteenth Century Drama* database: www.eighteenthcenturydrama.amdigital.co.uk.
14 For a full collection of biographies of Macklin, see Paul Goring (ed.), *Charles Macklin* in *Lives of Shakespearian Actors*, Part I, vol. 2, *David Garrick, Charles Macklin and Margaret Woffington by Their Contemporaries*, ed. Gail Marshall, et al. (London: Pickering, 2008).

sometime in 1754, culling from his Commonplace Books, but the majority of the notes and outlines, as Paul Goring has described, were lost on a ship carrying his effects from London to Ireland.[15] However, my interest here is not in these attempts to draw the character of the man but rather to consider Macklin's contribution to the making of the novel and to the ways in which the novel's rivalry with the theatre's capacity to deliver popular entertainment was responded to in the theatre itself.

Macklin as actor in the novel

MACKLIN'S ONE APPEARANCE AS HIMSELF in a work of prose fiction so far identified is in Maria Edgeworth's *Harrington* (1817). Critical attention has largely focused on this novel as an act of thoughtful reparation for an unthinking anti-Semitism in Edgeworth's earlier work, which was brought to her attention in a letter from a young American Jewish woman, Rebecca Mordecai, in the summer of 1816.[16] Edgeworth immortalizes Rebecca in the character of Berenice Montenero, a lovely young Jewish heiress with whom the hero Harrington becomes smitten when he sees her embarrassment at the theatre. This is a conventional novel device, familiar from *Evelina*, in which the heroine wins a lover's attention by her awkwardness when she sees the visible parallel between her own situation and that of the onstage representation. Here, the parallel is drawn between Berenice and Jessica, in a performance of *The Merchant of Venice*, with Macklin playing Shylock. Harrington, early trained into an aversion to Jews by a corrupting maidservant, is as a young man learning to leave behind his prejudice and his attraction to Berenice, daughter of a wealthy Jewish financier, only furthers the process. And these proceedings are apparently accelerated by an earlier encounter with Macklin himself. It is of course noteworthy that in the end Harrington's 'conversion' is brought about by few actual Jewish characters. Berenice, it transpires, is in fact Christian (since her mother was Christian

---

15 Paul Goring, 'The Sinking of Charles Macklin's Scholarship', *Notes & Queries* 66.4 (2019), 577–81. See also Amanda Weldy Boyd, *Staging Memory and Materiality in Eighteenth-Century Biography* (London: Anthem Press, 2017), 45.
16 See Catherine Craft-Fairchild, 'The "Jewish Question" on Both Sides of the Atlantic: *Harrington* and the Correspondence between Maria Edgeworth and Rachel Mordecai Lazarus', *Eighteenth-Century Life* 38.3 (2014), 30–63; Michael Ragussis, *Figures of Conversion: 'The Jewish Question' and English National Identity* (Durham, NC: Duke University Press, 1995); Neville Hoad, 'Maria Edgeworth's *Harrington*: The Price of Sympathetic Representation', in Shelia A. Spector (ed.), *British Romanticism and the Jews: History, Culture, Literature* (New York: Palgrave Macmillan, 2002), 133–34.

and raised her in that faith) and Macklin was a Protestant convert from Irish Catholic stock. His performance of Jewishness was much celebrated for its authenticity, informed by diligent research into Jewish dress and manners and transforming the presentation of Shylock from that of a comic pantomime villain to a complex and conflicted man.

Harrington is introduced to Macklin as 'the real, original Jew of Venice' in the fifth chapter of the novel.[17] Edgeworth lifts virtually wholesale a passage from William Cooke's *Memoirs of Charles Macklin* (1804) to give us Macklin's 'own words' and acknowledges Cooke as the source in her footnote. Emily Anderson comments that Edgeworth is here making a claim for the novel as a mode with the capacity to integrate and interpolate the biographical and the autobiographical in ways not available to other forms of depicting persons and lives. As she puts it, 'Edgeworth integrates Macklin's "own words" effortlessly into her own fictional tale: fiction, because it is fiction, has the ability to encompass not only real people but also the personal narratives of real people without compromising its own fictional nature'.[18]

It is not perhaps surprising that Macklin could serve as the mediating figure not only between the claims to realism of both fiction and the stage but also between English national identity and the 'others' that were often cast as threats to its integrity. His very public and performed Irishness made him a representative of his kind and kin, a role not taken on by the many Irish immigrants who lived and worked in the metropolis both in the theatrical and the publishing industries. However, when we consider *Harrington* in the context of the kind of role an actor can take in a novel we might also note that Macklin's presence also serves as a strange impediment, indeed a kind of digression, which misdirects the young hero's process of reformation. Harrington and his friend Mowbray (later revealed to be a deep-dyed villain conniving to destroy Harrington's growing sympathy for Jews) are seeking the home of a Spanish Jew recommended to Harrington but whose address he has lost: 'I was puzzled among half a dozen different streets and numbers'.[19] 'At last, tired and disappointed', Mowbray offers to console him for the loss of the chance to meet the Spanish Jew (Montenero, later revealed to be Berenice's father) by introducing him 'to the most celebrated Jew that ever appeared in England. Then turning into a street near

---

17 Maria Edgeworth, *Harrington*, in Marilyn Butler, Mitzi Myers, and W.J. McCormack (eds), *The Novels and Selected Works of Maria Edgeworth*, 12 vols. (London: Pickering & Chatto, 1999), III.199.
18 Emily Hodgson Anderson, 'Autobiographical Interpolations in Maria Edgeworth's *Harrington*', *ELH* 76.1 (2009), 9.
19 Edgeworth, *Harrington Novels and Selected Works*, III.198.

one of the play-houses, he knocked at the door of a house, where Macklin the actor lodged'.[20] In seeking a Jew, Harrington finds (or is led) to meet an actor who played the Jew. Macklin is carefully characterized: the famous '*cordage* of his face' is remarked upon as it was remarked upon by the rival actor James Quin and recorded by Cooke.[21] But nonetheless, his appearance in the fiction is ornamental rather than instrumental, a kind of realist decoy or cover to an overt ideological project recognizably ill-suited to the project of the novel as a form. Actors, it seems, do not make good characters in fiction; nor do they help in fiction to restore or alter the dominant modes of representing national or type 'character'.

In this respect, do fictionalized versions of theatrical actors contrast negatively with fictional treatments of real historical 'actors'? See, for example, the treatment of Charles Edward Stuart ('Bonnie Prince Charlie') in Walter Scott's hugely successful *Waverley; or, 'Tis Sixty Years Since* (1814),[22] a novel Scott wrote in imitation of Maria Edgeworth's pioneering invention of the national tale. There are similarities between this work and Edgeworth's *Harrington*. In both, an impressionable young man learns values of toleration and openness through his encounters with an ethnic group apparently threatening to his native loyalties of English Protestantism (Scottish Jacobites in *Waverley*, emigrant Jews in *Harrington*). In both, the hero's violent attraction to a young woman of that ethnic group (Berenice Montenero, Flora Mac-Ivor) contributes to his interest in the political fate of her people, an interest also prompted through a significant encounter with a real historical figure (Macklin and Charles Edward Stuart). In both, the hero is eventually married to a woman of the same ethnic group as his own (Berenice is revealed to be adopted by her Jewish father, Waverley shifts his affections to the border heiress, Rose Bradwardine).

Edward Waverley is brought into the presence chamber of a 'young man, wearing his own fair hair, distinguished by the dignity of his mien and the notable expression of his well-formed and regular features':[23]

> Unaccustomed to the address and manners of a polished court, in which Charles was eminently skilful, his words and his kindness penetrated the

---

20 Edgeworth, *Harrington*, *Novels and Selected Works*, III.198.
21 Cooke reports that the actor James Quin answered in response to the observation that Macklin would make a good actor because of the 'strong lines' in his face that 'I see nothing in the fellow's face, but a d——n'd deal of *cordage*' (Cooke, 19). Cordage is the rope used in rigging a ship.
22 Walter Scott, *Waverley; or, 'Tis Sixty Years Since*, ed. Claire Lamont (Oxford: Clarendon Press, 1981), 192–96.
23 Scott, *Waverley*, 192.

heart of our hero, and easily outweighed all prudential motives. To be thus personally solicited for assistance by a prince, whose form and manners, as well as the spirit which he displayed in this singular enterprise, answered his ideas of a hero of romance; to be courted by him in the ancient halls of his paternal palace, recovered by the sword which he was already bending towards other conquests, gave Edward, in his own eyes, the dignity and importance which he had ceased to consider as his attributes. Rejected, slandered, and threatened upon the one side, he was irresistibly attracted to the cause which the prejudices of education, and the political principles of his family, had already recommended as the most just. These thoughts rushed through his mind like a torrent, sweeping before them every consideration of an opposite tendency,—the time, besides, admitted of no deliberation,—and Waverley, kneeling to Charles Edward, devoted his heart and sword to the vindication of his rights![24]

The distinction between the effectiveness of Charles Edward Stuart's integration into *Waverley* and Macklin's awkward interpolation into *Harrington* may, however, lie more in the narrative style than the nature of the person fictionalized. Scott's free indirect discourse (a third-person narration in which the voices of character and narrator are purposefully fused) provides the reader with an ironic distance on the experience of the lead protagonist. We are aware, where Edward Waverley is not, that the encounter has been staged by the cunning Mac-Ivor chieftain to exploit the young hero's sense of inadequacy and alienation and win him to the Jacobite cause through the magnetic appeal of the man at its centre.

Harrington's first-person narration fails to communicate the same irony. In fact, his guide, Lord Mowbray, is himself distracting and displacing Harrington from the latter's quest to meet the Spanish Jew Montenero, by presenting him with an actor who plays a Jew. But neither Harrington nor the novel reader is yet aware of Mowbray's villainy. The visit to Macklin takes the shape of a curiosity of literary tourism hard to interpret as integral to the plot and sentiments of the novel as a whole.

Mowbray introduces Macklin as 'the most celebrated Jew in all England, in all Christendom, in the whole civilized world', and Harrington reports:

> No one, better than Mowbray, knew the tone of enthusiastic, theatric admiration, in which the heroes of the stage like, or are supposed to like, to be addressed.
> Macklin, who was not easy to please, was pleased.
> The *lines*, or as Quin insisted upon their being called, the *cordage* of his face relaxed. He raised, turned, and settled his wig, in sign of satisfaction; then with a complacent smile gave me a little nod, and suffered Lord Mowbray to

---

24 Scott, *Waverley*, 196.

draw him out by degrees into a repetition of the history of his first attempt to play the character of Shylock.[25]

Harrington diverts us, his readers, with a meticulous observation of the gestural style of the actor. A glimmer of self-knowledge about the narrator's own character is provided as Harrington describes his response to Macklin's account (taken from Cooke's *Memoir*):

> The emphasis and enthusiasm with which Macklin spoke pleased me— enthusiastic people are always well pleased with enthusiasm. My curiosity too was strongly excited to see him play Shylock. I returned home full of the Jew of Venice; but, nevertheless, not forgetting my Spanish Jew.[26]

Like Waverley, Harrington's character responds to that of the figure with whom his encounter has been carefully engineered. Harrington mirrors Macklin's enthusiasm. It is that enthusiasm on the part of both young heroes that makes them capable of the quick sympathies required of feeling protagonists in the novel but also makes them vulnerable to manipulation by stage performances learned through careful rehearsal. In both encounters, however, it is not the 'actor' (Charles Edward Stuart and Macklin) who is pulling the stage levers but the man (Mac-Ivor and Mowbray) who effects their introduction to the hero of the work. However, as we have seen, the historical actor Charles Edward Stuart is more fluidly integrated into the immersive novel world than the stage actor Charles Macklin.

Fictionalized versions of actors in 'bit parts' or set-piece encounters such as Macklin's in *Harrington* lead readers away from the new naturalism sought by the novel. The presence of the theatrical actor disrupts the immersive experience in a (prose) fictional world in a way that the presence of a historical actor appears not to, perhaps because novelistic narration can treat the historical person as one among a number of other equally plausible renderings of historical persons. The actor, by contrast, appears to have been 'interpolated' into that fictional world in ways that disorient an audience and undermine the fiction of real presence maintained in the made-up world of the novel. Actors thrive rather better when we find their stories and characteristics transposed into fictional characters in novels, especially when they take lead or principal roles. This we will see when we consider versions of Macklin rendered in the guise of fictional *characters* in contemporary novels.

---

25 Edgeworth, *Harrington, Novels and Selected Works*, III.199.
26 Edgeworth, *Harrington, Novels and Selected Works*, III.200.

Macklin as character in the novel

EDWARD KIMBER—traveller, travel-writer, and editor of the *London Magazine* from 1755—published in 1756 a two-volume fake biography with the title *The Juvenile adventures of David Ranger, Esq.*[27] This was the third of those works Simon Dickie terms 'ramble novels' (episodic, comic novels) in which Kimber was to build such reputation as he did as a novelist.[28] In these works a young man gets into comic scrapes in his travels and this particular rendering had the added attraction of offering readers a peek into the life of David Garrick or the backstory of one of his famous roles, the rake Ranger, in Benjamin Hoadley's *The Suspicious Husband* (1747), discussed below. In the event, they got neither, although the early and later parts of the narrative do suggest some relation to the known facts of Garrick's life despite giving him an Irish origin and extended kinship. David Ranger is small, energetic, especially celebrated in tragedy like his namesake. However, the humble Irish background of the hero also suggests some association with Garrick's onetime friend and mentor. Macklin is a shadowy potential alternative source for David Ranger's fictional 'back story'. But he is also given a character in his own right in the novel, in the shape of the loyal, passionate actor, Captain MacKenzie.

Kimber's Ranger, like other libidinous young heroes with essentially good hearts in the picaresque tradition, is largely engaged in romantic scrapes. Richard Ranger, a Cork merchant, lives in Playhouse Street and his wife Penelope raises David, the youngest of five children, with a passion for tragedy. As Garrick did, David forms a close friendship with an older fellow actor: he meets the strolling player, Captain MacKenzie, in a tavern and it is Mackenzie's acting company David joins for his first professional stage appearances. In the second volume of the *Juvenile Adventures*, David saves MacKenzie from attempted suicide and restores him to mental equilibrium. In their first joint appearances, David Ranger and Captain Mackenzie are the star players who eclipse all other performers; they occupy the stage and the full attention of their audience:

> the two gentlemen were themselves the support of the company, for the others, both men and women, were merely spouters, and had not good sense or discernment sufficient to enter into the characters they assum'd: They serv'd

---

27 Edward Kimber, *The Juvenile adventures of David Ranger, Esq; from an original manuscript found in the collections of a late noble Lord. In two volumes*, 2nd edn (London, 1757).
28 See Simon Dickie, 'Tobias Smollett and the Ramble Novel', in Garside and O'Brien, *The Oxford History of the Novel in English*, II.92–108.

indeed for some good ends, they supply'd the absolutely necessary parts, and were a sort of foils to set off more clearly the beautiful action and manner of their principals.[29]

Macklin appeared with Garrick on many occasions at Drury Lane, but he did also appear with him when Garrick played Ranger; Macklin, despite the differences between the two, took the part of the jealous husband Strictland for the first performance of *The Suspicious Husband* of 5 December 1747. And the fluctuating fortunes of Macklin's friendship with Garrick provided a rich seam for translation into this fiction, one among many, about contemporary theatrical life and personalities. Here, as elsewhere, however, the vividness of Macklin's character is consistently imagined as better invoked in his theatrical presence than in descriptions of it in published prose.

Macklin on novel character in the theatre

MACKLIN MAKES FEW ALLUSIONS to novels in his writing for the theatre. In making a case for the importance of the novel in his stage writing, I might be seen to be stretching my own cordage. By comparison with Fielding, Garrick, Goldsmith, or Sheridan, Macklin appears to be almost entirely a creature made in and for the stage: playing key parts in his own works. However, the threat of novelistic character overtaking the precarious attraction of actorly stage performance can be traced in his work.

The impression that Macklin cared little for the novel as a form is borne out by the evidence of the small number of prose fiction works in the auction catalogue of the over 3,000 books of his library that were sold in 1797 to support his widow.[30] Paul Goring and Rebecca Vollan, in their tagging of the different kinds of work in his library, identify only seventy-five works of prose fiction: small by comparison with other literary collections such as drama (247 works) and poetry (138 works). The majority of volumes in the prose fiction list are French (28), and they indicate a preference for the romance over the novel. Seventeenth-century English romances in the collection include Philip Sidney's *Arcadia* and Barclay's *Argenis* as well as Calprenède's *Pharamond*. Other European works of world literature included (and unsurprisingly so given their influence in plays of the period) are eighteenth-century English translations of the works of Cervantes, Boccaccio's *Decameron*, Le

---

29 Kimber, *David Ranger*, I.155.
30 See the digital catalogue prepared by Goring and Vollan, which is included as one of *Librarything*'s 'Legacy Libraries': www.librarything.com/profile/CharlesMacklin (accessed 10 August 2021).

Sage's *Gil Blas* and *The Devil on Two Sticks*, a 1763 edition of the *Arabian Nights Entertainments*, and Fénelon's *Telemachus* (Macklin's version was the translation by John Hawkesworth). Popular late seventeenth- and early eighteenth-century fictions such as a 1718 seven-volume edition of Paulo Marana's *The Turkish Spy*, several different collections from the fabulist Jean de La Fontaine, Poisson de Gomez's *Les Cent Nouvelles Nouvelles*, and a selection of works by Daniel Defoe (*A Collection of the Writings of the Author of the True-born Englishman* of 1703) are also found.

From among his contemporaries, there is a decided preference for modern works of sensibility and sensation: Jean-Jacques Rousseau's *Julie ou la Nouvelle Héloïse* (1761), Horace Walpole's *The Castle of Otranto* in an edition of 1782, Henry Mackenzie's *Man of Feeling*, and an eight-volume set of Laurence Sterne's complete works (1790) alongside the popular selection *The Beauties of Sterne* (1785). Perhaps worth noting is the presence of fictional works by female contemporaries: Sarah Fielding's *Familiar Letters Between the Principal Characters in David Simple*, Clara Reeve's *Old English Baron*, and the relatively obscure *Fitzroy; Or, Impulse of the Moment* by Maria Hunter. It is perhaps surprising that there are no copies of the works in the library list that we now see as most significant in elevating the novel as an ethical as well as popular medium—books by Henry Fielding and Samuel Richardson—especially the former, with whom Macklin was well acquainted as a fellow playwright and manager of repertory companies.

Paul Goring concludes that Macklin was a 'serious' reader from the evidence of the library. He reminds us that a library does not capture everything that a person reads nor can it indicate favourite books from among the list; indeed, it may not only represent the taste of the owner but also that of family and kin (see 'Macklin's Books' in this volume). However, we can see evidence in his few references to novels in his plays of Macklin's alertness to the contemporary pulse of enthusiasm for the novel. In particular, Macklin was an accomplished comedian as playwright and performer: and the novel provides material for his comic talents in his dramatic writing.

Macklin composed and delivered a prologue for the first play by Henry Fielding to be staged after the passing of the Licensing Act: the comedy *The Wedding-Day* (1743).[31] Macklin summons Fielding the author's absent spirit in the conventional apology for and plea for critical attention. As we have seen him do elsewhere, Macklin substitutes for Garrick. The latter, he reports, is so overwhelmed by the copiousness of his part as the rakish hero Millamour

---

31 *The Wedding-Day*, in Bertrand A. Goldgar and Hugh Amory (eds), *Miscellanies by Henry Fielding, Esq.*, *The Wesleyan Edition of the Works of Henry Fielding*, vol. 2 (Oxford: Oxford University Press/Wesleyan University Press, 1993).

that he cannot come on stage to deliver his own prologue. Macklin took the relatively small part of Mr Stedfast, the too-old prospective husband of Millamour's love-interest Charlotte (the part played by Peg Woffington). The author, Macklin tells us, first instructed him not to bother with a prologue but changed his mind when Macklin warned the audience would damn the play without it. The author then asks Macklin to deliver the prologue himself because he has a *'good long, dismal, Mercy-begging Face'*.[32] Rather than taking on this role of surrogate, Macklin points out the author in the audience and indeed invites comparison between his dismal face and the inappropriate merriment of that of the author in the face of a likely critical panning for a lacklustre script. Fielding has been lifting his 'spirits' with 'alcohol':

> *'Sir, your humble Servant: You're very merry'. 'Yes,' says he; 'I've been drinking*
> *To raise my Spirits; for, by Jupiter! I found 'em sinking.'*
> *So away he went to see the Play; O! there he sits:*
> *Smoke him, smoke the Author, you laughing Crits.*[33]

In a further attempt to divert a potential disaster, Macklin gestures to another absent (and entirely fictional) character to underwrite the play's value. This is a character he views as more likely to gain applause from the audience: the virtuous, generous cleric, Parson Adams, in Henry Fielding's novel *Joseph Andrews* (1741).[34] Macklin speaks directly to the author (whose presence he has smoked in the audience) inviting a comparison of Fielding's face and his own:

> *What think you now? Whose Face looks worst, yours or mine?*
> *Ah! thou foolish Follower of the ragged Nine,*
> *You'd better stuck to honest Abram Adams, by half:*
> *He, in spight of Critics, can make your Readers laugh.*[35]

Fielding's powers as an author and Macklin's as an actor are here represented as exhausted and under threat. Fielding can no longer ask actors to stand in his place and defend him from criticism, but his experiments in novelistic character—especially the foolish, learned, virtuous Adams—may protect him.

As in this prologue to *Wedding-Day*, Macklin's one-act afterpiece in defence of Benjamin Hoadley's *The Suspicious Husband* (1747) also deploys

---

32 Fielding, *The Wedding-Day*, *Miscellanies*, II.24.
33 Charles Macklin, 'Prologue', in Fielding, *The Wedding-Day*, *Miscellanies*, II.155.
34 *Joseph Andrews*, ed. Martin C. Battestin, *The Wesleyan Edition of the Works of Henry Fielding* (Oxford: Oxford University Press/Wesleyan University Press, 1966).
35 Fielding, *The Wedding-Day*, *Miscellanies*, II.156.

forms of virtue identified with novel characters to revive a flagging post-licensed stage. In this clever metatheatrical work entitled *The New Play Criticiz'd or the Plague of Envy*, the envious playwright Canker enlists two critics, Plagiary and Grubstreet, to help him undermine Hoadley's first night. All three have works that are languishing: a comedy from Canker, a masque from Grubstreet, and a tragedy from Plagiary. Canker distributes the labour of maligning *The Suspicious Husband* saying the three must work together through 'Journals, Epigrams and Pamphlets' to critique the play: 'you [Grubstreet] must Attack the Characters,—you the Sentiments and Dialogue [Plagiary], while I expose the Moral and the Fable'.[36]

Canker's jealousy is as corrosive as that of the husband in Hoadley's play but is easily countered by the plotting of the girl he is courting, Harriet, and her worthy suitor, Heartly. Harriet and Heartly feed the admiration of the circle of Lady Critic for *The Suspicious Husband*, recruiting two rival critics who are foolish followers of fashion, Nibble and Trifle. Harriet insists that she will not accept Canker's suit unless he reverse his temper and take her as his 'Minerva' with whom he will consult before scribbling applause or blame. To prove his reform she tells him to attend the comedy the next night and cry and laugh 'as soon as you see M[r]. Strictland acknowledge his Error, and sue to be reconcil'd to his Wife, if you have one humane particle in your Composition I insist upon your sympathising with his conscious Heart by dropping a Manly Tear along with him'.[37] Canker is not put to the test since his envious criticism results in an argument with Lady Critic and both repudiate the potential match with either of her nieces.

Macklin concludes his play with a metatheatrical twist. Heartly proposes that the last hour's dialogue should be turned into 'an agreeable Polite Piece' of theatre, itself composed by Lady Critic and Heartly. The former expresses her concern that Canker's 'Character is so very high the Audience will never allow it to be natural', to which Heartly responds, 'That part of the Audience who would know the Copy by themselves might condemn it, thro' Policy as being exaggerated, but the Candid and Judicious, who could not be hurt by it, and who know the Nature of Envy would approve it'.[38] Lady Critic and her party leave the stage to compose the play, agreeing on the title, '*The New Play Criticiz'd*'. They also leave Canker behind to compose a bad-tempered

---

36 Charles Macklin, *The New Play Criticiz'd; or, The Plague of Envy* (*The Suspicious Husband Criticized; or The Plague of Envy*), John Larpent Collection, Huntington Library, LA 64. Also available from Adam Matthew Digital, *Eighteenth Century Drama* database.
37 Macklin, *The New Play Criticiz'd*, 8.
38 Macklin, *The New Play Criticiz'd*, f. 42.

epilogue since his envy precludes him from contributing to a work intent on praising *The Suspicious Husband*.

The manuscript submitted to the censor in the Larpent collection at the Huntington Library concludes with a rough draft of an Epilogue in a different hand,[39] in which a shabbily dressed poet complains that authors for a theatre are subject to the whims of envious brother critics and thoughtless fashion. Here, then, Macklin defends a 'brother' author from the attack of envious fellow writers posing as critics when they review in print journalism or work up the crowd to hiss at a performance. He contrasts the envious critic with those who are frivolous followers of fashion and easy prey to flattery (Lady Critick's circle). Heartly and Harriet speak for and with an audience they compliment by suggesting that they are free of such vices, 'candid', and thus able to judge fairly. And both bear the hallmarks of the 'new' and novelistic sentimental hero and heroine, their sympathetic nature and respectful mutual love imported from the novel to promote 'new' forms of stage drama.

Macklin's fairly unsuccessful two-act satire, *The Covent Garden Theatre; or, Pasquin Turn'd Drawcansir*,[40] which enjoyed only one performance, on 8 April 1752, provides us with a more overt reference to the novel. Macklin appeared as Pasquin. Pasquin is master of ceremonies whose assistant Marforio brings on a series of city fools and villains to be publicly shamed before the (actual) audience.[41] Popular entertainments are satirized—along the lines of Fielding's *Authors of the Town*, including pantomimes, harlequins, and masquerades. And, of course, novels.

Typically, when the novel-reader appears on stage as a character, he or she is female, foolish, frivolous, and libidinous. Miss Diana Single-Life is so described as 'a maiden Lady of Youth , Beauty, Chastity, & Erudition: who has read more Romances, Novels, Poems & Plays, than there are Acts of Parliament in the English Language'.[42] Diana Single-Life is exposed in Act 2 as a fraud by Lady Lucy Loveit:

---

39 Macklin, *The New Play Criticiz'd*, f. 43.

40 Charles Macklin, *The Covent Garden Theatre; or, Pasquin Turn'd Drawcansir* (1752), Augustan Reprint Society, no. 116, ed. Jean B. Kern (Los Angeles: William Andrew Clark Memorial Library, University of California, 1965).

41 Fielding's *Covent-Garden Journal* advertised the play on 14, 18, 21, and 28 March 1752. Esther M. Raushenbush, in 'Charles Macklin's Lost Play about Henry Fielding', *Modern Language Notes* 51.8 (1936), 505–14, has argued that Macklin was not attacking Fielding but trading on the popularity of Fielding's 'Enquiry into the Causes of the Late Increase of Robberts' (January 1751). Helen Burke builds on this argument in this volume.

42 Macklin, *Covent Garden Theatre*, 30.

her Head, like the Study of Don Quixot, Stuffed with the exploded—Romances—of the two last Centuries—her Style the quaint Quintessence of Romantic Fustian, and her Manners those of a Princess in an Inchanted Castle. [...] The vain Creature endeavours to pass upon the World for five and twenty—A Maid & Strictly Virtuous—but is fifty at least—grey as a Badger—has had three Children—one by her Coachman—One by a Horse Granadier [sic]—and one by her present Friend—the tall Straping [sic] Irishman, whom they call the Captain. ha, ha, ha.[43]

As in *The New Play Criticiz'd*, Macklin concludes his play with a metatheatrical move which implicates his own character in the very satire in which he ostensibly deals. If Canker is both an object of satire *and* a version of Macklin himself (consumed with jealousy of those friends who surpassed his talent and enjoyed more success than he did, especially Garrick), so too is Pasquin a version of Macklin as satirist, inclined to prefer the sound of his own voice to the sound plotting that will retain an audience's attention. Marforio informs Pasquin at the end of the play that he has no more offenders to bring forth except 'one Charles Macklin, Comedian, of the Theatre Royal in Covent Garden' who 'hath written a strange hotch-potch Farce, and puff'd it upon the Town as written after the manner of Aristophanes and the Pasquinades of the Italian Theatre'.[44] Pasquin says they will wait to bring him in person to the next court day. And Hydra, 'the North Star of the Pit', warns that 'the Critics will Condemn your Piece for want of a Plot'.[45]

And this may be the lasting mark of Macklin's character—both in and of the novel: that his character and his portrayal of stage character tended to engross the business of plot. In many ways, Macklin stands as the sign of a resistance to the novel, a refusal of the stage to adapt itself to the new industry (or at least the new mediations) of prose fiction gaining traction through the novel. The evidence discussed in this article points to Charles Macklin's unusually close identification in his own and the public mind with the world of theatre by comparison with other figures who moved, or were moved, more flexibly between the industries of theatre and novel production (such as Henry Fielding, David Garrick, and Elizabeth Inchbald). He typifies the problem of the actor in and beyond the novel—or at least the way the novel often casts character. The actor's real presence comes to be perceived as a hindrance not only to the advancement of plot but also to the identification with character. He remains stubbornly resistant to the kind of interior projections and imaginative immersions increasingly associated with the world(s) of fiction:

---

43 Macklin, *Covent Garden Theatre*, 46.
44 Macklin, *Covent Garden Theatre*, 62–63.
45 Macklin, *Covent Garden Theatre*, 64.

a character or action, of man deeply invested in conserving his own property and embodied presence in a world increasingly prone to the circulation of character through textual presence. It is a testament to that resistance, and a monitory reminder of the danger of over-investing the novel with agency in the literary economies of the eighteenth century, that he sustained a career of this type so long and with such indomitable charisma.

Theatre

6

Macklin as Theatre Manager

Matthew Kinservik

The British Library contains a remarkable annotated transcription of a deposition given by Charles Macklin, relating to a lawsuit between George Colman the Elder and Thomas Harris and James Rutherford. Colman, Harris, and Rutherford were uneasy partners in the management of the Covent Garden theatre in the decade after John Rich's death in 1761. Tensions between the partners broke into open conflict in September 1767, when Colman took the unprecedented action of dismissing long-serving performers and hiring in their places lesser-known (and hence cheaper) performers. Colman further raised eyebrows by signing these new performers to multi-year contracts. And not just performers—he also hired stage crew and other theatrical personnel to long-term contracts. These were innovations that Colman implemented without consulting his partners. When Harris and Rutherford questioned him, Colman called the actors and other theatrical personnel to a meeting on 1 November 1767 at the Bedford Arms Tavern in the Piazza in Covent Garden. He complained that his partners were meddling unduly in his business practices contrary to the articles they agreed to earlier that same year and asked for the support of the company in his dispute.

Macklin was among the group that evening and he, along with others, agreed to come to the theatre the following morning for a meeting between Colman, Harris, and Rutherford. But when they met the next day, Harris and Rutherford read aloud the articles of agreement the partners had signed the previous spring. One of those articles stipulated that Colman was to oversee the day-to-day management of Covent Garden, but Harris and Rutherford had a veto over his actions. In Macklin's deposition, he describes the scene this way. After having read from the agreement:

> every P[er]son. remained silent some little time & then Harris & Rutherford appealed to the Dept. [i.e., Macklin] & desired him in par[ticu]lar as one who had known the Stage & the management of it many Years to Speak his thoughts on the matters then Agitated w[h]ich Dept. eather [sic] Declined doing by saying that the matter in dispute was a point of Law & not of managem[en]t. & that their (mean[in]g. all the Proprietors) own Good sense & good Humour wo[ul]d. Decide it or the Lord Chancellor must.[1]

But after having declined to give his opinion on the matter, Macklin was pressed to concede that Harris and Rutherford were in the right. Macklin claimed to be a stranger to them before this meeting, but says that he was,

> at that time intimate with Mr. Colman whom Dept. then Directly advised not to Embarrass & Plague himself about a contention for the Sole Power for that according to Depts. opinion of com[m]on Language & of the com[m]on justice that appeared to Govern the sd. Art[ic]le. relating to their managem[en]t. the Point was clearly against him the sd. Mr. Colman & Dept. saith that the sd. Colman then did allow that Harris & Rutherford was Intitled to Exert a negative by the sd. Art[ic]le. & did promise that for the future he wo[ul]d. observe their negative.[2]

This must have been an acutely embarrassing outcome for Colman. He was undermined in a highly public fashion in front of the entire company and by Macklin, whom he considered to be an ally.

But what is most remarkable about this episode is that although Macklin was not part of the management, he was called upon to settle the dispute, 'as one who had known the Stage & the management of it many Years'. Harris and Rutherford had no theatrical background and Colman, an established playwright, was new to management. So who better than Macklin to mediate the case? As it turned out, the dispute did not end there and so Macklin later swore his very long, very detailed deposition as part of a Chancery suit between the partners. In it, Macklin speaks at length about standard management practice, the relative quality of the individual performers hired and fired by Colman, and the puzzling innovation of offering long-term contracts to lesser performers and other theatrical personnel. He speaks in the deposition, as he did in that November 1767 meeting of the company, with the authority of 'one who had known the Stage & the management of it many Years'.

---

1 British Library, Add. MS 33218, f. 69.
2 British Library, Add. MS 33218, f. 69.

By the time of these events, Macklin had been performing on the London stage and elsewhere for four decades. His long theatrical career included work as a performer, playwright, acting instructor, lecturer, and manager. The lion's share of scholarship has focused, naturally, on his achievements as an actor and playwright. But more attention is owed to his labours as a theatrical manager. He is never listed among the more famous actor–managers of the long eighteenth century. Betterton, Cibber, Garrick, and Foote are the models we have in mind when we think of an actor–manager. They personally held royal patents or licences for London theatres that they oversaw for extended periods of time. Macklin's case is different because his managerial work was sporadic and included work done in London, Dublin, and provincial towns. As a consequence, this element of his career has been overlooked. That is unfortunate because his managerial work occurred at moments of instability and change on the London and Dublin stages and because his role as a manager offered him important opportunities as an actor and playwright (and vice versa).

The relationship between Macklin's managerial labours and his achievements as an actor–playwright has never been explored, and this exploration is long overdue. For example, he is known to have been the operational stage manager for Charles Fleetwood at Drury Lane in the early 1740s. These were the years when the Shakespeare Ladies Club effectively advocated for more Shakespearean performances on the London stage. Not coincidentally, that included the restoration of Shakespeare's *The Merchant of Venice* in 1741 with Macklin in the role of Shylock. After a falling-out with Fleetwood, Macklin set up shop in the Little Haymarket, leading an acting school. He then established the British Inquisition, a dining and lecture hall that he directed. This was followed by a brief period as a manager at the Crow Street Theatre in Dublin, partnering with Spranger Barry and others. Macklin is most often thought of as an actor–playwright, but we need to add 'manager' in order to fully appreciate his long and varied career.

Deputy manager at Drury Lane

MACKLIN'S FIRST MANAGERIAL EXPERIENCE came in the 1734–35 season. Charles Fleetwood had assumed management at Drury Lane, but, with no experience in the business, he was heavily dependent on Theophilus Cibber, who served as his lieutenant for a season until Fleetwood dismissed him in favour of Macklin. Evidence of exactly what it meant to be 'Fleetwood's lieutenant', as William W. Appleton calls Macklin, is hard to come by. Appleton claims that by 1735 Macklin's managerial position 'was an entrenched one. Provincial schooling in all aspects of the theatre had made him invaluable to the irresponsible manager'. Appleton later says that by 1738 Macklin's managerial 'responsibilities increased'.[3] These claims may be true, but the evidentiary basis of them is a combination of Macklin's fragmentary Commonplace Book in the Folger Shakespeare Library and Macklin's earliest biographers. And those biographers, of course, rarely cite any source material. This is frustrating because it means that what we mostly have are vague assertions about Macklin's role but none of the operational detail that would tell us what his duties actually were. The source material cited by modern scholarship has had to rely on anecdotes and theatrical lore committed to paper soon after Macklin's death.[4] That doesn't mean that these facts are wrong. But we have to admit that they lack specificity and are unsubstantiated.

The lack of evidence regarding Macklin's managerial duties at Drury Lane is endemic to the historiography of theatrical management itself. Joseph Donohue long ago lamented the 'ambiguity of the manager's position', noting that 'the records of his endeavors are sometimes nonexistent or else so sketchy as to be inadequate to the task of providing materials with which to build a coherent historical account'.[5] This problem is compounded when the subject in question is also an actor and playwright, roles that lend themselves more readily to the literary, text-based nature of traditional theatre history. As Donohue observes, 'We have no term, unfortunately, to comprehend the functions of *choregus*, master, manager, and producer. Where no word exists, understanding remains fragmented'.[6] Tiffany Stern's study of theatrical rehearsals in the period does an excellent job of identifying the myriad managerial tasks associated with producing a play.[7] She points out that these tasks were carried out by a range of people, including prompters, playwrights, '"untheatrical" managers' like Fleetwood, and 'actor–managers' like Colley Cibber. To describe Macklin's role under Fleetwood, Sterne uses the term 'stage manager'.[8] This seems appropriate because Macklin had no financial interest in the patent, but he assisted the 'untheatrical' Fleetwood by tending to things like rehearsals, training other actors, and repertory

---

3 *Appleton*, 29, 37.

4 Amanda Weldy Boyd, *Staging Memory and Materiality in Eighteenth-Century Theatrical Biography* (London: Anthem Press, 2018). Chapter 2 is on Macklin.

5 Joseph W. Donohue, Jr. (ed.), *The Theatrical Manager in England and America: Player of a Perilous Game* (Princeton, NJ: Princeton University Press, 1971), 5.

6 Donohue, *Theatrical Manager*, 4.

7 Tiffany Stern, *Rehearsal from Shakespeare to Sheridan* (Oxford: Clarendon Press, 2000), esp. chaps 5 and 6.

8 Stern, *Rehearsal from Shakespeare to Sheridan*, 198.

selection. Macklin was not the proprietor, but his duties were consequential and he assumed a large part of what David Taylor calls 'the complex authority of the manager'.[9]

Like Donohue before him, Taylor laments that theatre historiography has largely neglected the role of the manager. And this neglect is only compounded when the subject in question is, like Macklin, not the proprietor, but the lieutenant or stage manager. But some evidence exists of Macklin's duties and the nature of his subordinate managerial role under Fleetwood. Actress and playwright Charlotte Charke ridicules Macklin in the character of Bloodbolt and Fleetwood as Brainless in her 1735 farce, *The Art of Management*. In the preface, she refers to Macklin and Fleetwood as '*the Managers of* Drury Lane', giving them coequal status. She also doles out equal condemnation. Contrasting the current management with the stewardship of her father, Colley Cibber, and the other members of the Triumvirate, she writes, '*I don't know that there are any Persons there who can properly claim that Title* [i.e., manager], *for since the two Gentlemen (who governed six Years ago) have been dead, and the other quitted it, I don't know any one Circumstance that has look'd like Order or Decorum during that Time*'.[10] Without naming names, Charke refers to Macklin as a 'Bully' and blames him for her peremptory dismissal from the Drury Lane company.

The Art of Management is, in short, a very personal attack on Macklin. Charke portrays him as a Philistine who cashiers long-serving players and promotes low entertainment over spoken-word drama: 'I'll engage to furnish the House with a much better Company, and at a cheaper Rate, ay, and have Business carried on as it shou'd be;—I'll make a Bear Play Pierrot, or a Monkey, Harlequin, that shall out-do any we have now upon the Stage!' (16). This is, in one sense, conventional anti-managerial satire, representing Macklin as what Taylor calls, the 'manager-as-despot' (70). But Charke becomes more pointed and personal when she has Bloodbolt suggest that he will replace veteran performers with his Cook-Maid and Ostler, vowing, 'Egad! I'll soon teach 'em to come up to any Thing we have here' (16). This is an early reference to Macklin's efforts as an acting coach, a feature of his managerial duties that became more prominent as his career progressed.

For the most part, the farce offers a fairly generic and exaggerated picture of Macklin as an incompetent and despotic stage manager. Indeed,

---

9 David Francis Taylor, 'Theatre Managers and the Managing of Theatre History', in Julia Swindells and David Francis Taylor (eds), *The Oxford Handbook of the Georgian Theatre, 1737–1832* (Oxford: Oxford University Press, 2014), 70.
10 Charlotte Charke, *The Art of Management; Or, Tragedy Expell'd* (London, 1735), preface.

Brainless/Fleetwood figures only slightly into the play. Most of Charke's fire is directed at Bloodbolt/Macklin. In the end, Brainless is confronted by creditors and must forfeit his patent. The new proprietor, Headpiece, restores all the veteran personnel and fires Bloodbolt, musing, 'What a Head has he to think it worth his while to employ so much of his Time in what he absolutely knows nothing of? I think, tho', 'tis pretty plain that he had no legal Right to be concerned; if he had, I shou'd not so easily have got rid of him' (41). This last point was to prove prophetic, neatly describing the dilemma Macklin faced when he and Fleetwood came to be at odds during the actors' rebellion of 1743. Having no legal or financial claim to his managerial role, Macklin served at the pleasure of Fleetwood. Charke satirically exaggerates Macklin's conduct as a 'bullying Deputy' (45), making her play an unreliable source of information about his actual managerial duties, but she shrewdly characterized the precarious nature of his role and authority.

Acknowledging the problems and limits of our evidence about Macklin's managerial responsibilities under Fleetwood is important, but it is also important to note that two key claims can be corroborated by other evidence. These are that Macklin made himself indispensable to Fleetwood and that he used his position as a manager to boost his career as an actor. Reviewing different aspects of theatrical management in the period, Judith Milhous describes how managers without theatrical experience relied upon actor–managers like Macklin.[11] She calls Macklin, 'a forceful manager' who 'more or less restored order with the aid of an experienced staff. *Someone* had to keep a tight grip on things. If the owner did not do so, then he needed a strong manager who could and would' (26). Francis Congreve, Macklin's first biographer, says that Macklin was Fleetwood's 'favourite advisor and bosom friend'.[12] Another early biographer, William Cooke, calls Macklin a *'Theatrical Drill Serjeant'*, who relished his authority to oversee rehearsals and influence the repertory.[13] The key example, of course, is the Drury Lane production of *The Merchant of Venice* in 1741 that featured a return to Shakespeare's text and Macklin's revolutionary interpretation of Shylock. It is fair to say that had Macklin not been Fleetwood's 'favourite advisor and bosom friend', he probably would not have had the opportunity to produce *The Merchant of Venice* and perform the role that made him famous.

---

11 Judith Milhous, 'Company Management', in Robert D. Hume (ed.), *The London Theatre World, 1660–1800* (Carbondale: Southern Illinois University Press, 1980), 1–34.
12 *Congreve*, 20.
13 *Cooke*, 91.

For Macklin, however, such good times were never of long duration. Two years after his triumph as Shylock and a year after bringing the new hot commodity, David Garrick, to Drury Lane, Macklin made a fateful miscalculation and crossed Fleetwood. Macklin and Garrick led the failed Actors' Rebellion of 1743, protesting Fleetwood's impecunious and incompetent management of Drury Lane. The story of that failed rebellion is well known and its outcome was disastrous for Macklin.[14] Stung by Macklin's betrayal, Fleetwood ultimately agreed to rehire all of the rebel actors but Macklin. The latter was reduced to abjectly pleading for mercy, writing to Fleetwood in an attempt to both move his sympathy and remind him of Macklin's value as Shylock. Playing Portia to Fleetwood's Shylock, Macklin writes:

> You must imagine, sir, that by this time I am in no small distress, and distress, they say, even in an Enemie, will excite Humanity. Revenge, at such a time, being cruel, as forgiveness is generous: the one is the noblest office of the mind; the other becomes only the cruelty of a coward.[15]

Just as Portia failed to persuade Shylock that mercy was the noblest virtue, so did Macklin's appeal to Fleetwood fall on deaf ears.

Perhaps surprisingly, the pamphlet war that broke out over the Actors' Rebellion of 1743 offers virtually no insight into Macklin's managerial role at Drury Lane. Clearly, Fleetwood relied on Macklin's expertise, and his refusal to rehire Macklin or his wife after the rebellion is an indication of how terribly betrayed he must have felt. But the only references to Macklin's managerial responsibilities come in a back-and-forth exchange with Garrick over the issue of reducing overall acting salaries. Garrick claims that in the season prior to the rebellion Fleetwood increased Macklin's pay from £6 to £9 per week. The reason for the increase was Macklin's purported influence over Garrick, which (it is implied) might help to rein in Garrick's exorbitant salary demands.[16] For his part, Macklin claimed that he was offered a £200 bribe by Fleetwood to exert his influence with the other performers to keep calm when Fleetwood reduced the salaries of Garrick, Kitty Clive, and others. Fleetwood denied this, but it is not a stretch to think that he might have proposed this to Macklin. Citing Colley Cibber's *Apology*, Milhous notes that Christopher Rich relied upon an actor–manager, 'partly because he needed

---

14 Judith Milhous and Robert D. Hume, 'The Drury Lane Actors' Rebellion of 1743', *Theatre Survey* 42.1 (1990), 57–80.
15 Quoted in *Appleton*, 71–72. The manuscript letter is preserved in the William Appleton Collection of Theatrical Correspondence and Ephemera, 1697–1930, in the Billy Rose Theatre Collection, New York Public Library, Box 4, Folder 14.
16 Charles Macklin, *Mr Macklin's Reply to Mr Garrick's Answer* (London, 1743), 18–19.

expert assistance to get plays staged, but also to serve as a buffer between himself and the company when he lowered salaries or made other unpopular decisions'.[17] If it is true of Fleetwood and Macklin, then Charke's characterization of them in *The Art of Management* is close to the mark. Macklin claims to have refused this bribe but suggests that Garrick must have agreed to something similar when he came to terms with Fleetwood and led the rest of the company back to Drury Lane at reduced wages.[18] This is probably not the case. In point of fact, Macklin begged to be rehired at greatly reduced wages and Garrick and the other principal actors sought to prevail on Fleetwood to rehire Macklin. Garrick even offered to forego a significant portion of his own salary if Fleetwood rehired Macklin. Garrick and the others surely would not have done this if Macklin was as incompetent and malicious as Charke portrayed him to be. Instead, their efforts offer compelling evidence that he was an effective stage manager at Drury Lane.

Macklin's exclusion from the company at Drury Lane marked the end of a decade of steady employment there and ushered in a much longer period of professional uncertainty that lasted the rest of his career (nearly another five decades). During that time, he exhibited an entrepreneurial spirit that can only be appreciated if we look beyond his acting and playwriting and consider the managerial dimensions of his career. In 1744, he was begging the patentee of Drury Lane for work as an actor. By 1772, he was proposing to offer his acting services to Covent Garden, 'but not as a Comedian'.[19] More specifically, he meant that he was offering his services, but not *merely* as a comedian. And, indeed, he was identified in one publication from around that time as 'Deputy Manager' at Covent Garden, something akin to the role he had under Fleetwood.[20] How did he get from the low point of 1744 to a much higher point after 1772?

Acting coach and projector

Beginning in the winter of 1744, Macklin was desperate to make a living. The project he hit upon was to offer acting instruction to interested amateurs. Among his first pupils were Samuel Foote, John Hill, and Francis Blake Delaval. Macklin instructed his students and then

---

17 Milhous, 'Company Management', 8.
18 Macklin, *Mr Macklin's Reply to Mr Garrick's Answer*, 29–30.
19 Macklin's characterization of a December 1772 letter to Colman, offered in his Answer to the Mgrs. Original Bill of Complaint, 13 March 1778. Preserved in the National Archives, Kew, C 12/1667/30.
20 Anon., *The Poetical Review, A Poem* (London, n.d.), 21.

exhibited their talents in a public performance of *Othello* at the Little Theatre in the Haymarket.

As with the legendary *Merchant of Venice* production a few years earlier, Macklin not only instructed the others in their parts, he also had Iago and Othello 'new dressed after the manner of his country'.[21] In order to evade the Stage Licensing Act's prohibition on unlicensed performances, the event was advertised as a concert of music with the play performed gratis between the two halves of the concert. Performances of *Othello* and other plays occurred between 6 February and 3 July 1744, after which point Macklin abandoned the project and left to act on the provincial circuit.

Apart from the Little Haymarket *Othello*, Macklin was known to have instructed others in acting. In March 1751, he again instructed Delaval and other friends from high life in a one-off amateur production of *Othello* at Drury Lane that was attended by the Prince and Princess of Wales along with many members of the House of Commons, which adjourned early that day to attend the performance. Macklin is reputed to have coached Garrick in his breakthrough role of Richard III. According to Cooke, Garrick asked Macklin to 'sit in judgment' on the first night he performed Lear, noting later the advice Macklin offered.[22] Cooke also claims that prior to appearing in the role of Abel Drugger in Jonson's *The Alchemist*, Garrick privately rehearsed the part before Macklin and others.[23] Macklin is similarly reported to have coached Spranger Barry in his most celebrated role, Othello. Of all Macklin's pupils, he was certainly proudest of having trained his daughter, Maria. She enjoyed a successful career of her own and frequently performed with her father on her benefit nights.[24]

Training others to act was a constant feature of Macklin's career, spanning from the 1730s to the 1780s. Samuel Foote, who benefited from Macklin's instruction, nevertheless later ridiculed him in the character of Puzzle in a scene he added to *The Diversions of the Morning* (1758). Foote portrays the instruction as the ridiculous exaggeration of wildly contrasting emotions in the course of a single speech. Sterne seems to take this representation of Macklin as an acting coach at face value, observing that it 'illustrates how Macklin, who for a time ran an acting school, was inclined to treat his

---

21 Quoted in *Appleton*, 69.
22 *Cooke*, 104.
23 *Cooke*, 110.
24 For a recent perspective on Maria Macklin's theatrical career, see Felicity Nussbaum, 'Straddling: London-Irish Actresses in Performance', in David O'Shaughnessy (ed.), *Ireland, Enlightenment and the English Stage, 1740–1820* (Cambridge: Cambridge University Press, 2019), esp. 48–56.

players as vehicles for his own performances'.[25] But Foote's play is hardly a reliable source of information, and if Macklin were truly as ridiculous as Foote portrays him, then surely the likes of Garrick and Barry would not have sought out his advice. Nevertheless, judging from the evidence found in Macklin's own letters, his methods as an acting coach later in life are not difficult to caricature. In a draft letter from 1782, Macklin writes to a female pupil, telling her, 'I found you very deficient in your Utterances and totally a Stranger to such correctness of Speaking as is indispensible & necessary in an actress'.[26] He then says that he resolved to treat his student 'as an Infant' and correct her faulty speech by beginning with the alphabet: 'accordingly I got you a Spelling Book and practised with you by uttering Consonants vowels & syllables daily'. Not surprisingly, the student seems not to have taken this demeaning treatment well. Macklin concludes his draft by observing, 'your Conduct to me Since you came to Town has been of Such a nature as to deserve a name of a very disagreeable Quality'. And lest we presume that this is an unrepresentative characterization of Macklin's teaching style, we have this brief letter Macklin sent to a Miss Leeson in 1773:

> Madam
> For three months last past you have been making Excuses for not coming to me to rehearse your Parts according to my Requests.—first your Cloaths were so damaged by the Rain in travelling that you were ashamed to appear in them at my Lodging, then you were ill & could not Stir out—and, by your note of the Seventh Instant you Say you have gotten a most Severe cold, and therefore can not Stir out, and yet it is notorious that you have been almost every night at the Playhouse in Crow street. These answers madam are triffling and insidious. I look upon them as breaches of your Contract as an apprentice, & I believe the Law and every honest man must interpret them in the Same manner. Once more I insist upon your coming to rehearse the part of Celia in my new Play at my Lodging in Bolton Street this afternoon at four o'Clock. I desire you will Send me an Answer in writing whether or no I may expect you. Should it be in affirmative pray name the hour that I may Settle my Business accordingly.
> I am
>   Madam
>   your huble Servt
>   Charles Macklin
> Feb: 9th: 1773
> three o'Clock
> P.S. If you may take a chair I will pay for it.[27]

---

25 Stern, *Rehearsal from Shakespeare to Sheridan*, 266.
26 Fragmentary letter draft from Macklin to an unidentified pupil, c.1782. Preserved in the Theatre Museum's Charles Macklin Biographical File held by the Victoria and Albert Museum.
27 Charles Macklin Biographical File, Victoria and Albert Museum.

Coming from Macklin himself, this is damning evidence of his conduct as an acting coach later in his career, not to mention his effect on his pupils. Claims of his effectiveness as a teacher come from earlier in his career, and as he aged he evidently became a more peremptory and less skilful instructor.

Macklin's inclinations as a pedagogue went beyond acting lessons and manifested themselves in a great mid-career experiment. The British Inquisition, discussed in detail in this volume by Markman Ellis and Helen Burke, might in fact best be understood as a pedagogical experiment. He retired from the stage (for the first time) in 1753 and spent a year fitting up a coffeehouse under the North Piazza in Covent Garden. He spent lavishly on the project and opened for business in March 1754. Over the next several months, he continued to spend money fitting up the rooms over the coffeehouse and in November 1754 he opened the British Inquisition. Advertised as being modelled on 'the plan of the ancient, Greek, Roman, and Modern French and Italian Societies of liberal investigation', the establishment promised to explore 'subjects in Arts, Sciences, Literature, Criticism, Philosophy, History, Politics, and Morality, as shall be found useful and entertaining to society'.[28] In the first weeks of the enterprise, the topics under discussion were related to the theatre. But, as Appleton explains, 'before long he had pitched them on a less exalted plane and was discussing "the ingenious nation of the Pygmies" and the kidnapping of Elizabeth Canning'.[29] Not surprisingly, Macklin became a target for satire for his pretensions to learning. Samuel Foote ridiculed him both at the British Inquisition and on the stage in the Little Haymarket, and by January 1755 Macklin pleaded bankruptcy.

Irish adventurer

Having publicly retired from the London stage and then failed in his grand project of the British Inquisition, Macklin in his mid-fifties had no clear path forward. He was out of money, but never out of ideas. His early biographer, William Cooke, offers this shrewd observation: 'Amongst Macklin's oddities, he was always a great projector, and, like most people who take up this character from a certain restlessness of temper, his projects were generally unsuccessful'.[30] His next project was focused on the Dublin stage and, improbably for a recent bankrupt, involved him as a principal in the establishment of a new theatre. Immediately after the

---

28 *Public Advertiser*, 21 November 1754. Quoted in *Appleton*, 102.
29 *Appleton*, 104.
30 *Cooke*, 163.

failure of the British Inquisition, Macklin returned to teaching acting, but not long after that his one-time protégé Spranger Barry approached him to join this new project as a partner in establishing a new theatre in Crow Street, Dublin.

Having no money to invest, Macklin seems to have been an odd choice. But what he offered to the enterprise was his long experience in theatrical affairs, especially in management. John C. Greene says that Barry turned to Macklin 'evidently reluctantly'.[31] But letters between Barry and Macklin show that the initial overtures were far from reluctant. Barry sought out Macklin as a partner early on, and Macklin, looking for a route back to theatrical employment, was an eager accessory.[32] And even though Macklin had no money to invest, what Barry offered him was a breathtakingly good deal. Barry proposed that Macklin should receive £1,200 a year and a quarter of the profits. Acknowledging the reality of Macklin's financial situation, Barry adds, 'and that you may not be distrest on account of the advancing the fourth of the Expenses, I will take the Joint security of yourself and Miss Macklin for it'.[33] This is all the more generous when one considers what followed in that same letter, which bears quoting in full because it sheds important light on Macklin's reputation as a stage manager. Barry writes:

> I will not say but that if [you] had dealt otherwise with me, I might have been induced to have taken your single security. But your own behavior has taught me prudence enough not to confide too much in you in a matter of consequence. [...] But in one thing it is requisite to be very explicit; and which you will perceive, contains the reasons above referred to. It is impossible for you to share any power of managing—for there are several People whom I have engaged, who would not Article with me till I had solemnly assured them that you were not to have any share of the management. They have experienced some inconveniences from your former Management at different places.[34]

This letter is in private hands and survives only in a partial transcription from a sale catalogue. But even in partial form it contains fascinating and tantalizing evidence of Macklin's reputation as a stage-manager at mid-career. Having initially approached Macklin as a performer and a partner in management, Barry and he evidently had a falling out ('your own behavior has taught me prudence enough not to confide too much in you'). As a consequence, Barry

---

31 John C. Greene, *Theatre in Dublin, 1745–1820, A History*, 2 vols (Bethlehem, PA: Lehigh University Press, 2011), I.215.
32 Matthew J. Kinservik, '*Love à la Mode* and Macklin's Return to the London Stage in 1759', *Theatre Survey* 37.2 (1996), 1–21.
33 Barry to Macklin, dated 31 May 1758. Quoted in Greene, *Theatre in Dublin*, I.215.
34 Cited in Greene, *Theatre in Dublin*, I.215.

shifted to engaging Macklin and his daughter only as performers, relying on their drawing power to support the fledgling venture.

Alarmed at the prospect of losing a theatrical monopoly in Dublin, Thomas Sheridan did everything he could to prevent the Crow Street Theatre from becoming a reality. Initially, he sent Benjamin Victor to London in March 1757, in order to persuade Barry to drop his plans. Instead, Victor offered Barry the united theatres in Aungier Street and Smock Alley, either in partnership with Sheridan or as sole manager.[35] After that failed, Sheridan sought a parliamentary limit on the number of theatres and campaigned against the Crow Street project in print. Wary of attacking the popular Barry, Sheridan fixed his sights on Macklin, observing, 'Mr. *Barry* has been urged to the Undertaking by Persons who had more ill-will to Mr. *Sheridan* than Friendship to Mr. *Barry*; and deluded also by the specious Arguments of artful Men, who being shut out of all Theatres, and consequently desperate, care not what dangerous Enterprize they involve him in'.[36] In Sheridan's telling, Macklin was playing Iago to Barry's credulous Othello and was 'the very Man whose Counsels have chiefly sway'd him in this Affair, whom he has taken by the Hand and brought over to this Kingdom as his *Mentor*' (76). Although Sheridan is mistaken about who was the prime mover in the Crow Street Theatre, this characterization is exactly right: Macklin was initially of value to Barry not as an investor but as a mentor in theatrical management. His literal management experience consisted of his work under Fleetwood at Drury Lane and assembling and leading a provincial company at Chester in 1749. And he recently oversaw a major construction project for the rooms in London that housed his coffeehouse and the British Inquisition. For an entrepreneur, failure is often a prelude to success, so Macklin's bankruptcy probably struck Barry as less important than the experience he gained by the project.

Unfortunately for Barry, Macklin proved to be more of a tormentor than a mentor. Despite contributing no money, he took an active and at times unreasonably demanding and intrusive role in the business. Before the curtain rose on the first performance at the Crow Street Theatre, Macklin was no longer part of the management. Instead, he parted ways with Barry and later joined the rival company at the Smock Alley Theatre, which Sheridan had by then sold to the actor Henry Mossop. According to Cooke, Macklin 'was not only concerned with him as a principal actor, but frequently employed as a kind

---

35 Benjamin Victor, *The history of the theatres of London and Dublin, from the year 1730 to the present time. To which is added, an annual register of all the plays, &c. performed ... in London, from the year 1712. ... by Mr. Victor, ... In two volumes* (London, 1761), I.223–26.

36 Thomas Sheridan, *An Humble Appeal to the Publick* (Dublin, 1758), 75.

of *Assisting Manager*—an office which he ever loved, but which always suited his inclination more than either his temper or his judgment'.[37] To my mind, this is the perfect characterization of Macklin's career as a theatre manager.

Playwright/actor-manager

Everything changed for Macklin upon the premiere of his incredibly successful farce, *Love à la Mode*, in December 1759. Before this, Macklin had spent sixteen eventful years, pursuing various projects, acting, teaching, writing plays, and assisting in management. After *Love à la Mode*—and because of it—he enjoyed singular bargaining power as a performer. As his correspondence with various managers shows, his jealous protection of exclusive performance rights to *Love à la Mode* allowed him to demand unusual employment contracts. In these contracts Macklin was able to dictate his performance schedule and roles and was on occasion also given authority over costuming, sets, music, and other aspects of production. Most actors were not in a position to set terms like these. But, with his long experience and the perennially profitable *Love à la Mode*, Macklin was unique. This helps us to understand why, when he was negotiating a contract with Colman in 1772, he specified that he sought employment at Covent Garden, 'but not as a Comedian'.

Macklin's vigilance in defending his property in *Love à la Mode* is legendary—and rightly so. As Jane Wessel explains, by keeping the play out of print, he was able to maintain exclusive performance rights to it throughout his career.[38] A revealing example is Macklin's lawsuit against James Whitley, Henry Owen, and Frances Weeler, for advertising and performing *Love à la Mode* for the benefit of Whitley on Friday, 17 May 1770, in Leicester. In his bill of complaint, Macklin asserts that

> he should not only have had and taken to himself the Sole and exclusive right to print and publish the Same and all the Profits to arise thereby but also should have had the Sole and exclusive right of having the said Comedy or Farce represented when and in such manner as he should think proper.[39]

For the purposes of this essay, the key claim Macklin makes is that he should dictate that the play can only be performed 'when and in such manner as he

---

37 *Cooke*, 266.
38 Jane Wessel, 'Possessing Parts and Owning Plays: Charles Macklin and the Prehistory of Dramatic Literary Property', *Theatre Survey* 56.3 (2015), 268–90.
39 National Archives, Kew, C 12/1327/5.

should think proper'. These are managerial decisions. By keeping his play out of print, Macklin vested these prerogatives in himself rather than surrendering them to the managers at various theatres. And when he consented to allow others to perform it, he exacted a price. Sometimes that was a 'gratuity' that others had to pay him. The defendants in this case claimed that Macklin 'had been frequently paid Twenty pounds a Night for Acting in and Superintending the Representation' of *Love à la Mode*. This is a steep price for a provincial performance, and the defendants claimed that their profit was about half this amount. But, again, what is striking is that Macklin was able to demand a gratuity for the right to perform the play and his insistence that he supervise any performance.

Macklin's use of *Love à la Mode* to assert what are, essentially, managerial prerogatives was not limited to the provincial stage. From early on he dealt with the managers of the London patent houses in much the same way. In correspondence with Garrick in 1763, Macklin stipulates that his contract be structured so that he is able to travel to Ireland to perform for part of the season and 'that the Sole Property of My Plays or Farces Shall be always vested in me!'[40] He indicates that he should not be required to perform in both the mainpiece and afterpiece on the same night, that he is willing to produce new farces or adapted older plays for the company to perform, and that his pay could be a nightly amount or a share of the profits during his time of employment. When one compares how precarious Macklin's fortunes were prior to *Love à la Mode* with the confidence of his negotiations with managers after, the value of maintaining the sole ownership of the play is clear. It was the difference between being a supplicant actor and a sort of actor–manager.

Macklin parlayed the success of *Love à la Mode* into a series of favourable engagements on the London, Dublin, and provincial stages for more than two decades. As shown below, he eventually grew weary of the play and became ambitious to write more and to try his hand at different roles. In his negotiations with George Colman the Elder for an engagement at Covent Garden in 1773, the seventy-four-year-old Macklin proposed the following:

1. To be contracted for three seasons, beginning 20 September and ending last day of April.
2. To act in common stock plays twice a week, but not in the play and farce on same night.
3. To act in new and revived plays as often as called upon.
4. To act in *Love a la Mode* 12 nights per season, if called upon.
5. To write one farce each season, which the managers can play as often as

---

40 Macklin to Garrick, 28 April 1763, David Garrick's Correspondence and Papers, 1717–79, Victoria and Albert Museum, F. 48. F. 22 (items #52–60).

they please, but upon the end of the agreement, all rights reside in Macklin alone.
6. To not act in Westminster or within five miles around it during the term of the agreement.
7. To perform one of his own plays on his or his daughter's benefit night.
8. To receive £400 in equal weekly payments and £100 per farce.
9. To receive a benefit night in February, paying customary house charges.
10. To be exempt from pantomimes, masquerades, and processions.[41]

Very few performers enjoyed this kind of bargaining power with managers, and fewer still could demand the kind of managerial prerogatives that Macklin did with Colman. In addition to the stipulations listed above, the negotiations with Colman also (and fatefully) extended to assigning Macklin both the role of Macbeth and the authority to oversee all aspects of the production '(which was to be dressed decorated and represented as near to the historical facts and manners of the times and action of that play as could be suggested)'.[42]

Colman agreed to employ Macklin on these terms, but he obviously did so with some reluctance.[43] In the context of a lawsuit, Colman later claimed that Macklin 'Insisted on performing the Characters of King Richard, Lear, and Macbeth and shewed the greatest reluctance to act Shylock and Sir Archy MacSarcasm wherein he Excelled'.[44] Eventually worn down by Macklin in negotiations, Colman, 'for the sake of peace consented that [Macklin] should try the Sence of the Publick in the character of Macbeth'.[45] However, Macklin claims that Colman, being uneasy with what they agreed to, then attempted to interfere with Macklin's rehearsals by ensuring that:

> the greatest part of the Stage of the said theatre was occupied by Carpenters and Scene shifters and they during the former and the greater part of the rehearsal were employed in hammering sawing hawling Timber and Scenes and bawling to and answering each other by which the rehearsal was greatly interrupted and disturbed and it was rendered impossible for your Orator to remember or think with any precision of the business of the Rehearsal or to hear or make himself heard with any good effect.[46]

In the event, Colman did not succeed in frustrating Macklin's production of *Macbeth*, which resulted in a riot, Macklin's dismissal, and then ten years

---

41 National Archives, Kew, C 12/1367/6, f. 10.
42 National Archives, Kew, C 12/1667/30.
43 National Archives, Kew, C 12/1342/35.
44 National Archives, Kew, C 12/1342/35.
45 National Archives, Kew, C 12/1342/35.
46 National Archives, Kew, C 12/1367/6, f. 10.

of lawsuits. That controversy, however, sprang from a dispute over Macklin taking the role of Macbeth from William 'Gentleman' Smith and is unrelated to the merits of the innovative production that Macklin oversaw.[47]

Conclusion

John C. Greene's *Theatre in Dublin, 1745–1820*, contains an anecdote about Macklin from the 1770–71 season that illustrates just how different he was from other actors of the period. Macklin had commissioned the dressmaker of the Opera House in the Haymarket to make fine dresses for a new tragedy he had written. He brought them to Ireland but failed to get the play staged and so rented them out instead for a performance of Garrick's *Jubilee*. But, as Greene notes, in this anecdote we see that Macklin 'even provided the costumes for at least one of his plays, suggesting that he exercised even greater control over the production of his works than formerly realized'.[48] The more one looks at Macklin's career through the lens of theatre management, the more one sees that simply considering him as an actor or even actor–playwright is insufficient. Appleton's 1960 biography is subtitled *An Actor's Life*, but this seems too limiting when one considers the evidence presented here.

This review of Macklin's career suggests that he ought to join the ranks of the famous actor–managers of the eighteenth-century stage. Although he never enjoyed the title of manager, his long career involved multiple forays into management, both formal and informal. His influence on eighteenth-century acting styles, Shakespearean interpretation, costuming, and actors' and playwrights' performance rights are all a result of his occasional and often informal exercise of managerial responsibilities. Especially later in his career, his long experience on the stage and close knowledge of theatrical management made him a unique and uniquely important figure in the eighteenth-century theatre world.

---

47 For more on Macklin's *Macbeth*, see Matthew J. Kinservik, 'A Sinister *Macbeth*: The Macklin Production of 1773', *Harvard Library Bulletin* 6.1 (1995), 51–76 and Kristina Straub, 'The Newspaper "Trial" of Charles Macklin's *Macbeth* and the Theatre as Juridical Public Sphere', *Eighteenth-Century Fiction* 27.3–4 (2015), 395–418.

48 Greene, *Theatre in Dublin*, I.402.

7

Macklin and Song

Ian Newman

THIS CHAPTER CONSIDERS Macklin's relationship to what scholars are beginning to understand was one of the defining characteristics of the eighteenth-century theatre: the robust presence of song. Singing was a prerequisite of a theatrical culture that was shaped by the centrality of ballad operas like *The Beggar's Opera* to the repertoire, by the interaction between legitimate and illegitimate theatre, and by the demands of audience members who required song as part of their evening's entertainment. Comic actors, in particular, were required to sing frequently and, for all his reputation for severity, Macklin was a comic actor. Singing was one of the diverse set of skills he needed in his early career as a strolling player. In one anecdote of Macklin's life on the road William Appleton records how he played both Antonia and Belvidera in *Venice Preserved*, a performance in which he also 'performed a harlequinade, sang three songs and danced a Irish jig'.[1] And later in his career Macklin took on a variety of singing roles, with Peachum in *The Beggar's Opera*, a particular favourite along with 'the rollicking chanties of Ben in *Love for Love*'.[2] So what was it like to hear 'leathern-lunged' Macklin sing?[3] The question is an intriguing one in part because Macklin was not known for the pleasantness of his voice, so his case forces us to confront the consequences of a theatrical culture in which song played so crucial a role: audiences must have been forced to endure many performances by mediocre

---

1 *Appleton*, 13.
2 *Appleton*, 14.
3 The term 'leathern-lunged' is William Appleton's, as I will discuss below. *Appleton*, 2.

singers, but yet they still demanded song. Why was this, and what does it reveal about the role song played in the theatre?

This question can be supplemented by a further investigation into Macklin's relationship to song, beyond those he sang. In addition to the songs he performed on stage himself, Macklin was also responsible for the development of plays in which song played a central role, such as his ground-breaking *The Merchant of Venice* for which Thomas Arne wrote two songs. Macklin also wrote songs. As the author of a number of plays, comic afterpieces, and Christmas entertainments, Macklin wrote the words to a number of songs, some of which enjoyed remarkable success, and have experienced significant afterlives. The aim in this essay is to explore Macklin's relationship to song in order to consider the affective role of song on the eighteenth-century stage and beyond it, in the hopes of better understanding how theatrical song shaped the culture of the eighteenth century more broadly.

In one sense, then, this essay offers an aural counterpart to the visuality discussed by David Taylor in the chapter 'Macklin's Look' in this volume, but it is worth emphasizing that the difference in medium is by no means trivial. To understand Macklin's look it is possible to rely on stable archival materials—graphic satires and paintings—through which we can view Macklin's appearance. Song, however, is a performed medium that frequently floats free from the print archives to which the historian is shackled. It is a category of performance, like the plays in which Macklin appeared, which is best understood in terms of the repertoire. The repertoire, according to Diana Taylor, is an alternative archive by which people 'produce and transmit knowledge through embodied action'.[4] For Taylor, the repertoire is a form of ongoing memory work, by which what is created in performance is transformed into gesture and behaviour, however consciously, in a way that theoretically enables it to be revisited and renewed.[5] The kinds of evidence we are able to marshal and our ability to understand it require a different set of analytical assumptions, as will become clear in some of the more speculative traces of Macklin's song uncovered below, in which I attempt to recover what Macklin's voice sounded like, the affective role that song played in Macklin's theatre, and ultimately how the songs that Macklin wrote experienced a life outside of the theatrical institutions in which Macklin worked.

---

4 Diana Taylor, *The Archive and Performance: Performing Cultural Memory in the Americas* (Durham, NC: Duke University Press, 2003), 24.

5 For a discussion of song as repertoire, see Ian Newman and Gillian Russell, 'Metropolitan Songs and Songsters: Ephemerality in the World City', *Studies in Romanticism* 58.4 (2019), 436–38.

Macklin's voice

IN HIS BIOGRAPHY, William Appleton opens his account of Macklin with a description of him in old age. Macklin's lapses in memory had forced him to retire from the stage in 1789, 'but for a decade afterwards he had haunted the Covent Garden district, strolling at noon under the arcades in threadbare clothes which oddly recalled the dead fashions of his youth. Time had not tamed his temper'. Appleton continues, 'Though usually amiable in manner, on occasion his great hawk eyes would blaze with sudden anger, and his leathern-lunged voice echo through the Piazza in tirades of undiminished vigor'.[6] This description of Macklin's 'leathern-lunged voice' is, of course, an imaginative recreation by Appleton who wrote nearly two hundred years after the events he described. Appleton never heard Macklin's voice in person, so can have no personal experience to draw on, but what he does have is a deep immersion in the Mackliniana published around the time of his death, and a compulsion to understand what Macklin sounded like. Appleton's desire to hear Macklin's voice captures the spirit of Peter Holland's desire to attend to the aural as well as the visual dimensions of theatrical history.[7] It also prefigures Judith Pascoe's genre-bending study *The Sarah Siddons's Audio Files*, which seeks, in spite of all the obvious hurdles, to understand what Siddons's voice sounded like.[8] There is a clear difference, however, in that both Garrick and Siddons were known for the beauty of their voices. Siddons, for example, was described by the artist Joseph Severn as possessing a 'deep touching voice whose tones, whether loud and impassioned or soft and pathetic, were very like the finest music, for they thrilled the air with melodious tones'.[9] No one described Macklin's voice in this way. Descriptions of Macklin's voice tend to focus not on its otherworldliness but on its otherness. In his 1799 biography, James Kirkman placed considerable emphasis on the challenges Macklin faced in overcoming 'the strong vernacular accent' with which he spoke on first coming to England, and described his 'efforts, for years, to get rid of his natural accent'.[10] Further, Kirkman suggested that his 'Irish brogue', as it was frequently described, was received differently in different places and

---

6 *Appleton*, 2.
7 Peter Holland, 'Hearing the Dead: The Sound of David Garrick', in Michael Cordner and Peter Holland (eds), *Players, Playwrights, Playhouses: Investigating Performance, 1660–1800* (Basingstoke: Palgrave Macmillan, 2007), 248–70.
8 Judith Pascoe, *The Sarah Siddons Audio Files: Romanticism and the Lost Voice* (Ann Arbor: University of Michigan Press, 2011).
9 William Sharp, *The Life and Letters of Joseph Severn* (London: Sampson, Low, Marston & Co., 1892), 14.
10 *Kirkman*, I.58, 62.

according to the predisposition of individual audience members. In Bristol, for example, where there was a considerable Irish presence, Macklin's accent proved less of a barrier than in other parts of England. 'With the judicious, his Irish accent was an objection which they allowed his acting, in a great degree, counterbalanced;—with the lower order, his being an Irishman was an objection, however admirably he might act'.[11] In Kirkman's account, what is initially understood more objectively as an impediment to comprehension quickly becomes a signifier with more ideological meanings. To *sound* Irish is necessarily to fail as an actor in England because prejudice deafens the audience.[12] Moreover, for Kirkman, Macklin's ability to overcome the obstacles associated with his voice played a central role in his development as an actor and hence to his ultimate success:

> The difficulties which his accent and provincial expression threw in his way, at first, though now in some degree surmounted, dwelt with lingering pain in his mind; and impelled him to use more than common efforts to get rid of them. He observed, too, that most of the actors who failed of success on the stage, had to attribute their failure to defective enunciation; and he could even see that the best of those, with whom he performed, were greatly deficient in that respect.[13]

The clear implication here is that Macklin's success in the theatre, his revolutionary style of acting, and his success as an acting teacher were directly tied to his preoccupation with his voice, and especially with the deficiencies of a voice which was 'naturally' hard to understand. For Kirkman, Macklin's success was enabled by his acute sensitivity to vocal nuance, born of his struggles to overcome his own vocal deficiencies.

Macklin joined John Rich's company at Lincoln's Inn Field, where he (probably) made his London debut on 11 October 1725 as Alcander in Dryden and Lee's *Oedipus*. According to Congreve's *Authentic Memoirs*, 'he spoke with so little of the then tragic cadence, that the manger was not satisfied and a separation in consequence then took place'.[14] William Cooke records Macklin himself commenting, 'I spoke so *familiar*, Sir [...] and so little in the *hoity toity* tone of the Tragedy of that day, that the manager told

---

11 *Kirkman*, I.64.
12 For a later example of an Irish actor in England who struggled to overcome the prejudice an English audience had towards Irish accents, see Oskar Cox Jensen, 'The Diminution of "Irish" Johnstone', in David O'Shaughnessy (ed.), *Ireland, Enlightenment, and the English Stage, 1740–1820* (Cambridge: Cambridge University Press, 2019), 79–97, esp. 80.
13 *Kirkman*, I.69.
14 *Congreve*, 12.

me, I had better go to grass for another year or two'.[15] The implication of Cooke's *Memoirs*, echoing Kirkman's earlier assessment, was that Macklin's new 'naturalistic' mode of acting depended on overcoming the limitations of his voice. It also involved overcoming the old style of acting, described by John Genest as the 'good old manner of singing and quavering out their tragic notes'.[16] The musical metaphors of this description—taken from Genest's *Some Account of the English Stage* (1832)—are apt in part because Macklin's voice, according to most accounts, was singularly ill-equipped to provide the musicality of the old style that this description emphasizes.

Whether Macklin was ever able to shake off the Irish strains that characterized his voice in the early years of his career was a matter of some debate. According to *Bell's Weekly Register*, Macklin fooled himself that he had developed 'a pure and correct delivery with the accent of genuine Anglicanism' when he gave his lectures at the British Inquisition in the 1750s. But the aural trace of his youth was not manifested in predictable ways. 'Though a native of the *humblest* description, he had not the least of the Irish *patois*', *Bell's* reported, 'but a *tone* was observable like the Scotch accent'. The point seems to be that while he had lost his Irish accent, he could never become fully English, and he succeeded merely in exchanging one form of otherness for another.

The otherness of Macklin's voice was not always so explicitly described. Often it was expressed in more subtly loaded assessments. According to Appleton, for example, 'Macklin was limited by his physique, voice and temperament. He could not submerge his personality and while he could play many roles acceptably, he excelled in those of a dark, saturnine cast'.[17] These assessments carry over into descriptions of Macklin's singing. In Appleton's account, 'To the end of his career, [Macklin] enjoyed bellowing the lusty songs of Peachum in *The Beggar's Opera* and the rollicking chanties of Ben in *Love for Love*'.[18] Though Macklin's voice can never be adequately recovered, these descriptions together describe a powerful, memorable voice, the resonance of which, read through the lens of his Irishness and his signature performance of Shylock, suggested a malevolence which Macklin could not escape. Over a hundred and fifty years after his death, Appleton still understands the 'tirades' that echoed around Covent Garden with 'undiminished vigor', not as admirably mellifluousness, but as 'leathern-lunged'.

---

15 *Cooke*, 13.
16 John Genest, *Some Account of the English Stage: From the Restoration in 1660 to 1830*, 10 vols (Bath, 1832), IV.162. See also *Appleton*, 74.
17 *Appleton*, 157.
18 *Appleton*, 14.

THE MERCHANT OF VENICE

THE UNDERSTANDING OF MACKLIN'S VOICE, then, depends on an understanding of Macklin the Irishman, which, as David Taylor suggests in his chapter on Macklin's look, became enmeshed with the role for which Macklin was most celebrated. Macklin's otherness at various points becomes entwined with Shylock's otherness and so for the purposes of understanding Macklin's relationship to song it is worth emphasizing that *The Merchant of Venice*, when it was performed as a vehicle for Macklin, had a significant musical component that helped to shape the audience response to the play. Following the success of Macklin's initial season in the role as Shylock, Thomas Arne wrote two new songs for the play, which were introduced the following season and became standard in performances of *The Merchant of Venice* until at least Kemble's 1797 production.[19]

In a discussion of Arne's music for the Drury Lane Shakespeare revivals of 1740–41, John Cunningham makes an observation that is helpful in understanding the role of song on the eighteenth-century stage. Comparing eighteenth-century theatrical song performance with music from Shakespeare's time, Cunningham notes that songs in the eighteenth-century theatre served as 'entertainments within the entertainment'.[20] On the early modern stage any music that was performed was usually part of the dramatic action, 'always part of the world of the play itself, heard and responded to by the characters on stage'.[21] By the nineteenth century, as Michael Pisani has discussed, music often underscored dialogue in the theatre, providing affective cues to the audience or suggesting time, place, ethnicity, or class—it formed the '*melos*' of melodrama.[22] The eighteenth century might be seen as

---

19 John Cunningham, 'The Reception and Re-Use of Thomas Arne's Shakespeare Songs of 1740–1', in Bill Barclay and David Lindley (eds), *Shakespeare, Music and Performance* (Cambridge: Cambridge University Press, 2017), 140. And see also Irena Cholij, 'Music in Eighteenth-Century London Shakespeare Productions', unpublished PhD thesis, King's College London (1995), 43. Cunningham claims that Arne's songs were introduced into the 1740–41 season. However, Arne's score states that the songs were performed by Thomas Lowe, who didn't appear in the play until the 1741–42 season, when he replaced William Havard in the role of Lorenzo, presumably in order to perform Arne's songs. This is corroborated by *The London Stage*, which notes that advertisements for the first performance in which Lowe performed, on 2 November 1741, mentioned that 'character songs will be introduced proper to the play'.
20 Cunningham, 'Reception and Re-Use of Thomas Arne's Shakespeare Songs', 135.
21 David Lindley, *Shakespeare and Music* (London: Thomson Learning, 2006), 112.
22 Michael Pisani, 'Music for the Theatre: Style and Function in Incidental Music', in Kerry Powell (ed.), *The Cambridge Companion to Victorian and Edwardian Theatre* (Cambridge: Cambridge University Press, 2004), 71. See also Michael Pisani, *Music*

an intermediary period as theatrical music negotiated the transition from being primarily diegetic to possessing a capacity for non-diegetic effects, but this broad teleology fails to account for some of the complex, and often surprising, possibilities of eighteenth-century theatrical music.

Cunningham notes that compared with the early modern theatre, eighteenth-century theatrical songs were more for the audience than for the other characters on stage, a feature of playgoing enabled by the rise in both the critical capacity of the audience (marking their approbation or contempt with cheering, hissing, rioting, and other forms of commentary) and in the culture of celebrity surrounding well-known actors and actresses.[23] Songs could stop the action of the play, as the actor moved to the front of the stage to address the audience directly, frequently interpolating songs from elsewhere as actors showed off their vocal abilities.

The treatment of song should be considered alongside the eighteenth-century theatrical practice of 'pointing', which involved delivering well-known speeches, together with standardized gestures, directly to the audience. Such 'points' constituted significant breaks from the action of the play, and, as Lisa Freeman has argued, audiences accepted points as moments that operated independently of the rest of the play and could be judged on their own terms.[24] According to William Worthen, pointing offered discrete moments that provided an opportunity to structure emotional responses and to 'coordinate the passions of the actor, character and spectator'.[25] These seemingly incongruous moments that stood apart from the rest of the play's action were clearly part of the appeal of going to the theatre, of a piece with the harlequinades, ballets, and afterpieces that made up the evening's bill of fare. Although, as I hope to show, this general observation can get complicated when individual songs are considered—as a song's relationship to its surrounding material is rarely as simple as being straightforwardly independent of it.

Both songs that Arne wrote for the 1741 *The Merchant of Venice*, were sung by Lorenzo, played in Macklin's production by Thomas Lowe, who had made his name in Arne's *Alfred*, first performed for Frederic, Prince of Wales, in 1740 (making Lowe the first performer of 'Rule Britannia'). Arne's first song is described as a 'Serenade' in $\frac{3}{4}$ time, with a speed marking of 'Amoroso', to be performed in the second act. In it, Lorenzo urges Jessica to escape from

---

for the Melodramatic Theatre in Nineteenth-Century London and New York (Iowa City: University of Iowa Press, 2014), xix–xxi.
23 Cunningham, 'Reception and Re-Use of Thomas Arne's Shakespeare Songs', 135.
24 Lisa A. Freeman, *Character's Theater: Genre and Identity on the Eighteenth-Century English Stage* (Philadelphia: University of Pennsylvania Press, 2001), 31–32.
25 William B. Worthen, *The Idea of the Actor* (Princeton, NJ: Princeton University Press, 1984), 72.

Shylock's house, suggesting that while Shylock has confined his daughter with steel, 'cruel love' is a more urgent form of slavery that 'inchains the mind', providing a greater impetus to escape than to stay. As Irena Cholij has pointed out, this was a setting, with some minor adjustments, of the final three stanzas of a seven-stanza poem, possibly written by Ambrose Phillips, originally published in Addison and Steele's *The Spectator* (no. 366) in April 1712.[26] In *The Dramatic Censor* of 1770, Francis Gentleman suggested that the song was inserted into the scene to allow Jessica (played by Miss Woodman in the 1741 production) time for a costume change when she appears for the first time in boys' clothes, suggesting that the use of song in eighteenth-century theatre provided practical functions besides audience pandering.[27] But the song has dramatic purposes beyond these practical considerations. It is replete with 4–3 suspensions (on, for example, the words 'long' and 'de-nies': see Figure 7.1), which evoke a sense of yearning, helping to characterize Lorenzo's amorous longing as he pleads with Jessica to abandon her repellent father and run off with him. In this sense, it contributes to Macklin's conception of Shylock, by engaging the audience's sympathies with Jessica, whom Shylock has kept in a form of 'slavery', and with her lover who pleads with Jessica to allow him to liberate her from her father's bondage—albeit with the contorted but characteristically self-involved logic that he too is in bondage, so by liberating Jessica he is in fact liberating himself.

There is, unquestionably, an irony in the fact that Lorenzo's 'Serenade' exhorts Jessica to 'haste away' in a slow, amorous plea in lilting triple time, seemingly undercutting the very message of urgency the song purportedly records. This does, however, helpfully illustrate the status of song in this production. Theatrical songs, like operatic arias, could suspend the action of the play in order to provide an opportunity for lyrical meditation on the unfolding action. But this reflective capacity was not entirely indifferent to the action it commented on, nor did it arrest the plot entirely, rather it slowed the action down, prioritizing emotional appeal over plot movement in order to heighten dramatic tension by forging a particular relationship with the audience. The song occupies a position simultaneously inside and outside of the plot, participating within the action, while making an affective appeal directly to the audience and anticipating the desired feelings an audience should have. This is a much more complicated mediation between performer, audience, character, and overall production than suggested by Cunningham's sense that songs were divorced from the dramatic context, and it suggests,

---

26 Cholij, 'Music in Eighteenth-Century London Shakespeare Productions', 42.
27 Francis Gentleman, *The Dramatic Censor; or Critical Companion*, 2 vols (London, 1770), I.282.

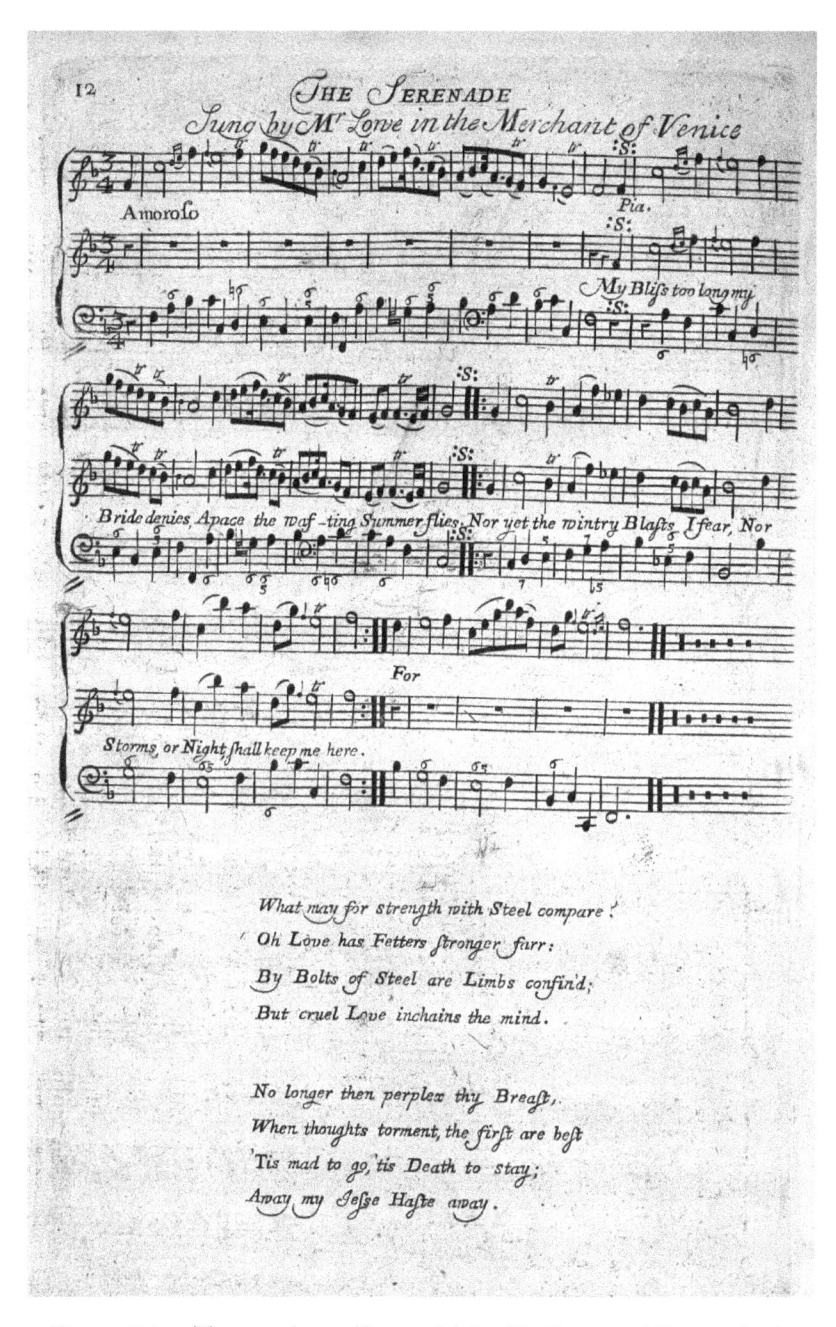

Figure 7.1: Thomas Arne, 'Serenade', in *The Songs and Duetto, in the Blind Beggar of Bethnal Green ... with the Favourite Songs Sung by Mr Lowe in the Merchant of Venice* (London, 1740). © The British Library Board (Music Collections G.320.f).

too, that beyond merely offering musical entertainment to an audience who had grown to expect it, theatrical song contributed to the impact of drama in meaningful ways.

Arne's second song has a similarly complicated relationship between plot, character, and audience, although in rather a different way (Figure 7.2). This song was inserted at the beginning of Act 5 during the scene in which Lorenzo and Jessica admire the shining moon and engage in a playful battle of wits—'out-nighting' each other, as Jessica has it—with variations on the phrase 'In Such a Night'.[28] Shakespeare's scene calls for music as Lorenzo delivers his speech 'How sweet the moonlight sleeps upon this bank/Here will we sit and let the sounds of music/Creep in our ears'. Arne abandoned the instrumental music called for in Shakespeare's text in favour of a song sung by Lorenzo, with the following lyrics:

> To keep my Gentle Jesse
> What Labour would seem hard
> Each toilsome Task how easy
> Her love the sweet reward.
> The bee thus uncomplaining
> Esteems no Toil severe
> The sweet reward obtaining
> Of Honey all the year.

It is a song that, through his discussion of music, Shakespeare partially authorizes, while Arne's symphonic setting, which includes several orchestral interjections, marks this out as a musical set piece; it is a diegetically justifiable song that goes beyond diegesis to become an occasion for concert performance.

Ostensibly, in the context of the play this song is performed by Lorenzo to woo Jessica, as he explains that any amount of labour would be a pleasure if he gets the reward of her love. But as soon as the orchestra strikes up, the audience would understand that Lorenzo is simultaneously stepping outside of the world of the play and performing also for them. They are thus being wooed by Lorenzo, on behalf of Arne and the production as a whole, inviting them to think metatheatrically about the labour of acting, and inviting them to grant the 'sweet reward' of their approbation, signalled through applause. The point to emphasize here, though, is that Lorenzo's performance is neither exclusively for Jessica, nor exclusively for the audience, but *both simultaneously*, and it is part of the ontology of eighteenth-century playgoing—indeed,

---

28 William Shakespeare, *The Merchant of Venice*, in Stanley Wells and Gary Taylor (ed.), *The Complete Works* (Oxford: Oxford University Press, 1988), 5.1.23.

Figure 7.2: Thomas Arne, 'To Keep my Gentle Jesse', *The Songs and Duetto, in the Blind Beggar of Bethnal Green ... with the Favourite Songs Sung by Mr Lowe in the Merchant of Venice* (London, 1740). © The British Library Board (Music Collections G.320.f).

probably all playgoing—that audience members are able to recognize themselves as both witnesses to and recipients of performance. Affectively, this means that while Lorenzo performs this song audiences are aligned with Jessica, the diegetic audience, while forging a close relationship with Lorenzo who attempts to woo them through his singing, which effectively puts them in competition with Jessica for Lorenzo's affection. This tension between alignment and alienation with Jessica is underscored in contemporary editions of *The Merchant of Venice*, which places Jessica's line 'I'm never merry, when I hear sweet music' directly after Lorenzo's song. This line might, of course, be said in any number of ways (sighingly, admiringly, playfully, sarcastically), but however it is played it offers a challenge to the audience's assumed applause for Lorenzo's star turn, emphasizing the difference between diegetic and non-diegetic receptions of theatrical song.

There is one other notable feature of the music for Macklin's *Merchant*, which is, I think, revealing of the affective functions of song in the eighteenth century: and that is the *lack* of a song for Portia, played by Catherine 'Kitty' Clive, widely regarded as one of the best singers on the eighteenth-century stage.[29] Clive enjoyed a particularly fruitful relationship with Thomas Arne, who set several songs for her, including two in the other Shakespearean revivals of the 1740–41 Drury Lane season. In both cases, the songs were interpolated from elsewhere. The first was in *As You Like It*, in which Clive played Celia for whom Arne wrote 'When Daisies pied' (known as 'The Cuckoo Song'), which was taken from *Love's Labour's Lost*, presumably in order to give Clive a song to perform, although it remained standard in productions of *As You Like It* until the nineteenth century. The second was for *Twelfth Night*, in which Clive played Olivia, and for which Arne borrowed the song 'Tell me where is Fancy Bred' from Act 3 Scene 2 of *The Merchant of Venice*, sung by an anonymous singer as Bassanio studies the caskets before choosing the one that is revealed to contain Portia's portrait.[30] It is particularly surprising, then, that Clive had no songs as Portia in the 1741 *The Merchant of Venice*—there would certainly have been nothing preventing Clive from singing 'Tell me where is Fancy Bred' in both *Twelfth Night* and *The Merchant of Venice*. We might, then, suggest that a singing Portia would have been incommensurate with Macklin's conception of the play as a whole, which sought to play down the role of Portia (which Clive played unapologetically for laughs) in order to play up

---

29 For a discussion of Clive, see Felicity Nussbaum, *Rival Queens: Actresses, Performance at the Eighteenth-Century British Theater* (Philadelphia: University of Pennsylvania Press 2010), 151–88.

30 Cunningham, 'Reception and Re-Use of Thomas Arne's Shakespeare Songs', 138–39.

the menace of Macklin's Shylock.[31] While songs might be viewed in some ways as incongruously independent of the plays into which they interpolated in the eighteenth-century theatre, they were not simply part of a miscellaneous jumble, but had an important role in determining the meanings and emphases of the plays in which they appeared. It is song's ability to inform an audience's response to a play, to transcend the moment of the drama, and to take on a life independent of the theatre, that a consideration of the songs that Macklin included in the plays he wrote can help inform.

Macklin's songs

As my discussion of Arne's contribution to Macklin's greatest stage success suggests, music and song played an important role in mediating between actors, characters, and audience members on the eighteenth-century stage. Indeed, song was part of the very texture of the theatrical experience, a point that Macklin understood well and incorporated into the fabric of the plays he wrote. The full extent to which Macklin used song is difficult to ascertain as we are reliant on the Larpent manuscripts for the texts to many of his plays. Frequently the words for songs were not submitted to the censor, with stage directions such as 'singing and dancing the Harlequin' (as in *The Covent Garden Theatre; or, Pasquin Turn'd Drawcansir*) making clear that songs were present, but without indicating the precise nature of the song. Even the plays for which Macklin oversaw authorized printed editions can be imprecise about the nature of the music, with stage directions such as 'Enter Lady Rodolpha, singing a music paper in her hand' providing testimony that song was part of the theatrical experience, but giving little away about the songs that were performed.[32] What is clear, however, is that song frequently had important resonances for the plays as a whole, such as in *The True Born Irishman*, where Pat Fitzmungrel enters 'drunk and singing' in a moment which plays off the stereotypes of Irishness as they had been constructed on the stage.[33] The association of song with drunkenness is a conspicuous feature too of *The Man of The World*, first performed in Covent Garden in May 1781, in which Lord Lumbercourt (in the words of the stage directions of the 1793 edition) 'sings without flushed by wine'. Unlike in *The True Born*

---

31 On Macklin's influence as a theatre or stage manager, see Matthew Kinservik's chapter in this volume.
32 Charles Macklin, *The Man of The World, A Comedy* (London, 1793), 48.
33 Charles Macklin, *The True Born Irishman; or, Irish Fine Lady, A Comedy of Two Acts* (Dublin, 1783), 37.

Irishman, though, this is not generic drunken singing. The words to the song are specified in the 1793 printing as 'What have we with day to do? ... Sons of Care 'twas made for you'. This song was a well-known drinking song, better known as 'By the Gaily Circling Glass', which was first written for a stage adaptation of John Milton's masque *Comus*, by John Dalton, with music once again by Thomas Arne. Dalton's adaptation of Milton's poem had been a staple of theatre for much of the eighteenth century, with a notable performance in 1750 in which Garrick spoke a prologue written by Samuel Johnson. The song 'The Gaily Circling Glass', however, experienced a considerable popularity independent of the play, being frequently performed in the convivial societies that flourished in the second half of the eighteenth century, and reaching its apex in the 1780s. As a song it had all the traits valued by convivial clubs including the standard emphasis on present enjoyment because life is short and the world outside the social circle is full of care:

> By the Gaily Circling Glass
> We can see how minutes pass;
> By the hollow cask are told,
> How the waning night grows old,
> How the waning night grows old.
> Soon, too soon, the busy day
> Drives us from our sport and play;
> What have we with day to do?
> Sons of care, 'twas made for you,
> Sons of care, 'twas made for you.

It was a song that was remained popular throughout the century and was included in dozens of convivial songbooks that were published in large quantities from the 1770s until the end of the eighteenth century, such as *The Vocal Union* (London, 1772), *The Syren* (London, 1770), *An Anacreontic Garland, The Aviary, or Magazine of British Melody* (London, 1750), *The Bacchanalian Magazine and Cyprian Enchantress* (London, 1793), *The Bacchanalian Songster* (Winchester, 1783). The tune was also used for other Anacreontic songs, such as 'The Bacchanalian Crew' printed in *The Bacchanalian Magazine* (London, 1793). Macklin's use of the song in the *Man of the World* is clearly intended to signal Lord Lumbercourt's participation in the convivial culture of late-night revelry that was a feature of the London social scene of the late eighteenth century, in which many of his male audience members would have participated. The song then suggests a shared repertoire of song and forges a continuity between audience and stage. It was, in a sense, a song that belonged to the audience, or at least certain male members of the audience, the pleasure of which would have been the recognition of seeing one of *their* songs performed in the play. At the same time, the reframing of the song through stage representation could offer a new perspective on the song itself as these same audience members recognize their own convivial behaviour held up to scrutiny by the play. In this sense one could see the performance of the song as a criticism of the boorish masculine behaviour of some of the audience members, albeit a criticism likely to be received as light-hearted fun-poking, however seriously it was intended—and there probably was a serious intention behind these criticisms. Elsewhere in this volume, David O'Shaughnessy argues for the consistency of the intellectual project of social reform that can be found throughout Macklin's plays, even in the notably playful and bawdy content that got expunged by the censor. We might extend this intellectual project to include Macklin's Coffeehouse, as discussed by Markman Ellis and Helen Burke, which could be viewed as an attempt to reform the boorish conviviality associated with the Covent Garden area into something more refined, and indeed improving. It seems likely then that Macklin had serious intentions to hold a satirical mirror up to his own audience's value-systems, but, as Macklin's career amply demonstrated, with the 1772 Macbeth riots being only the most obvious example, an author's intentions could not determine an audience's response.[34] The inclusion of 'The Gaily Circling Glass' in *The Man of The World* crystallizes the process of meaning-making as it is forged between character, audience, and author: for Lumbercourt, the song is an opportunity to forge a connection with the audience members who know the song, for the audience, it is an opportunity to hear a familiar song featured on the public stage, for Macklin it is an opportunity for social critique. The meaning of the song in the context of the play is a result of the interplay of these various motivations and impulses.

In *Love à La Mode*, the connection between singing and conviviality takes a more indirect path, but an interesting one all the same. Here *Sir Callaghan O'Brallaghan* sings 'You never did hear of an Irishman's fear' sung to what the printed version calls 'An Old Irish Tune'. While the tune isn't specified in the printed version of the play, the song appears in *The Irish Musical Repository* of 1808 set to 'Ballinamona Ora'—a tune that has since become known as a 'traditional' Irish jig (Figure 7.3a–c).[35] Gaps in the print archives prevent us from saying with any certainty whether this was the tune that was used in the original production, but if we rely less on archives for proof and more on the

---

34 For a discussion of Macklin's *Macbeth*, see Matthew J. Kinservik, 'A Sinister *Macbeth*: The Macklin Production of 1773', *Harvard Library Bulletin* 6.1 (1995), 51–76 and Kristina Straub, 'The Newspaper "Trial" of Charles Macklin's *Macbeth* and the Theatre as Juridical Public Sphere', *Eighteenth-Century Fiction* 27.3–4 (2015), 395–418.

35 *The Irish Musical Repository: A Choice Selection of Esteemed Irish Songs Adapted for the Voice, Violin, and German Flute* (London, 1808), 119–21.

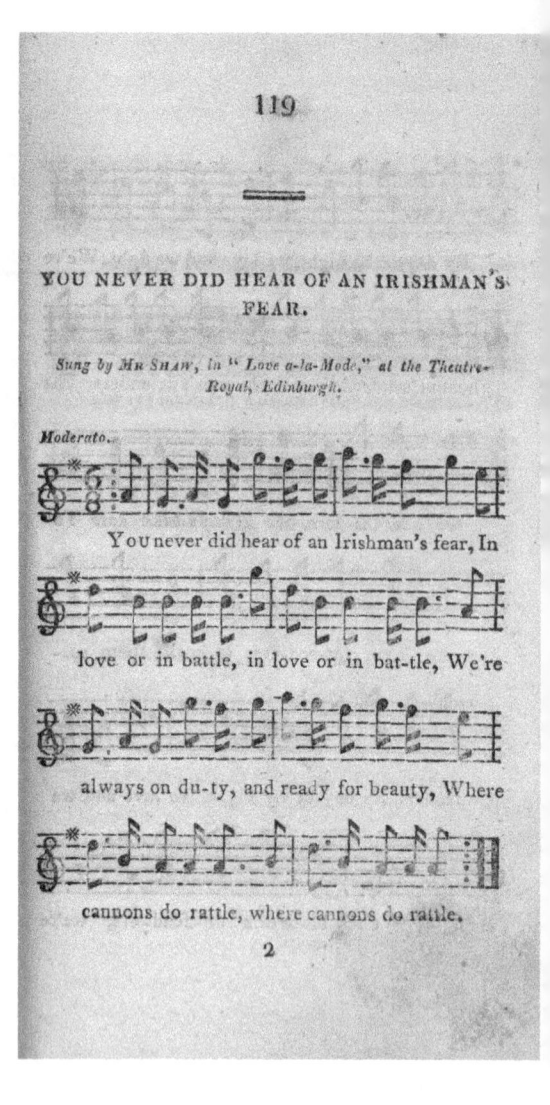

Figure 7.3a–c: 'You Never Did Hear of an Irishman's Fear', *Crosby's Irish Musical Repository* (London, 1813), 119–21. Reproduced from the original held by the Department of Special Collections of the Hesburgh Libraries of the University of Notre Dame, Indiana.

notion of 'repertoire', as conceived by Diana Taylor, we might at least claim with some authority that this was a tune that had an association with the song. The point is of interest because of other places that the same tune appears in the period, including, for example, being used as the tune for two of Captain Morris's celebrated political satires. The first, 'The Treaty of Commerce', began: 'Troth, Mr John Bull, y'are a pretty milch cow/What do you think of us Volunteers now?' The second was a song printed under the title, 'A New Song', with the opening lines: 'Sure Master John Bull, I Shan't Know Till I'm Dead/ Where the devil you're driving at Arse over head'. Both of these songs, dating from the mid-1780s, are told from the perspective of an Irishman who looks askance at English politics. It is impossible to say with certainty why Morris chose this particular tune for his satires, but given the popularity of Macklin's *Love à la Mode* and the association of the Irish soldier Sir Callaghan O'Brallaghan getting the better of his counterparts (including an Englishman), it is not hard to imagine that Macklin's play influenced the decision of tune.[36]

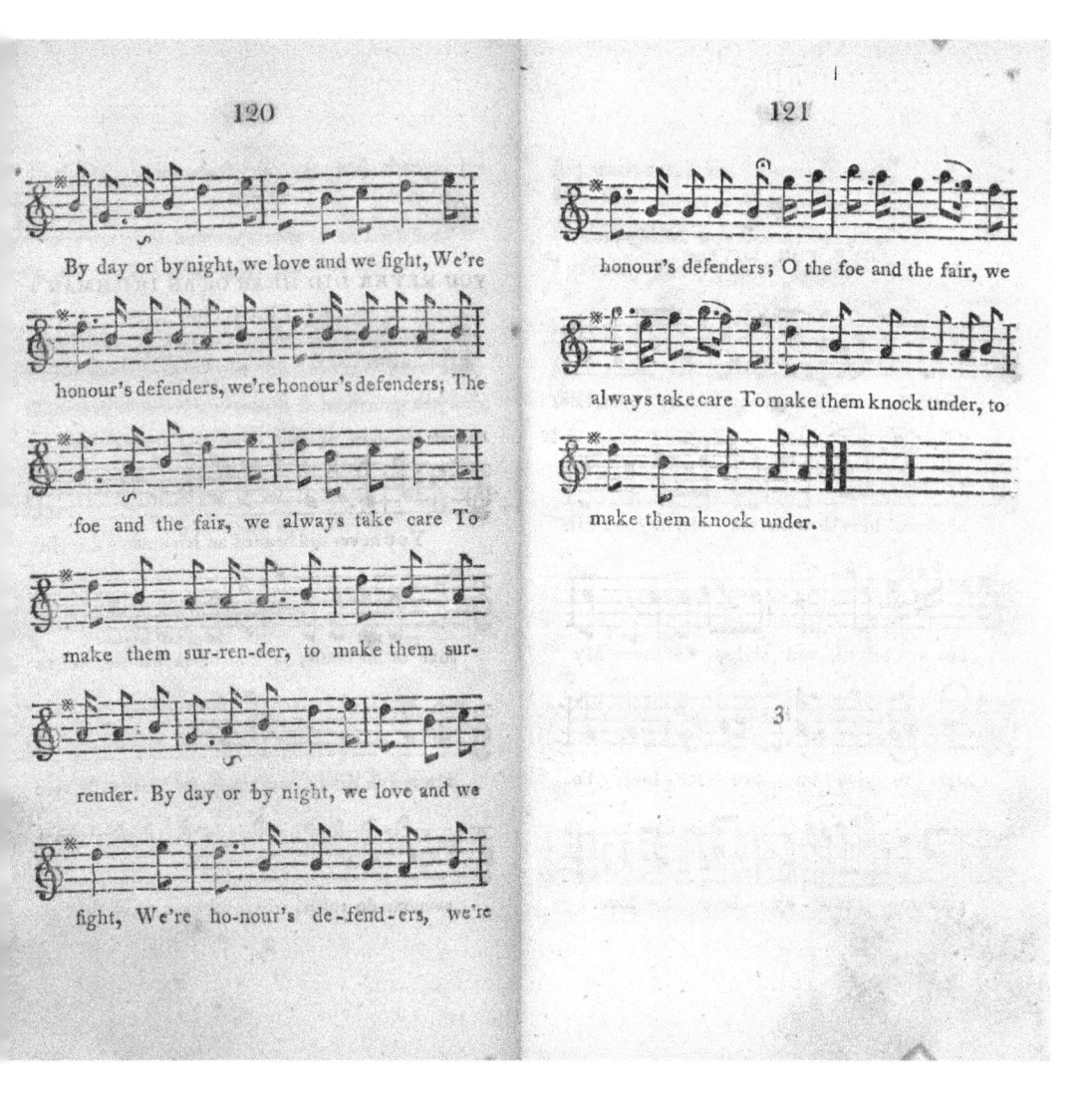

The same tune was used by Robert Burns for his song 'A Lass Wi' A Tocher', which praises the superiority of wealth over beauty ('Tocher'

---

36 For more on Morris, see Ian Newman, *The Romantic Tavern: Literature and Conviviality in the Age of Revolution* (Cambridge: Cambridge University Press, 2019), 113–48.

being a dialect word meaning dowry or marriage portion). 'A Lass Wi' A Tocher', originally printed with the title, "Awa' Wi' Your Witchcraft O' Beauty's Alarms', was one of the songs Burns wrote before his death in 1796 for George Thomson's *Select Collection of Original Scottish Airs*, upon which Burns's posthumous reputation chiefly rests.[37] Burns's use of an 'Irish tune' for Thomson's collection of ostensibly Scottish songs is suggestive of an assumed continuity between Irish and Scottish national airs, but it is suggestive too of the relationship between the use of dialect in song and in the theatre. If Burns's use of 'Ballinamona Ora' was influenced by Macklin's use of the same tune in *Love à la Mode* (a point that cannot be directly proven but—given Burns's enthusiasm for the theatre—is certainly feasible), it would be possible to read 'A Lass Wi' A Tocher' as a response to Sir Archy Macsarcasm, whose Scottish dialect comically ridicules Scottish masculine egotism.[38] In Macklin's piece, Sir Archy plays the amorous lover until he believes Charlotte's fortunes have been lost, at which point he quickly ends the connection so that he does not bring disgrace upon his family. Rather than offering a corrective to Sir Archy's misplaced pride, Burns's song plays into the role of the lover whose motivations are financial but translates them from the urban scene of the Covent Garden theatre to rural Scotland ('O gi'e me a lass that has acres o' charms,/O gi'e me the lass with the weel stockit farms'). In doing so, Burns uses a dialect form that authenticates the necessity of economic considerations as an admirably honest attitude, suggesting that the play's criticism of Sir Archy's mercenary nature, in false stage dialect, is all very well and good in the fabricated world of the London play, but is an affront to 'authentically' Scottish manhood, which has to prioritize financial matters over questions of beauty—that fades anyway.

The connection between Macklin's play, Captain Morris's political satire, and Robert Burns's song, which all use the same tune, are admittedly tenuous. As I have suggested, print archives cannot adequately forge the links between these disparate uses of the same tune, even when thematically they circle around similar concerns. I would argue that in the case of studying song history, a history which is dependent on ephemeral performance, speculation is necessary. Indeed, song history as a form of performance history exposes the

---

37 George Thomson (ed.), *A Select Collection of Original Scottish Airs for the Voice with Introductory and Concluding Symphonies & Accompaniments for the Piano Forte, Violin & Violoncello*, 4 vols (Edinburgh, 1793–1802), II.100.

38 For Burns's enthusiasm for the theatre, see, for example, his letters to William Nicol, dated 9 February 1790; to Louisa Fontaenelle, [22] November 1792; to Robert Gartmore Graham, 5 January 1793; and to William Robertson, 3 December 1793. *The Letters of Robert Burns*, ed. J. De Lancey Ferguson and G. Ross Roy, 2nd edn, 2 vols (Oxford: Oxford University Press, 1985), II.12, 160, 173, 264.

limitations of depending on print archives for 'historically verifiable' argument. If we depend only on what can be recreated by the concrete documentation of bureaucratic regimes it prevents investigation into probable, but not provable, scenarios. This is why Taylor's concept of the 'repertoire' is so helpful.

But I want to conclude by considering the other song in Macklin's *Love à la Mode*, the pathways of which are more verifiable. The song is entitled, 'Let Other Men Sing of their Goddesses Bright', sung once again by Sir Callaghan O'Brallaghan, and it occupies a particularly prominent position in the play, forming one of the turning points in the affections of the central couple, Charlotte and Callaghan. At the beginning of the play, Callaghan has all the characteristics of the stereotypical stage Irishman and seems as much of a buffoon as the other comic characters. Gradually throughout the play, however, Callaghan reveals his motivations in wooing Charlotte to be purer than the other characters, and when it is erroneously revealed that she does not have a fortune, he remains committed to winning Charlotte's hand. A key moment in this development is the scene in which Callaghan sings 'Let Other Men Sing of their Goddesses Bright', a song which has been frequently mentioned by Sir Archy Macsarcasm as a piece of absurdity and which will provide much amusement. 'Noo yee shall hear sic a song as has nair been penn'd sin the time they first clepp'd the wings and tails of the wild Irish', Sir Archy gleefully anticipates, before hiding with Squire Groom to overhear and ridicule Callaghan's attempt at wooing.[39] On stage, Callaghan sings to Charlotte a song that emphasizes how bad he is at the rhetorical manoeuvres expected of the wooer, but declaring nevertheless the strength of his feeling:

> Let other men sing of their goddesses bright,
> That darken the day and enlighten the night;
> I sing of a woman—but such flesh and blood,
> A touch of her finger would do your heart good.
>   With my fal, lal, lal, &c.
>
> Ten times in each day to my charmer I come,
> To tell her my passion, but can't, I'm struck dumb;
> For cupid he seizes my heart by surprise,
> And my tongue falls asleep at the sight of her eyes.
>
> Her little dog Pompey's my rival I seem
> She kisses, and hugs him, but frowns upon me:
> The, pr'ytee, dear Charlotte, abuse not your charms,
> Instead of a lapdog, take me to your arms.[40]

---

39 Charles Macklin, *Love à La Mode, a Farce* (London, 1793), 33.
40 Macklin, *Love à La Mode, a Farce*, 33–34.

After the song has concluded, Squire Groom and Sir Archy 'steal off' with very little comment, leaving Charlotte to say, 'Well, Sir Callaghan, your poetry is excellent, nothing can surpass it but your singing'. For Susan Cannon Harris, the song demonstrates that Callaghan's 'raw sexual energy has been domesticated by love', though this reading of the scene depends on a recognition that Macklin's play was an adaptation of Thomas Sheridan's *The Brave Irishman*, which may or may not have been uppermost in audience members' minds.[41] Certainly, in the recent productions of *Love à la Mode* directed by Colm Summers, discussed elsewhere in this volume, Callaghan's 'raw sexual energy' was nowhere palpable prior to the song. The song became the pivotal moment in the courtship, as Callaghan transitioned from an impotent buffoon to the strongest contender for Charlotte's hand. These recent productions made Callaghan an unfortunate understudy (filling in, allegedly, for 'Charlie McLaughlin') who was constantly in the wrong place at the wrong time, doing the wrong thing, until he skilfully sang this song, impressing all present, including Charlotte herself, Sir Archy and Squire Groom (who slink off with much consternation), and—crucially— the audience, who were for the first time impressed by the actor playing Callaghan. Clearly, whether in the Felicity productions (shown in colour plates 1–6 in this volume) or Macklin's own time, the success of the farce depends a great deal on songs' capacity to transcend the business of farce and to communicate a strength of feeling both to Charlotte and to the audience.

The tune for the song, once again, was recorded in *The Irish Musical Repository* of 1808 (Figure 7.4a–c).[42] No earlier instances of the tune have yet been recorded, suggesting that it may well have been written for the play—by Macklin or someone else. But it continues to have a significant performance history outside the play, thanks largely to the arrangement made by Ludwig van Beethoven for the first volume of George Thomson's *Select Collection of Original Irish Airs* (1814), where it appeared to new words written by a Mr T. Toms, with the title, 'Since Greybeards Inform us that Youth Will Decay'. Thomson's collection was an attempt to capitalize on the popularity of 'national airs', a moment which coincided with a boom in domestic music-making brought about by the availability of affordable fortepianos. Thomson had already published some Irish songs in his collection of Scottish Airs, as discussed above, but now he turned his attention to Irish Song, and

---

41 Susan Cannon Harris, 'Mixed Marriage: Sheridan, Macklin, and the Hybrid Audience', in Cordner and Holland, *Players, Playwrights, Playhouses*, 207. For an alternative discussion of the scene, see Michael Ragussis, 'Jews and Other "Outlandish Englishmen": Ethnic Performance and the Invention of British Identity under the Georges', *Critical Inquiry* 26.4 (2000), 787.

42 *The Irish Musical Repository*, 129–31.

he originally commissioned Joseph Haydn to arrange the melodies with words contributed by well-known poets such as Joanna Baillie, Byron, Helen Maria Williams, and Walter Scott. As Thomson explained in the preface to the edition, Haydn had already 'harmonized' (Thomson's term) a number of Scottish and Welsh melodies for Thomson's earlier collections, but his health was declining and many delays led Thomson to ask Beethoven instead. (In the meantime, Thomson's friend and collaborator Robert Burns died, which prompted Thomson to approach Thomas Moore to write words to the Irish Melodies he'd collected; Moore refused, deciding instead to work on a similar project for William and James Powers, which ultimately, much to Thomson's irritation, was published before Thomson's effort, and achieved considerable commercial success.[43])

Much could be said about this extraordinary conjunction of Scottish publisher, Irish song, and Austrian and German composers in the development of what is confusingly called 'national song', but, for the current purposes, what matters is the way Macklin's song 'Let Other Men Sing of their Goddesses Bright' becomes entangled in the development of national musical traditions. In the first instance, it makes explicit something that scholars have long known about 'traditional song'—that we can date with some precision the idea of national song to the end of the eighteenth century when it was self-consciously constructed by enterprising musical enthusiasts for commercial ends. It suggests, too, the intimate proximity of what we understand as 'classical' and 'popular' music. But the presence of Macklin's song at the heart of this nexus also helps us understand several important ideas about theatrical song.

Most obviously, it suggests the ease with which song from the theatre passed into popular musical traditions. More precisely, the presence of Macklin's song in Beethoven's canon helps us understand the *kinds* of song that crossed over and enjoyed a vigorous afterlife in the world outside the theatre. Clearly, the fact this was a song that was sung by an Irish character in a play that dealt with ethnic representation was important to Thomson's decision to send it to Beethoven: the song's 'Irishness'—despite being fabricated in London for an urban theatregoing audience—was its chief mark of distinction for Thomson.

---

43 For discussions of Thomson's collections of National Song, see Cecil Hopkinson and C.B. Oldman, 'Thomson's Collection of National Song, with Special Reference to the Contributions of Haydn and Beethoven', *Edinburgh Bibliographical Society Transactions* 2.1 (1938–1945), 1–64; C.B. Oldman, 'Beethoven's Variations on National Themes: Their Composition and First Publication', *Music Review* 12 (1951), 45–51; and, especially, Kirsteen McCue's introduction to *The Oxford Edition of the Works of Robert Burns*, vol. 4, *Robert Burns's Songs for George Thomson*, ed. Kirsteen McCue (Oxford: Oxford University Press, 2021), xxv–xcvi.

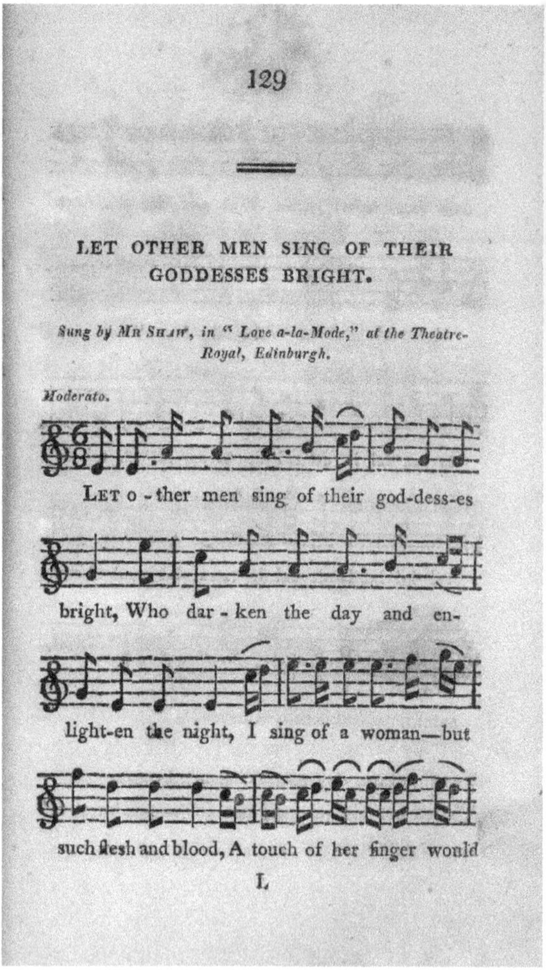

Figure 7.4a–c: 'Let Other Men Sing of their Goddesses Bright', *Crosby's Irish Musical Repository* (London, 1813), 129–31. Reproduced from the original held by the Department of Special Collections of the Hesburgh Libraries of the University of Notre Dame, Indiana.

But I would want to suggest too, albeit more speculatively, that its pivotal role in the plot of the play was also a significant feature of its capacity to move beyond the theatre. As I have suggested, the song occupies a critical moment in the development of relations between Charlotte and Callaghan, which is simultaneously a pivotal moment in the affective relationship between *the audience* and Callaghan, who from this moment on emerges as the only viable candidate for Charlotte's hand. One might argue that it does not especially matter if the song is performed with elegant beauty (as it was by Fionn Foley in the Felicity production, shown singing in plate 4 of this volume) or if it is played for laughs (as the 'Fal lal lal' chorus of Macklin's published script strongly suggests). What matters is that for a moment the action of the play is suspended and characters and audience alike become spectators together of

130

do your heart good. Wid my far ral lal lal tal de ta ral lal la, Wid my ta ral lal la de ral de ta ral lal la, tal de ral lal lal la de ral de ta ral lal la, And my smallilow, bubberoo, ditheroo, whack!

Ten times in a day to my charmer I come,
To tell her my passion, but can't——I'm struck dumb;

131

For Cupid so seizes my heart by surprise,
That my tongue falls asleep at the sight of her eyes.
 Wid my far ral lal, &c.

Her little dog Pompey's my rival, I see;
She kisses and hugs him, but frowns upon me:
Then pr'ythee, dear Charlotte, think more of your charms;
Instead of your lap-dog, take me to your arms.
 Wid my far ral lal, &c.

2.

this critical moment of courtship. The message of the song is that Callaghan cannot articulate the powerful feelings expected of the lover, but this does not mean he feels any less; it is a song that deals with the power of affect over hollow eloquence. This is an idea peculiarly well-suited to the strengths of song with relatively simple words combined with a tune that can carry the burden of communicating emotion. It is the kind of song that resonates affectively with a theatre audience.

The dramatic functions that songs possess contribute to the possibility of a song having an independent existence outside of the theatre. The emotional bonds that the song forges, between the characters on stage and between the characters and the audience, enables the possibility of the song's movement out of the theatrical space into the wider culture. To adapt

Cunningham's formulation, then, eighteenth-century theatrical songs provide an entertainment within and without the entertainment. What gets lost in these transactions, however, is the question of authorship, as the tunes become 'traditional' and so untethered from the words and productions which made them popular. As so often with Macklin, his achievements continue to have lasting legacies, even as we forget that it was Macklin, with his resonant, if not beautiful, voice, who initiated them.

8

Ethnic Jokes and Polite Language
Soft Othering and Macklin's British Comedies

Michael Brown

THE PLAYS OF CHARLES MACKLIN embody an interpretive puzzle; one that concerns a set of conflicting narratives historians and critics tell about the eighteenth century. At its simplest, the puzzle circles around the question of why people laugh. In that, this essay revisits the classic cultural history essay published by Robert Darnton in 1984, 'The Great Cat Massacre'.[1] Therein, Darnton deployed a novel set of methodological tools to unpick and interpret a strange sequence of events in a French print house, an approach primarily inspired by Clifford Geertz.[2] Involving an act of revenge against the master's wife—herself deemed haughty and unresponsive to her social responsibilities towards the workmen on the floor—the comedy came to the fore when the killing of her pet cat was re-enacted as a piece of impromptu theatre by one of the apprentices.[3] Darnton then posed the central question to which this essay also refers: what is so funny?

In thinking about the dramatic comedies of the Irish playwright and actor Charles Macklin, however, the moral issues are not those of animal cruelty

---

1 Robert Darnton, 'Workers Revolt: The Great Cat Massacre of the Rue Saint Séverin', in *The Great Cat Massacre and Other Episodes in French Cultural History* (New York: Basic Books, 1984), 75–106.
2 Clifford Geertz, *The Interpretation of Cultures* (London: Fontana, 2010).
3 This reading has been the subject of extensive criticism. See, for instance, Roger Chartier, 'Texts, Symbols and Frenchness', *Journal of Modern History* 57.4 (1985), 682–95; Dominick LaCapra, 'Darnton, Chartier and the Great Symbol Massacre', *Journal of Modern History* 60.1 (1988), 95–112; Harold Mah, 'Suppressing the Text: The Metaphysics of Ethnographic History in Darnton's Great Cat Massacre', *History Workshop* 31.1 (1991), 1–20.

and social inequality but of racial prejudice and social recognition. Yet his work still raises the question of the moral weight of comedy: what is it that makes his comedy funny? And why did audiences laugh at the comedy of ethnic prejudice? It begs the question as to how xenophobic comedy works and whether it is wholly, and solely, aggressive in its nature? Who is its audience and against whom is the humour aimed? And are their variations of texture, tonality, and coloration? What are we to make of the ethnic comedy of the eighteenth century, and what does it tell us about polite taste and refined manners in the period that such comedy was successfully deployed on the London stage?

If this set of issues is not problematic enough, Macklin poses a further problem in the interpretive puzzle alluded to above. This involves the difficulty that Macklin's comedies do not subscribe to the preordained narrative of racial stereotyping and nation-building that underpins the literature around Britishness and the creation of the British Enlightenment's imperium. This argues for a thickening of national identity in the last decades of the century and a consequent reification of the language, manner, and social performances of the south of England as the apogee of that identity. This process of solidification was prompted by the trauma of the loss of the American Colonies in the 1770s but was characterized by the continued global military conflicts with France and the twinning of economic improvement with a sense of a cultural mission to spread behavioural norms that accorded with British sensibilities. If this trajectory were to be followed, Macklin's comedy would have also thickened in its prejudice and xenophobia, accenting the English statecraft that underpinned the imperial project. Yet, as the following account suggests, his barbs if anything were less pointed towards certain castes of outsiders, the polemical tone concerning ethnic identity was increasingly relaxed and reduced. The humour Macklin deployed in the later phases of his authorial career thus poses questions about how we read the relationship between comedy and identity formation, between jokes and politics. Humour in his case seemingly trumps politics, recasting questions about when and in what way British nation-building occurred and the shape it took. What is offered then is a complicating case study in the comedy of nationalisms.

Playing the Jew

On its surface Charles Macklin made his acting career from racist typecasting. His breakthrough role came in the season of 1740–41, when he took to the stage as Shylock in Shakespeare's *The Merchant of Venice*. His turn was a triumph; his rendering of the merchant was, in John Gross's phrase, 'unyieldingly malignant'.[4] Having seen a performance in 1775, the German scientist George Lichtenberg recorded this perceptive account:

> Picture to yourself a rather stout man, with a coarse sallow face, a nose by no means lacking in any of the three dimensions, a long double chin; as for his mouth, nature's knife seems to have slipped when she carved it and slit him open on one side all the way to the ear. He wears a long black gown, long wide trousers and a red three-cornered hat [...] The first words he utters when he comes on are spoken slowly and deliberately. 'Three thousand ducats' the two *th* sounds and the two *s* sounds, especially the *s* after the *t*, which Macklin lisps voluptuously, as though he were savouring the ducats and all that they can buy—these sounds make an impression that nothing can efface.[5]

In his physical appearance, his attire, and his enunciation Macklin drew on the tropes of anti-Semitic caricature to amplify his performance. He rejected the tradition of playing Shylock for easy laughs; instead, he made the merchant a focus for animus that was fuelled by the presence of Jewish traders on the London stock exchange and rumours of their pernicious influence. William Appleton documents that Macklin even went to the Exchange and associated coffeehouses to converse with and study with London Jews in preparation for the part.[6] As Emily Anderson observes, he 'played off negative historical conceptions of Jewishness to depict Shylock as a terrifying villain'. It was a performance embedded in racial hatred, which, as Anderson goes on to note, most 'likely did much to encourage anti-Semitic attitudes among its audience'.[7]

It was a distaste for others that can be read as encompassing Macklin's career as a dramatist as well as that as an actor. Macklin, an Irish immigrant, was one of many 'outlandish Englishmen'; ethnic interlopers entangled in the weave of intra-British rivalries.[8] He was actively moving away from an Irish origin—anglicizing his name as well as converting to Anglicanism—at the same time as he was crafting a sneering Scotophobia that informed his work as a playwright.[9] In this, Macklin was both characteristic of

---

4 John Gross, *Shylock: A Legend and its Legacy* (London: Simon & Schuster, 1992), 112.
5 Quoted in Gross, *Shylock*, 113–14.
6 *Appleton*, 46.
7 Emily Hodgson Anderson, 'Celebrity Shylock', *PMLA* 126.4 (2011), 941.
8 'Outlandish Englishmen' comes from Macklin's *Love à la Mode*. The term is explored in Michael Ragussis, 'Jews and Other "Outlandish Englishmen": Ethnic Performance and the Invention of British Identity under the Georges', *Critical Inquiry* 26.4 (2000), 785.
9 Macklin's antagonistic view of the Scottish was also housed within the discourse of Irish Patriotism in the 1770s. See Martyn J. Powell, 'Scottophobia versus Jacobitism: Political Radicalism and the Press in Late Eighteenth-Century Ireland', in John Kirk, Michael Brown, and Andrew Noble (eds), *Cultures of Radicalism in Britain and Ireland* (London: Routledge, 2016), 49–62.

and a central creative force in the shaping of the 'Stage Scot' and 'Stage Irish' personas, which informed the appearance of the British nationals in the London theatre scene in the latter half of the eighteenth century.[10] As Joep Leerssen has extensively documented, the Stage Irishman was commonly put to comedic use in the period, with his drunkenness and his inherent violence subsumed under his social incompetence, his rudeness, and his vaunting ambition.[11] This Irish adventurer was a comedic foil to the sullen, grasping, and stingy Scot, and both stood in turn against the proud antiquarian Welshman, whose sole ambition seemed to be to connect his lineage with the sons of Noah, and to declare himself a 'True Briton'. As a cohort, these staged national identities allowed the English audience to laugh at the threat they posed to their economic, political, and social interest. They reinterpreted the menace of British interlopers by remarking on how the politics of imitation always degraded the imitator to the same extent as it flattered those being imitated. In that, it reassured the English middling sort of the efficacy, virtue, and desirability of the polite commercial society of London and its surrounds.

The plays are in fact shot through with the typical concerns of the middling sort who patronized the pit: marriage, inheritance, social respectability. These concerns were signalled in the titles of the plays to be considered here: *Love à la Mode* (1759), with its blend of emotional commitments and transient fashions; *The True Born Irishman* (1767), with its declaration of national pride and concern with authenticity; and *The Man of the World* (1781), with its commitment to masculine virtue and cosmopolitan sophistication. These plays are thematically linked, with the success of *Love à la Mode* probably inspiring Macklin to project a sequence of four 'multi-ethnic spectacles'—a term which Michael Ragussis has coined to indicate 'a new kind of popular subgenre [...] in which several different ethnic figures shared the stage at the same time [...] typically fused onto the traditional comedic marriage plot'.[12] As Macklin told James Boswell, the ambition was to script 'a trueborn Scotsman, a trueborn Englishman, a trueborn Irishman and a trueborn Welshman' in an extended survey of the make-up of the United Kingdom's national persona.[13] The Scottish drama was first performed in Dublin in 1764 before receiving extended revisions and re-emerging as *Man*

---

10 For Macklin's development of a revisionist stage Irish persona, see Paul Goring, '"John Bull, pit, box and gallery said No!": Charles Macklin and the Limits of Ethnic Representation on the Eighteenth-Century London Stage', *Representations* 79.1 (2002), 67–71.
11 Joep Leerssen, *Mere Irish and Fíor-Ghael* (Cork: Cork University Press, 1997), 85–168.
12 Ragussis, 'Jews and Other "Outlandish Englishmen"', 778.
13 *Appleton*, 207–8.

of the World for its London debut seventeen years later.[14] The Irish text duly followed, although, despite revisions (including the title being reworked as *The Irish Fine Lady*) aimed at accommodating itself to an English audience, it closed after a sole performance on 28 November 1767.[15] The difficulties of staging these works and their mixed reception in London ensured Macklin abandoned the project before he completed his imaginative theatrical tour.

Despite their mixed reception, in disparaging the claims of the ethnic interlopers that populate these works, Macklin's British comedies were self-consciously playing to the crowd, performing a comic turn for the groundlings. In this sense, Macklin's career turns on and in turn informs the standard narrative about the emergence of a common British standard, which is focused on the cultural norms and social etiquette of the south-east corner of England. Lynda Mugglestone, in *Talking Proper* (2003), has written of how the desire to standardize pronunciation focused on reifying an intersection between the court and the city, and identified southern spoken forms as norms from which the regions were to be understood as derivations and dialects.[16] Hence, alongside a social hierarchy that demanded that Macklin's characters accord to a certain wealth and standing to be considered legitimate protagonists, there was also an understated ethnic and regional hierarchy that informed social exchange, which Macklin's comedy made explicit.

From another angle, chronologically, the last quarter of the century saw a solidification of the norms of expression grounded in a prioritization of the south-east of England.[17] And this finds further confirmation within the work of Dror Wahrman's *The Making of the Modern Self* (2006). Wahrman has argued for a rise in essentialism in the ideas of gender and race in the wake of the American conflict: as the threat of imperial descent was made manifest, the British calcified their identities around southern English norms and expectations to stabilize their sense of diminishing authority.[18] So too Roxann Wheeler has argued that racial categories grounded on skin colour replaced a more open idiom of identity markers in the latter half of the century. As she summarized the issue,

---

14 See Matthew J. Kinservik, 'New Light on the Censorship of Macklin's *The Man of the World*', *Huntington Library Quarterly* 62.1–2 (1999), 43–66.
15 See Goring, '"John Bull, pit, box, and gallery, said No!"', 63–64; 74–76.
16 Lynda Mugglestone, *Talking Proper: The Rise of Accent as a Social Symbol* (Oxford: Oxford University Press, 2003), 16.
17 See Ossi Ihalainen, 'The Dialects of England since 1776', in Robert Burchfield (ed.), *Cambridge History of the English Language*, 6 vols (Cambridge: Cambridge University Press, 1994), V.197–232.
18 Dror Wahrman, *The Making of the Modern Self: Identity and Culture in Eighteenth-Century England* (New Haven, CT: Yale University Press, 2006).

in eighteenth-century Britain, the ideology of human variety broadly changed from being articulated primarily through religious difference, which included such things as political governance and civil life, to being articulated primarily through scientific categories derived from natural history that featured external characteristic of the human body—colour, facial features, and hair texture. At the end of the century, the contours of racial ideology were more established than a century before, a solidification that accompanied the more important role of race and racism in the intellectual pursuits and structures of everyday life in Britain.[19]

The earlier iteration of human variety allowed for civilizing processes founded on religious conversion, the emulation of British manners, the adoption of British fashion, and, crucially, the taking of a British spouse. As these emblems of emulation diminished in symbolic power the paths to assimilation became more varied and more contentious. Macklin's cultural mockery of the Celtic adventurers—the Scots, Irish, and Welsh who sought their fortune on the English marriage market—seems to conform to this cultural narrative of identity formation and racial rejection.

Competitive regionalism

Yet despite this apparent congruity, Macklin's career does not sit easily in this story of racial border walls and the calcification of British identity around an English core.[20] His work accords instead with a different narrative of the relationship between British identity and English nationhood, one that is complicated by the Celtic caricatures with whom he populates his comedy. At stake is more than just a problem of chronology, but that is a good place to start.

Macklin's high-water mark as an author came with *Love à la Mode* (1759). It is simultaneously a comedy of manners and marriage and a satire mocking the social ambition of ethnic outsiders.[21] The simple conceit of the play is a reverse of the Judgement of Paris, with a series of suitors presenting themselves to the eligible Charlotte. These are a Jew, Mordecai; a Scot, Archy Macsarcasm; an Irishman, Sir Callaghan O'Brallaghan; and, intriguingly, a Yorkshireman, Squire Groom; the four men act as a comic representation of the metropole

---

19 Roxann Wheeler, *The Complexion of Race: Categories of Difference in Eighteenth-Century British Culture* (Philadelphia: University of Pennsylvania Press, 2000), 289.
20 On the erection of border walls and the decline in state power, see Wendy Brown, *Walled States, Waning Sovereignty* (Cambridge, MA: MIT Press, 2010).
21 Charles Macklin, *Love à la Mode*, in J.O. Bartley (ed.), *Four Comedies by Charles Macklin* (London: Sidgwick & Jackson, 1968), 41–77.

(Mordecai is a moneylender and hence a trader in the city), the two Celtic kingdoms, and the English provinces. Although it is not made explicit, Charlotte can thus be read as representative of the English home counties, and her guardian Sir Theodore Goodchild as a Tory landed gent.

Much of the comedy is generated from the suitors' pained efforts to win Charlotte's affections. And, in this, much is made of their appearance and their modes of speech. When Mordecai enters for the first time, singing an Italian air suggestive of love but also of decadence, Charlotte takes note of his new suit, saying: 'Quite elegant. I don't know any one about town deserves the title of beau, better than Mr. Mordecai'.[22] This deployment of a term of fashion, and one which was loaded with some degree of distain in the parlance of the day, is taken quickly to heart by the vain suitor:

Mordecai: O dear madam, you are very obliging.
Charlotte: I think you are called Beau Mordecai by every body.
Mordecai: Yes, madam, they do distinguish me by that title, but I don't think I merit the honour.
Charlotte: No body more.[23]

If Mordecai's entry marks him out as a vain metropolitan, the arrival of the Scot Macsarcasm, which quickly follows, sees him identified by his manner of speech that Macklin rendered as a broad brogue, almost incoherent on the page and clearly intended for hamming up on stage. His opening line sets the tone. Speaking to his servant, he demands: 'Randol, bid Sawney be here wi' the chariot at eight o'clock axactly', before addressing Mordecai, declaring: 'Ha, Ha, ha! my cheeld of circumcision, gi' us a wag of thy loof; hoo dun ye do, my bonny Girgishite?'[24] Completing the early set of comic turns, the Irish adventurer Sir Callaghan O'Brallaghan is rapidly lampooned for his martial, not his marital, inclination. Asked if he had needed to return to the war in Germany, he confirms that, 'Yes, madam, it was quite over, but it began again: a true genius never loves to quit the field till he has left himself nothing to do; for then, you know, madam, he can keep it with more safety'.[25] Only in the second act does the English caricature Squire Groom make his appearance, having decanted his way from York to London overnight, arriving drunk and in command of little more than a hunting obsession and a run of losses at the gambling table.[26]

---

22 *Love à la Mode*, in *Four Comedies by Charles Macklin*, 48.
23 *Love à la Mode*, in *Four Comedies by Charles Macklin*, 48.
24 *Love à la Mode*, in *Four Comedies by Charles Macklin*, 49.
25 *Love à la Mode*, in *Four Comedies by Charles Macklin*, 54.
26 *Love à la Mode*, in *Four Comedies by Charles Macklin*, 65.

Each character, then, plays to a stereotype: a fashionable and money-minded Jew, an uncouth and provincial Scot; a militaristic, violent Irishman, and a reckless and immoderate northerner.[27] Macklin has supplied little for Charlotte's genteel Englishness to choose from. As she tells her guardian at the opening of the play, 'since the days of giants and enchanted castles, no poor damsel has been besieged by such a group of odd mortals'.[28]

All of the proposed lovers seemingly disqualify themselves, not by who they are but by what they are. Thus, Macklin's treatment of the Irish hero O'Callaghan is loaded with humour founded on his awkward use of martial analogy. As he tells Macsarcasm, 'I intend to carry the place like a solider, *à la militaire*, as we say abroad; for I make my approaches regularly to the breast work, before I attempt the covered way'.[29] If the Irish figure is mocked for his rough wooing, Macsarcasm himself is dismissed as overly proud of his ancient lineage: 'Conseeder, madam, there is nai scant of wealth or honour in oor faimily. Lady, we hai in the hoose of Macsarcasm twa Barons, three Viscoonts, sax Earls, yean Marqueesate, and twa Dukes—besides Baronets and Lairds oot of aw reckoning'.[30] And in making this foolish claim he is overly quick to degrade the English stock from which Charlotte hails: 'In Scotland, aw oor Nobeelety are sprung frai Monarchs, Warriors, Heroes, and glorious achievements: noo here i' th' Sooth, ye are aw sprung frai sugar hogsheads, rum puncheons, wool packs, hop sacks, iron bars, and tar jackets'.[31] One suspects this kind of dismissive treatment is not the way to a girl's heart.

The laughter then is largely grounded on the audience's awareness of how inappropriate and how unusual these suitors' advances are. In this, Macklin's humour appears to accord with the theories of laughter offered by Thomas Hobbes. In a passage in 'Human Nature', part one of *The Elements of Law*, he argues that laughter was

> nothing else but a sudden glory arising from sudden conceptions of some eminency in ourselves, by comparison with the infirmities of others, or with our own formerly: for men laugh at follies of themselves past, when they come suddenly to remembrance, except they bring with them any present dishonour.[32]

---

27 On this kind of comparative racial humour, see Alan Dundes, *Cracking Jokes: Studies of Sick Humor Cycles and Stereotypes* (Berkeley, CA: Ten Speed Press, 1987), 79–93.
28 *Love à la Mode*, in *Four Comedies by Charles Macklin*, 45.
29 *Love à la Mode*, in *Four Comedies by Charles Macklin*, 58.
30 *Love à la Mode*, in *Four Comedies by Charles Macklin*, 52.
31 *Love à la Mode*, in *Four Comedies by Charles Macklin*, 53.
32 Thomas Hobbes, *The Elements of Law Natural and Politic* (Oxford: Oxford University Press, 1994), 54–55.

This superiority theory of laughter produces a comedy in which the mishaps and foolishness of ethnic outsiders is displayed to the genteel and polite for their astonished entertainment. It is the comedy of the freak show, and the key element in many racist jokes. It is also the comedy of 'socially sanctioned aggression'.[33]

The exception to this rule is in the final treatment of the Irish adventurer. While O'Brallaghan's militarism is keenly mocked in Act I, in the denouement to the play his loyalty and valour shine through and he is marked out as a worthy lover for Charlotte. To discern the shortcomings of her suitors, she proposes to her guardian the playing of a simple deceit. She is to have it reported that a failed business adventure has left her penniless, revealing whether those courting her are motivated by love or profit. Each of the other men make their excuses and withdraw their petition. Their insincerity is accentuated by the vivid display of ethnic difference. Here is Macsarcasm beating his retreat in his markedly dialectical prose and his exaggerated concern for the clan's view of the proposed match:

> Madam, I am sorry to be the messenger of ill tidings, but aw oor connection is at an end; oor hoose has heard of my addresses till ye; and I hai had letters frai the dukes, the marquis, and aw the deegnetaries of the family remonstrating— nay, axpressly proheebeting my contaminating the blood of Macsarcasm wi' ainy thing sprung frai a hogsheed, or a coonting hoose.[34]

And here is Mordecai, accounting for his withdrawal in terms of money and economy. It is, in his word, a 'business', suggesting that now Charlotte is destitute she is a decidedly poor investment: 'matrimony is a subject I have never thoroughly considered, and I must take some time to deliberate, before I determine upon that inextricable business. Besides, madam, I assure you, my affairs are not in a matrimonial situation'.[35]

Only with O'Brallaghan does Charlotte find an honourable partner. His declaration comes as a surprise to his rivals, but is a heartfelt expression of his trustworthiness on the field of love as on the field of battle:

> When she was computed to have a hundred thousand pounds, I loved her, 'tis true, but it was with fear and trembling, like a man that loves to be a solider, yet is afraid of a gun; because I looked upon myself as an unequal match to her—but now she is poor, and that it is in my power to serve her, I find something warm about my heart here, that tells me that I love her better than

---

33 Dundes, *Cracking Jokes*, 17.
34 *Love à la Mode*, in *Four Comedies by Charles Macklin*, 73.
35 *Love à la Mode*, in *Four Comedies by Charles Macklin*, 73–74.

when she was rich, and makes me beg she will take my life this instant, and all I have, into her service.[36]

In this moment, the Irish adventurer is recuperated and his true character shown to be worthy of the love of the home counties heiress, whose value is in turn re-established with the revelation that her bankruptcy was indeed a ploy. As Joep Leerssen has noted, this is to reverse the expectations of the stage Irishman, giving his persona a positive spin. As he recognizes, 'When Mordecai and Sir Archy try to portray Sir Callaghan's military character in as ridiculous a light as possible, their attempts are stymied by the Irishman's refusal to be funny'.[37] O'Brallaghan's barbarism is understood as authenticity; his violence is now read as bravery; his passions are revealed to be unwavering; his heart is seen to be true.[38]

As the recuperative revelation of O'Brallaghan's decency and integrity suggests, Macklin was aware that not all laughter is inherently aggressive. The possibility that Irish authentic virtue might complement English polite decorum suggests that there are avenues by which the identities of the British Isles might either triangulate or combine to germinate something other than simple antagonism. And it is here that Macklin's trajectory as a playwright complicates the narrative of emergent racism and the rise of Anglo-nationalisms.

Certainly, O'Brallaghan's constancy is suggestive that Macklin retained some semblance of patriotic ardour for the land of his birth and early life.[39] So too the dismissive caricaturing of Macsarcasm supports a reading of Macklin's work as informed by what Martyn Powell has nicely termed 'Competitive Celticism', in which the Irish and the Scots compete for the fortune and favour of the English.[40] Macklin's comedy is clearly created by the way the four beaus traduce their rivals' claims. Macsarcasm and O'Brallaghan even come to blows after arguing about Sir Archy's incomprehensibility.[41] The rendering of the

---

36 *Love à la Mode*, in *Four Comedies by Charles Macklin*, 75.
37 Leerssen, *Mere Irish*, 134.
38 Leerssen suggests that the impact of this positive portrayal was long lasting as 'from the 1760s virtually all Irish characters on the British stage are sympathetically characterized and their Irishness seems to be meant to contribute to their positive nature'. Leerssen, *Mere Irish*, 140.
39 This assertion is also supported by his authoring of *The True Born Irishman*, first performed in Dublin's Crow Street Theatre in 1762.
40 Martyn J. Powell, 'Celtic Rivalries: Ireland, Scotland and Wales in the British Empire, 1707–1801', in H.V. Bowen (ed.), *Wales and the Overseas British Empire: Interactions and Influences, 1650–1830* (Manchester: Manchester University Press, 2016), 62–86.
41 *Love à la Mode*, in *Four Comedies by Charles Macklin*, 60.

exchange as enacting competitive Celticism is complicated in part by how it is the Scot, not the Irish soldier, who first turns to weaponry. So too the play's wider narrative of Irish–Scottish rivalries is disrupted by the presence of Mordecai and Squire Groom. Yet these characters do accord with the wider shift identified by Mugglestone to reify south-east England at the expense of either the capital or the other regions, for, as Michael Ragussis has noted, 'the Jew was located centrally in the redefinition of England as a commercial nation', and was to that extent emblematic of London's mercantile power.[42] Similarly, he notices how on the stage 'audiences were treated to a host of comic dialects, not least was that of the Yorkshire county clown, a kind of native exotic who frequently was placed beside the Irishman and the Scot in the multi-ethnic spectacle'.[43] Both figures are here in Macklin's treatment also positioned as supplicants for the southern belle's sexual and material favours.

Offensive sociability

The interpretation of Macklin as staging forms of competitive Celticism—and competitive regionalism—is buttressed by his 1762 play, *The True Born Irishman*. Staged successfully in Dublin it failed to capture the affections of the London audience when it was restaged at Covent Garden in 1767 as *The Irish Fine Lady*, even though, as with *Love à la Mode*, much of the comedy draws on ethnic comparisons. In this work, the butt of the humour is the fashionable 'Macaroni', Count Mushroom.[44] He is seeking to seduce the wife of the eponymous trueborn Irishman Murrogh O'Dogherty. The dramatic action, such as it is, is filled out by the shifting attitude of Mrs Diggerty, who at first is starry-eyed about her encounters with the English capital, what her husband terms 'the London vertigo'.[45] In the second act she comes to her senses, being convinced of the need to abandon her foolish infatuation both with London and with its personification, Count Mushroom. O'Dogherty ultimately gains his revenge by exposing the lecherous Londoner to acute social embarrassment: Mushroom's disdainful attitude to the Irish beau monde is exposed, as well as his nefarious attempt to bargain a reduction in the lease over which he acts as middleman in exchange for the sexual favours of Mrs Diggerty.

---

42 Ragussis, 'Jews and Other "Outlandish Englishmen"', 783.
43 Ragussis, 'Jews and Other "Outlandish Englishmen"', 796.
44 On 'Macaronies', and other victims of the London fashions, see Wahrman, *The Making of the Modern Self*, 60–65.
45 Charles Macklin, *The True Born Irishman*, in *Four Comedies by Charles Macklin*, 85.

Much of the play is concerned with the problem of names. The distance between the spouses is marked by Mrs Diggerty's adoption of an English variant on the Irish surname O'Dogherty—retained by the husband—as well as her pursuit of an honour for her spouse. 'There's a necessity for a peerage', she declares as the second act opens, vexed as she is by how she is

> affronted for want of a title: a parcel of upstarts, with their crownets upon their coaches, their chairs, their spoons, their handkerchiefs […] creatures that were below me but t'other day, are now truly my superiors, and have the precedency, and are set above me at table.[46]

Social prestige is attached here to the name you present the world.

So too dialect plays its part in marking out difference, with O'Dogherty bemoaning his wife's adoption of 'London English'.[47] She in turn mocks the Irish rendering of English, remarking to Mushroom on how 'I fancied, being just come from England, that the very dogs here when they barked, had the brogue'.[48] Yet in a sharp reversal of expectations, in Macklin's handling here it is Mrs Diggerty's words that are given dialectical markers, such as when she reflects on her attendance at a feast hosted by the Lord Mayor of London: 'I went with her grace, a friend of mine, and a peerty of the court, as one of the household—but the minute I went in every eye was upon me: Lord, it was veestly pleasant to see how the she grocers, the she mercers, the she dyers, the she hosiers, and the she taylors did stare at me'.[49] Here her language marks her out as a parvenu as much as her lack of awareness of the reason she garnered such stares from the lower orders as an obvious outsider to the scene.

The extent to which Mrs Diggerty has had her head turned by London's social whirl is underlined by how she risks her reputation by fraternizing with Count Mushroom. He in turn is positioned as a neat reversal of the Irish adventurer, a lascivious seducer passing as a fine gentleman. He ends the play having donned women's clothes, in a forlorn attempt to escape the attentions of O'Dogherty, displayed in a case for the humour of the audience; the Irish are literally making a show of an English adventurer. O'Dogherty underscores the moral, noticing how the Count and his behaviour are now 'objects for a farce'.[50] In other words, O'Dogherty is now asking the audience to join him in laughing with the Irish, rather than laughing at them.

Macklin was highly conscious of the nature of this request, for in the

---

46 *True Born Irishman*, in *Four Comedies by Charles Macklin*, 100.
47 *True Born Irishman*, in *Four Comedies by Charles Macklin*, 111.
48 *True Born Irishman*, in *Four Comedies by Charles Macklin*, 95.
49 *True Born Irishman*, in *Four Comedies by Charles Macklin*, 96–97.
50 *True Born Irishman*, in *Four Comedies by Charles Macklin*, 121.

prelude of its London performance he rhymed out his anxiety that his treatment of O'Dogherty as a proud provincial might meet with resistance:

> In fair defiance of this Gothic Law.
> Milesian sprung, confess'd in every part,
> Hibernia's Seal impress'd on Tongue and Heart.
> Nay more, our Bard still rises in Offence,
> And dares give Irish Tones a sterling Sense.
> But what is stranger still, indeed a wonder,
> He hopes to make him please, without a Blunder.[51]

In asking the audience to stay their criticism he asked them to accept that his ambition was to bring harmony to a discordant British community: 'Our work's a Farce,—Our end to mend the Heart'.[52] In that, he looked to a shared sensibility in which social preening and commercial luxury were rejected in favour of local pride and emotional investment.

As Simon Critchley expresses it, 'in listening to a joke, I am presupposing a world that is shared, the forms of which the practice of joke-telling is going to play with'.[53] To get the joke, both the joker and their audience needs to understand the nature of the social expectations and rational norms that are being played upon.[54] Here Macklin is generating a sympathetic connection between the audience and his characters, humorously dramatizing the complexity of Anglo-Irish relations by indulging the idea that either might be out of place in passing themselves off in the other kingdom. The source of the humour lies in the complicity of the English in the shared predicament of traversing a diverse polity, allowing the English to laugh along with the Irish, rather than consistently laughing at them.

This sense of comedy as grounded in the sociability inherent in shared predicaments was articulated by the moral philosopher Francis Hutcheson.[55] In 'Reflections upon Laughter', Hutcheson openly rejected Hobbes's thesis concerning humour, suggesting he had confused laughter with ridicule, and posited instead a thesis that sourced comedy in human sociability. He underscored that laughter is commonly a communal activity: we laugh with others. As he stated, laughter 'is plainly of considerable moment in human society. It is often a great occasion of pleasure, and enlivens our conversation

---

51 The preface, transcribed from manuscript, is in Goring, '"John Bull, pit, box, and gallery, said No!"', 75.
52 Goring, '"John Bull, pit, box, and gallery, said No!"', 75.
53 Simon Critchley, *On Humour* (London; Routledge, 2002), 4.
54 Critchley, *On Humour*, 1.
55 Hutcheson was also expressive of the incongruity theory of humour. See Paul McDonald, *The Philosophy of Humour* (Penrith: Humanities-Ebooks, 2012), 49–50.

exceedingly when it is conducted by good nature'.[56] Laughter, he averred, relied upon and expressed 'a kind instinct of nature, a secret bond between us and our fellow creatures'.[57] Laughter is here treated not as an act of aggression but as a means of bonding with those whom you see as part of your own moral community. It allows you to carefully delineate the outsiders against whom you can be defined as an insider.

Soft othering

As Elliott Oring has noted, racist comedy, as much as with other forms of joking, 'implies a community; a fellowship of laughers with whom the humor is shared'.[58] Indeed, it can go further: by voicing prejudice, jokes based on stereotypes can 'communicate [...] that racism can and should be open and explicit. They show that there is nothing to fear from liberals, the politically correct or the law [...] They attempt to create a climate, perhaps even a culture of racism'.[59]

This doubling effect can be illustrated through the looming presence of the aptly named Sir Pertinax Macsycophant in Macklin's last major play, *The Man of the World* (1781).[60] Macsycophant personifies the graceless and truculent Scot whose resentment at the post-Union predicament results in a dislikeable and disorderly dependency. He openly rejects the demands of political principle, favouring connections and telling his son to vote for the corrupt minister to promote his own interests. When Egerton protests, weighing his conscience in the fight, Macsycophant rails, 'Conscience! why, ye are mad! Did ye ever hear ainy mon talk of conscience in poleetecal maiters? Conscience, quotha? I hai been in Parliament these three and thratty years, and never heard the tarm made use of before'.[61] In all this, Macsycophant matches the common caricature of the Scot at the time as overweening, unprincipled, calculating, and grasping.[62] This kind of thick

---

56 Francis Hutcheson, 'Reflections upon Laughter', in James Arbuckle (ed.), *Hibernicus Letters*, 2 vols (Dublin, 1729), I.102.
57 Hutcheson, 'Reflections upon Laughter', 86.
58 Elliott Oring, 'Humor of Hate', in *Engaging Humor* (Urbana: University of Illinois Press, 2003), 56.
59 Oring, *Engaging Humor*, 56.
60 Charles Macklin, *The Man of the World*, in *Four Comedies by Charles Macklin*, 199–270.
61 *The Man of the World*, in *Four Comedies by Charles Macklin*, 250.
62 On how the layering up of negative characteristics ensures a longevity for ethnic stereotypes, see Alan Dundes, 'The Jew and the Polack in the United States: A Study of Ethnic Slurs', in *Cracking Jokes*, 99.

description of the Scottish intruder into English affairs relayed and reworked the tropes of English Scotophobia in cartoons and prints.[63]

In embodying this negative stereotype so fully, Macsycophant provides the audience with an ability to laugh together at their anxiety over Scottish adventurers and the threat they pose to an English national culture. In this, the play works within the confines of the anti-Scottish sentiment stoked up against the Prime Ministerial administration of the Earl of Bute and which John Wilkes virulently articulated in the pages of the *North Briton*. It was this political context, Matthew Kinservik persuasively argues, that informed the decision of the Lord Chamberlain to reject the petition to stage the play in 1770 and again in 1779, only allowing it to proceed, with revision, in 1781.[64] In co-opting and building on this public sentiment, Macklin enabled a release model of humour in which the anxiety is diminished by laughter. The threat, such as it is, to identity and community, is not to be taken seriously. Macsycophant at once allowed the audience to express their anxiety, and the laughter he elicited created a sense of a shared predicament that they were confronting together.

Macklin's caricatures may be guilty of that kind of othering, mocking the proud if dependent Scot and celebrating the values of the home counties in so doing. But it also speaks to another source of laughter, that of appropriate incongruity. As identified by Elliott Oring, appropriate incongruity is the comedy of mismanaging associations, or, as he frames it, 'the perception of an appropriate relationship between categories that would normally be regarded as incongruous'.[65] The militaristic imagery of O'Brallaghan in his depiction of love affairs is one example; the misplaced ethnic pride of a financial dependant enunciated in the speeches of Macsycophant is another.

As with the other theories, incongruity theory had a contemporaneous advocate: in this case the Scottish philosopher and poet James Beattie. Writing in an extended essay on the subject, he observed how 'Laughter arises from the view of two or more inconsistent, unsuitable or incongruous parts or circumstances, considered as united in one complex object or assemblage, or as acquiring a sort of mutual relation from the peculiar manner in which the mind takes notice of them'.[66]

---

63 See Gordon Pentland, '"We Speak for the Ready": Images of Scots in Political Prints, 1707–1832', *Scottish Historical Review* 90.1 (2011), 64–95.
64 Kinservik, 'New Light on the Censorship', 43.
65 Oring, *Engaging Humour*, 1.
66 James Beattie, 'An Essay on Laughter and Ludicrous Composition, written in the Year 1764', in *Essays on Poetry and Music, as they Affect the Mind, on Laughter and Ludicrous Composition; on the Usefulness of Classical Composition* (Edinburgh, 1776), 347.

For Beattie, then, the real cause of laughter lies in the ludicrous and the ridiculous. The first he thinks can 'excite pure laughter, the latter excite[s] laughter with disapprobation or contempt'.[67] And both of these are generated by highlighting 'an opposition of suitableness and unsuitable', resolved by the realization that the two are connected in some unlikely fashion.[68] And Beattie goes on to suggest that 'the greater the number of incongruities that are blended in the same assemblage, the more ludicrous it will probably be', as the complexity of the resolution is enhanced.[69]

Unlike Beattie's version of the incongruity theory of laughter, for Oring, appropriate incongruity does not admit of simple resolution. Unlike riddles, for instance, which have a solution, jokes that depend on appropriate incongruity 'are open ended and relatively unpredictable'.[70] Oring also accepts, however, that 'a joke will only be successful if the listener can identify and access the background knowledge without which verbal humour cannot proceed'.[71] In other words, the audience needed to know the stereotypes on which Macklin's comedy was founded if they were to be 'in' on the joke. The incongruity of the behaviour of the Irishman in his wooing of the girl was dependent on the audience recognizing the casting of the Irish as military servicemen across the continent; the mocking of the Scot relied on the cliché of the Scot on the payroll of the despised countryman-cum-Prime Minister, the Earl of Bute, whose patronage of the Scots so irritated John Wilkes in the 1760s. Despite Wilkes's overt commitment to English identity, Macklin was supportive of his critique of Bute's administration, which he thought to be intruding untrustworthy Scottish placemen into power, contending that

> they mix in every part of society, from the cabinet council, the king's closet, the senate, down to the lowest dregs of the people—coffee-houses, taverns, beer-houses, private families, clubs and every kind of public meeting, in which they first flatter, and then betray to the ministry every sentiment respecting politics, religion, morality and all the human dealings.[72]

Yet, in drafting the character of Egerton, Macklin disrupted the easy binaries of national comparison (Scottish is bad, English is good) by personifying a rather different kind of moral community, and one the English

---

67 Beattie, 'Essay on Laughter', 326–27.
68 Beattie, 'Essay on Laughter', 348.
69 Beattie, 'Essay on Laughter', 349.
70 Elliott Oring, *Jokes and their Relations* (Lexington: University Press of Kentucky, 1992), 6.
71 Oring, *Jokes and their Relations*, 6.
72 *The Monthly Mirror* 7 (May 1799), 276 quoted in *Appleton*, 209.

bride Constantia was being invited to join. In this Macklin is imagining a pan-British identity which is enlightened in its tolerance of the regional differences of the archipelago; he is staging a case for integration.

Although Macsycophant dismisses his son's values as irrelevant to the commercial landscape of the contemporary world—'preenciples that meeght hai done vary weel among the aunvient Romans, but are damned unfit for the modern Britons'—Egerton's case proves the folly of that view.[73] Egerton is actually proposed by the play as an ideal modern Briton. His commitment to a shared polity is articulated in the fight with his father, stated by way of a vow of patriotic allegiance:

> *Egerton*: Only shew me how I can serve my country, and my life is hers. Were I qualified to lead her armies, to steer her fleets, and deal her honest vengeance on her insulting foes—or could my eloquence pull down a state leviathan, mighty by the plunder of his country—black with the treasons of her disgrace, and send his infamy down to a free posterity, as a monumental terror to corrupt ambition, I would be foremost in such service, and act it with the unremitting ardour of a Roman spirit.[74]

It is his moralism and patriotism—directed not to Scotland but to Britain—that also makes him the ideal romantic partner for the virtuous Constantia.

In Egerton we find a Scottish hero, albeit one that is not characterized by his pronouncedly provincial traits. He is in that sense subject to what might be termed 'soft othering'. He is as distant from his father's aggressive posturing about Scotland as he is from the English by way of birth and patrimony. He is capable of adapting to the English ways—his name has been changed to reflect his English inheritance—but his political and moral commitments reside above the regional fray in a British superstructure that sets aside local, ethnic, and regional difference in favour of incorporating union and imperial outreach. It is not without significance that it is wealth derived from the Empire—in this case from India—that ensures the match with his English bride is financially as well as emotionally secure.

Here, then, instead of venerating England, Macklin's plays created conceptual space for ethnic adventurers. By the time of writing *The Man of the World* Macklin was committed to the idea that exaggerated provincial pride was boorish and counterproductive. It was also hypocritical in that it failed to register the nature of the interdependency the provinces enjoyed with each other. This political stance empowered his comedy by asking his audience to laugh about false pride in provincialism, instead of mocking the regions for

---

73 *The Man of the World*, in *Four Comedies by Charles Macklin*, 260.
74 *The Man of the World*, in *Four Comedies by Charles Macklin*, 251.

their backwardness. In making this critique, Macklin was able to speak to the value of a pan-archipelagic identity that was finding focus and form in the years in which he wrote.

Making the English Laugh

CHARLES MACKLIN WAS A RELIGIOUS CONVERT to the established church, an actor who made his way by playing outsiders and ethnic others, and an Irish adventurer making his way on the London stage.[75] Yet what is unusual, and puzzling, about Macklin's comedic trajectory is that far from solidifying and calcifying the ethnic basis of his humour, he came over the years to reject the reification of the south of England in favour of a form of integrationist Britishness. In this, his work complicates the narratives of ethnic identity offered in the work of Lynda Mugglestone and Dror Wahrman. Instead, Macklin's case confirms John Kerrigan's sense that

> The potency of English identities, and their expansive influence around the archipelago, can be critically represented without the overall perspective becoming Anglocentric. What one discovers is that Englishness was a contested resource as much for writers engaging with readers as for leaders mustering armies, and that 'England' was a shifting entity, open to reconceptualization, defined against and meshed with its neighbours.[76]

This awareness of the unsettled nature of the British identity across the eighteenth century allows us to return to the question posed at the beginning, and which echoed that of Robert Darnton: why did the audiences laugh? In part, the humour in Macklin is driven by both the comedy of superiority and that of social identification. However, there is in Macklin's work a twist which at once perplexes and complicates the story of the hardening of ethnic prejudices in the second half of the eighteenth century; and it is the open-ended nature of appropriate incongruity that reveals it. The irony laced into the subtext of Macklin's crude ethnic humour is that it is dependent upon and expresses the parochial prejudices of the southern English middling sort.

Yet southern English provincialism is just as acute, Macklin hints, as that of the overbearing Scot; their displaced violent urges are just as disruptive

---

75 On the wider context of this community of actors, see David O'Shaughnessy, 'Introduction: Tolerably Numerous: Recovering the London Irish of the Eighteenth Century' and Toby Barnard, 'The Irish in London and the "London Irish", ca.1680–1780', *Eighteenth-Century Life* 39.1 (2015), 1–14; 15–40.
76 John Kerrigan, *Archipelagic English: Literature, History and Politics, 1603–1707* (Oxford: Oxford University Press, 2008), 12.

as those of the overtly military Irish. Indeed, their greed and mercantile ambition are thought to match those projected onto the Jewish community; and their boorish concern with drink and gambling is a match for their northern countrymen. In sum, the southern English, despite their pretensions to sophistication and *politesse*, are just as small-minded as those they claim superiority over. The appropriate incongruity of Macklin's work, then, hinges on the revelation that English prejudice is the real source of the racial humour. That is what is exposed by the end of each play: in both *Love à la Mode* and *The Man of the World* the play's resolution is reached by the protagonists realizing the virtue of regional difference and the necessity of uniting in happy matrimonial union. In *The True Born Irishman* it is to be found in a renewed affiliation with the region of origin and a rejection of the seductive power of metropolitan sophisticates and cosmopolitans. (Mrs Diggerty's attempts to pepper her speech with French is duly mocked in the revised London staging of the work; she exclaims: 'jenny-see-quee' and 'moundew'.)[77]

The plays thus move less along the route of ethnic solidification, and more along the lines of developments in the theory of laughter—from Hobbes to Hutcheson to Beattie. Macklin begins by drawing laughs by mocking ethnic others; he then redirects his comedy towards laughing with them. Ultimately, the plays conclude by laughing about the nature of prejudice itself. As Alan Dundes has written, 'Stereotypes are a factor in the formation of prejudice, and prejudice often prevents people from accepting one another as individuals'.[78] That is the failing that Macklin was highlighting and the failure was being located amongst the southern English who sought to place themselves at a time of state formation and identity solidification at the pinnacle of the regional hierarchy. It is their faux sophistication and their actual prejudice which are being targeted.

By contrast, Macklin was providing an alternative vocabulary of national identity and a discourse that enabled the combination of ethnic groupings, through social co-operation and intimate marital relations. This was the purchase of his Britishness; a political identity actively being forged in a theatrical mode. Macklin was quite literally acting it out for the edification of his parochial and bigoted audience. This was the premise of his argument in a letter to the Lord Chamberlain upon resubmitting *The Man of the World* for consideration in 1779. He attested that 'The Author's chief end [...] was to ridicule & by that means to explode the reciprocal national Prejudices that equally soured & disgraced the Minds both of English & Scotch Men'[79]

---

77 *The True Born Irishmen*, in *Four Comedies by Charles Macklin*, 95, 96.
78 Dundes, 'Slurs International', 92.
79 Quoted in Kinservik, 'New Light on the Censorship', 63.

In all this, Macklin rejected the reification of southern England as a cultural lodestone, to which the Irish and the Scots ought necessarily to be attracted. The Celtic cousins are recast as having something valuable to contribute to a blended identity, one that is inhabited by self-consciously British islanders. Britishness may in turn have a nationalistic basis of its own; one which keeps out colonial subjects. So too it carries its own anxieties about imperial failure; it is no surprise that Britishness finds focus in the epoch of the loss of the American colonies and the conflict with the French republic. But for an Irishman like Macklin British identity is resonant of possibilities, both for the Irish and the Scots, in the empire and domestically. The only residual barriers are the narrow focus of the Celts on their provincialism and the English resistance to Celtic acculturation.

So it is that while much of the humour in the British comedies of Charles Macklin seems to be directed at the foolish behaviour and false pride of the British regions—London, the north, Ireland, and Scotland—the real purpose of the dramas is to illuminate how it is the southern English, who claim cultural supremacy, who are the real bigots and the ones who fail to understand the British dispensation. The English, in that sense, are always the butt of the joke, and that is why they laugh.

9

Macklin and Censorship

David O'Shaughnessy

The business of the Stage is to correct vice, and laugh at folly.

Charles Macklin[1]

THE INTRODUCTION OF THE STAGE LICENSING ACT in 1737 would limit many forms of satire and indecorousness but it was immediately most effective in stifling theatre's capacity to critique the political sphere. This is of course unsurprising given that the major impetus behind the legislation's introduction was the increasing irritation of Robert Walpole at being pilloried on stage.[2] The first play to be refused a licence under the legislation was Henry Brooke's *Gustavus Vasa*, in March 1739, a play that attacked Walpole's regime on grounds of corruption. This set the tone for the early years of the legislation with a number of plays being prohibited by the Examiner, not least because of the willingness of John Rich at Covent Garden and Charles Fleetwood at Drury Lane to stage opposition drama,

---

1 Charles Macklin, 'Essay on Censorship', lost manuscript, cited in *Kirkman*, II.278.
2 The most thorough background to the introduction of the legislation is given in Vincent J. Liesenfeld, *The Licensing Act of 1737* (Madison: University of Wisconsin Press, 1984). See also L.W. Conolly, *The Censorship of English Drama, 1737–1824* (San Marino, CA: Huntington Library Press, 1976) and the essays by Thomas, Swindells, Kinservik, Newey, and Davis in Julia Swindells and David Francis Taylor (eds), *The Oxford Handbook of the Georgian Theatre, 1737–1832* (Oxford: Oxford University Press, 2014). For a selection of manuscripts censored during the course of the long eighteenth century, including Macklin's *The Man of the World* and *Covent Garden Theatre*, see https://tobeomitted.tcd.ie.

193

encouraged by Frederick, Prince of Wales, who was a persistent thorn in his father's side.³ James Thomson's *Edward and Eleonora* was the second play to be refused a licence in late March 1730, also for its bold and very thinly veiled attack on the government. William Paterson's *Arminius* was submitted in December 1739 and in January it became the third play to be denied a performance under the new legislation. Paterson's play attacked the government on the grounds of weak military leadership as Britain tepidly— in the opposition's view at least—contested a war with Spain; moreover, it also included the almost obligatory personal jibe at Walpole.⁴ John Kelly's *The Levee* (1741), a farce, was also turned down, for going one further and making Walpole look foolish as well as corrupt. After this initial flurry of censorship, Walpole's resignation in 1742 removed the primary butt of dramatic satire and heralded the commencement of a much more assertive war policy. The combination of these events heralded the effective demise of drama coloured by party political vitriol. The Jacobite threat in 1745 saw theatres become hotbeds of patriotism: anti-Catholic plays—such as Cibber's *The Non-Juror* and Ford's *Perkin Warbeck*—filled the playhouses and the tradition of singing God Save the King after performances began.⁵ With theatres becoming bastions of loyalism, brimming with jingoistic fervour, the Examiner of Plays was little troubled by political dissent, right through the 1750s and 1760s, as the manuscripts of the John Larpent Collection testify.⁶ The 1750s were very quiet indeed, with no play refused a performance licence, while there were only a couple of plays in the 1760s that were denied permission: the anonymously authored *The Bourbon League* (1762) and William Shirley's *Electra* (1763). This is not to suggest that plays were not subject to some censorial intervention: from 1737 onwards, a considerable proportion of plays were required to make minor deletions or amendments prior to performance as a matter of course. And it hardly needs noting that playwrights and managers had naturally internalized the culture

---

3 Conolly, *Censorship of English Drama*, 52–56.
4 Conolly, *Censorship of English Drama*, 61.
5 *Daily Advertiser*, 28 September 1745, cited in Emmett L. Avery, et al. (eds), *The London Stage, 1660–1800: A Calendar of Plays, Entertainments & Afterpieces together with Casts, Box-Receipts and Contemporary Comment, Compiled from the Playbills, Newspapers and Theatrical Diaries of the Period*, 5 parts, 11 vols (Carbondale: Southern Illinois University Press, 1960–1968), Part 3, II.1183.
6 The John Larpent Collection is held at the Huntington Library, San Marino, California. It is named after the man who held the office of the Examiner of Plays, 1778–1824, and comprises over 2,500 theatrical manuscripts—plays, operas, prologues, epilogues, songs, etc.—which were submitted to the Lord Chamberlain for approval in advance of performance at the patent theatres for the period 1737–1824. Larpent manuscripts referenced in this essay will be indicated as LA ##.

of censorship so they operated, generally speaking, within the parameters of this disciplinary framework with a degree of self-interested caution.

I provide this brief recap of the first couple of decades of theatre censorship as it helps us appreciate just quite how explosive the snarling Hector MacCrafty's (later Pertinax Macsycophant) sardonic unveiling of the truths of British political life in *The Man of the World* would have been in 1770. As Conolly outlines, *The Bourbon League* had plenty of abuse of Britain's enemies and praise for British liberties and *Electra*'s Jacobite leanings were couched in allegory—measures aimed to deflect accusations of partisanship.[7] But there was little restraint shown by Macklin's political critique of British political institutions; it was strident, specific, and splenetic. It took three submissions—and a second Examiner of Plays—before it made it onto the Covent Garden stage in 1781.

The ins and outs of the evolution of Macklin's satire on corrupt Westminster political life and its susceptibility to self-interested ethnic groupings has already been told in detail.[8] Recently, I have argued that the political critique contained within the play can be traced to the very beginning of his playwriting career. While the ignominious fate of *King Henry VII; or, The Popish Impostor* (Covent Garden, 1746) has ensured that critics have largely ignored it,[9] there are striking parallels between it and *The Man of the World* in Macklin's early Whiggish critique of a weak monarchy corrupted by devious and self-interested courtiers.[10]

This chapter engages with the censorship of Macklin's plays in two ways. First, it will offer a brief survey of the other breaches of theatrical protocol

---

7 See Conolly, *Censorship of English Drama*, 73–74.
8 Dougald MacMillan, 'The Censorship in the Case of Macklin's *The Man of the World*', *Huntington Library Bulletin* 10 (1936), 79–101; Matthew J. Kinservik, 'New Light on the Censorship of Macklin's *The Man of the World*', *Huntington Library Quarterly* 62.1–2 (1999), 43–66; Matthew J. Kinservik, *Disciplining Satire: The Censorship of Satiric Comedy on the Eighteenth-Century Stage* (Lewisburg, PA: Bucknell University Press, 2002), 184–95.
9 An honourable exception is provided by Michael M. Wagoner's 'The "Merry Tragedy" of *Henry VII* as written by "Charles Macklin, Comedian"', *New Theatre Quarterly* 31.4 (2015), 372–80.
10 The play's prologue invokes Algernon Sydney's thought as a model for ameliorating the British polity and the telling evidence of the Examiner's excisions on the manuscript make clear that Macklin's political edge was formed at least as far back as then. It is notable that he was not intimidated into silence at a moment when he might be forgiven—as an Irishman of ill repute in London just after the '45—for keeping his head down. For a full discussion, see David O'Shaughnessy, '"Bit, by some mad whig": Charles Macklin and the Irish Enlightenment', *Huntington Library Quarterly* 80.4 (2017), 559–84.

identified by the Examiner, particularly those made on grounds of sexual explicitness, with a view to providing a fuller sense of Macklin's dramatic esprit. I will further speculate that he was emboldened to do so by a particular freedom allowed by benefit nights and because he was acting with his wife, Ann Macklin (née Grace). Capturing this broader perspective of his censorial breaches offers us a more playful view of Macklin than we currently hold. Second, this chapter will use censorship as a lens to complicate Matthew Kinservik's take on Macklin's satiric strain. Kinservik dismisses *Covent Garden Theatre* as an immature work, an 'awkward topical revue'. For him, *Covent Garden Theatre* is a far cry from Macklin's best plays such as *The Man of the World*, which feature 'psychologically complex, metaphorical characters' and where the 'satiric method is decidedly sympathetic and reform-oriented'.[11] While I would concur with this assessment to a large degree, I want to tease out a strain of hitherto unidentified personal satire—directed ostensibly at Elizabeth Chudleigh (c.1720–1788)—in the farce. But I want to further argue that the critique of Chudleigh is actually a means of pointing out the fallibilities of the monarchy and its circle. In addition, I will also suggest that *The Man of the World*'s Hector MacCrafty may be more than a 'metaphorical creation' intended to cast general aspersions against Bute's government by suggesting that there are grounds for arguing that Lawrence Dundas (d.1781) was in Macklin's mind when he wrote the piece.[12] This too then might be thought of in the category of personal satire. These observations suggest that there is greater consistency in Macklin's satirical approach through the decades than previously thought; the interfusion of personal and political satire is a thread we can trace though much of his work. We may indeed prefer the greater psychological depth of *The Man of the World* but we should also acknowledge that the reforming drive of Macklin's personal satire offers a coherent way to reflect on his oeuvre and to nuance the common image of Macklin as an 'ardent Wilkesite'.[13]

The whole picture of Macklin's censorship

Let us begin with a quick run through the manuscript evidence of Macklin's censorship infractions. If we consider his body of work, we can find examples of political sharpness which anticipate the thrust of *The Man of the World*. Shark, the slick servant of *A Will and No Will; or, A Bone for the*

---

11 Kinservik, *Disciplining Satire*, 173, 172.
12 Kinservik, *Disciplining Satire*, 179.
13 *Appleton*, 209.

Lawyers (LA 58; 1746), reflects ruefully: 'The Stateman's Skill like mine is all Deceit/What's Policy in him—in me's a Cheat/Titles and Wealth reward his noble Art/Cudgells and Bruises mine—sometimes a Cart' (f. 17v).[14] The Larpent manuscript for *The School for Husbands* (LA 184; 1761) has: 'This is in the Man of the World', pencilled in a contemporary hand in the margin beside these lines:

> Nay, Madam, it is the Character of them all [the gentry], Fortune and Pleasure are the Deities they sacrifice to. The Temple of Virtue is quite erased. Give them but a fine Equipage; deep play, & an admired Wanton, & a Minister of State may Convert the Honour of every Man of them into a Vote, that wou'd sell the Nation to Prester John & their boasted Liberties to the Great Mogul. (f. 43v)[15]

In *The Trueborn Irishman* (LA 274; 1767), Mr O'Dogherty rails against political cronyism in familiar words, provoking the Examiner's pencil at various points: 'For I now find that a Courtier is just as honest a Man as a Patriot—my dear' (f. 4v). These sentiments are taken from Thomas Gordon and John Trenchard's *Cato's Letters* (1724), a key Whiggish text and found in Macklin's library.[16] Similar sentiments can be found recorded in his Commonplace Book.[17] His most well-known play, *Love à la Mode*, is also believed to have come under the scrutiny of the Lord Chamberlain: Horace Walpole recorded that Lord Bute, angered at the representation of the Scots in the character of Sir Archy Macsarcasm, tried to have it suppressed.[18]

---

14 Sir Isaac Skinflint's refusal to be reconciled after he is outmanoeuvred by Shark and Lucy in *A Will and No Will* also anticipates Sir Pertinax Macsycophant's protestations of revenge in *The Man of the World*.
15 There is also some suspicion that alleged references to a real life philandering aristocrat in *A School for Husbands* (LA 184; 1761) got through the censor unnoticed but not past the audience, even if Kirkman gave Macklin the benefit of the doubt: 'Several exceptionable passages, pointed out by the Audience at the first representation, were expunged, and the Piece ran nine nights. [...] There was a strong opposition made to this Comedy, from the belief, that Mr. Macklin intended, by his character of *Lord Belville*, to satirize a gentleman then living; but this certainly was not the case'. Kirkman, I.424.
16 Thomas Gordon and John Trenchard, 'Of Parties in England; how they vary, and interchange Characters, just as they are in Power, or out of it, yet still keep their former Names', *Cato's Letters: Or, Essays on Liberty, Civil and Religious, And other Important Subjects*, ed. Ronald Hamowy, 4 vols (Indianapolis, IN: Liberty Fund, 1995), II.687–93.
17 Charles Macklin, 'Commonplace Book, 1778–1790' [manuscript], Folger Shakespeare Library, M.a.9, f. 11v.
18 Matthew J. Kinservik, '*Love à la Mode* and Macklin's Return to the London Stage in 1759', *Theatre Survey* 37.2 (1996), 8.

Politics was at the core of Macklin's dramatic agenda but, as we can see, the Examiner of Plays often reined in those tendencies.

While politics provided the main reason for the interventions, the censor also had other causes to brandish his pen at Macklin's plays. There are emendations on the grounds of religion: there is a brief jibe at Methodists in *A Will and No Will*[19] and in *The New Play Criticiz'd* Sir Patrick suggests that the bishops of England have an unhealthy interest in playing backgammon.[20] *The New Play Criticiz'd* takes Benjamin Hoadley's *The Suspicious Husband* (1747) as its subject and it debates various dramaturgical innovations in this successful comedy; a number of specific mentions of Hoadley and the play are marked by the Examiner for deletion—references to real people often provoked censorial rebuke. But the most eye-catching changes were demanded because of references and allusions to sexual impropriety, particularly in *A Will and No Will* and *The Covent Garden Theatre; or, Pasquin Turn'd Drawcansir* (LA 96; 1752).

Macklin wrote *A Will and No Will* for his wife Ann Macklin's benefit night and it was performed on 23 April 1746 at Drury Lane Theatre.[21] The plot, inspired by Jonson's *Volpone* and Jean-François Regnard's *Le Légataire universel*, sees Sir Isaac Skinflint betray his nephew Bellair by planning to disinherit him and marrying Bellair's fiancée Harriet Lovewealth. Shark and Lucy, servants to Sir Isaac but loyal to Bellair, hatch a scheme to ensure that Skinflint is duped so that the lovers can be enriched and united as planned. Shark disguises himself first as another one of Skinflint's nephews and then as his niece. In these personae, he expresses some outrageously licentious sentiments in order to shock the wealthy man into discounting the nephew and niece as beneficiaries of his fortune.

The Examiner's office demanded a number of cuts from the Larpent manuscript. There is, as is often the case for the period, some uncertainty over who is responsible for the cuts. It seems more likely that those cuts made in pen, similar to *Covent Garden Theatre*, were made by the Examiner's office and the other cut made by the manager Lacy. In any case, the censorship is what matters; who imposes it is very much a secondary concern. When Shark, disguised as Skinflint's niece and trying to portray her as sexually wanton, tells Skinflint that 'she' is pregnant again (for the second time since the death of her husband), he follows this up with an

---

19 John Larpent Collection, Huntington Library, LA 58, f. 20r.
20 John Larpent Collection, Huntington Library, LA 64, f. 13v.
21 The play had further performances on 22 March 1748 (benefit for Charles Macklin); 29 March 1748 (benefit for Richard Yates); 31 March (benefit for William and Mrs Havard); 21, 22 April 1748; and 29 March 1756 (benefit for Maria Macklin).

unseemly invitation to Skinflint to 'feel if you please' (f. 19v), marked for excision. Puzzled at this surprising conception, Skinflint asks her to explain who had been her 'Bedfellow' (the term underlined for deletion) and Shark responds:

> *Shar*: I took a Religious Gentleman, a very good man to bed with me—an Itinerant Methodist, one Doctor Preach Field.
> *Skin*: Doctor Preach Field, I have heard of him.
> *Shar*: O he's a very good Man, Uncle, I assure you, and very full of the Spirit.

This passage has various pen marks in the margin, consistent with the style of the Examiner's office, indicating that this dialogue was too lewd for his taste, particularly the pun on 'Spirit'. Most extraordinary of all, is this exchange between the disguised Shark, Skinflint, and Lucy (Figure 9.1):

> *Shar*: [to Skinflint] I have heard too, that for several years past, you have been an Old Fornicator, and that you have led a most wicked Life with this Girl.
> *Lucy*: With me Madam.
> *Shar*: Yes you Naughty Creature, and that your Fornication would have had carnal Symptoms, but that he took most Unnatural Methods to prevent your Pregnancy. (f. 20v)

This explicit reference to contraceptively inspired anal sex is underlined by the Examiner in—rather heavily inked—pen, rather than simply flagged in the margin like most of the other interventions. Adding fuel to the fire, Macklin has Lucy suggestively invite Sir Isaac to 'slip up the back Stairs' (f. 21v) a few lines later, although this appears to have been missed by the Examiner (that said, the innuendo is lost once the initial lines have been cut). Quite how Charles Macklin envisaged getting this risqué material through the censorship process is frankly baffling but worth, perhaps, some consideration.

We know that Macklin played the part of Sir Isaac Skinflint. We also know that the piece was for Ann Macklin's benefit, thus, although we cannot be certain, it seems very probable that she played Lucy, the female lead of the comedy. Thus the 'Fornication' that Shark suggests takes place between Sir Isaac and Lucy winks bawdily in the direction of the Macklins' marital bed: Macklin's rather knowing exchanges between himself, his wife, and the audience are quite deliberate, rather than evidence of a rush of blood to the head and a tawdry attempt to poke the Examiner in the eye. The physical comedy possibilities of this scene for the two married actors are considerable. An earlier scene when Skinflint has just told his nephew that he intends to marry the young Harriet himself includes some comparable

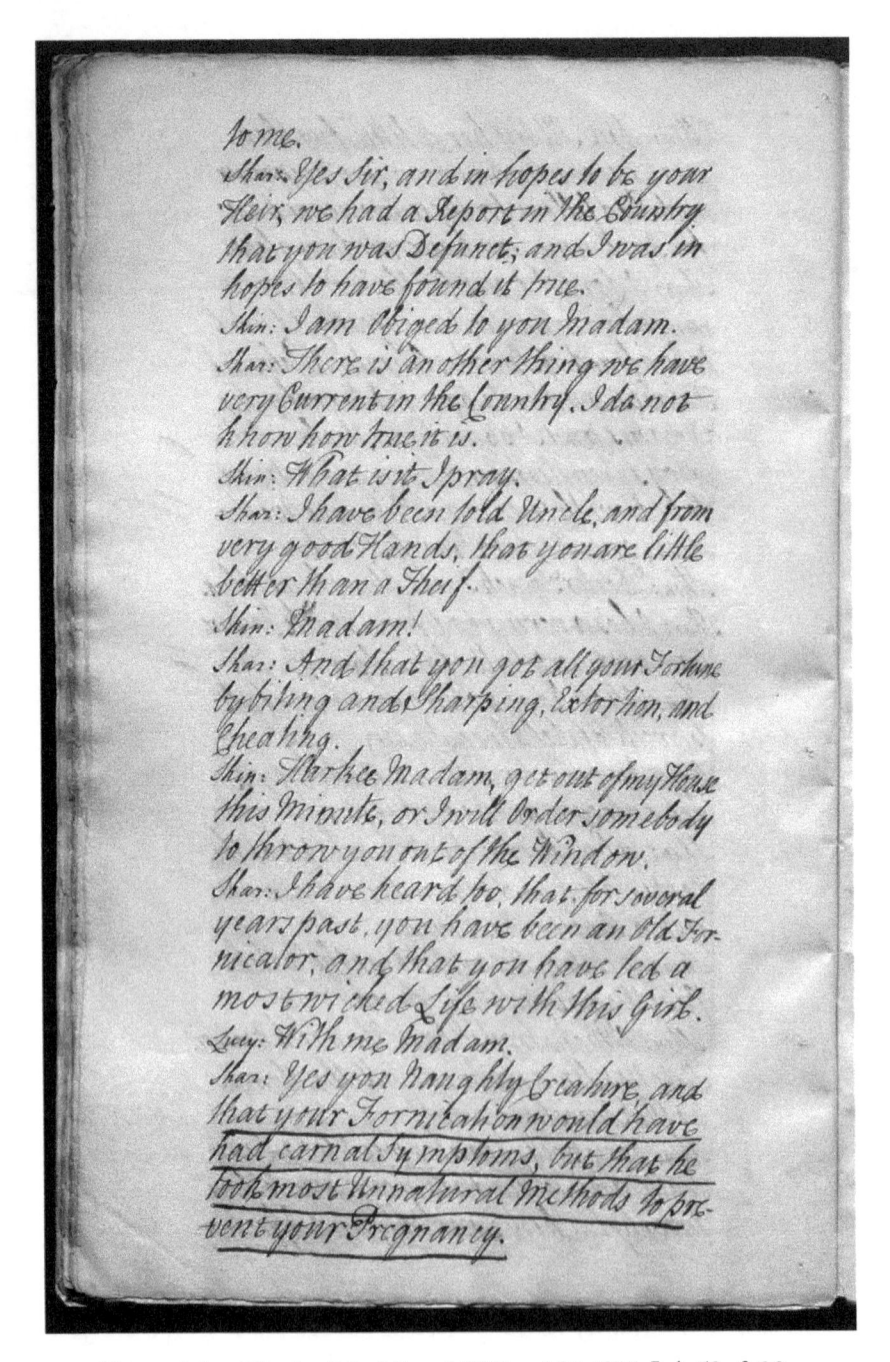

Figure 9.1: Charles Macklin, *A Will and No Will*, LA 58, f. 20v, John Larpent Collection, The Huntington Library, San Marino, California.

innuendo (although this time it was passed through by the Examiner without comment):

> *Skin*: Why nephew notwithstanding—I am so shatter'd with Age—and Infirmities—I assure you I have more Vigour than People Imagine: what think you Lucy?
> *Lucy*: Your Eyes Sir look very Sparkling and lively—but I think a-um—your other parts are not quite so brisk.
> *Skin*: Why ay, tis true, my other parts are a little—a little morbific, or so, as the Doctors say; but Harriet is very young, and she will be a Charming Bedfellow. (f. 10r–v)

One can easily imagine the humour of a sardonic Mrs Macklin bemoaning her husband's lack of briskness to the audience. And when Sir Isaac announces to Harriet shortly after, 'your charms will be a vivifying nostrum, to the morbific parts' (f. 11v), we can also readily imagine the humorous possibilities of physical comedy open to Mrs Macklin, as her character is present at this exchange.

What is less easy to imagine is the Examiner's leniency in allowing these references to impotence to pass through unscathed. They are quite lewd and it is not in keeping with a generally unforgiving attitude towards sexual references in plays from the period. Perhaps impotence was considered fair game? We might also speculate that the event's status as a benefit mattered as did the marital status of the two actors. Although it is unclear whether Macklin and Mrs Macklin were legally married, they were certainly understood to be so by their audience.[22] Thus the provocative lines are mediated through that real-life relationship and, to a degree, sanitized by it. Part of the advantage of their mutual success was their being facilitated in exploiting their marriage for commercial and dramatic reward. It may be that the Examiner, cognizant of the actors playing the parts and also of the economic importance of the benefit night to their profession, allowed special licence on this occasion.[23] But we can see that there is more than political or 'outsider' anger in Macklin's plays; there was a sense of bawdy fun and playfulness that does not often get discussed.

---

22 *Appleton*, 39.
23 The cover note from the manuscript submission by Lacy reads: 'Sir I have given Mrs Macklin leave to act this farce for her Benefit provided it meets with the Approbation of my Ld. Chamberlain'.

COVENT GARDEN THEATRE AND 'THE WHOLE HOUSE IN A TITTRE'

Bawdiness, as we shall see, is perhaps most apparent in *Covent Garden Theatre*, also discussed in Helen Burke's essay elsewhere in this volume. The plot of the two-act farce is slight. Pasquin, a self-appointed Drawcansir, or Censor of the nation, surveys and ridicules a number of 'Bon ton' characters who represent the foibles of London's modern life; he is assisted in this task by Marforio.[24] Characters who appear on stage for gentle ridicule include Miss Brilliant, Bob Smart, Sir Conjecture Positive, Sir Eternal Grin, Sir Roger Ringwood, Miss Diane Single-Life, and Lady Lucy Loveit. Sir Solomon Common Sense provides a foil to their collective inanity. The farce concludes with the customary obeisant gesture to the audience's good character and taste and an affirmation of the dangers of gambling to public morality inspired by Fielding's *Enquiry into the Causes of the Late Increase in Robbers* (1751). Literary debts are also owed to George Villiers's *The Rehearsal* (1671), Henry Fielding's play *Pasquin* (1736) and his periodical *Covent-Garden Journal* (1752), in which he used the pseudonym Sir Alexander Drawcansir.

Covent Garden Theatre was performed on 8 April 1752 at the eponymous theatre. The two-act farce was offered as an afterpiece to Colley Cibber's *The Provok'd Husband* and was a benefit performance for Macklin who most likely played the lead, Pasquin. The farce was never repeated. There is only one account of the production, which appeared in *Have at You All; or, The Drury-Lane Journal*, a periodical written by 'Madam Roxana Termagant', the pen name of Bonnell Thornton. Thornton's short-lived *Drury-Lane Journal* (16 January–9 April 1752) was specifically conceived in order to attack Fielding's *Covent-Garden Journal* by parodying his style.[25] Although *A Condemnation, or (according to the Technical Term) DAMNATION of the Dramatick Satire, call'd PASQUIN turn'd DRAWCANSIR* is ostensibly an attack on the play, it is clear that Thornton was quite sympathetic to Macklin's efforts. For instance, one of the criticisms Termagant levels is that 'it affronted a great part of the company, and obliged some very polite people in the boxes to decamp in a hurry, least their confusion of countenance should seem to betray a consciousness that they or their intimate acquaintance were aim'd at'—which suggests that Macklin's satire hit some of its marks.[26] While there are certainly issues with the quality of

---

[24] Pasquin and Marforio are names taken from the 'talking statues' of ancient Rome where satirical squibs would be placed at night by irreverent citizens.

[25] See Lance Bertelsen, '*Have at You All*: Bonnell Thornton's Journalism', *Huntington Library Quarterly* 44.4 (1981), 263–82.

[26] *Drury-Lane Journal*, 12 (1752), 283.

the drama, one might also observe that its failure was to a degree assured, given the extent of the censorship evidenced in the Larpent manuscript. As a piece heavily dependent on humorous references to contemporary people and events, their exclusion meant that there was little left for an audience to enjoy.[27] But, as we shall see, Macklin's piece was also rather earthy.

The sexual material in this play is unusually explicit insofar as mid-century Georgian theatre goes. There is a lurid suggestion that actresses 'might in time become Adamites, and go without so much as a Figleaf' (f. 21r). This follows a ribald exchange on Miss Giggle's exposure of her breasts that is marked for deletion in its entirety:

> *Mar[forio]*: But there is a further Charge against this Lady; She is said to be a common Nusance at the Theatres; and that She frequently Sets the whole House in a Tittre to the Confusion of the Actors, & the general disturbance of the Audience, by constantly exposing her Nudities to Publick View, contrary to the Ideas of female Modesty, and the Laws of Decency.
> *Miss Dy[Diana Singlelife]*: O fye Seignior, how can you make use of so indelicate an Expression. A Lady's Nudities, why, you might as well have said—I vow it is almost plain English, I protest such an Expression is enough to get your Farce hiss'd off the Stage—
> *Pas[quin]*: I am extremely Sorry the Phrase offends your Ladyship, but if you will Substitute any other.
> *Dia[na Singlelife]*: I think Mr. Drawcansir when those Objects are to be expos'd that—a Lady's Proturberances, her Snow balls, or her Lover's Amusements—wou'd be much more delicate.
> *Sr. Rog[er Ringwood]*: You are very right Madam, and if they happen to be of the immense kind—Cupid's Kettle Drums Mr. Pasquin, wou'd not be an—unelegant Phrase, ha, ha, ha.
> *Omn[es]*: Ha, ha, ha, ha. (ff. 19v–20r)

As already noted, it is often extremely difficult to be certain who makes particular interventions in Larpent manuscripts and this is again the case with this manuscript. It seems probable that those marks made in pen are by Edward Capell, deputy to William Chetwynd, the Examiner of Plays. We might speculate that it is the theatre manager, John Rich, who makes the pencilled marks here but it could be Macklin, some other theatre functionary, or perhaps even (although improbably) the Lord Chamberlain. Given what is at stake for the theatre, however, it seems the manager is the safest bet.

---

27 Esther M. Raushenbush offers the fullest treatment in a sympathetic piece, which provides a useful overview of the play: 'Charles Macklin's Lost Play about Henry Fielding', *Modern Language Notes* 51.8 (1936), 505–14. *Appleton*, on the other hand, is somewhat less kind, declaring it a 'loosely-constructed, witless piece' (95).

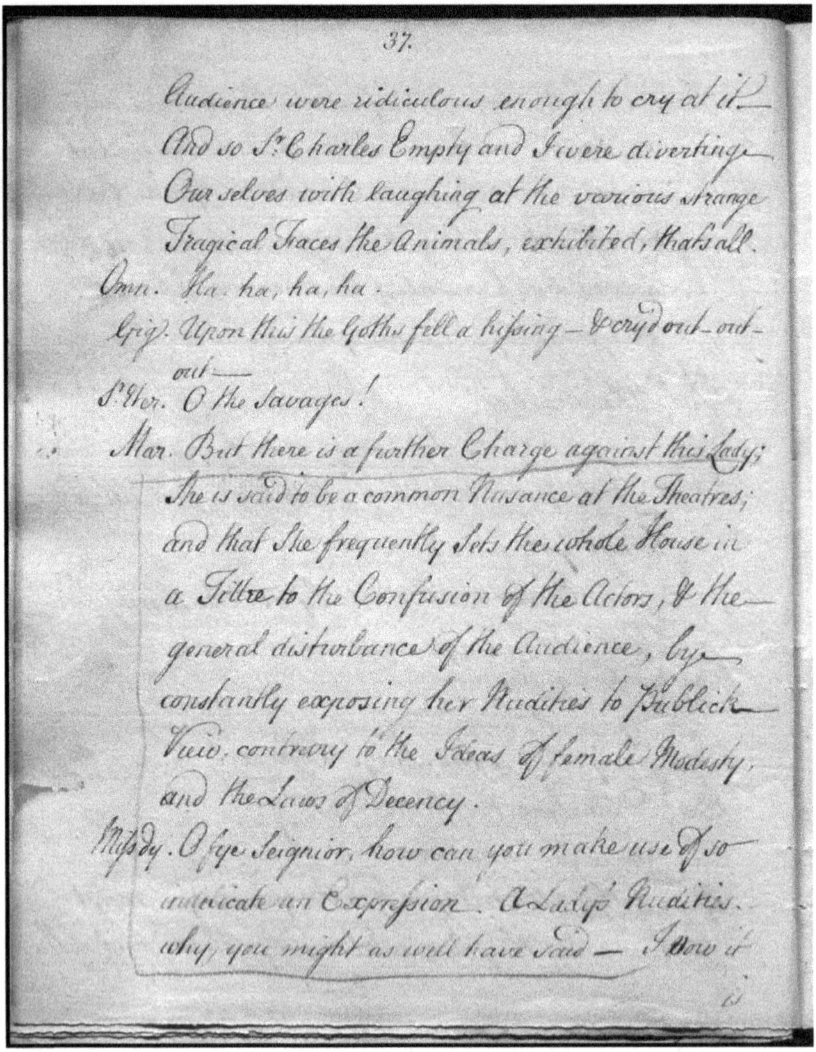

> 37.
>
> Audience were ridiculous enough to cry at it —
> And so S.r Charles Empty and I were diverting
> Ourselves with laughing at the various strange
> Tragical faces the Animals exhibited, that's all.
> Omn. Ha, ha, ha, ha.
> Grig. Upon this the Goths fell a hissing — & cry'd out — out —
> out —
> S.r Per. O the Savages!
> Mar. But there is a further Charge against this Lady;
> She is said to be a common Nusance at the Theatres;
> and that She frequently sets the whole House in
> a Titter to the Confusion of the Actors, & the
> general disturbance of the Audience, by
> constantly exposing her Nudities to Publick
> View, contrary to the Ideas of female Modesty,
> and the Laws of Decency.
> Melody. O fye Seignior, how can you make use of so
> indelicate an Expression. A Lady's Nudities.
> why, you might as well have Said — I know it

Figure 9.2: Charles Macklin, *Covent Garden Theatre*, LA 96, f. 19v, John Larpent Collection, The Huntington Library, San Marino, California.

I hazard then that the 'Adamite' reference is struck out by Capell (marked in pen in the margin) and the longer passage by John Rich (boxed in pencil and partly visible in Figure 9.2). But is there anything more to this colourful description of female breasts than cheap titillation?

In fact, there is a very specific reference in these lines. Macklin is invoking recent memories of Elizabeth Chudleigh's scandalous appearance at a royal masquerade at Somerset House in May 1749. Chudleigh was a figure of some notoriety in English society; one biographer has called her 'truly representative of the cosmopolitan society woman of the eighteenth century'.[28] She had been appointed a maid of honour to Princess Augusta in 1743 but this significant position had not constrained her lifestyle. As well as secretly marrying Augustus John Hervey, she was friendly with genteel female company such as committed cardplayer and socialite Lady Harrington (formerly Lady Caroline Fitzroy). Lady Harrington and her peers 'rioted in dissipation' and Chudleigh was 'constant at the midnight orgies of their pleasures'.[29] To mark the peace with France brought about by the Treaty of Aix-la-Chapelle, the king ordered illuminations and masquerades. At one of these masquerades, the twenty-nine-year-old Elizabeth set London alight with scandal when she went dressed—rather scantily—as the mythological Iphigenia: '[She] covered such parts of her skin, as a strict conformity to the character she had assumed, with flesh-coloured silk, which, however, had at least an indelicate appearance, and induced the Princess of Wales to give her favourite a tacit reproof, by throwing a veil over her'.[30]

The choice of costume certainly got Chudleigh the attention she sought. King George II, who was himself dressed in a friar's habit, was smitten and subsequently organized a jubilee ball in her honour where he bought her a watch for 35 guineas, pointedly telling her that he was paying for it himself rather than chalking it down to expenses on the civil list.[31] Elizabeth Montagu archly observed: 'Miss Chudleigh's dress, or rather undress, was remarkable; she was Iphigenia for the sacrifice, but so naked, the high priest might easily inspect the entrails of the victim'.[32] As Figure 9.3 indicates, the story became something of a minor urban legend and both written and visual accounts have her wearing fig-leaves and little else.[33]

---

28 Beatrice Curtis Brown, *Elizabeth Chudleigh, Duchess of Kingston* (London: Gerald Howe, 1927), 9.
29 *The Life and Memoirs of Elizabeth Chudleigh, Afterwards Mrs Hervey and Countess of Bristol* (London, [1788]), 10.
30 *Life and Memoirs of Elizabeth Chudleigh*, 10.
31 Brown, *Elizabeth Chudleigh*, 33.
32 Cited in Brown, *Elizabeth Chudleigh*, 32.
33 *Life and Memoirs of Elizabeth Chudleigh*, 10.

Figure 9.3: 'Iphigenia' (Elizabeth Pierrepont [née Chudleigh, later Hervey], Duchess of Kingston), by unknown artist. Attributed to Charles Mosley. © National Portrait Gallery, London.

It is not surprising that Macklin felt he could garner dramatic material out of the episode: London's newspapers referred to it for years after. In 1752, the same year as *Covent Garden Theatre* was performed, Thornton's satirical *Drury-Lane Journal* (9 April) advertised a Ranelagh Jubilee with a burlesque offering: patrons could avail of 'Naked dresses, in imitation of their own skin. And other natural disguises'.[34] Charles Churchill's *Gotham* (1764) contains the lines 'Summer, in light transparent gauze arrayed,/Like maids-of-honour at a masquerade'. Chudleigh also did her bit to remain in the public eye by writing *Britannia in tears* on the death of Prince Frederick in 1751, which got some press attention.[35] And, as has been well documented, the build-up to the 'hyper-public event'[36] of her trial for bigamy in the House of Lords in 1776 proved irresistible to Samuel Foote who also found comic potential in Chudleigh's life: the pair had a very public spat in the newspapers regarding his *A Trip to Calais*, a play which was refused a performance licence.[37] Chudleigh was a scandalously public woman and was referenced as Iphigenia in satirical prints until at least 1776.[38]

Macklin's boisterous bawdiness seems a little naïve: a man of his theatrical experience should have known better than to present material of this nature for the stage. Why be so bawdy? Was this a post-Lenten ebullience on his part? Did he wish to be in step with a public interest in masquerades?[39] Perhaps it may also be that Macklin felt that as it was a benefit night there might have been some allowance made for him, as we have speculated with *A Will or No Will*. However, I want to argue that the truth is much more straightforward. Macklin was writing, as Kinservik suggests, with a 'moral seriousness' that was unusual for the mid-eighteenth

---

34 *Drury-Lane Journal* 13 (1752), 286, cited in Charles E. Pearce, *The Amazing Duchess Being the Romantic History of Elizabeth Chudleigh*, 2 vols (London: Stanley Paul & Co., 1911), I.163.

35 *Britannia in tears: An elegiac pastoral on the death of Frederick, prince of Wales. By a Maid of Honour* (London, 1751). Chudleigh's authorship is noted in the *General Advertiser*, 19 April 1751.

36 Gillian Russell, *Women, Sociability and Theatre in Georgian London* (Cambridge: Cambridge University Press, 2007), 153.

37 The play was refused and staged as *The Capuchin* in 1776. Kinservik, *Disciplining Satire*, 161–63. For a fuller treatment, see Ian Kelly, *Mr Foote's Other Leg* (London: Picador, 2012), 294–323.

38 John Hamilton Mortimer, 'Iphigenia's late procession from Kingston to Bristol.—by Chudleigh Meadows' (1776). British Museum object number 1868,0808.4541.

39 There are four references to characters going to or dressing for a masquerade in the farce. A haberdasher advertised in the same week as the performance that he 'Has made up MASQUERADE DRESSES in all Characters entirely new, and never exposed to view', *Daily Advertiser*, 3 April 1752.

century.[40] He was using theatre's capacity to interrogate publicly the behaviour of the ruling classes, not Elizabeth Chudleigh. Bear in mind that the king had not only purchased a 35 guinea watch for this young and attractive maid-of-honour, he had also agreed to appoint her mother to the vacant housekeeper's post at Windsor, a post which came with a generous salary of £800. *Covent Garden Theatre*—and its odd tirade on fig leaves and breasts—was intended to rail against the salaciousness of the ruling classes certainly but also the corrupt allocation of places precisely as he would do in *The Man of the World*. Macklin, blinkered by his enthusiasm for a theatre of political reform, simply lost sight of what was or was not possible. Leaving aside its eyebrow-raising explicitness, the piece could not have passed through the Examiner's office. This is personal satire with a reformist bent, writ large and boisterous.

There is also a secondary level of satire in play as Macklin assesses 'the Ton's' capacity to assimilate the emerging assertion of women for a place in the public sphere. As Gillian Russell has shown, the growing discursive presence of elite women in the new sites of the public sphere was troubling to the 'homosocial integrity' of the club and the coffeehouse. As Russell argues,

> the developments in fashionable sociability in the 1760s and '70s was a sign that women had encroached profoundly upon the concept and practice of an authentic public sphere based on the male homosociality of the coffeehouse, tavern and club, with possible implications for the latter's claims to political and cultural legitimacy.[41]

Macklin's 1752 play anticipates the gendered realignment of the public sphere that unfurled over the subsequent decades.[42] In the bawdy commentary by ill-informed and vacuous commentators such as Sir Roger and friends, incapable of coping with the confident and enterprising poise of women such as Chudleigh, Macklin adroitly underlines the failings of post-1745 London to fulfil the Enlightenment claims of the newly reaffirmed Hanoverian project. In *Covent Garden Theatre*, we can trace some of the intellectual roots of the subsequent coffeehouse project, a project that offered women a participatory platform in 'an attempt to reform the boorish conviviality associated with the Covent Garden area into something more refined, and indeed improving', as Ian Newman suggests above.[43]

---

40 Kinservik, *Disciplining Satire*, 172.
41 Russell, *Women, Sociability and Theatre*, 87.
42 See also Markman Ellis's suggestion that the gendered transformation of public entertainment in mid-eighteenth-century London took place earlier than the 1770s. Ellis, 'Macklin's Coffeehouse', in this volume.
43 Ian Newman, 'Macklin and Song', 163.

The Chudleigh example shows how a play that has been understood to deal in generic types actually uses a very specific example in order to advocate a generalized moral reform. Macklin's slight farce thus challenges the behaviour, not only of Chudleigh, but the collective dissolution of all of those societal elites gathered in Somerset House, not least the king, prefiguring the attack on the levee of *The Man of the World*. In this later play, common consensus has been that there is a general critique of Scottish politicians associated with Lord Bute in the early 1760s.[44] This is undoubtedly the case; however, I want to suggest, more by way of a coda than a conclusion, that Macklin may have had a specific person in mind as he wrote the character of Hector MacCrafty, but, like *Covent Garden Theatre*, with a view to making a general case for political reform.

Coda

Sir Lawrence Dundas (1712–81) was known as the 'Nabob of the North', having amassed enormous wealth and land over his career.[45] After beginning as a wine merchant, he began to generate serious money as commissary for bread and forage in Scotland. Further positions followed and Dundas was able to get himself elected to parliament for the borough of Linlithgow Burghs, having paid what the duke of Argyll described as 'the greatest sum to purchase an election that was ever known in the country'.[46] Argyll, incensed at Dundas's corruption, stalled his ascent with the support of the prime minister Henry Pelham and Dundas was unseated for electoral corruption in 1748. The Seven Years War saw an upsurge in his fortunes and he generated enormous profits—estimated at £600,000 to £800,000— from supplying the Hanoverian army with bread and other goods during this conflict. In 1762, Lord Shelburne went to Bute on Dundas's behalf and acquired him a baronetcy; he also became MP for Newcastle-under-Lyme. Around this time he also became one of the great landowners

---

44 Dougald MacMillan describes it as a 'caustic satire of the Scotch politicians who swarmed into London and of political corruption in general'. 'The Censorship in the Case of Macklin's *The Man of the World*', 86.
45 I am very grateful to Aaron Graham for first pointing me towards Dundas. For the details on Dundas's career that follows, I am indebted to G.E. Bannerman, 'The "Nabob of the North": Sir Lawrence Dundas as Government Contractor', *Historical Research* 83 (2010), 102–23.
46 Cited in R.P. Fereday, 'Dundas family of Fingask and Kerse (*per.* 1728/9–1820)', *Oxford Dictionary of National Biography* (2008): https://doi.org/10.1093/ref:odnb/64103 (accessed 12 February 2020).

of Britain. Here is MacCrafty describing his rise to wealth to his son Marcus Montgomery:

> Sir I wriggled & wriggled, & wrought, & wriggled till I wriggle mysel among the very thick of them—hah!—got my snack of the Cloathes, the foraging, the contracts, the lottery tickets and aw the political bonuses; till at length, Sir I became a much wealthier man, than one half of the golden calves I had been so long a bowing to and was not that bowing to some purpose Sir, Ha? (f. 21r-v)

The foraging, the contracts, the political wriggling and conniving all offer explicit parallels with Dundas. Moreover, Dundas also engineered the marriage of his son Thomas to Lady Charlotte Fitzwilliam, a niece of the marquess of Rockingham, in April 1764—a political marriage that anticipates MacCrafty's desired union for his son. As G.E. Bannerman observes, 'the marriage had political consequences, linking Dundas with the opposition to the Grenvilles, but the social consequences were no less important—the marriage indicated that he intended his family to follow the well-worn path of integrating "new wealth" into aristocratic circles'.[47] The marriage and the political manoeuvring took place in the early 1760s when Macklin was writing his play and so it is at least plausible that Macklin channelled some of him into his composite Scottish bogeyman of political corruption, connecting personal satire with the general satirical swipe.

Macklin was a more serious dramatist than the picture of him as a truculent Wilkesite allows. Political reform is certainly a facet of Enlightenment but the censorship imposed on Macklin's oeuvre is broader than previous accounts have suggested; looking at the whole sweep of interventions, we get sight of a man aiming beyond party politics for a broader Enlightenment sense of societal reform. His jibes at religious hypocrisy are important but it is the earthy sexual material in his plays that offer us a radically different perspective on his work, his dramatic relationship with his wife, his attitudes to women more generally, and reveal a hitherto unacknowledged Rabelaisian streak. Moreover, the connections we can trace in his plays between personal and political satire give his oeuvre—from *King Henry the VII* to *Covent Garden Theatre* to *The Man of the World*—a degree of consistency with which he has not been credited. Macklin is a character who had a colourfully erratic career trajectory, one punctuated by tumultuous events (manslaughter, feuds, British Inquisition, law courts, and so on). Critics have had a tendency—not without cause—to look to his irascible nature as a unifying theme that explains his professional waywardness. But this distorts the character of the man, and not simply at the level of his personality. Tracing his clashes with

---

47 Bannerman, 'Nabob of the North', 118.

the Examiners of Plays delineates an intellectual project that brings much of his work together, a practice of Enlightenment that sustains itself through a variety of different engagements with the London stage and its theatrical practitioners over some decades. This chapter has shown how working towards social reform through the medium of corrective personal satire remains a consistent thread in his dramaturgical practice and can be traced further in other aspects of his life such as his British Inquisition lectures and his library, discussed elsewhere in this volume. This fuller understanding of the breadth of Macklin's capacity to irk the Examiner of Plays, and his rationale for doing so, bolsters Enlightenment claims we can make on his behalf.

Sociability

10

Macklin's Coffeehouse
Public Sociability in Mid-Eighteenth-Century London

Markman Ellis

IN 1753, AGED AROUND FIFTY-FOUR YEARS, Charles Macklin retired from the stage to establish a coffeehouse in the Piazza of Covent Garden. Macklin's Coffeehouse was an innovative commercial enterprise that blended together several different kinds of sociable space that were already familiar to his customers. In a luxuriously appointed set of rooms, his business offered a coffee service, together with food and drinks, conversation and gaming, oratorical lectures and public debates. Furthermore, it was open to women as well as men. There was nothing quite like it, but after an initial period of popularity, Macklin's enterprise was overcome by debt, and he was forced into bankruptcy in January 1755, having been open less than a year. This chapter examines Macklin's project in relation to notions of sociability, defined as the practice of convivial mixing, and explores the diverse models of sociability to which the project appealed. Macklin's Coffeehouse opened in March 1754, and nine months later, in November and December, for about a month and a half, the coffee-room hosted twenty-three performances of the event he called the British Inquisition, which combined an oratorical lecture with a debating society. William Appleton (1960) and Mary Thale (1999), both working within a tradition of theatrical history, have devoted focused attention to the British Inquisition, as does Helen Burke in this volume.[1] In this chapter, I will use the

---

1 The fullest account of Macklin's venture is *Appleton*, esp. 98–108. See also Mary Thale, 'The Case of the British Inquisition: Money and Women in Mid-Eighteenth-Century London Debating Societies', *Albion: A Quarterly Journal Concerned with British Studies* 31.1 (1999), 31–48. Debating societies, but not the British Inquisition, are

term 'Macklin's Coffeehouse' to refer to the whole enterprise, and reserve the name the British Inquisition for the performances advertised under that title.

The wider context for Macklin's Coffeehouse is the gendered transformation of public entertainment in mid-eighteenth-century London. Many contemporaries noticed that there had been a marked expansion in the number and variety of 'Places of Public Diversion' in the period. In 1754, newspapers like the *Public Advertiser* gave notice of a remarkable range of public diversions, including the theatre and opera, pleasure gardens, assemblies and masquerades, exhibitions and museums, lectures, clubs, learned societies, taverns and debating clubs. This represented a significant expansion of commercial public entertainments, and, as Gillian Russell has argued, women were the main beneficiaries of this 'revolution in modes of sociability'—although it is worth noting that she dates the change to a later period, beginning in the 1770s.[2] The increasing accessibility of public entertainment for women can be contextualized by arguments about gender and the separate spheres of public and private in eighteenth-century society. Amanda Vickery and Lawrence Klein (among others) have argued that the dialectical polarity of the 'separate spheres' construction encouraged historians to locate women in the private domestic sphere of the home, and men in the public. Instead, in the 1990s, Klein suggested 'that the public and private realms are less well segregated from one another and less exclusively gendered than they are sometimes represented to be'.[3] Numerous historians since then have explored this hypothesis in detail, contesting especially the assumption that women were excluded from the public world of associational sociability. The revisionist account describes how the significant extension of the genteel leisure industry in the period made it more visible and diversified in its locations, and women were increasingly producers as well as consumers. The culture of public entertainment, and practices of polite sociability, was being feminized, although when that occurred, and the dimensions of the transformation, are open to debate.

The concept of sociability has played a prominent part in recent research on social and cultural history, especially in the eighteenth century. The concept has been traced by some to the early twentieth-century German sociologist Georg Simmel's 1911 essay on *Geselligkeit*, or sociability, which in his analysis

---

also discussed in relation to gender in Betty Rizzo, 'Male Oratory and Female Prate: "Then Hush and Be an Angel Quite"', *Eighteenth-Century Life* 29.1 (2005), 23–49.

2 Gillian Russell, *Women, Sociability and Theatre in Georgian London* (Cambridge: Cambridge University Press, 2007), 10–15.

3 Lawrence E. Klein, 'Gender, Conversation and the Public Sphere in Early Eighteenth-Century England', in Judith Still and Michael Worton (eds), *Textuality and Sexuality: Reading Theories and Practices* (Manchester: Manchester University Press, 1993), 102.

was a form of social interaction that was 'freed from all ties with contents' existing 'for its own sake and for the sake of the fascination which, in its own liberation from these ties, it diffuses'.[4] But sociability was also a central concept in eighteenth-century Enlightenment thought on the origins of human society: essential to the work of Pufendorf, Shaftesbury, Hutcheson, and Hume, amongst many others.

Macklin showed some interest in this Enlightenment philosophical discussion of sociability. All his comedies, from *A Will and No Will* (1746) through to *The Man of the World* (1781), can be considered to some extent as reflections on sociable principles. His Commonplace Book, at the Folger Shakespeare Library, shows that he also engaged with contemporary philosophical debate on sociability. In it there is, for example, an abbreviated and undated reference to the abstract term 'Sociability', which references a discussion of sociability in an untraced encyclopaedia ('the word Sociability, p. 658. Vol: 38').[5] Elsewhere in the Commonplace Book Macklin argues that mankind was motivated by five necessities: curiosity, sociability, esteem or self-love, piety, and love of liberty. In his notes on 'LOVE or Sociability', Macklin says:

> we wish to Love and to be beloved our selves; as the honest means of our own happiness. & of the happiness of our fellow-creatures. Love is the prime principle of Benevolence.—Kindness, Humanity, and Compassion; the Bond of Domestick Society, the Seed of Friendship. It is that pulse of the Heart that expresses its own happiness in its feeling, the happiness of all.[6]

Macklin suggests love of esteem drives 'our acting in every part of our dealings and Conduct thro Life with the nicest Propriety and the strictest most liberal honesty'.[7] His discussion of sociability casts him as a sentimentalist, who sees benevolence and love for others as natural; for whom friendship and

---

4 Georg Simmel, 'The Sociology of Sociability', trans. Everett C. Hughes, *American Journal of Sociology* 55.3 (1949), 254–61; Brian Cowan, 'Public Spaces, Knowledge, and Sociability', in Frank Trentmann (ed.), *The Oxford Handbook of the History of Consumption* (Oxford: Oxford University Press, 2015), 251.

5 Charles Macklin, 'Commonplace Book, 1778–1790' [manuscript], Folger Shakespeare Library, M.a.9, No. 68, f. 23r. The commonplace book entries are not dated, but almost certainly derive from a period after 1770. *Encyclopédie, ou Dictionnaire raisonné des sciences, des arts et des métiers, par une société de gens de lettres. Mis en ordre & publié par M. Diderot … & quant à la partie mathématique, par M. d'Alembert* (Lausanne: Sociétés Typographiques, 1781–82), 36 vols (octavo). The volume and page references suggest that Macklin was reading one of the Swiss reprintings from the 1770s or 1780s: these quarto and octavo editions came in 36 or 48 volumes, but the reference itself has not been traced.

6 Macklin, 'Commonplace Book', No. 135, f. 40v.

7 Macklin, 'Commonplace Book', No. 136, f. 40v.

kindness is natural, not learned or mandated by authority; and for whom politeness and propriety drives moral probity. The Commonplace Book itself, both in its contents, and the structural forms and habits of thought it suggests, shows Macklin's intellectual landscape to have been sophisticated and closely engaged with Enlightenment philosophy. Macklin's Commonplace Book was a manuscript notebook of the author's reflections and observations, together with extracts from and summaries of other thinkers and writers, mostly without attribution or dating. The material is entered under a keyword into numbered cells (two to a page) and indexed alphabetically at the end. It shows his interest in philosophical approaches to modern urban life, and his awareness of and ambition in Enlightenment knowledge collation systems. Commonplacing systems both recorded information and facilitated its retrieval, which allowed *virtuosi* to seek new empirical information. Commonplacing further addressed the problem faced by many scholars that the amount of information they acquired exceeded their personal capacity to deal with it, and compromised the usefulness of its storage in larger scientific archives.[8] Macklin's notebook shows that he adopted commonplacing as a practice of note-taking, memory, and information control, but also repurposed and transformed that practice, so as to a create an idiosyncratic but flexible system for creative composition, in which information retrieval allowed Macklin to establish synchronic connection between topics and ideas.

Macklin's Enlightenment interests further locate him within recent studies of the diasporic Irish Enlightenment operating in London and other centres, comprising a network of Irish migrants, pursuing professional and intellectual activities, some of whom achieved relative prosperity in the middle classes.[9] David O'Shaughnessy has described how their

> influence within professional fields such as medicine, banking, and the law meant that they constituted a powerful interlinked and overlapping ethnic network with all the trimmings of a vibrant metropolitan constituency, including a Masonic lodge.[10]

---

8 Richard Yeo, *Notebooks, English Virtuosi, and Early Modern Science* (Chicago: University of Chicago Press, 2014), 5, 13–25; Richard Yeo, 'Notebooks as Memory Aids: Precepts and Practices in Early Modern England', *Memory Studies* 1.1 (2008), 115–36.

9 The complex historiography of the term Irish Enlightenment and its application within the 'London Irish' is discussed in Ian McBride, 'The Edge of Enlightenment: Ireland and Scotland in the Eighteenth Century', *Modern Intellectual History* 10.1 (2013), 135–51; David O'Shaughnessy, 'Introduction: "Tolerably Numerous": Recovering the London Irish of the Eighteenth Century', *Eighteenth-Century Life* 39.1 (2015), 1–13.

10 David O'Shaughnessy, '"Bit, by some mad whig": Charles Macklin and the Theater of Irish Enlightenment', *Huntington Library Quarterly* 80.4 (2017), 563.

The theatre was one such field, albeit one that tended to precarious finances. However, Irish actors and dramatists found popular success, and used that to pursue a kind of distributed collaborative enquiry into Irish identity. Macklin was embedded in the 'active and ambitious Irish networks in London', especially through his friendship and sociability with others in such networks with theatrical interests, including Spranger Barry, Arthur Murphy, Francis Gentleman, and Edmund Burke.

In this essay, I will recover as much as can be known of Macklin's Coffeehouse from primary documents, especially newspapers and periodicals. His coffeehouse was a real place, but also a conceptual formation that brings all the contexts above into contention with each other: the gendered transformation of public entertainment, the philosophy of Enlightenment sociability, and the Irish intellectual diaspora. The essay will explore the sociability of Macklin's project, analysing what it means when he describes it as, variously, a coffeehouse, tavern, ordinary, and subscription room, and then later, as a place which stages the lectures and debates of the British Inquisition. Macklin's medley will be examined as a form of hybridized 'polyhedonic sociability': one that seeks to offer a range of sociable pleasures that are more generally contraindicated or in tension. The range of sociable activities Macklin's project allowed may have made it more amenable both to London Irish culture and to philosophic enquiry. The hybridity of Macklin's venture is made more complex by its openness to women, and again, by the degree to which it can be ascertained women actually participated. The chapter will end by drawing some conclusions about women and gendered behaviours in the 'polyhedonic sociability' of Macklin's Coffeehouse.

Mr Macklin's 'House and Rooms in the Piazza'

IN MIDSUMMER 1753, Macklin contracted with the Duke of Bedford's steward for a set of rooms under the arcades of the North Piazza of Covent Garden. The lease of this 'Capital Messuage' was for twenty-one years at the annual rent of £45, providing he agreed to make repairs estimated at £368: he was offered cheaper rent to mitigate the considerable repair bill. Macklin employed a local builder, John Tinkler, to carry out the repairs and to make improvements.[11] Macklin built a two-storied extension at the back of the building ('at the North of Back Front'), adding

---

11 *Public Advertiser*, 22 April 1754.

two rooms one above another, and another building of one storey. This cost £700. Then, in addition, Macklin contracted with Tinkler to build, for a further £900, a building beyond that which fronted onto Hart Street. For his total investment of £1,968, Macklin had a large building that ran from the North Piazza of Covent Garden right though to Hart Street.[12] This was in close proximity to the Theatre Royal Covent Garden, the Shakespeare Tavern, and the Bedford Coffeehouse; as such, at the centre of the London theatrical world. This location coloured perceptions of the enterprise, given that this corner of Covent Garden had historically enduring connections with illicit and bawdy sociability, especially drinking, gambling, prostitution, and theatre. Rival coffeehouses in the area included Button's and Tom's in Russell Street, once but no longer known as the wits' or poets' coffeehouses, but also Moll King's, in a shed in the Piazza, famous for its late hours, its eclectic clientele, and the assignations made there between them. This combination of architectural splendour and libertine notoriety gave this corner of Covent Garden what some historians have anachronistically called a sleazy bohemian glamour.[13]

The finished result of Macklin's rebuilding was a large and luxuriously appointed suite of rooms. A story in the *Public Advertiser* in March 1754 enthused about the scale of 'Mr Macklin's House and Rooms in the Piazza':

> Two of the Rooms are fifty by twenty-five, and twenty feet high; and the third is eighty by thirty, five and twenty Feet high; which, with other Apartments, form a Suite of Rooms two hundred and thirty Feet deep.[14]

There are no extant visual records, but we might assume that these rooms were luxuriously appointed, with mirrors and gilt—along the lines of later assembly rooms such as Almack's. The only details of the interior that have

---

12 Details about the renovations are found in Philip Yorke, Lord Hardwicke, 'In the matter of Charles Macklin a bankrupt', 31 July 1755, in John Doran, *'Their Majesties Servants': Being an Annal of the English Stage from Thomas Betterton (1635–1779) to Edmund Kean (1787–1833). Illustrated with Drawings, Engravings, Caricatures, Autograph Letters, & Play Bills*, 5 vols, extra-illustrated (1888), III.(opp.)109. Houghton Library, Harvard Theatre Collection TS 934.5F.

13 On Button's, see Peter Smithers, *The Life of Joseph Addison*, 2nd edn (Oxford: Clarendon Press, 1968), 243–44. On Moll King's, see Markman Ellis, 'The Coffee-Women, *The Spectator* and the Public Sphere in the Early Eighteenth Century', in Elizabeth Eger and Charlotte Grant (eds), *Women and the Public Sphere* (Cambridge: Cambridge University Press, 2001), 35–39. On Covent Garden and the history of bohemianism, see Vic Gatrell, *The First Bohemians: Life and Art in London's Golden Age* (London: Allen Lane, 2013).

14 *Public Advertiser*, 11 March 1754.

emerged are that the decorations involved 'paper hangings' (printed decorative wall paper) and there were 'water closets', both of which signal luxury appointments.[15] When the building was finished, Macklin paid Tinkler £1,300, and the remaining sum of £668 was owed as a debt or mortgage that the business had to pay off.[16] Macklin's finances are somewhat mysterious, and it is unclear whether the cash payment to Tinkler was covered by a loan or partnership with unknown investors, or whether the sum represents the actor's career savings. In any case, Macklin had significantly overspent his budget on renovation and rebuilding works and remained in Tinkler's debt.

Macklin sometimes described his property as a 'Great Room'. As Richard Altick explains, this was a term used in eighteenth-century London to describe 'any rentable room large enough to accommodate concerts or exhibitions'.[17] A 'great room' was a flexible space in which a large number of people could assemble for sociable and cultural purposes. In 1753 alone, there were at least eight different 'great rooms' advertised in London in the newspapers. These included Mr Ogle's Great Room in Dean Street, that hosted regular subscription music concerts by Handel and others, as well as balls and assemblies;[18] Hickford's Great Room in Brewer Street that also hosted music concerts;[19] the Great Room near Exeter Change that hosted exhibitions and Dr Lucas's course of lectures on Chemistry;[20] the Great Room at Old South Sea House in Old Broad Street that hosted Mr Jack's course of forty 'Lectures on Natural and Experimental Philosophy';[21] and Mr Ford's Great Room in St James's Haymarket;[22] the Great Room of the Antigallican Coffeehouse in Threadneedle Street;[23] and Mr Browning's Great Room over the Royal Exchange, that all hosted auctions of various kinds.[24] There was also a Great Room at Ranelagh. As this suggests,

---

15 *London Gazette*, 18–22 March 1755. These items are listed in the notice of the coffeehouse's forced sale after bankruptcy. The term 'water closet' in this period meant both 'A small room fitted out for a person to urinate and defecate in, with a water supply to flush away the waste' and 'A fixed receptacle used for urination and defecation' (*Oxford English Dictionary*).
16 Hardwicke, 'In the matter of Charles Macklin a bankrupt'.
17 Richard Daniel Altick, *The Shows of London* (Cambridge, MA: Belknap Press of Harvard University Press, 1978), 54 n.
18 *Public Advertiser*, 14 March 1753.
19 *Public Advertiser*, 9 May 1753.
20 *Public Advertiser*, 30 January 1753; *London Evening Post*, 6 October 1753.
21 *London Daily Advertiser*, 7 March 1753.
22 *Public Advertiser*, 2 April 1753.
23 *Public Advertiser*, 22 October 1753.
24 *Public Advertiser*, 12 November 1753.

the metaphor of the Great Room was used for a wide variety of indoor commercial public entertainments.

In preparation for opening the business, Macklin acquired permission to operate as a tavern keeper from the local authority.[25] News of his plans began to spread. Thomas Birch wrote to his patron Philip Yorke on 15 September 1753 that Macklin had 'taken the House formerly Lord Mornington's under the Piazza, & [was] intending to fit up a magnificent Coffee Room & School of Oratory, which he says is a great Desideratum in our Country'.[26] In November 1753, Macklin announced his intention to retire from the stage,[27] and on 20 December, he gave his final benefit performance of *The Refusal* by Colley Cibber, at which he hinted at this new venture in a 'Farewell Epilogue'.[28] In the Epilogue, written by David Garrick, Macklin announced that he was to 'quit the Trade' for 'A Scheme I have in Hand will make you stare!' The Epilogue plays around with the idea of the actor serving his audience like a waiter serves his customers, but does not give much away about the nature of the new 'Scheme', except that it was going to be in the sociability business. The Epilogue said:

> My Plan is this—Man's form'd a social Creature,
> Requiring Converse by the Laws of Nature.[29]

Garrick's epilogue repeats a conceit first expressed in Aristotle, and recalls the phrasing of *The Spectator*'s ninth essay, where Addison proposed that 'Man is said to be a Sociable Animal'.[30] The expression makes the claim that sociability was the cornerstone of community, urban life, and human society. Whatever Garrick knew of Macklin's actual plans, he suggests that his post-retirement project was to be based around sociability and conversation.

---

25 Middlesex County Records, Recognizances: L.v. (W) 69/929, 20 September 1753; renewed L.v. (W) 70/1155, 5 September 1754.
26 Birch to Yorke, 15 September 1753, British Library, Add. MS 35398, ff. 159–160 (f. 160r).
27 *Public Advertiser*, 24 November 1753.
28 Macklin played Sir Gilbert Wrangle, a wealthy Director of the South Sea Company, who has his pockets full of letters and petitions from those who want his favour.
29 *Gray's Inn Journal*, 14 (29 December 1753), 84.
30 Joseph Addison, *The Spectator* 9 (10 March 1711), in Joseph Addison and Richard Steele, *The Spectator*, ed. Donald F. Bond, 5 vols (Oxford: Clarendon Press, 1965), I.39. Aristotle, *Politics*, trans. H. Rackham (Cambridge, MA: Harvard University Press, 1932), 1252b, 9. See also Fred D. Miller, *Nature, Justice, and Rights in Aristotle's Politics* (Oxford: Clarendon Press, 1997), 61.

Murphy's satire on the female coffeehouse

The prospect of Macklin's Coffeehouse attracted the attention of the satirists. In the *Gray's Inn Journal* for 5 January 1754, Arthur Murphy addressed the new venture while construction was still continuing.[31] Murphy was the son of a merchant in Dublin, and in 1754 was twenty-five years old, a generation younger than Macklin. He was seeking a career in the law and in literature, in pursuit of which he cultivated friendships amongst dramatists and actors, at both the theatre and the Bedford Coffeehouse. He went on to become a successful dramatist in the late 1750s and was called to the bar in 1761. Murphy played opposite Maria Macklin in the 1755 performances of Congreve's *The Mourning Bride* at Drury Lane. Macklin and Murphy were later to become friends, and Murphy became Macklin's legal counsel in the 1770s.[32] Murphy's *Gray's Inn Journal* began as a regular essay in *The Craftsman*, and after forty-nine numbers, started again at number fifty as a half-folio pamphlet in September 1753. Murphy's essay on Macklin's Coffeehouse venture, something between an affectionate puff and an incredulous satire, introduces two beautiful sisters, Harriet and Charlot Millefont, whose characteristic perfections are 'Politeness, Good-nature and Affability'. They are also practised at the new female public sociability: they are as familiar with 'the Opera and the Burletta' as they are with the theatre; they also attend the new fashionable assemblies known as masquerades, and 'Routs and Drums'. Harriet comments that she had even been in the theatre when Macklin had given his last performance, but, having not understood 'the Hint in the Epilogue', asks about *'Macklin's* new Scheme'.[33]

Charles Ranger, the editorial persona of the periodical, explains what he knows of Macklin's plan.

> He has built two magnificent Rooms, and intends to furnish them in an elegant Manner; the Apartment on the Ground-Floor to be a public Coffee-Room, and the other to receive such of the Nobility and People of Fashion as may think proper to subscribe to his Undertaking.

---

31 [Arthur Murphy], *The Gray's Inn Journal, By Charles Ranger*, 'Numb. 15' (5 January 1754), 85–90. A considerably revised version was reprinted as 'No. 61, Proposal for a Female Coffee-House', in *Gray's Inn Journal*, 2 vols (London, 1756), II.50–55. See Roy E. Aycock, 'Arthur Murphy, the *Gray's-Inn Journal*, and the *Craftsman*: Some Publication Mysteries', *Papers of the Bibliographical Society of America* 67 (1973), 255–62.

32 John Pike Emery, *Arthur Murphy: An Eminent English Dramatist of the Eighteenth Century* (Philadelphia: University of Philadelphia Press, 1946), 27, 140. See also David Worrall's chapter in this volume.

33 Murphy, 'Numb. 15', 85–87.

Two rooms, one open and public called a Coffee-Room, and the other a selective and exclusive room to hold a members' subscription club for the polite and fashionable elite. Harriet responds obliquely: she observes that a coffeehouse, despite what Ranger says, is not really open to the public, because it excludes women. Harriet says:

> it's a vexatious Thing to see how these Men are always contriving Places for their own Accommodation, without Troubling their Heads about the Women. The odious Things are always herding with one another, and the Ladies are Sequestred from all the Joys of these convenient Meetings.

She characterizes the coffeehouse in general as homosocial space with narrow and restricted discourse, 'sequestered' from the full openness of heterosocial encounter. As such, she concludes, they encourage immorality. Instead, Harriet makes a proposal of her own: '—Whip me, but I wish the Women would agree to have a Coffee-House of their own, to be revenged of the Fellows'. Harriet presses Ranger to pursue the idea of a female coffeehouse in his publication: this essay is the result.[34]

The essay continues with Ranger's considerations of Harriet's suggestion. He agrees with her criticism that the normative homosocial coffeehouse experience has a corrupting effect on male manners: 'most of those Places', he says, are

> frequented entirely by Bucks, Bloods, and Rakes of all Denominations, from whom there is nothing to be acquired except a Swagger in the Gait, a drunken Totter, a noisy riotous Deportment, a Volly of Oaths, and a total Want of what is called Good-Breeding.

He explicitly identifies the absence of women as the cause: men who go to the coffeehouse are missing

> any Connections in genteel Families, or any Acquaintance with the amiable Sex, without which no one can ever properly be said to relish Society, or to possess that Polish in his Manners, which is necessary to distinguish the Gentleman. Perhaps this Opportunity of detaching themselves from the Ladies in Coffee-House Clubs is the Cause of that Aukwardness.

Insulated from female company, men in the coffeehouse are boorish or awkward, unsuited to polite mixed company.[35]

Any apparent seriousness with which Ranger considers Harriet's proposal is undermined in the rest of the essay. A female coffeehouse, Ranger suggests,

---

34 Murphy, 'Numb. 15', 87.
35 Murphy, 'Numb. 15', 87.

would also corrupt women, as they would there give free reign to mindless trivialities, pantomimes, gossip, and gambling. Ranger ends with 'A System of Rules, &c' for the conduct of a female coffeehouse.[36] These rules suggest that women should pay for their drinks; that 'Actresses' should be admitted; that women should be permitted to play at cards; and that they might be admitted as members of the club. There was something of a fashion for mock regulation of female intellectual sociability in these years: Bonnell Thornton had satirized the rules of a 'Disputant Society for the Female Sex' in the *Drury Lane Journal* the year before, and the rules of a 'Female Parliament' were discussed in *The Connoisseur*, the journal Thornton co-edited with George Colman, later in 1755.[37] These satires all pull in the same direction, describing regulations that prohibit, and so advertise, various forms of supposedly characteristic social behaviours associated with women, familiar from misogynist satires. Rather than reforming women, these rules are a description of misogynist beliefs about the sociability of women: that women are riven with jealousy, cheating, sexual intrigue, and quarrelling, and that this is their nature and their fate.

Coffeehouse, tavern, ordinary, subscription room

On 11 March 1754, the *Public Advertiser* wrote that 'Mr Macklin's House and Rooms in the Piazza are finished, and will be opened next Week. [...] The whole is judged, by all which have seen it, to be much the most elegantly fitted up, of any Place of public Entertainment in Europe'.[38] A series of newspaper reports underlined the high costs of 'Macklin's Room below Stairs'.[39] The next day the same newspaper announced

> To-morrow Macklin's will be open'd. The lower Apartment is for a Publick Coffee-Room, where nothing will be taken but Silver. The large Room above Stairs is for a select Number of Subscribers, who have form'd themselves into a balloting Club, upon the Plan of White's and George's. The other Part of the House is for a Tavern; and the whole is fitted up in a most expensive and elegant manner.[40]

---

36 Murphy, 'Numb. 15', 88–89.
37 'Rules to be observed by the new Disputant Society for the Female Sex', *Have at You All; or, the Drury-Lane Journal* 7 (27 February 1752), 149–50; *The Connoisseur*, 49 (2 January 1755) and 57 (3 April 1755).
38 *Public Advertiser*, 11 March 1754.
39 *Public Advertiser*, 25 March 1754.
40 *Public Advertiser*, 26 March 1754.

The announcement indicates that Macklin's venture blended into one establishment a coffeehouse, tavern, and subscription club room. These are all sociable spaces, with a focus on conversation, but also with a fundamentally inconsistent expectation about the attendance of women. Furthermore, while the 'coffeehouse', and 'tavern', were distinct places of assembly, operating under different regulatory regimes or behavioural expectations, their offer nonetheless overlapped in important ways. Each type of business, each name, in other words, is a metaphor for a certain alliance of consumables, regulations, behaviours, and states of feeling. The next section of the paper will consider how these names describe different kinds of space, each of which contributes different and somewhat contradictory expectations to Macklin's hybrid sociability project. Inevitably, these descriptions will be schematic.

As a coffeehouse, the sociability Macklin encouraged was centred on a hot beverage service, around which was associated conversation and discussion, on politics, culture, and religion, but also gossip, together with provision of printed news and literature, and materials for writing and smoking. A French visitor, Henri Misson, described the multiple pleasures of the coffeehouse:

> Coffee-Houses, which are very numerous in London, are extremely convenient. You have all manner of news there; you have a good Fire, which you may sit by as long as you please; you have a Dish of Coffee; you meet your Friends for the transaction of Business, and all for a penny, if you don't care to spend more.[41]

A coffeehouse appealed to customers because it offered a warm and convivial coffee-room; newspapers and a library of other reading matter; pen, ink and paper; tobacco and pipe; the company of like-minded men ready to engage in conversation, gossip, and debate. Access was open to all men, and within the coffee-room, an equality of status was assumed between individuals, a form of interaction metonymically indicated by the common table around which some customers were seated. Women of middle-class propriety were not ordinarily encountered in the coffeehouse, although many women worked there as staff and managers.

Coffeehouses were normally inexpensive places of resort. Misson noted that a penny at the bar covered the cost of a dish of coffee and the rest, a price that remained the norm for most of the century. But Macklin's 'Publick Coffee-Room', as the newspapers excitedly noted, would take no money but silver. The smallest silver coins were the sixpence and the shilling,

---

41 Henri Misson de Valbourg, *M. Misson's Memoirs and Observations in his Travels over England*, trans. Mr Ozell (London, 1719), 39–40, a translation of *Memoires et observations faites par un voyageur en Angleterre* (The Hague [La Haye], 1698), called 'Caffez', in French, 37–38.

implying a price that pitched entry and drinks well above that of the common coffeehouse, and closer to the cost of elite entertainments like the Pantheon or Vauxhall (at a shilling entry). There is not much detailed evidence about the coffee service at Macklin's. However, when it closed, the new management advertised that business would continue as before, serving

> the Best of Coffee, Tea, Chocolate, Eaugeat, Capillaire, &c. &c. at the same Prices, and every Thing else upon the same Footing, as at the Bedford and other Coffee-houses.[42]

Like other coffeehouses, Macklin's served coffee, tea, and chocolate, augmented with some now unfamiliar drinks. 'Eaugeat' or orgeat (Thackeray says it was pronounced *orjaw*)[43] was a sweet almond-flavoured syrup, while 'capillaire' was an orange-flower syrup, both used in or as cold drinks. The same newspaper advertisement suggests that the coffee room possessed 'a scarce and most valuable Collection of almost all the Plays and Farces in the English Language'. It was not unusual for coffeehouses in the early 1750s to maintain a collection of pamphlets and books for their clients.[44] This collection reinforced Macklin's association with theatre and theatre criticism. These details concerning Macklin's coffee-service might be seen as mere curiosities, but they reiterate that Macklin was in the hot beverage business, even when he was also managing a literary or theatrical establishment. When Macklin's Coffeehouse failed, it was arguably the former which destroyed the latter: if so, then the beverage service, and its efficient management, is significant.

Macklin's venture was also a tavern. An important part of Macklin's planning for his new business was gaining the authority to open a tavern, in the form of a recognizance from the Justices of the Peace at the Middlesex Sessions in September 1753.[45] The recognizance licensed the individual rather than the business, it had to be renewed annually, and renewal could be refused without good behaviour. Having a licence to run a tavern allowed Macklin

---

42 *Public Advertiser*, 10 January 1755 and 11 January 1755. The evidence is the advert from Thomas Lawrence when he took over the coffeehouse on 10 January 1755, where he was probably continuing everything as is. Lawrence also claims that 'Gentlemen may have Coffee a la Crem, Canappe, Bavaroise, and Chicken Milk, as in the Coffee-houses at Paris'. These items include coffee prepared or served with cream, alongside other restoratives.

43 William Makepeace Thackeray, 'Jerome Paturot', in *Miscellaneous Essays, Sketches and Reviews* (London: Smith, Elder, 1885), 45: 'a glass of orgeat (pronounced *orjaw*)'.

44 Markman Ellis, 'Coffee-House Libraries in Mid-Eighteenth-Century London', *The Library: Transactions of the Bibliographical Society* 10.1 (2009), 3–40.

45 Middlesex County Records, Recognizances: L.v. (W) 69/929; 70/1155.

to sell wine and beer, and covered his coffee selling. The tavern licence underpinned the whole business, providing the basis of its legal regulation and the core of its activities. Given this, it is even more notable that Macklin called the venture a 'Publick Coffee-Room'.

A tavern was an establishment licensed to sell alcoholic beverages, including wine. The regulatory framework of the tavern related it to other businesses that sold alcoholic drinks, namely the alehouse and the inn. Although the legal distinctions between such premises were being eroded, the reputation of the tavern placed it between the alehouse and the inn. While an alehouse keeper could only sell beer, a tavern licence also permitted its keeper to sell wine and punch. An inn, on the other hand, was a more substantial enterprise that offered in addition accommodation, for both people and their horses. These distinctions, however, were fluid, and were culturally as much as legally determined. Even among taverns there was considerable variation between the greatest and least of their kind. Some taverns sustained literary coteries, such as the theatrically-minded clientele of the Shakepeare's Head Tavern in Covent Garden in the 1730s, and the critics who gathered at the Turk's Head Tavern in 1750s. Although not built until 1768, The London Tavern in Bishopsgate Street was constructed on a notably grand architectural plan, offering substantial dining rooms with elegant fittings.[46] Tavern sociability was centred on drinking alcohol, and could degenerate into dissipation. But, Ian Newman argues, although tavern sociability was associated with exchanging gossip, singing songs, and drinking healths, the tavern was also a site for serious conversation, intellectual debate, and discussion of politics, culture, and religion. Taverns were particularly conducive to the associational culture of the period, as Peter Clark argues, hosting clubs, dining societies, learned and scientific societies, intellectual, artistic, and book groups, and sporting clubs.[47] These clubs were primarily masculine and urban in their orientation, though women, and fashionable sociability, were not excluded absolutely. Newman confirms that taverns were closely allied with 'masculine, urban association', but also argues that tavern spaces supported a diversity of sociable activities. In this way, 'the male-dominated clubs and societies that met in them' and 'the broader range of activities that the tavern supported' help to make visible 'the place of the associational world in the broader constellation of Georgian sociability'. The tavern was thus associated most strongly with a convivial form of sociability that was idealized, Newman

---

46 Ian Newman, 'Edmund Burke in the Tavern', *European Romantic Review* 24.2 (2013), 127–31.

47 Peter Clark, *British Clubs and Societies, 1580–1800: The Origins of an Associational World* (Oxford: Oxford University Press, 2000), 39–40.

suggests, under the three principles of humour, sentiment and mutuality.[48] Although Habermas specifically identified the coffeehouse as one of the new institutions in the emergence of the public sphere, similar arguments have since been made about the tavern.[49]

That Macklin named his venture a coffeehouse imprinted it with certain expectations, proposing that its central activity was the sober and intellectual sociability that was associated with the coffeehouse. He thus relocated it away from the tavern's associations with both the more loquacious discussions conducted under the influence of alcohol and the vulgar forms of dissipation that ensued. Macklin's naming scheme inscribed the coffeehouse sociability onto the regulatory framework of the tavern, creating a hybrid space that brought together the two most important sociable meeting places in which urban elites assembled for business and trade, for the exchange of gossip and information, for the discussion of politics and culture, and the practice of various social behaviours of the middling sort.

The third sociable space at Macklin's was the subscription room or club, in the 'large Room above Stairs', intended 'for a select Number of Subscribers, who have form'd themselves into a balloting Club'. Subscription-room sociability was founded on expense and exclusivity, forming a club that was only open to members who had paid their subscriptions. The forebear of the expensive, male-only, gentleman's club that flourished in the Victorian period, the sociability of the subscription room was based around conversation, gossip, and gaming. Macklin's room was to be a balloting club 'upon the Plan of White's and George's': that is, the number and composition of the membership would be controlled by the current members, any one of whom could reject any application, by a secret ballot in which applicants who received only one black ball would be rejected. This method helped maintain congeniality and the sociable ethos of the status quo but was also notably exclusive.

The opening of the room on 30 March was announced in the *Public Advertiser*: 'Macklin's Subscription Room will be open'd To-morrow, at Seven o'Clock in the Evening'.[50] Macklin apparently made a mistake, however, by not informing all the prospective members of the event. He placed a notice in the *Public Advertiser* on 1 and 3 April expressing his apologies:

> Mr Macklin humbly hopes that those Gentlemen whose Names are in the Original Nomination for his Subscription-Room, will excuse his not having

---

48 Ian Newman, *The Romantic Tavern: Literature and Conviviality in the Age of Revolution* (Cambridge: Cambridge University Press, 2019), 17.
49 Adam Smyth (ed.), *A Pleasing Sinne: Drink and Conviviality in Seventeenth-Century England* (Cambridge: D.S. Brewer, 2004); Newman, *Romantic Tavern*, 2–3.
50 *Public Advertiser*, 29 March 1754.

sent them Notice before the opening: The Omission not arising from Neglect, or the want of Respect, but from an Incident not in his Power to prevent; but as soon as possible Notices will be dispatched to every Gentleman.[51]

As this suggests, prospective members were all men of elite status, who had completed a 'Nomination Form' expressing their interest in belonging. Unlike the public-facing openness of the coffee-room and tavern, the subscription room was closed, subject to administrative regulation, and bureaucratic management of the membership. Gambling and cards-playing were certainly a feature of Macklin's subscription room: not only piquet but also faro. Macklin's rooms had been formerly occupied, before his renovations, by a gambling establishment known as Lord Mornington's, which Macklin seems to have attended or at least have heard of. Little is known about Lord Mornington's club, which may have been run under the auspices of a wealthy Irish peer, Richard Wesley (d.1756) of Dengan in Co. Meath, created Baron Mornington in 1746 and known as Lord Mornington. That Macklin maintained a 'Gaming-Table' at his Coffeehouse is also mentioned in Stephanus Scriblerus's boisterous satire in *The Censor* (1755).[52] High-stakes gambling of this kind, associated especially with the sociability of wealthy and aristocratic men, created a voyeuristic spectacle of luxury and money.

Macklin's model, as he stated, was both White's and George's. In a bon mot attributed to Foote (first published in 1805), Macklin is said to have quipped that his establishment should be called '*Black's* coffee-house, in contradistinction to *White's*'.[53] White's Chocolate House, in St James's Street, had begun as a coffeehouse in the 1690s, but had transformed into a subscription club in 1736.[54] At its foundation, the membership was dominated by noblemen, courtiers, and 'gentlemen of fashion'.[55] In the 1750s, it was notorious for luxurious dining and reckless high-stakes gambling: whist was played 'for

---

51 *Public Advertiser*, 1 April 1754, repeated 3 April 1754.
52 Stephanus Scriblerus, *The Censor. Numb. I. To be continued occasionally* (London, 1755), 4.
53 William Cooke, *Memoirs of Samuel Foote, Esq.: with a collection of his genuine bon-mots, anecdotes, opinions, &c. mostly original: And three of his dramatic pieces, not published in his works*, 3 vols (London, 1805), II.119.
54 Kate Loveman, 'The Introduction of Chocolate into England: Retailers, Researchers, and Consumers, 1640–1730', *Journal of Social History* 47.1 (2013), 27–46. See also Percy Colson, *White's, 1693–1950* (London: Heinemann, [1951]); Algernon Bourke, *The History of White's* ([London: Waterlow and Sons for Algernon Bourke, 1892]); Anthony Lejeune, *White's: The First Three Hundred Years* (London: A & C Black, 1993).
55 Members' list, in Bourke, *History of White's*.

the trifle of a thousand pounds the rubber'.[56] But while the membership and gambling-book was exclusively male, the club participated in the wider feminization of public entertainments through the masquerade balls it organized at the Haymarket Theatre, the social world of the beau monde it sustained, and the discourse of love and gallantry its members practised.

George's Coffeehouse, on the Strand, at the corner of Devereux Court, next to Temple Bar, was a less splendid enterprise, but was a well-established place of resort for literary gentlemen. Leased in 1750 by George Harding,[57] the regulars supported a subscription club that maintained an extensive library of books and pamphlets, especially poetry, for the use of subscribers.[58] When William Shenstone first came to London in 1741, he paid a shilling to become a member.

> My company goes to George's Coffee-house, where, for that small subscription, I read all the pamphlets under a three-shilling dimensions; and indeed, any larger ones would not be fit for coffee-house perusal.[59]

In 1754, George's was the home of a self-denominated Board of Critics (also known as the Parliament of Critics), later satirized, albeit affectionately, in an anonymous mock-georgic verse pamphlet entitled *George's Coffee House* (1761).[60] George's and White's both operated by subscription, and White's was selective, using a ballot to select among the applications. Both were exclusive social spaces, although their exclusivity pulled in different directions. White's tended to attract and accept the upper echelons of the nobility and the court, while George's was geared towards the arguably more meritocratic elite of the literary sphere. In both cases, these were male-oriented homosocial spaces, even though their range of interests tipped them towards the sociable world of the town and the beau monde. For Macklin to name them both as his model implied an ambition to emulate and entertain an odd mixture of the learned wits and the fashion-conscious beau monde.

---

56 *The Connoisseur*, 1 and 19 (1754).
57 M[iddlesex] L[and] R[egister], 1749. Hugh Phillips, *Mid-Georgian London: A Topographical and Social Survey of Central and Western London about 1750* (London: Collins, 1964).
58 Markman Ellis, 'Poetry and Civic Urbanism in the Coffee-House Library in the Mid-Eighteenth Century', in Kyle Roberts and Mark Towsey (eds), *Before the Public Library: Reading, Community, and Identity in the Atlantic World, 1650–1850* (Leiden: Brill, 2017), 52–72.
59 William Shenstone, to Richard Graves, London, soon after 13 February 1741, in Marjorie Williams (ed.), *The Letters of William Shenstone* (Oxford: Basil Blackwell, 1939), 21.
60 *George's Coffee House. A poem* (London, 1761).

The fourth sociable space in Macklin's Coffeehouse was an 'ordinary', or meal service. His 'public Ordinary' was held 'every Day, at Four o'Clock, Price 3s per Person', and included such 'Port, Claret, or whatever Liquor' as chosen by each customer.[61] It was a fixed-price all-you-can-eat offer, which was the norm for a public ordinary, but with unlimited alcoholic drinks supplied. An ordinary usually presented a short bill of fare for a fixed price: Macklin retained the fixed price, but the food was both very expensive and unusually generous. In the first few months of its operation in 1754, evidence in the newspapers suggests that Macklin's establishment was popular amongst people of fashion, and renowned for excess and over-indulgence. The decidedly unfashionable Henry Fielding thought the excess of the ordinary was characteristic of the enterprise, deriding the whole place as 'the temple of luxury under the Piazza where Macklin the high priest daily serves up his rich offerings to [the] goddess'.[62] The satirist George Alexander Stevens (1710–1784) eulogized this overindulgence in a mock-heroic poem called *The Birth-Day of Folly*, published in April 1755.[63] He noted that dinner was served promptly at four, by a company of unsmiling servants in spectacular uniforms: 'Ten Waiters drest like modern beaux/In Folly's livery, parti-colour'd cloaths'. The poem, which ridiculed all the orators contending for the London audience that season, including Foote, Henley, and Macklin, mocked Macklin especially for his empty pretensions to learning and universal knowledge, and for the mixed metaphors of his establishment's sociability. In the poem, a hungry audience interrupts Macklin's lecture when they smell the 'savoury scent of supper', finding a table laden with dishes:

> A jowl of Codd, Chubbs, Gudgeons in a dish;
> Wit-damping puddings, tripe in butter fry'd,
> Fat chitterling and goose on every side:
> Stern at the bottom grinn'd, still breathing dread,
> The bristly horrors of a huge hog's head.

Macklin loaded his table with a Rabelaisian surfeit of luxury foods and a wide range of drinks.

---

61 *Public Advertiser*, 18 November 1754.
62 Henry Fielding, *The Journal of a Voyage to Lisbon, Shamela, and Occasional Writings*, ed. Martin C. Battestin (Oxford: Oxford University Press, 2008), 635.
63 George Alexander Stevens, *The Birth-Day of Folly, an heroi-comical poem, by Peter: with notes variorum, for the illustration of historical passages relating to the hero of the poem, and other remarkable personages* (London, 1755), ll. 242–43. 'This Day was publish'd, Price 1s.', *London Evening Post*, 1 April 1755.

Full pots of porter, three threads, stale and stout,
Bumpers of punch, and nipperkins of stum,
Of windy cyder, and of mawky rum.[64]

The Menippean hubbub of this feast of folly, which in this satire was enough to draw the attention of the magistrates, suggests to Stevens that Macklin's establishment represented a confusion of values, unhelpfully mixing luxury with excess, sobriety with drunkenness, learning with fashion, high with middle.

The British Inquisition

ON 18 NOVEMBER 1754, the *Public Advertiser* announced the opening performance of the British Inquisition on 22 November. Over the following month and a half, there were twenty-three performances of the British Inquisition: usually three a week, often Monday, Wednesday, and Friday, although Macklin experimented with every night of the week, including Sunday. As Horace Walpole said on 24 December 1754, 'The new madness is Oratorys'. He went on: 'Macklin has set up one, under the title of the British Inquisition; Foote another against him; and a third man has advertised another to-day. I have not heard enough in their favour to tempt me to them'.[65] As well as Macklin, Walpole here noted Foote's performance in the 'Writ of Inquiry' at the Little Theatre in the Haymarket, a burlesque mock-trial on the Inquisitor.[66] The third was George Alexander Stevens's 'Comic Lecture' on 'Orators and Inquisitions' at the Lecture Room in James Street, 'Ladies to be admitted—not to speak'.[67]

At performances of the Inquisition, Macklin presented, in the medium of a lecture, a demonstration of oratory, often on a theatrical subject, that might also include exemplary speeches from the plays. The topics for each performance were announced the *Public Advertiser*. Some of these lectures were written or devised by others:

> N.B. Any Question, Lecture, or Essay, upon Trade, Morality, Literature, Arts or Sciences, or upon any Subject of public Utility or Entertainment will be thankfully received, and delivered to the Public from the Rostrum; or if any

---

64 Stevens, *Birth-Day of Folly*, ll. 243–48; 276–78.
65 Walpole to Richard Bentley, Strawberry Hill, 24 December 1754, *The Yale Edition of Horace Walpole's Correspondence*, 48 vols (New Haven, CT: Yale University Press, 1937–1983), Letter 414, XXXV.200.
66 *Public Advertiser*, 23 December 1754.
67 *Public Advertiser*, 23 December 1754; 24 December 1754.

Gentleman or Lady is inclined to speak their own Productions, the Inquisition is at their Service.[68]

The oratorical performances were dominated by topics on the theatre, including Shakespeare, on techniques for public speaking, on Macklin's contest with Samuel Foote (which probably includes those on cuckoldry), and on the enterprise of the British Inquisition itself (see Table 10.1).

Table 10.1 British Inquisition lecture topics

Lecture topics	Number	Proportion
Theatrical	6	25 %
Public speaking techniques	5	21 %
Samuel Foote scandal	4	17 %
British Inquisition	2	8 %
Cuckoldry	2	8 %
Other (gambling, Canning, the Sabbath, Roman History, Pygmies)	5	21 %

Macklin delivered the lecture to an audience that was ideally quiet and attentive (perhaps more like a sermon, than a theatrical performance). Visual satires of oratory performances suggest this ideal was not always achieved: the anonymous satire entitled *The Robin Hood* (1 June 1752; Figure 10.1), which depicts a weekly meeting of the club presided over by the president Caleb Jeacocke, suggests that the audience was at times fractious and distracted.[69] The content and form of the lectures may be indicated by extant drafts in Macklin's hand at the Folger Shakespeare Library.[70] Four scripts address theatrical topics: one concerns the rivalry between managers and actors for control of the green room; another addresses kinds of actors and characters, directed against Foote and the role of the mimic, and another discusses the improvement of commerce, developing into a discussion of political corruption. The lectures read like an occasional essay on the model of *The*

---

68 *Public Advertiser*, Wednesday, 4 December 1754 [in fact, Monday, 2 December].
69 *The Robin Hood* (publish'd according to act of Parliament, 1 June 1752). Lewis Walpole Library, Yale University, 752.06.01.01+.
70 Charles Macklin, 'Item 1–6. Miscellaneous notes on various subjects including the venality of the stage, [1754–1760?]', in Autograph papers of Charles Macklin [manuscript], [1754–1787], Folger Shakespeare Library, Y.d.515 (1–6).

Figure 10.1: *The Robin Hood* (1 June 1752), Lewis Walpole Library, 752.06.01.01+. Courtesy of the Lewis Walpole Library, Yale University.

Spectator, although they are angrier in tone and more vituperative. They are not intended to produce a comic effect.[71]

In addition, each evening Macklin hosted a debate, on the model of the Robin Hood debating society. Macklin set two or three questions to be addressed and publicized them in the *Public Advertiser*. As in a debating society, customers were encouraged to participate. Unlike the Robin Hood, women as well as men were invited to participate in the debate, a significant innovation, as Thale rightly argues. Amongst the other topics addressed are questions on bashfulness, bankruptcy, patriotic sacrifice, suicide, seduction, and a new Thames bridge (see Table 10.2). Many more reflected further on theatrical topics: suicide for example, related to Addison's *Cato*, in performance during that season. One participant in a debate, the satirist George Alexander Stevens, printed his contribution to the first debate in the *Gentleman's Magazine*: it is a witty but shallow denunciation of the corrupting influence of French manners on English sincerity.[72] The range of topics at the British Inquisition resemble those canvassed in an essay periodical, albeit with more focus on theatre and oratory than most: that is to say, broadly within the popular culture of the Enlightenment in Britain.

Table 10.2 British Inquisition debate questions

Debate questions	Number of questions (total = 43)	Proportion
Theatre, including Foote	6	14 %
Marriage and female manners	5	12 %
Public speaking	4	9 %
Slavery	3	7 %
Education	3	7 %
Miserliness	3	7 %
Other	19	44 %

---

71 These fragmentary notes may not relate to performances at the Inquisition (no. 2 has a section, perhaps added separately, that refers to books published in 1758). They were sold at Sotheby's on 15–16 May 1902 as 'Autograph notes of Lectures on Theatrical and other subjects delivered by Macklin at the school of oratory, instituted by him in the year 1754 under the title "The British Inquisition"' (p. 22).

72 George Alexander Stevens, 'XXIII. Humorous speech at Macklin's', *Gentleman's Magazine*, 24.12 (December 1754), 568–69. The question was 'Whether the People of Great Britain have profited by their Intercourse with, or their Imitation of the French Nation', *Public Advertiser*, 22 November 1754.

The British Inquisition, and also the Coffeehouse space that hosted it, were not closely associated with the Irish diaspora, though of course it is likely that Irish actors, orators, and writers attended. Edmund Burke and Oliver Goldsmith are known to have attended debating societies like the Robin Hood Society, as well as being habitués of coffeehouses and taverns.[73] Arthur Murphy was curious enough about the project to write his satire on the female coffeehouse. But there is no direct evidence they attended, nor what they thought of it. In its self-representations in the newspapers, Macklin's Coffeehouse was not coded as Irish. The topics discussed at the performances of the British Inquisition also do not show much curiosity about Irish affairs, although they do engage with some topics that broadly overlapped with Enlightenment philosophical debate, such as marriage, female manners, slavery, and oratory.

Macklin's performance of the British Inquisition was initially popular: the newspapers stated that the first night had 'an Audience of Seven hundred and fifty eight Gentlemen and Ladies, and 'tis computed that as many went away that could not get in'.[74] But the vogue did not last, especially after Macklin was drawn into a bad-tempered ad hominem quarrel with Samuel Foote, in which Macklin, in his role as the Inquisitor, was viciously satirized as a pompous know-nothing. Appleton describes this quarrel in some detail.[75] It is clear that, at the same time, the business was also struggling. Signs of financial distress can be observed from early December, when an advertisement gave notice that *all* customers had to pay for what they call for at the bar, rather than to the waiters (this suggests endemic pilfering).[76] On 31 December, Macklin announced abruptly in the *Public Advertiser* that '☞ The Ordinary is discontinued'. Gauging from some of the satires, the dinner service at the ordinary was perhaps what Macklin's was most renowned for, but it must also have been not only loss-making, but ruinously so. Ten days later, on 10 January, he declared bankrupt, and the coffeehouse, as the business was described, was taken over by a jobbing coffee-man called Thomas Lawrence. On 25 January 1755, the *London Gazette* reported that a Commission of Bankrupt had been issued against Charles Macklin, a 'Vintner, Coffeeman and Chapman'.[77] This description is significant, for as

---

73 Mary Thale, 'The Robin Hood Society: Debating in Eighteenth-Century London', *London Journal* 22.1 (1997), 38; Newman, 'Edmund Burke in the Tavern', 136.
74 *Public Advertiser*, 23 November 1754. *The Gentleman's Magazine* said there were 'near eight hundred present the first night' (24 November 1754), 532.
75 *Appleton*, 104–8.
76 *Public Advertiser*, 9 December 1754.
77 *Public Advertiser*, 27 January 1755; *London Evening Post*, 28 January 1755; *Whitehall Evening Post or London Intelligencer*, 28 January 1755.

a business owner, he could declare bankrupt; whereas, as a private person, such as an actor, he would have been a debtor, and as such, confined to debtors' prison.[78] Macklin was declared bankrupt by creditors who included John Tinkler, the builder who had undertaken the renovations in the winter of 1753–54. His case was complicated, and eventually required Lord Hardwicke, the Lord Chancellor, to resolve it. Hardwicke's memorandum noted that Tinkler submitted that he had completed work to the value of £1,000 and £1,077, but also that Tinkler's account overlooked or ignored Macklin's payment of £1,300 towards these costs. For this imposture, Hardwicke discharged Tinkler as a commissioner of the bankruptcy as an improper person and appointed a Surveyor to establish how much Macklin owed his creditors.[79] Evidence suggests Macklin's Coffeehouse was in trouble in November and December, but it may have been that his creditors acted precipitously in forcing the bankruptcy so early in January 1755. In response to the total wreck of his plans, Macklin moved back to Dublin, where, by 1758, he was acting again. He eventually retired from the stage, for the second time, thirty-one years later, in 1789.

Conclusion: Macklin's 'polyhedonic' coffeehouse model

Macklin's Coffeehouse ended in failure: a failure that was commercial, cultural, and ideological. Macklin identified, or attempted to identify, a new hybrid sociable space, but was unable to make it work successfully. That it failed, while attracting large audiences to some events, is interesting. Macklin's biographers, from Cooke to Appleton, examine the decline of the business within the context of the satirical contest fought between Macklin and Foote. Macklin's inability to counter Foote's attacks may have been disheartening to Macklin and may have led to some decline in audience.[80] But the enterprise had wider difficulties, and it is more likely that it failed as a business—a coffeehouse—not a theatrical performance.

Mary Thale has argued that the British Inquisition was a reforming institution that commercialized and regendered the debating society. Amateur debating societies had been popular for a decade or so, and were typically held in cheap tavern rooms, with drinks restricted to beer or punch.

---

78 On 12 April 1755, his 'Certificate of Bankrupt' was approved by the Lord Chancellor, Philip Yorke, Earl of Hardwicke, and gazetted (officially published in the *London Gazette*, as required by the legislation). See *London Gazette*, 12 April 1755.
79 Hardwicke, 'In the matter of Charles Macklin a bankrupt'.
80 *Cooke*, 200–12; *Appleton*, 104–8.

Women were not expected to attend, although there were rumours that some women had attended in male clothing ('breeches'). Thale argued that the entry charge to Macklin's Inquisition effectively commercialized a previously amateur sociability. Opening the space to women was also thoroughly innovative. Thale argued this was a significant repositioning of the debating society in the culture of public entertainments in London.

What does Macklin's venture say about gender, politeness, and sociability? Macklin's project was a multi-modal centre for public entertainments, providing a variety of pleasures and diversions in spaces that functioned as or were described as a coffeehouse, a tavern, an ordinary, a subscription members' club, a performance space, and a debating club. It was, in this sense, a 'polyhedonic sociability', appealing to a range of different convivial pleasures (Table 10.3). These disparate modes of interaction were all oriented towards a public sociability, but in different ways, and, as they occupied the same spaces, there was some interesting friction or tension between them. As there were more sociable models in play than rooms, some must have been coextensive and coincident. That women were actively courted as customers for some of these sociable spaces added to the venture's hybrid strangeness. But the commercial and gendered innovations at Macklin's Coffeehouse extended beyond the debating society, to the other sociable dimensions of the project. Generally, the tavern, coffeehouse, and ordinary were commercial premises predicated on open access to all who could afford the beverages sold there, but Macklin's Coffeehouse, in charging for entrance, signalled that the place was reserved for the polite elite. The shilling entry-price restricted attendance to a higher, more elite, and arguably more polite audience, than a coffeehouse, tavern, or ordinary would normally attract—although, if over seven hundred people attended on some nights, Macklin's can hardly be described as exclusive. The entry price of a shilling was not prohibitive but was considerably more than the free entry to other coffeehouses. The sum was equivalent to that charged by Vauxhall Pleasure Garden, a sociable space that, as numerous satires made clear, was coded as a polite entertainment, but in fact was attended by a wide variety of people.[81] Macklin repositioned the sociability to appeal to a higher status audience, but in doing so he exacerbated the internal contradictions of his coffeehouse idea.

This chapter began by appealing to Gillian Russell's hypothesis about the gendered transformation of public sociability in the mid-eighteenth century. She argues that the considerable expansion in commercial public

---

81 David Coke and Alan Borg, *Vauxhall Gardens: A History* (New Haven, CT: Yale University Press for Paul Mellon Centre for Studies in British Art, 2011).

Table 10.3 Macklin's model of 'polyhedonic sociability'

	Organizing practice	Status	Sociable activities	Gender
Coffeehouse	Coffee	Open Polite Middle Commercial	Conversation Gossip Debate News Print culture	Male Homosocial
Tavern	Alcohol	Open Mixed Low Commercial	Conversation Gossip Debate Song culture Drinking healths	Heterosocial Male-centred
Ordinary	Food	Open Mixed Low Commercial	Conversation Gossip Eating Drinking	Heterosocial Male-centred
Subscription Club	Gaming	Exclusive Polite Elite Commercial	Conversation Gossip Gambling Drinking	Heterosocial Male-centred
'Inquisition' lecture	Lecture	Ticketed Polite Mixed Commercial Passive	Lecture Gossip Fine dress Spectating	Heterosocial Feminocentric
'Inquisition' debating society	Debate	Open Mixed Low Free Participatory	Oratory Debate Drinking	Heterosocial

entertainments aimed to attract a new audience that was polite and elite. Women were able to access this fashionable urban culture, not least because its sociability was modelled on their behaviours. Macklin's Coffeehouse pre-dates the period in which Russell argues this transformation happened by a decade or so: Russell focuses on the period 1770–90, after 'the crisis of the 1770s', as she calls it. Macklin's approach to women as audience members, as consumers of his food and beverage services, and, most especially, as participants in oratorical debate, suggest that Macklin prefigures Russell's revolution, providing a taste of things to come. Macklin's Coffeehouse experiment is, in effect, one of the 'abandoned schools of pleasure' Russell's work is dedicated to uncovering in the history of gendered public sociabilities.[82] Such a conclusion reflects well on Macklin's ambition and innovation, but not on his acumen as a cultural entrepreneur and coffee-man.

Celebrating Macklin's innovations sharpens the focus on the failure of the enterprise, especially as its collapse was so rapid and so calamitous. Macklin's bankruptcy had local causes: Foote's satires, for example, and his dispute with the builder John Tinkler, who (probably) foreclosed on the mortgage on his property. But it is interesting, in the light of Russell's argument, to speculate about the internal inconsistencies and frictions imposed by Macklin's Coffeehouse, tavern, ordinary, club, and oratory. Macklin's greatest innovation, the presence of elite women in polite heterosocial public spaces devoted to entertainment and luxury consumption, may also have created turbulence and tension with other aspects of his venture more traditionally identified as homosocial and masculine (especially the coffeehouse, tavern, and club). Macklin's hybrid space made its innovation by introducing women of the polite classes, with their association with refined manners and elite pricing; but perhaps he also failed to exclude enough of that masculine rowdy and vulgar sociability that was associated with the coffeehouse and the tavern, the club and the ordinary.

---

82 Russell, *Women, Sociability and Theatre*, 11–12.

11

Macklin's Talking 'Wrongheads'
The British Inquisition and the Public Sphere

Helen Burke

AN INTERESTING THOUGH HITHERTO OVERLOOKED source of information on Charles Macklin's short-lived oratorical and debating institution, the British Inquisition, is the engraved print listed in the British Museum holdings as 'The British Inquisition or Common Sence in Danger/ Oh Thou Head of the Wrongheads' (Figure 11.1).[1] At its most obvious level, this image purports to represent what Michael Warner in his discussion of different kinds of publics calls the 'theatrical public' or 'concrete audience', which, in this case, would have been visible to itself and to Macklin in his great room on Hart Street on Friday, 13 December 1754.[2] On that day, as we know from newspaper advertisements, the 'Inquisition' focused on 'the Moral and Physical Nature of Elizabeth Canning's Story. And the Conduct of the Parties, for and against that unhappy Woman', a topic which had generated much heated debate in London during the previous two years.[3] This case centred on the alleged abduction and imprisonment in 1753 of Canning, a servant girl, by a brothel keeper, 'Mother' Wells, and the 'gypsy', Mary Squires, and it resulted initially in sentences of hanging for Squires and branding for Wells. After the Lord Mayor of London, Sir Crisp Gascoyne, reviewed the evidence, however, that verdict was overturned, and Canning herself was sentenced to transportation for perjury, much to the dismay of

---

1 British Museum Prints and Drawings, 1868,0808.3977. The catalogue description of this print makes no mention of Macklin.
2 Michael Warner, *Publics and Counterpublics* (New York: Zone Books, 2005), 66.
3 *Public Advertiser*, 13 December 1754.

a large section of the public who continued to believe in her innocence. A paper war ensued between these supporters (the 'Canningites', led by Henry Fielding) and the supporters of Squires (the 'Egyptians', led by Gascoyne and John Hill), and over the course of the period from 1753 to 1754 some forty pamphlets on this topic saw the light of day.[4]

The visual representation of Macklin's event suggests that the Inquisition audience was equally divided on the outcome of the case. The standing speaker, labelled #1 in the image, is identified as the 'Canning Prosecutor' in the key below the bottom caption, and, in a later hand below that, as 'Sir Crisp Gascoyne'. His speech bubble ('Mr. Inquisitor General, I give you the Prefference') would seem to suggest that Macklin, like the other standing gentleman who says 'The British find happiness in Transportation' (#2 in the image and in the key), are all on the anti-Canning side of this controversy.[5] The lady speaker (# 5 in the image and in the key), who says, 'Let them be carried to the Tripet' (Tyburn), meanwhile, would seem to be arguing the opposite case, echoing those who urged the gallows for Squires and Wells. The remaining, non-speaking, part of the audience for the most part would seem to be enjoying this exchange and the social interaction it is producing. While a few, like the gentleman in the right-hand corner of the image, look away in apparent disdain, others gaze intently at Macklin or check the responses of fellow audience members for their reaction, evidently entertained by this lively verbal sparring.

But the verbal captions and key that frame this animated scene, as well as the speech that is ascribed to Macklin, also reinterpret this live performance for what Warner calls a 'modern' type of public, the wider, less-defined audience that came into being as a result of print and the circulation of texts, and this remediation casts this whole event in a far more negative light.[6] Mimicking a theatrical advertisement, the print gives the British Inquisition a subtitle ('Common Sence in Danger') that suggests it is a subversive production, and it elaborates on this danger by linking the scene's central actor, Macklin, to two other much ridiculed characters, one drawn from the playhouse, the other from a rival oratorical venue. The top caption, 'Oh, Thou Head of the Wrongheads', is a line from Sir John Vanbrugh and Colley

---

4 See Judith Moore, *The Appearance of Truth: The Story of Elizabeth Canning and Eighteenth-Century Narrative* (Newark: University of Delaware Press, 1994).

5 This second standing gentleman resembles 'Sir' John Hill, one of the most vocal of Canning's opponents.

6 Warner, *Publics and Counterpublics*, 11 and *passim*. I am using the term 'remediation' as Jay Bolter and Richard Grusin use it: that is, to refer to 'the representation of one medium in another'. *Remediation: Understanding New Media* (Cambridge, MA: MIT Press, 2000), 45.

Figure 11.1:
'The British Inquisition or Common Sence in Danger/Oh Thou Head of the Wrongheads', British Museum, London (Ref. 1868,0808.3977).

Cibber's popular comedy *The Provok'd Husband* (1728), and it is spoken by the play's normative character, Mr Manly, in reference to Sir Francis Wronghead, the foolish country squire who endangers the well-being of his whole family when he comes up to London in the hope of finding a government 'place' and repairing his fortune.[7] In assuming the role of orator, the caption implies, Macklin, like this booby squire, is attempting a social role for which he is similarly ill-equipped, while neglecting his true calling—in this case, acting. Sir Francis Wronghead, as contemporaries would have known, was one of Macklin's best-known comic roles.[8] More damningly, however, the numbered key (#3 & 4 'Orators Henley & M—n') and the speech that is attributed to Macklin ('I am Martin Luther') link him to John Henley, the dissenting minister whose ('wrong') head appears in the far right corner of this representation. Henley had been outraging orthodox believers since the late 1720s when he began preaching what he described as a purer, 'primitive' brand of Christianity in his 'Oratory' over a meat market in central London, and he was still preaching there (though to declining numbers) when Macklin turned orator in 1754.[9] Macklin had ventured into Henley's religious territory, too, when in the only Inquisition event to be held on a Sunday, he gave a 'moral Lecture on the Institution and Nature of the Sabbath, and the Duty of Man in relation to that Day', followed by a recitation from Milton 'in the Manner of the Antediluvian, and Primitive Christian Orator'.[10] And either at that event or on some other occasion, if we are to credit a much repeated claim by his opponents, Macklin referred to himself as 'the *British* Martin Luther' who had come to 'reform all *Covent Garden*'.[11] The print bubble ascribed to Macklin, then, reminds viewers of this rash claim while also linking his reforming effort to that of Henley, the preacher whom Alexander Pope had famously dubbed the 'Zany of his Age'.[12]

Henley is also remembered today, however, for his role in popularizing the concept of the public debating society, an associational structure which over the course of the eighteenth century served to expand the British public

---

7 Sir John Vanbrugh and Colley Cibber, *The provok'd husband; or a journey to London* (London, 1728), 64. The actual line is 'Ah, thou Head of the *Wrongheads!*'
8 *Kirkman*, I.251.
9 See Paula McDowell, *The Invention of the Oral: Print Commerce and Fugitive Voices in Eighteenth-Century Britain* (Chicago: University of Chicago Press, 2017), 117.
10 *Public Advertiser*, 28 November 1784; 29 November 1754.
11 *M-ckl-n's Answer to Tully* (London, 1755), 19. On 19 December 1754, George Colman also noted in his journal that 'the great *Orator Macklin*' frequently called himself 'the *Martin Luther* of the age'. *Connoisseur*, 2 vols (London, 1755), I.278.
12 Alexander Pope, *The Dunciad in Four Books* in *The Poems of Alexander Pope*, ed. John Butt (New Haven, CT: Yale University Press, 1963), 759.

sphere, and I will suggest that the attack on Macklin and his 'Wrongheads' must also been seen as part of the ongoing resistance to that Enlightenment project. As Paula McDowell notes in her groundbreaking study of eighteenth-century oral culture, Henley's Oratory was designed not only to provide religious instruction but (as he himself stated) 'to supply the want of an university, or universal school in this capital, for the equal benefit of persons of all ranks, professions, circumstances, and capacities'.[13] To that end, this preacher promoted a lecture/disputation model of interaction on topics drawn from across the disciplinary fields, and he opened his lecture/debating forum to all comers, women as well as men, artisans and tradesmen as well as gentlemen. But no less significantly, as McDowell points out, Henley created a new model of 'oral commerce', using strategies and methods borrowed from the theatrical and print industries (he used the same kind of tiered price system as the playhouse, for instance, and he promoted his events by means of a journal and regular eye-catching newspaper advertisements).[14] This set off a fierce struggle between his new oratorical/debating kind of entertainment and these older ones, thus triangulating that enmeshed relationship between print media and the theatre which Stuart Sherman, Daniel O'Quinn, and others have described.[15] Publications like *The Grub Street Journal* (1730–37), and stage performances like Henry Fielding's *Author's Farce* (1730) and Christopher Smart's 'The Old Woman's Oratory, or, *Henley in Petticoats*' (1751–52), for instance, mimicked Henley's tactics and repurposed his oratorical material, even as they mocked his attempt to open the field of public debate to a wider cross-section of the British population.[16]

When he set up the British Inquisition, then, Macklin took up this fight. His lecture and debating institution was, on the one hand, another one of those 'improving' entertainments that followed in the wake of Henley's Oratory, the most famous of which was the Robin Hood Society, a working man's debating association established in the late 1740s.[17] In his journal *The Connoisseur*, George Colman also noted that connection when he sneeringly complimented 'the great *Orator* Macklin' for joining 'the plans' of these two

---

13 Cited in McDowell, *The Invention of the Oral*, 130.
14 McDowell, *The Invention of the Oral*, 5, 125–30, 135.
15 Stuart Sherman, 'Garrick among Media: The *"Now"* Performer Navigates the News', *PMLA* 126.4 (2011), 966–82 and '"The General Entertainment of My Life": The *Tatler*, the *Spectator*, and the Quidnunc's Cure', *Eighteenth-Century Fiction* 27.3–4 (2015), 343–71; Daniel O'Quinn, *Entertaining Crisis in the Atlantic Imperium, 1770–1790* (Baltimore, MD: Johns Hopkins University Press, 2011).
16 See McDowell, *The Invention of the Oral*, 144, 118, and the discussion below.
17 See Mary Thale, 'The Robin Hood Society: Debating in Eighteenth-Century London', *London Journal* 22.1 (1997), 33–50.

establishments together with the British Inquisition.[18] But the Inquisition was also an imaginative intervention into the cycle of appropriations and remediations that Henley had set off—one which, in this instance, represented an intrusion on the part of public debating into two spaces that had been central to the development of the bourgeois public sphere in Britain: the coffeehouse and the periodical journal.[19] In what follows, I will track the development of Macklin's daring crossing act, as well as analysing in more detail the backlash it provoked. This opposition, as we will see, exposed the class, gender, ethnic, and religious limits of the British public sphere and, by extension, the failure of the British Enlightenment to live up to its own ideals of rationality, tolerance, and inclusivity.

MACKLIN'S 'STRANGE HOTCH-POTCH FARCE': *THE COVENT GARDEN THEATRE; OR, PASQUIN TURN'D DRAWCANSIR*

MACKLIN BEGAN HIS INTRUSION into the fields of oratory and print with *The Covent Garden Theatre; or, Pasquin Turn'd Drawcansir*, a two-act afterpiece, which he wrote for his benefit night at Covent Garden theatre on 8 April 1752.[20] In giving his play that title, he was undoubtedly seeking to capitalize on Henry Fielding's celebrity. *Pasquin* (1736), of course, was one of Fielding's most famous dramatic satires, and 'Sir Alexander Drawcansir, Knt. Censor of Great Britain' the pseudonym under which he wrote *The Covent-Garden Journal*, a publication that was still appearing regularly at the time of Macklin's play. Contrary to what some have argued, however, this play was not in any simple sense 'about' Fielding.[21] The mention of oratory in the advertisement for this afterpiece—the 'Satire to be introduced by an Oration and to conclude by a Peroration. Both to be spoken from the Rostrum in the

---

18 *Connoisseur*, I.278.
19 For the seminal account of the public sphere, see Jürgen Habermas, *The Structural Transformation of the Public Sphere*, trans. Thomas Burger with Frederick Lawrence (Cambridge, MA: MIT Press, 1991), esp. 1–56. For more recent analyses, see Brian Cowan, 'Mr Spectator and the Coffeehouse Public Sphere', *Eighteenth-Century Studies* 37.3 (2004), 245–366 and Ann C. Dean's *The Talk of the Town: Figurative Publics in Eighteenth-Century Britain* (Lewisburg, PA: Bucknell University Press, 2007).
20 Charles Macklin, *The Covent Garden Theatre; or, Pasquin Turn'd Drawcansir* (1752), Augustan Reprint Society, no. 116, ed. Jean B. Kern (Los Angeles: William Andrew Clark Memorial Library, University of California, 1965), 62. References are to this edition.
21 See Esther M. Raushenbush, 'Charles Macklin's Lost Play about Henry Fielding', *Modern Language Notes* 51.8 (1936), 505–14 and W.L. Cross, *The History of Henry Fielding*, 3 vols (New Haven, CT: Yale University Press, 1918), II.410–13.

manner of certain Orators by Signior Pasquin'– indicates that it was rather another in those cross-genre forms of entertainment that were so much in demand by a novelty-seeking public at this time and, as this announcement made clear, the part of 'Pasquin Drawcansir' was designed solely 'for the Interest' of this drama's 'Censorial Highness', Charles Macklin.[22]

The oration which Macklin delivered from a rostrum on the stage at the opening of his play provides further information on the genesis of this production. London, Pasquin/Macklin told his audience, is the 'Universal Rendevouz of all the Monsters produced by waggish Nature and fantastick Art', and because he has heard of this audience's fondness for such 'Monsters', he has come (he says) 'to exhibit mine, the newest, and I hope the greatest Monster of them all'. As he described the 'common bank' from which he drew his new kind of 'monster', he then provided a description of these other anomalous entertainments, a list which included, amongst others, 'Mother Midnights, Termagants, Clare Market and Robin Hood Orators, Drury Lane Journals, Inspectors, Fools, and Drawcansirs' (4–5). Noting the number of periodical writer pseudonyms in this list, Manushag Powell plausibly reads this speech as Macklin's commentary on the paper-wars which broke out in 1752 after Fielding ('Drawcansir') and John Hill (the 'Inspector') began battling each other in the pages of their respective periodicals, and she suggests that when Macklin spoke of 'monsters' he was critiquing the kind of 'intergeneric' entertainments that these periodical writers produced in the effort to profit from this conflict and satisfy a public hungry for novelty.[23] However, as this speech made clear, Macklin was not so much critiquing these hybridized forms of entertainments as seeking to compete with them and, as he implied when he included 'Mother Midnights, Termagants, Clare Market and Robin Hood Orators' among these 'monsters', these intergeneric forms of entertainment, including his own, were as much the product of the current oratorical wars as the ongoing paper wars.

'Mother Midnights' was a reference to the character which the cross-dressed Christopher Smart assumed in his nightly parodies of the 'Clare Market Orator' (Henley) on the stage of the Haymarket Theatre, a satire which Smart amplified in a section entitled 'From the Rostrum' in his journal *The Midwife: or, The Old Woman's Magazine*.[24] 'Robin Hood Orators', 'Termagants', 'Drury Lane Journals', and 'Drawcansirs', meanwhile,

---

22 Cited in Kern, Introduction, *Covent Garden Theatre*, iii.
23 Manushag N. Powell, *Performing Authorship in Eighteenth-Century English Periodicals* (Lewisburg, PA: Bucknell University Press, 2012), 85–87.
24 See Graham Midgley, *The Life of Orator Henley* (Oxford: Clarendon Press, 1973), 51–54, 179–80, 185–92.

alluded to another front in this war, one which opened up in response to the establishment of the Robin Hood Society in the late 1740s. Writing under the name 'Madam Roxana Termagant', Bonnell Thornton began satirizing this society in his *Drury-Lane Journal* on 23 January 1752, and, five days later, 'Drawcansir' (Fielding) entered the fray in his *Covent-Garden Journal*, using ethnic as well as class stereotypes to satirize what he saw as the ignorance, illiteracy, and irreligious attitudes of this Society's members.[25] Fielding's burlesque account of a debate on the question of 'whether Relidgin was of any youse to a Sosyate', for instance, features remarks in favour of the abolition of religion not only by a barber, James Skotchum, but also by student, Mr Mac Flourish, a pedantic Scot, and a solicitor, Mr OCurry, a bull-making, self-described Irish Catholic ('I am of it myself', OCurry says of this religion, 'though I don't very well know what it is [...] Something about Beads, and Masses, and Patty Nosters, and Ivy Marys') (61, 62, 63). Fielding and Thornton continued these Robin Hood attacks in two subsequent issues of their respective journals in an apparent effort to outdo each other in their mockery of this plebian debating society.[26]

When he used Drawcansir in his title, then, Macklin hinted that his dramatic Pasquinade would be another in this satiric vein, and he dropped that hint again in the expanded notice which he placed in the *General Advertiser* on the day of his performance. Purporting to be responding to a correspondent, he stated at the bottom of this advertisement that 'The hint concerning the Robin Hood Society will be complied with'.[27] But if the audience came to his play with the expectation of enjoying another laugh at the expense of these 'Robinhoodians' (60), as Fielding called them, they would have been disappointed. Macklin's drama worked to subvert rather than to reinforce the assumptions of social and ethnic inferiority behind such satires, a turning of tables that can be explained by this playwright's own close association with that debating society. A year later, William Kenrick would explain the term '*Macklin* religious' in his satiric poem *The Pasquinade* (1753) with a footnote identifying the playwright as 'a famous player, and author, particular celebrated for his harangues on religious subjects, at the oratory of the *Robin-Hood*'.[28] And the actor and poet George Alexander Stevens

---

25 [Thornton, Bonnell], *Have at You All; or, the Drury-Lane Journal, By Madam Roxana Termagant*, 2 (23 January 1752), 42; *The Covent-Garden Journal*, ed. Bertrand A. Goldgar (Middletown, CT: Wesleyan University Press, 1988), 60–65. References are to this edition.

26 See *Covent-Garden Journal*, 66–71 and *Drury-Lane Journal* 5 (13 February 1752), 108–12.

27 *General Advertiser*, 8 April 1752.

28 W.B. Kenrick, *The Pasquinade. With Notes Variorum* (London, 1753), 21.

would say something similar about Macklin's connection to that institution in his satire *The Birth-Day of Folly* (1755), a poem which was written shortly after the closing of the British Inquisition. Locating the 'great Inquisitor' just after Orator Henley in the parade of dunces who have come to celebrate the birthday of the Goddess Folly, Stevens states that Macklin has

> Just from the Robin-hood come piping hot,
> Where once a week Religion goes to pot;
> Here Barbers, Taylors, Tinkers take degrees,
> And vent their new-laid notions as they please.[29]

Like these barbers and tailors, Stevens also suggests, 'studious M—n' has derived his 'new laid' religious and political notions from reading such writers as [John] Toland, [Bernard] Mandeville, and [Henry St John] Bolingbroke, and he implies that he is now spreading these dangerous ideas with his public lectures (13–15). These allegations had not yet been made explicitly when Macklin took the stage as Pasquin in 1752. But Fielding's representation of those who questioned religion at the Robin Hood as 'the Dregs of the People' (67) and his inclusion of a bull-making Irishman among such doubters could not have pleased him. Nor would he have been happy with the introduction of a player with a name similar to his own in Thornton's subsequent satirical account of a Robin Hood debate in his *Drury-Lane Journal*. This debate, which is on the question of 'Whether this Society be a Proper Subject for the Drama', leads a speaker to sketch out the possibility of such a play, one that would include 'the impudent PLAYER ... (MACLAINE for example)' who 'having his cue given him, makes his speech and at the conclusion makes his exit'. Most readers would have identified Macklin with that 'impudent Player', just as they would have identified Thornton's opponent, Fielding, with the 'storming hero, *Sir Alexander Drawcansir*' who (the same speaker supposes) could bring about the resolution of this drama by examining the proceedings of the Robin Hood Society and sending all its members to the House of Correction.[30]

Macklin was responding to this kind of mockery, then, with his Pasquin/Drawcansir act, and by providing an oratorical frame around his censorial court (the play's central conceit) he figuratively reappropriated the debating space that Thornton and Fielding had sought to command. In this space, however, it is the imagined audience for these Robin Hood Society print satires—'Hydra' or the 'Town'—which is the object of the disciplinary gaze,

---

29 [George Alexander Stevens], *The Birth-Day of Folly, an Heroic-Comical Poem by Peter* (London, 1755), 13. Subsequent references are to this text.
30 *Drury-Lane Journal* 5 (13 February 1752), 108, 110, 112.

while Macklin himself, elevated by the rostrum which he mounts at the beginning and at the end of the play, assumes the position of the classical censor. The eloquent and moralizing speeches that he delivered during the play would also have worked to contradict the view that Robin Hood orators (Macklin among them) are either illiterate or dangerously irreligious. After he delivers his long speech against the evils of gambling, for instance, Bob Smart, a character who is introduced as an 'Eminent Orator at the Robin-Hood Society' (18), states that 'he [Pasquin/Macklin] would make a good Figure at the Robin Hood Society' (58)—a comment which might seem ironical if it were not for the fact that the speech itself has the same high moral seriousness as the passage on gambling in Fielding's *Enquiry into the Causes of the Late Increase in Robbery* (1751). Critics indeed have invoked the similarity between Macklin's speech and this text to support the argument that, in this play, Macklin is simply playing Fielding.[31]

Macklin made explicit his desire for self-vindication, too, when, towards the end of the trial of unruly town offenders, Pasquin is asked to hear a 'Presentiment against one Charles Macklin, Comedian' on the charge that the latter has written 'a strange hotch-potch Farce, and puff'd it on the Town as written after the manner of Aristophanes and the Pasquinades of the Italian Theatre' (62–63). Perhaps following the precedent that Fielding had set when he brought his novel *Amelia* (1751) before the 'Court of Censorial Inquiry' in his *Covent-Garden Journal*, the play delivers no clear verdict on Macklin's guilt or innocence; the 'Town', as represented by the assembled characters on the stage, are divided on the question and, on those grounds, Pasquin puts off the final verdict until the next day (63). The fact that Macklin did not repeat this piece, however, indicates that the verdict was ultimately against him, and this is suggested too by the admittedly tongue-in-cheek 'Damnation' by 'the Town' which appeared in the *Drury-Lane Journal* the day after the performance.[32] But, as Macklin made clear two years later when he stepped through the fourth wall and set up a lecture and debating institution over a coffeehouse in Covent Garden, this setback did not cause him to relinquish his desire to assume an oratorical, Drawcansir-like role. His *Covent Garden Theatre* play, hindsight suggests, was rather a rehearsal for his next oratorical/periodical/theatrical act: the British Inquisition.

---

31 See Kern, Introduction, *Covent Garden Theatre*, iii.
32 The piece, which may well have been inserted by Macklin as a pre-emptive strike against his critics, attributes totally frivolous and contradictory reasons for the condemnation of this play, among them the charge by the 'Town' that the 'poor guilty culprit of a scribler, palpably laugh'd at us to our faces; instead of confessing his own faults'. *Drury-Lane Journal* (9 April 1752), 283.

Macklin's 'Live' Periodical: The British Inquisition

Among the dramatic entertainments for 1754, the *Gentleman's Magazine* included an item for 22 November that began: 'Mr. Macklin exhibited a new entertainment at his great room in *Hart-street*; he calls it the *British Inquisition*, and he proposes in the character of Inquisitor to analyze the art of speaking in public'.[33] As Markman Ellis's detailed analysis shows, this 'great room' was part of a multi-purpose entertainment complex which Macklin had begun the previous summer in the Covent Garden/Hart Street area, a set of structures which would ultimately include not only this room but also an elegant eating house, a coffeehouse, a tavern, and a gentlemen's club.[34] Macklin also began drumming up public interest in this soon-to-be opened establishment in the winter of 1753. In the 'Farewell Epilogue', which he spoke from the Drury Lane stage on 20 December, he hinted at the role he would play in this new venue, while also providing some teasers on the type of entertainment which he would be providing:

> A scheme I have in hand will make you stare!
> Tho' off the stage, I still must be the play'r.
> Still must I follow the theatric plan,
> Exert my comic pow'rs, draw all I can,
> And to each guest appear a diff'rnt man.
> I (like my liquors) must each palate hit,
> Rake with the wild, be sober with the cit,
> Nay sometimes act my least becoming part—the wit.
> With politicians must nod—seem full—
> And act my best becoming part—the *dull*.[35]

The gustatory metaphors in this speech pointed most obviously to the host character that Macklin was to assume in the eating and drinking part of his proposed establishment. In his capacity as maître d', he implied, he would need to adapt his manner of speaking and behaving to the varied nature of his clientele, just as he would need to adapt his dishes to their various tastes. But, as Powell notes in her discussion of periodical literature, 'the ability to imagine the self *as* a persona' was also a defining element both of Adam Smith's 'impartial spectator' and the spectatorial self popularized by Addison and Steele in their *Spectator* papers.[36] And, even in the process of describing how he would need to 'appear a diff'rent man' to each of his guests, Macklin

---

33 *Gentleman's Magazine*, 24 (November 1754), 532.
34 See Markman Ellis, 'Macklin's Coffeehouse', in this volume.
35 *The London Magazine, Or Gentleman's Monthly Intelligencer*, 22 (December 1753), 611.
36 Powell, *Performing Authorship*, 7.

was demonstrating his capacity to assume such a self-reflexive, disinterested character. In so doing, he was setting the stage for his appearance as the impartial 'Inquisitor' who (as was suggested in subsequent British Inquisition advertisements) would oversee an inquiry aimed at an 'Acquisition of Truth in matters of Fact'.[37]

In the months that followed, Macklin also made aggressive use of print media to promote his multifaceted entertainment centre, and with these puffs, too, he set the scene for the opening of his lecture and debating venue. No print outlet was more active in this regard than the *Gray's Inn Journal*, a periodical paper then edited by Macklin's fellow Irishman Arthur Murphy. As biographers have noted and David Worrall discusses in this volume, Murphy was a lifelong friend of Macklin, advising him on the drafts of *Love à la Mode* (1759), for instance, and supporting him in his old age by publishing by subscription an elegant edition of Macklin's plays.[38] This friendship also accounts for the *Gray's Inn Journal*'s enthusiasm for Macklin's 1754 venture. Just after the opening of the first part of his establishment in late March, a puff, which appeared in Murphy's paper under the heading 'Macklin's Coffee-House', stated that this venue was 'magnificently prepared for the Reception of all the Choice Spirits of the Age'. And the following week, this paper related that these 'Choice Spirits' were literary critics who had formed themselves 'into a Kind of Committee, in which several Debates arose a few Nights since'.[39] This description, like the subsequent account of a debate on Milton's *Paradise Lost*, was designed to show that 'Macklin's' was that kind of polite and civilizing coffeehouse that Addison and Steele had described in their periodical papers—'a site for conversable sociability conductive to the improvement of society as a whole', as Lawrence E. Klein has put it.[40] The link to this idealized coffeehouse is made more explicit, too, in a later puff that compares 'Macklin's' to the now closed Will's Coffee-House, the locus for the *Tatler*'s discussion of poetry.[41]

Macklin clearly intended the public, then, to see British Inquisition's lectures and debates as an extension of this polite coffeehouse conversation, and to this end he appropriated tropes and concepts from the periodical, the literary genre that purported to represent that conversation.[42] The

---

37 *Public Advertiser*, 18 November 1754.
38 *Cooke*, 226–28, 325–28.
39 [Arthur Murphy], *Gray's Inn Journal* 27 (29 March 1754), 162; *Gray's Inn Journal* 28 (6 April 1754), 167.
40 Lawrence E. Klein, 'Coffeehouse Civility, 1660–1714: An Aspect of Post-Courtly Culture in England', *Huntington Library Quarterly* 59.1 (1996), 33.
41 *Gray's Inn Journal*, 27 (27 April 1754), 186.
42 See Dean, *The Talk of the Town*, especially chap. 1.

lecture that was written by Macklin and delivered by him in the persona of the 'Inquisitor' at the beginning of each Inquisition event, for instance, was the oral equivalent of the essay or leader in periodical papers, and, like the fictional personae of periodicals, he encouraged members of the public to correspond with him and submit questions or ideas for discussion. A number of early advertisements for the Inquisition ended with the following notice:

> Any Question, Lecture, or Essay, upon Trade, Morality, Literature, Arts or Sciences, or upon any Subject of public Utility or Entertainment will be thankfully received, and delivered to the Public from the Rostrum; or if any Gentleman or Lady is inclined to speak their own Productions, the Inquisition is at their Service.[43]

If subsequent advertisements are to be believed, Macklin did receive suggestions from the public on topics for discussion, and these real or imagined letters, like those that appeared in contemporary periodicals, served as a strategy for highlighting the collective and participatory nature of his oratorical entertainment. The advertisement for the evening of 13 December, for instance, acknowledges receipt of three such letters, including one from a female correspondent who, in an evident allusion to the female Roman orator of that name, named herself 'Hortensia'; this latter letter elicited the response that 'the Inquisitor will gratefully obey her Commands'.[44]

Other features of the British Inquisition event, such as its thrice-weekly staging, a tempo which Macklin settled into by the third week of production, would also have seemed familiar to contemporary readers of periodicals (Richard Steele's *Tatler* [1709–11], Lewis Theobald's *Censor* [1715–17], and Fielding's *Champion* [1739–43] all followed that production schedule). Nor would such readers have been surprised by the variety of topics discussed and debated at this forum. Subsequent biographers have cited the inclusion of such sensationalist topics as the Canning affair as evidence that Macklin was unable to sustain the high cultural note which he struck in his initial few events when he devoted his lectures to such topics as the theatre, the art of public speaking, Shakespeare, and Milton.[45] But such shifts in content and tone were characteristic of periodical literatures since, as Scott Black notes in relation to the *Spectator*, such papers were

---

43 See, for instance, *Public Advertiser*, 5 December 1754 and 7 December 1754.
44 *Public Advertiser*, 13 December 1754. For Hortensia (42 BC), see Joyce E. Salisbury, *Encyclopedia of Women in the Ancient World* (Santa Barbara, CA: ABC-CLIO, Inc., 2001), 161–62.
45 See *Appleton*, 104.

structured not by classical literary models but rather 'by the variety of the mundane' and the 'quotidian dynamics of friendship and conversation'.[46] A closer look at the advertisement for the 13 December Inquisition event (the date that focused on the Canning affair) also dispels the notion that there was any notable falling off in the seriousness of this institution's discussions around that time. The third question set for debate on that day, it is true, raised a relatively minor matter of social etiquette ('Whether the greater Man in Public Assembly, or other Place, ought first to take off his Hat to his Inferior, or his Inferior to him'). But the two other debate questions related to the theatre and to social policy, and the latter in particular—a debate on the question of 'Whether the Poor of Great-Britain may not be more effectually provided for than they are at present, and what are the best Means?'– addressed a topic of the greatest social significance.[47] The British Inquisition lecture and debate topics in the previous week were similarly varied in content and in degree of seriousness. The lecture for the previous Wednesday (11 December), for instance, was on the nature of the Inquisition itself, and 'what everyone says of the Undertaking, and the Undertaker, and what he says of every Body', a talk which would have furnished Macklin with the opportunity to engage in that (sometimes playful) self-scrutiny, which, as noted above, was a feature of the periodical authorial persona. The first debate question on that evening, however (and one that was described as being repeated 'by particular Desire of several Gentlemen'), was 'whether it is consistent with Humanity, Religion, or true Policy, for a free Nation to makes Slaves of Human beings'.[48] That question, like the first one discussed on the previous Saturday—'Whether Ireland or our Colonies, ought by Policy, to have equal Advantage with the Mother Country'[49]—would have opened up a discussion of the deepest moral as well as social and political significance, one that bore on the rights and freedom of peoples across the empire.

Unlike the coffeehouse discussions that periodical writers purported to relate, however, these British Inquisition discussions were open to all comers who could cover the price of admission and, this economic limit notwithstanding, this added a radically different social dimension to this debating forum, transforming what had been a restricted and virtual site

---

46 Scott Black, 'Social and Literary Form in the *Spectator*', *Eighteenth-Century Studies* 33.1 (1999), 26, 27. Readers' interest in the mundane and the sensational also explains why Fielding, for instance, included in his journal a section that carried the sordid details of the actual cases which came before him in his capacity as magistrate.
47 *Public Advertiser*, 13 December 1754.
48 *Public Advertiser*, 11 December 1754.
49 *Public Advertiser*, 7 December 1754.

of conversation into a live, potentially more democratic one.⁵⁰ Taking its published claims about the upscale nature of this enterprise at face value, critics have tended to assume that the British Institution was an elitist institution, and, indeed, as the emphasis on elegance in his advertisements reveals, Macklin actively courted a genteel clientele.⁵¹ During his event's second week, he also announced that 'by the particular Desire of several Persons of Distinction', 'the Disposition' of his great room had been 'theatrically altered' so that 'some Seats are enclosed, and that the price for those seats was now two shillings and sixpence'.⁵² The admission to that part of the room was thus the equivalent of admission to the pit in the playhouse, a section frequented by male 'wits' and the more affluent among the 'middling' sort. General admission to Macklin's forum, however, remained at its first announced price of one shilling, the equivalent of the entry fee to the playhouse's upper gallery, and while that was admittedly more than the sixpence required for admission to the Robin Hood Society, it would not necessarily have prohibited those from the lower echelons of society (small tradesmen, clerks, artisans, for instance) from attending this entertainment, any more than it prevented them from going to see a play.⁵³ As theatre historians have shown, throughout the eighteenth century, the lower orders were well-represented in the so-called 'gods'.⁵⁴

The satire that was directed against the British Inquisition also makes it clear that, like the playhouse, Macklin's venue was seen as a socially volatile site, one which, in this case, had the potential to disrupt not only the gendered norms of public debating societies, as Mary Thale and Markman Ellis have noted, but also the class, ethnic, and religious norms that upheld the eighteenth-century public sphere in Britain.⁵⁵ As we have seen above, Macklin did encourage the 'Ladies' to speak at his forum, and the depiction of a lady speaker in the British Museum British Inquisition image suggests

---

50 On the periodical's 'virtual' public sphere as a carefully policed and restrictive site, see, for example, Cowan, 'Mr Spectator and the Coffeehouse Public Sphere', 348 and *passim*.
51 See Ellis, 'Macklin's Coffeehouse', in this volume.
52 *Public Advertiser*, 29 November 1754.
53 For playhouse admission prices, see Robert D. Hume, 'The Value of Money in Eighteenth-Century England: Incomes, Prices, Buying Power—and Some Problems in Cultural Economics', *Huntington Library Quarterly* 77.4 (2014), 383. For the Robin Hood Society admission price, see Thale, 'The Robin Hood Society', 36.
54 See Leo Hughes, *The Drama's Patrons: A Study of the Eighteenth-Century London Audience* (Austin: University of Texas Press, 1971).
55 See Mary Thale, 'The Case of the British Inquisition: Money and Women in Mid-Eighteenth-Century London Debating Societies', *Albion* 31.1 (1999), 31–48 and Ellis, 'Macklin's Coffeehouse', in this volume.

that at least some women took him up on this offer. When the famous comic mimic Samuel Foote spoke at the Inquisition in the dress of a woman, then, he was undoubtedly ridiculing this intrusion into what had been traditionally a masculine preserve and, as Thale notes, George Alexander Stevens and others continued this gendered assault at the Little Theatre and at the New Theatre at the Haymarket with such parodic productions as the 'Female Lyceum' and the 'Female Inquisition'.[56] But these attacks were part of a broader counter-theatre that engaged the satiric talents not only of actors but of periodical writers, pamphleteers, poets, and print-makers, and for some in this second group, Macklin's unforgiveable offence was the ambition he promoted in the lower orders, both by his lectures on the art of public speaking and through his own example.

The attacks connecting Macklin's debating forum to the Robin Hood Society are instructive in this respective. As noted above, Stevens in his 1755 poem, *The Birth-Day of Folly*, spoke of 'the great Inquisitor' as having come 'piping hot' from the Robin Hood Society, a place where, as he derisively notes, 'Barbers, Taylors, Tinkers take degrees'. In an issue on the 'Power of Speaking' in his short-lived journal *The Tuner* (1753–54), Paul Hiffernan, a writer who had gained notoriety in his native Dublin for his attacks on Charles Lucas (subsequently dubbed the 'Irish Wilkes'), took this imputed Robin Hood/Inquisition connection a step further, suggesting that the latter institution, under Macklin's leadership, was an outgrowth of the former. Like Satyrus, the Greek actor who recognized Demosthenes' oratorical talents even when others did not, Macklin saw the oratorical potential of his Robin Hood colleagues, Hiffernan suggested, and he set up his Inquisition for the purpose of providing a better outlet for that hitherto confined 'Genius':

> Macklin, the Modern *Satyrus*, having perceived many eloquent Amplificators cramp'd and bamboozled by the *Robin-Hood*'s limited Time of speaking, being but five Minutes, short Period for those, who have a Speech-flux! and having also perceiv'd the Unsonoreity of the low-roofed Porter-quaffing Academy, has invited those of warm and prurient Genius, to let it out, in his newly erected spacious Museum.[57]

In developing this mocking Satyrus/Macklin comparison, Hiffernan, who had been educated first in a Catholic seminary in Ireland and then in a university in France, was arguably attempting to differentiate his genteel, classically educated kind of Irish immigrant from the more plebian, less-educated variety that Macklin represented, and, to that end, too, he parodied

---

56 Thale, 'The Case of the British Inquisition', 44.
57 *Tuner* 5 (January 1755), 6. Subsequent references are to this text.

the latter's style of speaking, showing, for instance, how Macklin violated the tenets of classical rhetoric.[58] But in addition to ridiculing Macklin, Hiffernan also mocks his 'oratorical Clutch, his little unfledg'd Demosthenes' (7), and as he develops this strand of his satire, he gives us more information on the social make-up of the Inquisition audience. If it included university-educated men like Samuel Foote (or, for that matter, like Hiffernan himself), it also included 'young Adventurers, *Embryo-Demosthenes*' who were hissed after their first effort at speaking (5), and 'young *Pudding-Row* and *Hart Street Orators*' who fear to show their '*Idiotism*' in knowing only their 'Mother Lingo' (9); and, as Hiffernan's text implies, this group of less-experienced and less-literate speakers had come not to mock Macklin but to learn from him with the hope of moving up in the world. After receiving a half-hour of Macklin's instruction in the art of speaking, Hiffernan sardonically asks, 'who is the Person, nay the humblest Tradesman, that may not hope, sometime or other to become a Member of the Body corporate of the Place he lives in, and have an Opportunity of displaying whatever *Power of Speaking* Nature or Application may have endowed him with?'(11).

That Macklin had a following among this small trader and artisan class is also suggested by 'Stephanus Scriblerus', the anonymous author of the first and only issue of a journal called *The Censor* (1754). This publication is chiefly concerned with exposing what the writer sees as the contrived and self-serving nature of the quarrel that developed between the Inquisitor and Foote at the Haymarket. But it also contains an 'Epistolary Dedication to Orator Mack—n' in which the Inquisitor is ironically hailed as '*the Father of Grub-street Eloquence*' and praised for his role in teaching those who were traditionally excluded from public debate, either on the basis of age or social status.[59] '*At his publick Speaking Room*', this writer states,

> [Macklin] *instructed the Youth of this Kingdom in universal Arts and Sciences, and was the first that formed the mouths of Cobblers, Barbers, and Apprentice-Boys, to vomit out a Cataract of Metaphors, and Allegories. So that, to the Erudition of this Great Man, it is to be ascribed that we are now a Nation of Orators.* (iv)

If Macklin was dubbed the 'Head' of the 'Wrongheads', then, it was, in part, because he was perceived to be leading this nationally disruptive oratorical movement, one which was bringing plebian speakers out of obscurity into

---

58 For Hiffernan's ongoing struggle to establish himself as a man of letters in London, see Norma Clarke's *Brothers of the Quill: Oliver Goldsmith in Grub Street* (Cambridge, MA: Harvard University Press, 2016), 64–73.

59 Stephanus Scriblerus, 'Dedication to Orator Mack—n', *Censor* 1 (1755), v. Subsequent references are to this text.

middle-class coffeehouses and lecture rooms, the arena where public opinion was shaped and decided. But Macklin also earned this dubious title, the evidence suggests, because as an immigrant from a 'low' native Irish and Catholic background, he was himself an overdetermined example of all the differences that the public sphere sought to exclude—differences, which as we have seen in the Fielding satire on the Robin Hood Society above, centred not only on social status and education but also on ethnicity and religion.

The twenty-six-page anonymous pamphlet, *An Epistle from Tully in the Shades, to Orator Ma———n in Covent Garden* (1754) also illustrates how opponents used these overlapping categories to expose Macklin's 'wrongness' when it came to his public speaking role. Using the persona of the dead Tully (Cicero), the author of this pamphlet pretends initially to praise him for the originality of his 'Orations and Philosophy'.[60] But, like other Inquisition mock-panegyrics, this text reveals instead Macklin's distance from the classical ideal, whether in oratory or learning. 'Like a Mushroom from Dung and Ordure' (4) or 'like the Eagle rising from a Carcass', Tully tells Macklin, you have risen to the greatest heights of fame, and all 'without waking over Books, Application to Study, mixing in learned Company, translating from foreign Languages, or even understanding your own' (5–6). Macklin's Irishness is invoked, then, to further discredit his oratorical and philosophical claims, and, to add that dimension to his satire, the writer draws on Irish stereotypes from a wide variety of sources. The suggestion, for instance, that Macklin was born in a deep 'cavern' in his native city to a mother who ate only roots throughout her pregnancy, echoes early fantastical accounts by travellers about the barbarism of the so-called 'wild Irish'. But to ridicule Macklin's claim to be an authority on Shakespeare, the writer borrows from a more recent source, recasting the Irishman as another one of those monstrous 'Macs' who, in Dryden's 'Mac Flecknoe', shut out the light of true English genius. On hearing his reading of *Lear*, Tully tells Macklin, Shakespeare's ghost ran mad through Elysium, lamenting '*alas! the mighty Macloughlin comes, and like the dusky and opaque Moon passing between my Works and me, eclipses all my world of glory*' (12).

Reference to Catholicism, Macklin's faith before he converted to Anglicanism, works likewise to suggest the inappropriateness, if not the danger, of his attempt to lecture the British public on religion and morals. Picking up the Luther trope mentioned above, Tully informs Macklin that the shade of this reformer trembled lest the Inquisitor's 'Arguments for Protestantism' should eclipse his (Luther's) legacy, and thus restore 'papal Power, the

---

60 *An Epistle from Tully in the Shades, to Orator Ma———n in Covent Garden* (London, 1754), 4. Subsequent references are to this text.

establish'd Religion of your Land' (23). The implication here—namely that Macklin is a crypto-Catholic who is working to overthrow the Protestant Reformation—is, on the face of it, ridiculous. His biographers tell us that, at the age of forty, he became a Protestant after reading the seventeenth-century anti-Catholic tract, 'The Funeral of the Mass', and there is no reason to doubt this, given his general distrust of authority and his commitment to the kind of rational inquiry that this pamphlet espouses.[61] But the suggestion that Macklin was secretly working to overthrow the established church was nevertheless an inflammatory one since it tapped into long-standing English suspicions about Irish migrants, especially when those migrants had Catholic family connections and/or recognizable native Irish names. As the caricatured depictions of Edmund Burke show, the professed Anglicanism of such Irishmen was frequently seen as merely a form of entryism, a passing act that masked more nefarious political and religious desires.[62]

If the British Inquisition was a short-lived affair, it was not only, then (as some have argued), because of its inability to survive the nightly ridicule heaped upon it by Foote, Stevens, and others at the Haymarket.[63] It was also because of print satires like the ones above which depicted this institution's clientele as illiterate and vulgar and the Inquisitor himself as the stereotypically ignorant and politically suspect Irishman.[64] The racialized dimension of these attacks serves as a reminder, too, that eighteenth-century British society was not always quite as tolerant and accepting as recent accounts of Irish 'middle-class' migration during that period would lead us to believe.[65] Macklin may well have thought of himself as one of the middling sort, and he may well have been part of 'London Irish networks with enlightenment aspirations', as David O'Shaughnessy has persuasively argued.[66] But, as the case of the British Inquisition makes clear, his self-identification and aspirations counted for little among those with entrenched anti-Irish

---

61 For this conversion anecdote, see *Cooke*, 75–76. For Macklin's anti-authoritarianism, see [Richard Lewis], *The robin-Hood Society: a satire. With notes variorum. By Peter Pounce, Esq*; (London, 1756), 70–71.
62 See, for example, Nicholas K. Robinson, *Edmund Burke: A Life in Caricature* (New Haven, CT: Yale University Press, 1996), 89.
63 *Appleton*, 105–8.
64 See also *M–ckl–n's Answer to Tully*. This tract portrays Macklin as being too ignorant and stupid to realize he is being mocked in the Tully letter, and it puts nonsensical blunders in his mouth which he seeks to excuse 'as from the Irishman' (4).
65 See Craig Bailey, *Irish London: Middle-Class Migration in the Global Eighteenth Century* (Liverpool: Liverpool University Press, 2013).
66 David O'Shaughnessy, '"Bit, by some mad whig": Charles Macklin and the Theater of Irish Enlightenment', *Huntington Library Quarterly* 80.4 (2017), 559–84.

prejudices.[67] This is not to suggest that we must now see Macklin through the lens of the older victim narrative about the Irish in Britain, a story that stressed this community's passivity in the face of oppression. As the history of eighteenth-century debating societies makes clear, those working men and women who were denied a voice in the British public arena never willingly accepted their exclusion, and neither did Macklin.[68] Though he never again mounted the rostrum as a public orator, he used his theatrical platform and his dramatic productions in subsequent years to defend his right (and by extension the right of other marginalized subjects) to speak publicly. In the Dublin prologue to *Love à la Mode* (1762), for example, he criticized Britannia for mocking accents that were not like her own rather than acknowledging that 'merit springs in *every* soil'. And he challenged such racialized cultural assumptions, outraging John Bull yet again, when he made 'a true-born Irishman' the genteel hero of his comedy of that name.[69] As evidenced by the lecture that he gave his audience after his controversial staging of *Macbeth* in 1773, Macklin continued up to the end of his career to battle his print opponents and others who would limit his right to speak. Clutching the newspaper reviews that took issue with this *Macbeth* performance, and over the calls 'off, off, off' that filled the playhouse, he reportedly cried out, 'I will be heard'.[70] He spoke here, it could be argued, for all those who pressed to have a voice in the eighteenth-century public sphere and who fought to make good the promise of the British Enlightenment.

---

67 As was illustrated by the furore over the 'Jew Bill' during the same period (1753–55), anti-Semitic prejudice was no less entrenched.
68 For an overview of this struggle, see Craig Calhoun, 'The Public Sphere in the Field of Power', *Social Science History* 34.3 (2010), 301–35.
69 See Helen Burke, *Riotous Performances: The Struggle for Hegemony in the Irish Theater, 1712–1785* (South Bend, IN: Notre Dame University Press, 2003), 252–53, 255–61 and Paul Goring, '"John Bull, pit, box, and gallery, said No!" Charles Macklin and the Limits of Ethnic Resistance on the Eighteenth-Century London Stage', *Representations* 79.1 (2002), 61–81.
70 *Hibernian Magazine*, 5 (November 1775), 649. For an excellent analysis of this event, see Kristina Straub, 'The Newspaper "Trial" of Charles Macklin's *Macbeth* and the Theatre as Juridical Public Sphere', *Eighteenth-Century Fiction* 27.3–4 (2015), 395–418.

Restaging Macklin

Among the inspirations for the conception of this volume were two revivals of Macklin's Love à la Mode *at Smock Alley Theatre in 2017 and 2018. This section considers those productions, photographs from which can be found in the colour insert to this volume. Nicholas Johnson, an academic and theatre practitioner, provides a detailed reflection on 'practice as research' in the modern academy and considers what is at stake in this kind of activity. This is followed by an interview with the director, Colm Summers, carried out by Johnson, where the politics and dramaturgical issues of reviving Georgian theatre for the present moment are debated. Taken together it is hoped that these pieces can help bridge what at times can seem an insuperable gap between the academic and theatrical industries—a problem that may seem, but need not be especially, acute for the eighteenth-century repertoire.*

12

Restaging Macklin

Nicholas Johnson

EIGHTEENTH-CENTURY DRAMA seems to be an especially endangered species, within the broadly threatened phylum of the live theatre. The socio-political environment in which Georgian plays were performed—not to mention the expectations of audiences, the material life of actors or managers, and even the architectural features of theatres—have migrated so far from original conditions that the texts may not seem immediate or relevant today. In practice-focused theatre education, eighteenth-century work is often viewed through the generalized lens of 'Restoration comedy', 'comedy of manners', or 'farce'—an amorphous (and often ahistorical) tradition in which a figure like Charles Macklin is lumped in with, and eclipsed by, names that have more reliably delivered twentieth-century box office success. Old farces, if they are taught at all, are generally held up as an example of 'external' or 'presentational' forms of performance, in contrast to psychological realism/naturalism, a tradition based in Konstantin Stanislavski's work at the turn of the twentieth century, but still dominant in actor training (and the popular imagination of acting) today.[1] Though architectural restoration has brought a Georgian theatre back to life at Bury St Edmunds, and though some

---

1 Notably, Stanislavski contrasted his own evolving 'System' of actor training with the tradition of farce, to which he is not kind: 'A talented actor is expected to be able to say silly things with a serious face, and tell spicy stories with a naïve expression, to make unnatural things seem natural, make something dull appear to be gay, give the aspect of wit to banalities—in a word he is supposed to edit the author or, better still, replace him'. See Constantin Stanislavski, *Stanislavski's Legacy*, ed. and trans. Elizabeth Reynolds Hapgood (New York: Routledge, 2015 [1968]), 57.

efforts have been made to encourage the recovery of a lost repertoire there, no regional theatre could sustain its life solely with theatre of the period; its loyalty must be to what audiences today want to see (in sufficiently large numbers), such that the venue can survive.[2]

In such conditions, few contemporary theatre-makers and even fewer audience members are steeped in the specific traditions of eighteenth-century drama; programmers are therefore not seeking out such work for commission. The fact that *Love à la Mode* came to audiences in Dublin in 2017 and 2018 at all is firmly linked to the academic study of the dramatic literature of the eighteenth century, rather than commercial imperatives. Nonetheless, this process exposed some of the ways in which the text itself, the author's legacy as a public figure, and the practices of this period of theatre continue to be vibrantly alive for theatre-makers and audiences alike. The academic environments in which the project originated and developed provided important avenues not only for research to flow usefully into the process, but also for the experiences of actors, directors, and designers to flow back towards scholarship and pedagogy. This chapter represents an effort to identify and disseminate some of the ephemeral insights from this theatrical work in a more durable form, exploring not only the practicalities of 'restaging' Macklin, but also the conceptual implications, challenges, insights, and values that arose from the process. It is hoped that this exploration will be of interest not only to scholars of Macklin who may not have local access to contemporary versions of this play on stage, but also to those interested in engaging with practice-as-research in their own academic contexts.

The first discussions about restaging Macklin, as so often in such projects, began with the idea of simply providing a staged reading or, at most, a one-off performance, as part of the February 2017 Dublin conference, 'The Irish and the London Stage: Identity, Culture, and Politics (1680–1830)'. David O'Shaughnessy, then based at the School of English at Trinity College Dublin, reached out to the department of drama in the summer of 2016 to identify possible actors for what could have been a singular event with strict parameters: transcribe and edit a script, rehearse a few times, and then present, either on book or memorized. Two factors contributed to the fact that this simple version of the project did not occur: first, the historical relationship of Charles Macklin to Dublin's Smock Alley Theatre,

---

2 David Taylor, who was a resident research consultant in the restored theatre for a period in 2010, notes that the programme 'does not operate within a museological or pedagogical framework, but within the commercially fraught and locally oriented parameters of regional theatre'. See David Francis Taylor, 'Discoveries and Recoveries in the Laboratory of Georgian Theatre', *New Theatre Quarterly* 27.3 (2011), 229.

restored in 2012, made the possibility of a fully mounted 'homecoming' staging extremely enticing; second, Trinity's drama department has spent much of the last decade building a community of practice around recoveries, adaptations, and interventions involving unperformed/under-performed, theoretically 'unperformable', or otherwise 'lost' works.[3] Such projects have been central to the growth of Trinity's interdisciplinary research theme in Creative Arts Practice, and it contributes to a national-level discussion—still relatively nascent in Ireland—around the methods and impact of practice-as-research in the performing arts.[4]

To engage fully with what it means to 'restage' Macklin in the landscape of contemporary theatre in Ireland, this chapter will explore the manifold ways in which theatre praxis travels across time through form, content, translation, interpretation, reception, and education. The troublesome link between 'thinking' and 'doing' theatre has wide-ranging pedagogical and philosophical implications, which must be considered alongside the actual 'findings' from the theatre-as-laboratory in which Macklin's *Love à la Mode* was the object of analysis. Beyond these methodological considerations, there is also new information to be mined about the work itself through its transformations over time. If genetic criticism focuses on the development of literature through the study of manuscripts, then performance represents an augmentation of the 'epigenetic' layer of information about the work itself: that which is changed, developed, or altered by the work's new environment as it migrates and adapts. Dirk Van Hulle writes that the 'work' of literature, so conceived, becomes 'a complex and fascinating dialectic between completion and incompletion',[5] in which the study of theatre is especially concerned with 'continuous incompletion'.[6] Though Van Hulle here is writing about manuscripts from twentieth-century aesthetic modernism, this

---

3 Key projects in this trajectory include the founding of the Samuel Beckett Laboratory (2013), the ensemble performance projects *Enemy of the Stars* after Wyndham Lewis (2014–15), *The David Fragments* after Bertolt Brecht (2015–17), and the recent VR/AR projects *Virtual Play* and *Augmented Play* after Samuel Beckett (2017–20).

4 Such discussions are international as well. The League of European Research Universities (LERU), of which Trinity is a member, released a briefing paper in 2012 exploring the potential in this area; Trinity was asked to address LERU on its own approach in 2017. See Martinus Buekers, Bas Nugteren, and Katrien Maes, 'Creative Arts and Research-Intensive Universities: A Crucial Partnership', LERU Briefing Paper: www.leru.org/files/Creative-Arts-and-Research-Intensive-Universities-A-Crucial-Partnership-Full-paper.pdf (accessed 31 May 2020).

5 Dirk Van Hulle, 'Modern Manuscripts and Textual Epigenetics: Samuel Beckett's Works between Completion and Incompletion', *Modernism/modernity* 18.4 (2011), 808.

6 Van Hulle, 'Modern Manuscripts and Textual Epigenetics', 804.

chapter suggests that a view of theatre as chiefly concerned with mobility and evolution also applies to eighteenth-century farce.

Rethinking 'restaging': form and content

THE FORMAL LINEAGE OF FARCE extends across so many theatre traditions and over so many centuries that it can be difficult to find agreement on its characteristics, and as a word used to describe a theatre piece it is notoriously flexible. Among practitioners, farces are often identified as difficult to direct, with prodigious technical challenges for designers and actors built in. Part of the tradition would suggest that to be successful at farce, actions must be highly choreographed and precise; from another angle, however, disarray, disorganization, and absurdity can be thought of as the main characteristics of the form. From an audience perspective, 'farce' may not seem especially complicated, since generally the testament to its success is simply laughter. But the conditions under which things appear funny are highly specific to a given culture at a given time—when the moral universe has shifted so far since the time a play was written, it is common to discover that what was once amusing to an audience is now more disturbing.[7] For a collective of self-described millennial theatre-makers—the troupe known as 'Felicity' that emerged simultaneously with the first iteration of *Love à la Mode*—the issues and questions raised by both the form and the content of Macklin's text were thoroughly contemporary.[8] In taking on the project while remaining loyal to today's artistic ethics, they had to ask: how possible is it to produce a *relevant* farce today? How to handle stereotypes that might offend current sensibilities? Especially when a script comes from the eighteenth century, how can such a play avoid appearing 'historical', 'stuffy', or the 'museum theatre' of a bygone era? Colm Summers's director's note from the February 2017 work-in-progress presentation is explicit about the troupe's quest to 'exceed anachronism', asking the question: 'what can eighteenth-century drama offer theatre in the twenty-first century?'[9]

---

[7] A clear example from *Love à la Mode* would be the way in which the figure of Mordecai the Jew is mined for comedy based partly on his religious affiliation, invoking tropes around money that are now widely thought of as anti-Semitic. Macklin himself, of course, famously noted that there was a '*geography* in *humour*'. Cooke, 270.

[8] See the next chapter in this volume, '*Love à la Mode* in Performance: A Dialogue', for the director's reflections on this topic.

[9] Colm Summers, 'A Note from the Director', *Love à la Mode* Programme (Smock Alley Theatre/Felicity, Scene + Heard Festival, Dublin 2017): https://cordis.europa.eu/docs/results/333/333592/final1-love-a-la-mode-programme.pdf (accessed 10 August 2021).

One answer to this question calls attention to the resurgence, or perhaps endurance, of Georgian theatrical strategies. Indeed, the numerous textual interventions in Macklin's original, supported by O'Shaughnessy's collaboration as dramaturg as well as a considerable research and inventiveness from the cast members themselves, made reference (in Summers's telling) to 'innovations offered to us by the Georgians: aside as dramatic constant, direct address, and above all, the explicit metatheatricality of their texts'.[10] The concrete outcome of this approach was that Macklin's text remained at the core of the event, but was penetrated by definitions and commentary by a female performer playing a 'Harlequin', as well as comedic moments that arose from gaps in performance style—most notably, gestures designed to critique the original—between the 'contemporary' actor in the room with the audience, and the 'historical' figure that they were asked to play. This porous text was preceded by a prologue delivered by Harlequin claiming (falsely) to be a rediscovered fragment from manuscript research, which itself was further framed by an opening delivered by the actor playing Mordecai, who— working in a mode akin to improv or stand-up comedy—got the audience to chant the word 'farce' before the play began.

Theatrical licence also extended beyond the confines of the performance itself. The company that claimed to be producing the play, 'Knaves', did not exist. A central comic conceit of both adaptations—the work-in-progress (2017) as well as the summer touring version (2018)—was that the role of Callaghan O'Brallaghan would be played by an understudy, because the actor originally cast—the elusive Charlie M'Laughlin—had experienced an unspecified mental breakdown in the course of rehearsals. This fiction was elaborately cultivated in the online world and word-of-mouth surrounding the play, through mysterious Facebook posts and gossip about rehearsal-room antics on the part of this invented actor (whose name is, of course, related to Macklin's own). This set of strategies worked to bring to life a central dramaturgical engine within Macklin's play: deceptions and lies. An audience member could believe at first that one actor on stage was new to the play; as this actor's performance steadily improved beyond the point where this was reasonable, they would realize they had been deceived; and when a figure appears at the play's end who could be M'Laughlin, the possibility of a still greater lie, or perhaps a truth beyond what they had thought of as a lie, opens up.

The idea of nested fictions within a drama, the 'play-about-a-play', and the actor having both a real persona and a character to play: all of these are associated by today's audiences and critics with 'postmodern' or sometimes

---

10 Summers, 'A Note from the Director'.

'postdramatic' dramaturgy, yet they resonate strongly with aspects of Georgian theatre practice. In addition to finding these connections across time through its structural choices, the play posed many opportunities for content to resonate for audiences as well. If one advertised a dramatic spectacle that engaged with the power dynamics that surround femininity, the rights that inhere in those who control wealth, and the meaning of national identity, audiences might think they would be attending political theatre that hit the hot-button issues of 2018. With national stereotypes abounding and jibes about origin, class, and family being traded among English, Scottish, and Irish characters, audiences in Dublin and London could not help but be reminded of the 2016 Brexit vote, about which debates and negotiations were ongoing passionately at the time of rehearsals and performances. Though these links were not made explicit, an understanding of theatre as essentially ideological would suggest that farce can be a capacious Trojan horse for such ideas. Comedy turns mostly on forms of social upheaval and human behaviour under stress. The laughter at things that are true of human beings, especially the messy things, licenses a subtle politics. To produce a farce today—especially this farce—is thus to sustain the value of an old text, as well as to reinvigorate it. Conversely, it also seeks to contribute to today's discourses by revisiting the past. In the thorny dialectic territory between precision and mess or between stereotype and satire, farce challenges the artists and audiences of today to find out what we learn when we follow our primordial impulses: namely, to go into a darkened room and laugh together at what is still, at some level, ourselves.

Rethinking 'Adaptation': *traduttore, traditore*

WHILE THE ACADEMIC ORIGIN of this restaged *Love à la Mode* was clearly indebted to the study of English literature—owing its funding, its dramaturgy, and much of its audience to Trinity's School of English—the project's ethics and praxis derived from the field of performance studies. Writing in 1995 about the complex emergence of this discipline, Dwight Conquergood argues that 'Performance studies is a border discipline, an interdiscipline, that cultivates the capacity to move between structures, to forge connections, to see together, to speak with instead of simply speaking about or for others'.[11] An ethnographer as well as a performer, Conquergood was attuned to the ethical and political dimensions of bringing stories to

---

11 Dwight Conquergood, 'Of Caravans and Carnivals: Performance Studies in Motion', *Drama Review* 39.4 (1995), 137–38.

life in a social context. Noting the durability of antitheatrical prejudice when theatre is considered as 'mere' *mimesis*—defined (mistakenly) for these purposes as being about 'sham and show'—he refers to the work of Victor Turner on concepts like social drama, liminality, and *homo performans* to justify a claim that performance had (already by the 1980s) become rather a form of *poiesis*, concerned with emergence, world-making, and 'coming into being'.[12] According to Conquergood, Turner's emphasis on 'the productive capacities of performance' has now given way to a more political and poststructuralist emphasis (which he credits to Homi Bhabha, among others) on performance as *kinesis*: 'breaking and remaking'; 'action that incessantly insinuates, interrupts, interrogates, antagonizes, and decenters powerful master discourses'; and 'those restless energies that transgress boundaries and trouble closure'.[13] Such intellectual underpinnings may go some way towards explaining the necessity of freedom and creativity in bringing young artists and young audiences to older works (whether unknown or canonical). In this admittedly simplified schema, *mimesis* of Macklin would have been the quest for historical reproduction of the play's most accurate possible performance text; *poiesis* would have entailed an interpretive journey to excavate the play's inner need to be, as a potter might release a pot from its surrounding clay. *Kinesis* is ultimately what occurred here: with carnivalesque irreverence, the play was flung from its original culture into our own, subjected to centrifugal forces in order to keep its ideas 'in play'—even if this gesture might entail distortion or outright rejection of the original.

Such thinking could only be considered innovative in relatively conservative theatre cultures like that of Ireland, where the writer has historically been empowered over the figure of the director. In the German theatre culture, *kinesis* of this kind is essentially the common standard, due both to its emphasis on directors and on its history of critically engaged theatre—a tradition identified most strongly in the twentieth century with Bertolt Brecht, but which clearly stretches as far back as Enlightenment figures like Gotthold Ephraim Lessing and Friedrich Schiller. German praxis highlights the importance of cultural context in how a drama is executed and embraces the idea that even classic texts require constant renewal and new directorial engagement that addresses the audience in the here-and-now. Hence, the 2017 work-in-progress festival showing of *Love à la Mode* could justify the

---

12 See Victor Turner, *Dramas, Fields, and Metaphors: Symbolic Action in Human Society* (Ithaca, NY: Cornell University Press, 1974) and *From Ritual to Theatre* (New York: PAJ Publications, 1982). The symbiotic collaboration between Turner and Richard Schechner in the 1970s and 1980s represents one of the origin narratives of performance studies.
13 Conquergood, 'Of Caravans and Carnivals', 138.

inclusion of aesthetics from stand-up comedy; the 2018 summer touring version for younger audiences included a newly penned rap about Charles Macklin, performed to the beat of 'Hypnotize' by the Notorious B.I.G. Such interventions typify *kinesis* by unsettling audience assumptions of eighteenth-century theatre, privileging access and engagement—and perhaps also 'fun'—over authorial fidelity.[14]

Though it is a truism that no two nights of performance are the same, the full implications of that difference are often subsumed in the presumption, or indeed the attempt, of repetition. Thus the art of theatre can either be an ordeal of unrepeatability, or it can celebrate and embrace the fullness of that morpheme 're'—understanding theatre as a process of recovery, restoration, revision, reinvigoration, resurrection, and revolution, which can only be achieved through rewriting and reworking the material at hand.[15] The widespread German practice of using the word *nach* instead of *von* when crediting authors of plays in production (i.e., 'after' instead of 'by') hints at this approach, privileging directorial or contemporary exigencies over fealty to the playwright or textual origins. As in previous practice-as-research projects emerging from the Trinity College theatre laboratory scene, the production was marketed as 'after' Macklin, a fact that did not escape the notice of Richard Jones in his review of the 2018 production in *Theatre Journal*, where he noted that 'prepositions are important'.[16]

Such thinking about how theatre must undergo 'translation' as it moves across time offers a productive nexus with concepts from translation studies. An early but now outmoded proposition, arising in relation to directing Samuel Beckett's precise late plays, was the claim that all performance is adaptation, in the sense that precise repetition of a play text is always already impossible, and so as the *object* of text enters into the logic of the *event*, it will change by necessity. An advantage that scholars of the eighteenth century might have over theorists of the theatrical avant-garde is that they are also

---

14 Richard Jones, in his review of the 2018 version, noted: 'the production's major attraction, apart from historical interest, was the cast's ebullience [...] if there were moments when it all became a little too self-referential, these were more than outweighed by a spirit of inclusion, of honestly desiring the audience to be part of the evening's sense of community'. See Richard Jones, 'Review of *Love à la Mode*', *Theatre Journal* 71.2 (2019), 226.

15 Suzan Lori-Parks, one of the leading living American playwrights, uses a strategy in writing that she calls 'rep & rev', for 'repetition and revision', which she indicates is derived from her engagement with jazz. It is, of course, not only directors who view theatre in terms of the consciousness of unrepeatability; numerous playwrights also compose with 'open' dramaturgy and provide spaces within texts that allow for variation.

16 Jones, 'Review of *Love à la Mode*', 225.

acutely aware of the instability of the underlying text, and the role that variance in manuscripts, printers, and sources always has to play in making a 'perfect' rendition impossible. The terms of this debate—establishing a continuum between fidelity to history on the one side and critical innovation on the other—have already been engaged in relation to both theatre spaces and dramatic repertoire by David Taylor. In his discussion of the restoration at Bury St Edmunds, he first notes the numerous differences between what the restored Globe has done for Shakespeare and what the Theatre Royal can do for the eighteenth-century repertoire, showing that the material conditions are not analogous.[17] He also parts company with those best known for 'restored' stagings (citing in particular Robert K. Sarlós's project on 'reconstructing' James Shirley's *The Triumph of Peace* in 1974), abjuring 'museum theatre' in the following terms:

> The programme at Bury exists not within a matrix of embodied scholarship but a regional theatre context in which archaeological dramaturgy is neither desirable nor possible. Indeed, the 'Restoring the Repertoire' programme seeks to 'retrieve' the Georgian repertory precisely by undertaking to embrace, rather than merely accommodate, the contemporaneity of its spectators. Restoration here is deployed in its Johnsonian sense: it suggests *regeneration* or *rehabilitation* (of an entire marginalized corpus), not *reconstruction* (of a discrete theatrical occasion).[18]

This impulse coincides exactly with Felicity's work with Macklin, and it seems to overlap productively with the Germanic tradition cited above, especially the way that the German theatre since the Enlightenment has treated canonical works such as Attic tragedy.

It is through parallel and ongoing research on Attic tragedy, particularly due to the work of Burç İdem Dinçel, that the word 'translation' has come to replace 'adaptation' in Trinity's current thinking about the interface between old text and new audiences. At first glance, it may seem that 'translation' is the narrower term, but there is ample theoretical room for an expanded notion of performance within its traditions. Following Taylor's line of flight, the 1755 *Dictionary of the English Language* by Samuel Johnson offers a foothold to support that the notion of difference and change through translation was

---

17 Taylor, 'Discoveries and Recoveries in the Laboratory of Georgian Theatre', 232.
18 Taylor, 'Discoveries and Recoveries in the Laboratory of Georgian Theatre', 233. Emphasis in the original. For more this project, in Sarlós's own terms, see Robert K. Sarlós, 'Performance Reconstruction: The Vital Link between Past and Future', in Thomas Postlewait and Bruce A. McConachie (eds), *Interpreting the Theatrical Past: Essays in the Historiography of Performance* (Iowa City: University of Iowa Press, 1989), 198–229.

fundamentally ingrained in the eighteenth-century understanding of the verb and its derivatives:

> TO TRANSLATE. 1. To transport; to remove. 2. It is particularly used of the removal of a bishop from one see to another. 3. To transfer from one to another; to convey. 4. To change. 5. To interpret in another language; to change into another language retaining the sense.
> TRANSLATION. 1. Removal, act of removing. 2. The removal of a bishop to another see. 3. The act of turning into another language; interpretation. 4. Something made by translation; version.
> TRANSLATOR. One that turns any thing into another language.[19]

As this Enlightenment-era understanding evolved through its encounter with aesthetic modernism in the twentieth century, the valorization of difference over repetition in thinking through the act of translation has become even more central. Especially salient in this regard is the contribution of the Russian formalists, particularly the concept of 'intersemiotic' translation developed by the theorist Roman Jakobson. Jakobson distinguishes three types of translation:

> 1) Intralingual translation or *rewording* is an interpretation of verbal signs by means of other signs in the same language. 2) Interlingual translation or *translation proper* is an interpretation of verbal signs by means of some other language. 3) Intersemiotic translation or *transmutation* is an interpretation of verbal signs by means of signs of nonverbal sign systems.[20]

The possibility of interpreting verbal signs by means of nonverbal sign systems, and vice versa, was a vital link that informed the development of *Enemy of the Stars* after Wyndham Lewis (2015), one of the 'origin projects' that fed the work of the ensemble that became Felicity. Jakobson applied his own third category to the realm of poetry, controversially claiming that 'poetry by definition is untranslatable',[21] writing that 'Only creative transposition is possible: either intralingual transposition—from one poetic shape into another, or interlingual transposition—from one language into another, or finally intersemiotic transposition—from one system of signs into

---

19 Samuel Johnson, *A Dictionary of the English Language*, 2 vols (London, 1755), II.2086. Johnson's examples have been elided between the numbered definitions. A discussion of this passage's relevance to current translation theory can be found in Daniel Weissbort and Astradur Eysteinsson (eds), *Translation: Theory and Practice* (New York: Oxford University Press, 2006), 175.
20 Roman Jakobson, 'On Linguistic Aspects of Translation', in Reuben Brower (ed.), *On Translation* (Cambridge, MA: Harvard University Press, 1959), 233.
21 Jakobson, 'On Linguistic Aspects of Translation', 339.

another (from verbal art into music, dance, cinema, or painting)'.[22] Jakobson's insights underpin what could be considered the 'first axiom of performability' that evolved out of the collective process around *Enemy of the Stars*: either everything is performable, or nothing is. If one defines performability as verisimilitude or alignment with an original, then no performance can exist that faithfully translates any text. Once we open the possibility of transmutation across forms and integrate it into our idea of fundamental action, then not only is everything—no matter how arcane, fragmentary, or occluded—performable, but also this moves the debate towards the more interesting territory of what values are being generated, upheld, set aside, or betrayed in our work as translators. This is also a Beckettian position proper to the terminology of the laboratory (a word also invoked in the title of Taylor's piece about Georgian theatre): failure is a precondition, and it does not prevent progress—quite the contrary.

Rethinking 'laboratory': praxis and pedagogy

Though many contemporary universities are interested in research-led teaching, the collaborations that buttress projects like *Love à la Mode* could be thought of as teaching-led research; such projects grow directly from relationships and practices first introduced and developed within the classroom. The concepts of 'ensemble' (an ethos of horizontal collaboration) and 'praxis' (the interweaving of practice and theory to create action) are core educational values in the teaching of theatre, and both have deep roots in history and theory, well beyond the narrow (and comparably young) fields of drama and performance studies. The creation of an ensemble in the theatre is a targeted use of the same physiological affordances and evolutionary forces that have shaped small social units throughout history, from the family to the military to trade guilds and unions. What is distinct in the theatre is the ephemerality of outcome from such collective effort, which does nothing to diminish the intensity of the commitment. Praxis, which has classical roots in the writings of Aristotle (but again was revised theoretically in Germany by both Hegel and Marx), is more of a disciplinary and academic term in theatre studies for the fusion of theory and practice. What has been discussed in this chapter as 'practice-as-research' could as easily be referred to as an 'ensemble research praxis'—but is this not also a definition of teaching? In these projects we form collectives; we research using all means at our disposal, including embodied practices; we move fluidly between libraries

---

22 Jakobson, 'On Linguistic Aspects of Translation', 339.

and studios as we prepare the work, and then fluidly between conferences, theatres, and publications as we disseminate it. The scripts arising from such projects can then return to the classroom for use by a different ensemble, among whom a 'contemporary' version of *Love à la Mode* can find greater traction with actors-in-training than an earlier edition without contemporary annotations or suggestive interventions.

During a period coinciding with the 2017 version of *Love à la Mode*, many of the same collaborators were in the late stages of a multi-year project called *The David Fragments* after Bertolt Brecht. This project again originated from an interdisciplinary relation to a fragmentary text: the Trinity Centre for Biblical Studies reached out with a request to co-produce Brecht's previously untranslated, unperformed, and unfinished fragments of a planned play about the biblical King David, written on and off between 1919 and 1921, well before Brecht became a famous German playwright or a major twentieth-century theatre theorist.[23] It is the Brecht project where perhaps there is the most fruitful comparative ground, since in addition to the ensemble's concurrent work on Macklin being, to some extent, composed in a post-Brecht theatrical universe, there may also be a direct relation (worthy of a more extended exploration than can be offered here) between Brecht's theatrical aesthetics and the theatre of the eighteenth century. Setting aside *The Threepenny Opera*, Brecht's most obvious debt to eighteenth-century English theatre in terms of content, his theatrical practice has much in common with earlier models too. To name only the most prominent connections, there is the priority given to social commentary in both production and reception of text; the centrality and visibility of the audience; and the tendency towards representational and gestural acting, over a narrow emotion-driven naturalism. In the process of restaging a work like Macklin's, and indeed in this particular adaptation of the work, Brecht looms large because he supplants the Stanislavskian 'what if' (the capacity of the actor to imagine and play within the bounds of an alternative but wholly coherent reality) with the 'not ... but' (the capacity of the audience to repeatedly observe the ways in which the performance is, entertainingly, wrong).[24] Brecht's directorial strategy of making the familiar slightly unfamiliar (and vice versa) plays into the performance of any text

---

23 For a comprehensive account of this project's theatrical process and outcomes, see chap. 5 in David J. Shepherd and Nicholas E. Johnson, *Bertolt Brecht and the David Fragments (1919–1921): An Interdisciplinary Study* (London: Bloomsbury, 2020).

24 For more on Stanislavski's 'what if', sometimes called the 'magic if', see Jean Benedetti, *Stanislavski: An Introduction* (New York: Routledge, 2005), 47–50. For more on Brecht's 'not ... but', sometimes written 'not—but', see David Barnett, *Brecht in Practice: Theatre, Theory and Performance* (London: Bloomsbury/Methuen, 2015), 61–64.

that does not necessarily 'belong' in today's repertoire, and licenses a blend of vaudevillian lightness—songs and jokes—with sincere and sometimes weighty truths.[25]

Writing collaboratively in our reflection on the 2014–15 *Enemy of the Stars* project, Colm Summers and I argued:

> Practice-as-research can be usefully understood as a Janus-faced activity, where one face is looking within to generate knowledge for the researchers themselves, and where one face is turning out towards the audience, the public, or other stakeholders. Within the laboratory, studio, or classroom, the work undertaken is inherently of value in the creation of the researcher's own knowledge. Studio work is thus akin to the private research stage of writing, at which one is learning and growing in thought through one's embodied activities, but is not yet burdened with their expression.[26]

A new element of the Macklin project, in comparison to the previous work done with Lewis and Brecht, was that a public-facing and commercial aspect was present from the beginning. There was no 'safe' conference setting envisioned for scratch-pad draft work or a specialist audience; tickets would be sold for the first outing. Although the university context provided crucial support both intellectually and financially, and while the festival setting in 2017 was technically a 'work-in-progress' showing, the pressure to succeed in public remained nonetheless, much more strongly than usual compared with past practice-as-research projects. Given the resonant context of Smock Alley Theatre as the site of the performance, the sense of indebtedness to Charles Macklin (whose portrait hangs in the lobby of that theatre today) also powerfully remained. While in most circumstances we would seek to avoid such pressure when undertaking laboratory theatre work in the name of research, in the case of eighteenth-century drama, it is in many respects essential: the centrality of the audience in this form of theatre, the charge that results from the presence of liveness and risk in their presence, and the affordances of engagement across what came (only in the twentieth century, of course) to be called the 'fourth wall' is an irreducible and necessary feature. Colin Blumenau, the first artistic director of the restored Theatre Royal and a director with experience of eighteenth-century work in the rehearsal room,

---

25 This formulation of 'one of the critical tasks that Bertolt Brecht had confronted in his search for a new dialectics of theatre' appears in the intercultural theory of Rustom Bharucha: 'to seek the familiar in the unfamiliar, the unfamiliar in the familiar'. See Rustom Bharucha, *The Politics of Cultural Practice: Thinking Through Theatre in an Age of Globalization* (Middletown, CT: Wesleyan University Press, 2000), 19.

26 Nicholas E. Johnson and Colm Summers, '*Enemy of the Stars* in Performance', in Philip Coleman, Kathryn Milligan, and Nathan O'Donnell (eds), *BLAST at 100: A Modernist Magazine Reconsidered* (Leiden: Brill, 2017), 162.

states this in resonant terms, saying, 'the Georgian theatre is an audience's theatre', and noting that the architecture of the theatre at Bury thus 'encourages intimacy, complicity, inclusivity'.[27] This is also a technological feature, arising from lack of dimmable lighting during the period, which resulted in the constant visibility of the audience to the actors. To encourage contemporary actors trained to ignore their presence to be 'adventurous, to embrace the audience', Blumenau describes rehearsing with a mute character on stage with the actors as a witness. A similar dynamic was visible in the rehearsal process for *Love à la Mode*; a slight feeling of deadness entered the rehearsals in the final week of both runs (even more so than usual), which only passed when strangers came into the room to hear the story for the first time. For us, to research *Love à la Mode* outside of a live theatre setting would be, essentially, to study the workings of an intricate machine while it is switched off: not necessarily useless, but hardly indicative.

Linking the Georgian theatre with the Brechtian dimension that comprises a basis for this praxis and even for the roots of drama in antiquity's *mimesis*, *poiesis*, and *kinesis*, there continues to be a politics implied by visibility of the audience today. Blumenau writes:

> Georgian drama is about engaging your audience, moralizing, educating, amusing, and diverting them through involvement so that they understand the dilemmas that the characters face emotionally, socially, and politically. An audience's collective spirit is composed of many different opinions—opinions about everything. Theatre works when it stimulates those opinions.[28]

In the same way that the use of ensemble pedagogy or collective practice-as-research reframes the ethical relation of director/actor or teacher/student, the shift implied in viewing the audience as co-conspirators, collaborators, or active participants engaged with the performers is a shift towards a more democratic theatre.[29] If the audience is to be a 'witness', this should be witnessing in its strongest and least passive sense—the action of a voter, a jury, a journalist, a citizen.[30] In *Love à la Mode*, Macklin seems to call on the

---

27 Colin Blumenau, 'Restoring a Georgian Playhouse: An Interview with Colin Blumenau', in Julia Swindells and David Francis Taylor (eds), *The Oxford Handbook of the Georgian Theatre, 1737–1832* (Oxford: Oxford University Press, 2014), 337.
28 Blumenau, 'Restoring a Georgian Playhouse', 339.
29 Blumenau writes: 'Thus the actors have to work *with* the audience if they want what they are saying and doing to be an experience which spectators are expected to entertain. The space is shared, the endeavour is mutual. It can be a truly democratic space' (338).
30 These terms intentionally echo Jacques Rancière's framing of an active audience in *The Emancipated Spectator*, trans. Gregory Elliott (London: Verso, 2009), where he

spectators to sit in judgement over the suitors' worthiness, and to discover that more perhaps hangs in the balance. If Macklin's laughter, arising from a critique of human desire, venality, bias, and nationalism, can resonate in 2018 above the same foundations where it rang out more than 250 years before, then perhaps there is hope that his enduring insights about truth, lies, and deception may still be heard.

Acknowledgements and Contributor Statement

The production on which this research is based was supported by grants from the European Commission's Marie Curie programme, as well as three sources at Trinity College Dublin: the Provost's Fund for the Visual and Performing Arts; the Faculty of Arts, Humanities, and Social Sciences; and the School of English. The research could not have progressed without the collaboration of the Trinity Long Room Hub, Smock Alley Theatre, and the conference committees for 'The Irish and the London Stage: Identity, Culture, and Politics (1680–1830)' at Trinity College Dublin (February 2017) and 'Charles Macklin & the Making of Eighteenth-Century Theatre' at Notre Dame London Global Gateway (June 2018). The author is especially indebted to collaboration with, and research by, Colm Summers (director) and David O'Shaughnessy (dramaturg).

In addition to the artists and sources identified in the bibliography and notes, the practice and research for this paper arose from a collective process with the theatre company Felicity, and the author wishes to acknowledge the full ensemble's contributions. Artists involved in *Love à la Mode* (2017) were: Jen Aust, Leonard Buckley, Honi Cooke, Morgan Cooke, Fionn Foley, Eugenia Genuchi, Colm Gleeson, Dara Hoban, Norma Howard, Charlie M'Laughlin, Seamus Ryan, Caitlin Scott, Michael Stone, and Annachiara Vispi. Collaborators who engaged in the 2018 full production and/or participated in its ancillary research process, correspondence, and interviews include, in addition to those named above, Fionnuala Gygax and Stephen O'Leary.

---

writes: 'Emancipation begins when we challenge the opposition between viewing and acting; when we understand that the self-evident facts that structure the relations between saying, seeing and doing themselves belong to the structure of domination and subjection' (13).

13

Love à la Mode in Performance
A Dialogue

Colm Summers and Nicholas Johnson

Nicholas Johnson (NJ): You lead a contemporary theatre company ('Felicity') that produced Charles Macklin's *Love à la Mode* early in its life.[1] A key question in our conversation will be how this play fits in with the trajectory and aims of your company, both conceptually and practically. How did the collective begin?

Colm Summers (CS): Felicity, a group of Dublin-based performance makers, held its first general meeting in April 2017. That inaugural meeting consolidated a collaborative bond of approximately five years for its ten core members, who hailed from Ireland, the United States, Italy, Moldova, and the United Kingdom, many of whom had worked together either as undergraduates in the Trinity College School of Drama or in the Dublin theatre scene itself.

NJ: One would be forgiven for suggesting that *Love à la Mode* looks like anything but the project a group of millennial theatre-makers might undertake. So why accept the offer to stage Macklin in the first place?

CS: My commitment to direct *Love à la Mode After Macklin*, the 2017 work-in-progress for what would become *Love à la Mode* (2018), pre-dates the official formation of Felicity. However, it marked a rehearsal process pivotal to the consolidation of the collective, and to what we now think

---
1 See Plates 1–6.

of as our catalogue and working method. Speaking as a freelance director, the draw for me in 2017 was a unique opportunity to work on a Georgian farce with relative freedom of intervention. Disregarding for a second the obvious challenges of performing in the Georgian vernacular, and indeed the notoriously treacherous form of farce itself, *Love à la Mode* is a unique challenge for the contemporary director, particularly in the arena of the actor–audience relationship, comic tempo, dance and fight choreography, intimacy direction, and anachronism, not to mention thematic and contextual issues such as nationalism and anti-Semitism.

Felicity emerged from a practice-as-research (PaR) context in theatre laboratories at Trinity College. As such, the challenges inherent to staging Macklin's play did not present themselves as 'problems' so much as 'solution opportunities'. Conceptually, the relative difficulty of *Love à la Mode*—its challenges to contemporary performance design—aligned with the legacy of our work together. Our works as an ensemble, which pre-dated the consolidation of the company, were even more clearly 'unstageable' than *Love à la Mode*—the Vorticist closet play *Enemy of the Stars* after Wyndham Lewis (Dublin 2014 and Fez 2015), for example, or our work on Bertolt Brecht's fragments for a retelling of the biblical David (Dublin, 2016–2017).[2] Compared to the extensive research and development processes we associated with the Lewis and Brecht projects, retelling Macklin's bawdy tale of suitors hoist by their own petards felt relatively straightforward. If anything, the fact that *Love à la Mode* was not contingent on a need to politically and spiritually forgive ourselves or the author (too much) was a welcome tonic to addressing the overt proto-fascism of Lewis or the personal misogyny of Brecht.

NJ: I know that feeling! When I got back from Lewis and Brecht into doing dramaturgy for living writers (without abysmal politics), or to directing the fully formed work of a playwright like Beckett, I remember that feeling of exhalation into (relative) stability. Beyond not having to compromise as much, did you actually find things that spoke to the contemporary moment within the Macklin text?

CS: Indeed. The arguable proto-feminism of Macklin's text, as well as its thematic commentary on European nationalism, felt essential. Like planets,

---

2 For full analysis of these past projects, see Nicholas Johnson and Colm Summers, '*Enemy of the Stars* in Performance', in Philip Coleman, Kathryn Milligan, and Nathan O'Donnell (eds), *BLAST at 100: A Modernist Magazine Reconsidered* (Leiden: Brill, 2017), 147–67, and Nicholas E. Johnson and David Shepherd, '*The David Fragments* in Performance', in *Brecht Yearbook/Brecht Jahrbuch* 44 (2019), 61–80.

plays are in orbit, and regardless of the theatrical zeitgeist, they come into focus when we look at them through the telescope of the present moment. In 2017–18, marital competition between intensely stereotyped subjects of the British Empire in *Love à la Mode* was resonant with the age of Brexit and #MeToo/#TimesUp, mainly in the sense that such extreme times imply extreme necessity of laughter.

It would be remiss at this point to overlook the fact that we were *commissioned* to make the work—work that we felt would in fact appeal to Dublin audiences—under the auspices of our alma mater, replete with institutional funding without which the production would have been more literally 'unstageable'. As such, *Love à la Mode After Macklin* in 2017 presented an opportunity to extend the aspirations of Felicity's mission statement in a semi-professional context with relatively low risk and high potential reward. Under those circumstances we could afford to take liberties that might otherwise have been impossible—for example: radical dramaturgical adaptation, a new prologue, queering Squire Groom, writing original music, and so on. When *Love à la Mode After Macklin* proved successful at the box office—by which time we had adopted the play as our own—we felt justified in a more high-stakes encounter with Macklin—i.e., a professional production and conference appearance in 2018.

NJ: As you mention bringing theatre work to conferences, I'm reminded that you've worked on both sides of the academic/artistic 'divide' (so to speak), doing PaR in university and university-associated settings, as well as professional gigs where you are working with the same collaborators and similar tools. What is the interplay between context and work in those different settings?

CS: 'So to speak' indeed. We can address the thorny issue of the 'divide' later in this dialogue, but suffice to say from the outset that we share a discomfort with what I would describe as an apparently arbitrary division of onto-epistemic practice in the arts and humanities. The idea that there is a difference being 'doing' and 'thinking' art is as absurd to me as the assertion that there is a hierarchy of research *in* art versus *on* art, a false dichotomy I hope this answer will address.

I have been fortunate, both in my work as a freelance director and as a member of the Felicity team, to have worked in PaR contexts on and off for the last five to six years. In my outline of Felicity's decision to stage *Love à la Mode* I emphasized the legacy of our ensemble experience with PaR projects, namely *Enemy of the Stars* and *The David Fragments*. By my own admission, this is a relatively limited experience, so I will proceed to examine the interplay in question from the position of an emerging artist, and my observations should be understood as such. That position has professional, financial, pedagogical prejudices I cannot ignore. I further acknowledge that my training has resulted in a bias towards PaR, from which this critique proceeds.

Before I engage with the question of how 'work' manifests itself in the context of the university versus the world of the professional theatre, I should address the presupposition among artists, scholars, and the 'hyphenated' cross-disciplinarians among us—artist–scholars and scholar–artists—that PaR work is contingent on *academic* outputs. By academic outputs I mean books, conferences, essays, and, indeed, scholarly dialogues. (Nobody panic!) In my experience of PaR, the subordination of *performance* outcomes, by which I mean theatrical presentations, can degrade the richness and subtlety of the 'research' outcomes implied by a practice-as-*research* process, and the potential of the practical presentation itself. Degradation at either end of that practice-to-research continuum could be avoided by rethinking our expectations of the continuum itself. A failure to do so results at worst in elitist theatre, and at best in justifiable accusations of navel-gazing. An in-depth analysis of audience expectation as a factor of performance analysis is not within the scope of this dialogue, but I will nonetheless attempt to summarize, based on my experience, the expectations of expert audiences to PaR presentations in university contexts versus 'inexpert' audiences in the professional world.

Implicit in PaR is an assumption that the work will be received as such. By that I mean that when we talk about the performance element of a PaR project in an academic context, we expect a 'workshop' performance, a work-in-progress, a provocation, or an experiment. We don't necessarily expect the presentation of a PaR project to occur before a public, paying audience. We expect, I think, that the piece will be intellectually or creatively accessible to the few, rather than the many. But for a person invested in artistry *and* scholarship, these expectations have serious implications. In the best-case scenario, before an expert audience, the piece will not just make sense, but will exceed that audience's expectations of what theatre can achieve, and how theory can be received. In the worst case, the expert audience is underwhelmed by the presentation's failure to exceed the imagination of the informed. Conversely, there is a sense that 'all will be forgiven'.

NJ: People who don't like jazz might say: 'play the tune, make a mistake, and call it jazz'. In this case, a shorthand for your concern might be: 'do the play, make bad theatre, and call it research'?

CS: The risk is that the unperformability of the piece is taken for granted, and failure is expected.

NJ: 'Unperformability' in what sense, from whose perspective? As we have rejected that term elsewhere as theatre-makers, declaring it axiomatic that 'everything is performable', we should be specific. Are you referring to 1) the play's internal demands not being formally or contextually achievable in the modern theatre, 2) venues' or producers' reluctance to engage with eighteenth-century drama, or 3) something more general about audience expectations and comprehension?

CS: I mean merely that audience expectation of failure is not conducive to success. Nor indeed is the weight of scholarship, which can inhibit the ability of academic audiences to consider the production on its own terms, inasmuch as any art is considered with any objectivity. Practically speaking, how could any performance outcome of a PaR project compete with the expectations of specialists for whom the research being practised—by non-specialist artists—represents not just a passion or expertise, but often a livelihood?

As a corollary to the above, when PaR-led projects appear in presentation before 'inexpert' audiences, by which I mean paying audiences in public theatre venues, the inverse is true. The horizon of expectations, in my experience, is limited to their assumptions of academia and of the artists in question. Audiences may imagine that the subject matter will be obscure, the form frustrating, the treatment technically lacking, or that what they are seeing is 'student theatre'. Due to the high proportion of theatre-makers among theatre audiences—much higher, for example, then the proportion of television-makers among television audiences—theatre audiences are generally more informed about theatre-making than other audiences, and the art form is necessarily local. As a result—but also as a result of the theatre's already marginalized position within the entertainment sector—PaR projects presented in public theatres are subject to additional scrutiny. Questions abound: what about *Love à la Mode* makes it essential to a theatre-going audience in contemporary Dublin? What is the currency of Charles Macklin's writing in 2018? Why is *this* play resourced by the university, when *that* play is not? These questions are justified. As hyphenated people on the PaR continuum, we should be asking ourselves these questions vigilantly. Paradoxically, it is scholarly and artistic expectations (and specifically the subversion of those expectations) which make PaR a worthy intellectual and artistic pursuit.

NJ: I'm interested in your language here of a 'continuum' associated with PaR and would love to hear more about how you conceive of this architecturally. Obviously, the work always does have different conditions and stakes, depending on the context and audience. Is that continuum a straight line in your view, i.e., from *practice* to *research* at two opposite poles, or is there a better way to conceive of that model spatially? I ask this because you are also nuanced in your rejection of the false binary between thinking and doing.[3]

CS: You're correct. Although I'm wary of contributing any arbitrary nomenclature to the field, I have come to think of the relationship between practice and research as a continuum, a sequence of relatable points between poles. One pole is *practice-as-research* (academics availing of artistic practices to produce new knowledge), while the other pole is *research-as-practice* (RaP: artists availing of academic research to innovate their work, advance their careers, etc.). People generally feel more at home in one space or the other, but both research and practice are going on at every point on this line.

I have hinted at how our expectations of a PaR outcome at either pole might generate stakes. By stakes I mean the share or interest of the individuals involved in any given PaR project. For example, a conference on Georgian theatre may be a good opportunity for Felicity member Annachiara Vispi to demonstrate her talents as a costume designer, but the conference is ultimately not what's at stake for Annachiara as an emerging artist. For Annachiara, even her fee is unlikely to generate the interest necessary to secure her collaboration and considerable skill. What is at stake is two things: one, the opportunity for peers to see her work, and hopefully to employ her in future; and two, her continued membership of a community of practice.

NJ: I agree that those are both important materially. I would add, however, the idea of the work itself as worthy of attention artistically, even spiritually. I am reminded of one of the early resources in our practice, the Marge Piercy poem 'To Be of Use', which ends with the line: 'The pitcher cries for water to carry/and a person for work that is real'.[4] In both academic and artistic spaces, I find myself more and more asking this question: is what I am about to spend time on 'real work'?

---

3 The rejection of what Dwight Conquergood calls an 'apartheid of knowledges' is foundational in performance studies; he critiques the 'false dichotomy that represses the critical-intellectual component of any artistic work, and the imaginative-creative dimension of scholarship that makes a difference'. Dwight Conquergood, 'Performance Studies: Interventions and Radical Research', *Drama Review* 46.2 (2002), 153.

4 Marge Piercy, *To Be of Use* (Garden City, NY: Doubleday, 1973), 49.

CS: Perhaps that is an idealism, or more properly a luxury, that comes more easily to permanent academics than to precarious artists. Alongside the money that is (hopefully) on the line in a PaR project, there is time, that special currency of academia and art. For those of us with the privilege to risk money and time on PaR/RaP, there is one more, very real risk: reputation. Let's not forget that for primary stakeholders in PaR/RaP, the outcomes along this continuum are not only representative of passion projects (with substantial financial and temporal costs) but often career milestones involving a vast network of professional connections, hard earned over years of hard work. As in all vocational work, in PaR/RaP, the personal is professional and vice versa.

You asked if there was a better 'architecture' or metaphor that might elucidate the idea of a continuum without the linearity. It is possible that a word like 'spectrum' provides a more nuanced way to think of this flow or exchange of work and ideas, since a spectrum implies that the nature of work on any given point of the PaR/RaP flow is classifiable and happening with greater dimension, not unlike how we might classify the colour band of white light as it emerges in its component parts as a rainbow. As for where *Love à la Mode* might fall along such a spectrum, it depends on how one characterizes either extreme, and which stage in the play's journey we're talking about.

NJ: I like 'spectrum', but an anxiety I have remains the latent binarism. We don't want to split the world into camps where we deny academics their artistry, nor artists their research. Where would you put the stages of this specific project on such a spectrum?

CS: Agreed: the characterization of either pole as purely one thing or the other is problematic in itself, and I would argue is antithetical to the whole project of PaR. For the purposes of plotting *Love à la Mode*, I will indulge the possibility that the research-as-practice pole (or if you like, the business end) of this continuum involves a 'professional' presentation in a receiving house open to the paying public, and that the PaR pole would, conversely, involve a private presentation for an 'expert' audience in an academic, or 'theatre laboratory' setting. In that model, I anticipate that *Love à la Mode After Macklin* (2017), a semi-professional work-in-progress, would fall somewhere in the middle of the spectrum: between a public, paying audience and a private, subsidised academic audience. *Love à la Mode* (2018) in its tour-ready dinner theatre production in the 200-seat main space of Smock Alley more closely resembles research manifested as practice.

NJ: That seems accurate. But both of these events still trouble our distinction somewhat. Both involve artists and academics; both proceed from research;

both involve a community of practice partly founded in academic structures and institutions, as well as cooperation from public-facing cultural institutions. The partnership would seem to have greatly enhanced both events, even if the slight taint of the 'less academic' is on the research, and if the slight whiff of the 'more academic' is on the practice, correct?

CS: I echo all your reservations about an emphasis on a binary between art and scholarship. Economists refer to those costs and/or benefits which a party does not choose as the 'externalities' of an economic project. Externalities can be positive or negative. Like trade, PaR (or artist–scholar collaboration) is subject to externalities. It is a trade, an exchange. Simply put, we artist-people trade our skills for your scholar-people resources—often cash and/or space—and, ultimately, we get to make work, you get to see it; we all get to 'use' it. Based on the inelegance of this trade relationship alone, we would be forgiven for imagining a perilous no-man's land between 'epistemic encampments'[5] at either end of the spectrum. Importantly, it is this no-man's-land of praxis that is most fruitful to both parties. It refers back to the idea of performance studies embracing the 'liminal-norm', consciously subverting attempts to neatly patrol its borders.[6]

But if their liminality helps events like ours to adapt and survive, ephemerality still threatens theatre as a whole, artists and scholars alike. The piece is there, then it is gone. The money is gone, the author is dead. All the interpersonal action, intellectual events, and artistic headbutting of the development process are among the most ephemeral externalities of theatre-making and PaR as such. These by-products of the labour of performance do not become 'objects' of study that can be referenced easily after the fact. In my experience, though, ephemeral processes are not synonymous with ephemeral externalities. Felicity, for example, was founded within a period of work bracketed by Macklin: between the February 2017 work-in-progress production and the fully fledged commercial production of June 2018. In that sense, the participation of the founding members in the *Love à la Mode* PaR project was a contributing factor in the founding of the company. Five founding members had taken part in at least two of the aforementioned laboratory projects each (that is, *Enemy of the Stars* and *The David Fragments*). So a positive externality of PaR is the formation of theatre companies from

---

5 Jonathan Heron and Nicholas Johnson, 'Critical Pedagogies and the Theatre Laboratory', *Research in Drama Education: The Journal of Applied Theatre and Performance* 22.2 (2017), 282.

6 See Jon McKenzie, *Perform or Else: From Discipline to Performance* (London: Routledge, 2001), 49–53, in which 'the liminal-norm' is introduced as one of the key meta-models of the discipline.

the communities of practice that grow up around them. 'Graduation' from the laboratory to semi-professional and then professional theatre environments is a testament to the pedagogical and experiential potential of PaR. There are more obvious positive externalities: the artist who becomes an artist–scholar by publishing their reflections with a colleague; the scholar who becomes a scholar–artist, undertaking the role of dramaturg; there are the secondary collections, articles, and reviews emerging from the research data working to make the revelations less ephemeral; and there is skill-acquisition and professional development of the artists and academics involved.

There are, unfortunately, less obvious, less savoury negative externalities. There is a feeling among some theatre makers that PaR is something like the cool older brother of 'museum theatre': something obtuse for intellectuals in ivory towers. The result for would-be professional artists involved in PaR can be a kind of reputation risk. An obscure work by an obscure writer presented in an academic institution is not something actors generally want to invite agents or casting directors to. Sadly, a negative externality of PaR for artists can be the pity, incredulity, or (at worst) the condescension of their peers.

For Felicity, composed of artists committed to work across the spectrum and sympathetic to the necessity of bridging the so-called 'divide', there is a need to reform expectations of the PaR/RaP process. If the differentiation between 'thinking art' and 'doing art' is a fallacy, then the truth is that any two-dimensional spectrum is a poor spatial metaphor to model PaR/RaP. The exchange characteristic of a successful PaR–RaP collaboration is more reminiscent of a sphere: one work begets another work, and one is hard pressed to say where the arts begins and scholarship ends, each work triangulated from at least three dimensions.

NJ: A heavy influence in our discourse and training at Trinity College Dublin is the 'theatre laboratory', a tradition that extends far back in the European twentieth century (Jerzy Grotowski, Peter Brook, Joan Littlewood, and many more used the term). A key issue in this approach is the focus on the process rather than the product, on observing and learning from the non-teleological progression (even perhaps the moments of 'play' more than 'rehearsal') of a theatre-idea coming into being. In what specific ways would Felicity rehearsals echo the training, pedagogy, and philosophy of the laboratory model?

CS: From a practical point of view, our rehearsal processes are marked by at least one full week of discovery before rehearsal begins in earnest. By discovery, I mean a period of play in which the text is subject to a systematic interrogation, experimentation, and autopsy. It is a process in which the ensemble train in, research on, and improvise around the text. It includes but is not limited to the dissemination of research dossiers on the show, long-form physical exercises, devising experiments, ensemble dramaturgical discussion, and in-depth tablework. We involve texts in a generative process with quantifiable research outcomes. We generate material around the text in the form of new writing, short performance pieces, and personal responses. We have created visual arts, film, music, and even a 'digital residency'.[7] For lack of a permanent rehearsal space, we have marshalled the start-up business model to streamline an artistic process which prioritizes play and exploration. In the company description that begins this dialogue, you may notice an emphasis on ensemble-led skill acquisition. In Felicity's research-as-practice processes, the traditional product/process hierarchy is problematized, and certain values and observations for PaR processes emerge as a result.

NJ: And what emerged here? What did you learn from the Macklin rehearsals about Macklin's play, and what did you learn about your own practice as a result of working on this particular text?

CS: Rather than present a performance analysis of findings from the Felicity theatre laboratory working on *Love à la Mode*, I should present my findings here in the form of a 'rehearsal analysis'. I do this for two reasons. First, Georgian theatre history will be better served by the performance analysis of Georgian theatre historians and scholar–artists, whose contributions also appear within this volume. I fear that as director of the show in question, my view of the results will be predictably biased. Second, I feel that by reporting back to base with some observations on our praxis, i.e., reporting what can be learned about *making* research-as-practice, that this dialogue will offer something that no one else could easily discover or articulate.

Many people think of research as something we do to find out, with increasing specificity, what something 'is', or, more philosophically, what we may understand it to be. RaP is most fruitful not when it yields information in which we are already confident, but when it facilitates conclusions that exceed

---

[7] Felicity was invited to produce a 'digital residency' by Live Collision International Festival 2018, which can be seen at www.livecollision.com/special-edition-2016/digital-residency-felicity-present-pseudaria/ (accessed 10 August 2021). Summers defined this as 'a formalization of a relationship which millennial artists already have to their work. We record, catalogue, and show work (and work-in-progress) online every day for display purposes, archival purposes, social media marketing, whatever. The useful thing about the word "residency" is that it suggests an online space where the work can "dwell" [...] a "live" virtual space activating the digital possibilities of the artistic process, rather than reproducing passive digital experience'.

our expectations and frustrate our prejudices. Grotowski said that 'creativity is rather to discover that which you don't know'.[8] For actors, designers, and directors developing a theatre piece, saying what something 'is'—especially early in the process—is risky. Simple definitions, particularly applied to complex theatrical works with nuanced performance histories, can be counter-productive. The kind of 'leads' which traditional research processes consider utile can be stifling to theatre-makers mid-process, because they can actually eliminate opportunities for discovery. Hence the non-teleological progression of the theatre-idea discovered through play in the theatre laboratory: the lab tables as many ideas as possible, for as long as possible. Ultimately, the need to present a performance outcome will necessitate choice.

I think the best crumb trail we can offer to the next people who dive back into Macklin, or indeed any challenging text, would be the values that operate when we make those necessary choices. These values include:

1) **Ensemble.** We remember that the principle of ensemble extends not only to the group of performers, actors, musicians, dancers, writers, and designers in the room, but also to stakeholders beyond the siege in the rehearsal studio. Furthermore, collaborative friction is productive so long as the stakes for all are communicated clearly, in time and transparently.

2) **Exigence.** A mutual commitment to exigence, by which I mean active pursuit of issues, problems, or situations which might cause someone to write or speak, i.e. to research, is a useful principle for PaR–RaP collaborations, as it locates rehearsal processes within an academic tradition of philosophical discourse (rhetoric) and encourages a scholarly approach to practice. An example of exigence in relation to *Love à la Mode* might be Colm Gleeson—the actor who originated the role of Mordecai—writing an etymological deposition of anachronisms like 'girgashites', 'zounds', etc. This really happened, and really helped.

3) **Essence.** Principles of ensemble and exigence will rapidly multiply the research outcomes of a process, with the result that the materials available for presentation will almost certainly exceed the available time in which to present them. Some of these outcomes will be of lesser interest to the majority of the stakeholders than others. It has been useful for me to adapt Paul Woodruff's proposition of 'essence', from his book *The Necessity of Theatre*, when making RaP choices. Woodruff tables the ontological problem, 'what makes a play the play it is supposed to be?' This is important to us, because we must be able to qualify our performance outcomes along the spectrum of PaR–RaP. In his example, Woodruff uses *Hamlet*:

---

8 Jerzy Grotowski, quoted in Thomas Richards, *At Work with Grotowski on Physical Actions* (London: Routledge, 1995), 117.

> What makes *Hamlet* worth watching to the end in every successful performance, and for every audience, is Hamlet himself, and the play is worth watching to the end because only then is the conflict between him and his elders worked out in a climax of revenge. (By a successful performance I merely mean one worth watching.) [...] Most of us, I suspect, would accept an Ophelia-free production as an abridged *Hamlet*, but some would not.[9]

Whether we would accept an Ophelia-free *Hamlet* is contentious, but what Woodruff is getting at is that the essential quality of what we may call a play, and by extension a performance of that play, and by extension a performance outcome for PaR–RaP, is what makes it worth watching. For Woodruff, 'theatre is the art by which human beings make or find human action worth watching, in a measured space and time'.[10] I propose that this question, 'why is this worth watching?' guide our choice-making in the art of PaR–RaP.

I hope these values will be useful to communities of practice engaged in PaR–RaP at either end of the spectrum. As an addendum to the findings above, I must also emphasize that diversity, equality, and inclusion should be the lowest common denominator of contemporary ensemble practice, and that the effect of quality assurance on research and practice outcomes in these processes increases exponentially when the space and time of theatre is occupied by a multiplicity of diverse stakeholders willing to commit to exigence—that is, discourse.

NJ: How did this project meet the ultimate test—the audience—from your perspective?

CS: The audience responses, ensemble experiences, and learning outcomes of work on *Love à la Mode* have been overwhelming. Whatever reservations anyone may have had about the performability of Macklin's play in 2017–18, the range of impassioned critical and academic responses to the work, including conversations like this one, have reinforced my confidence in the enduring power and sophistication of Macklin's playwriting. From a scholarly perspective, the outcomes for the theory and practice of Georgian theatre are self-evident. (You hold them in your hands or read them on your screen.) From a directing perspective, I feel that if I were to revisit the 2018 production, I would elaborate the theatrical frame (and the contingent *coup de théâtre*), as well as extend the central conceptual conceit of the piece.

---

9 Paul Woodruff, *The Necessity of Theatre: The Art of Watching and Being Watched* (New York: Oxford University Press, 2008), 54.
10 Woodruff, *Necessity of Theatre*, 19.

NJ: You feel the work isn't finished?

CS: Unluckily, the 2018 production lost its entire set design during get-in, with the result that the whole production was rethought on a dance-floor during tech. For some critics, my interventions in the text were unclear, and the 'ebullience' of the 'millennial' performers was overwhelming (drunk millennial audiences had no such problems with our ebullience). My intention in adaptation was simply to draw out the meta-theatrical potential of Sir Callaghan (performed, in our version, by an Understudy), not only as an avatar for a contemporary audience in the world of an otherwise arcane and unheard-of author, but also as an allegory about a contemporary Ireland in the time of Brexit and sexual revolution—to let Macklin really speak to my generation, through my generation. The 2018 version did that. I feel that a revival could then extend that project to satisfy (and further bamboozle) audiences with a codified expectation of farce, Georgian drama, and Macklin, as well as to inspire more singalongs from drunk and disorderly audiences whose tastes are less refined. *Love à la Mode* remains not just relevant in terms of research, but urgent and exciting work for a contemporary audience. The work is never finished.

Bibliography

Manuscript sources

British Library
Proofs for Plaintiffs and Counsel's notes in the action of Thomas Harris v. George Colman, part-proprietors of Covent Garden Theatre, arising out of disputes regarding the management of the same in 1767 and 1768. Add. MS 33218.
Letter from Thomas Birch to James Yorke, Bishop of Ely, 15 September 1753. Add. MS 35398.

Folger Shakespeare Library, Washington, D.C.
Autograph papers of Charles Macklin [manuscript], 1754–1787, Y.d.515.
Autograph letters signed from Charles Macklin to various recipients, 1767–1788, Y.c.5380.
Autograph letter from Maria Macklin, 9 December 1772, Y.c.5381 (2).
Charles Macklin, 'Commonplace Book, 1778–1790' [manuscript], M.a.9.
Charles Macklin, 'Covent Garden Riot', T.b. 23.
Diary of Isaac Reed, 1762–1804, M.a.117–131.
Part for the role of Shylock in *The Merchant of Venice*, 1772, Y.d.42.

Houghton Library, Harvard Theatre Collection, Harvard University, Cambridge, Massachusetts
Doran, John, *'Their Majesties Servants': Being an Annal of the English Stage from Thomas Betterton (1635–1779) to Edmund Kean (1787–1833). Illustrated with Drawings, Engravings, Caricatures, Autograph Letters, & Play Bills*, 5 vols, extra-illustrated (1888), III.(opp.)109: TS 934.5F.
Kirkman, James Thomas, *Memoirs of the life of Charles Macklin, Esq. principally compiled from his own papers and memorandums*, 2 vols (London, 1799), extra-illustrated, TS 943.2.

Huntington Library, San Marino, California
John Larpent Collection, MSS LA 1–2503.
Goldsmith, Oliver, *The Novel; or Mistakes of a Night* (LA 349, 1773).
Macklin, Charles, *The Covent Garden Theatre; or, Pasquin Turn'd Drawcansir* (LA 96, 1752).
—— *The New Play Criticiz'd; or, The Plague of Envy (The Suspicious Husband Criticized; or The Plague of Envy)* (LA 64, 1747).
—— *The School for Husbands* (LA 184, 1761).
—— *The Trueborn Irishman* (LA 274, 1767).
—— *A Will and No Will; or, A Bone for the Lawyers* (LA 58, 1746).

Middlesex County Records, Recognizances
L.v. (W) 69/929, 20 September 1753; renewed L.v. (W) 70/1155, 5 September 1754.
M[iddlesex] L[and] R[egister], 1749.

National Archives, Kew
Court of Chancery: Six Clerks Office: Pleadings, 1758–1800
Macklin v. Whitley (1771) C 12/1327/5
Macklin v. Colman (1776) C 12/1342/35
Macklin v. Harris (1776 and 1778) C 12/1367/6
Macklin v. Colman (1782) C 12 1667/30

New York Public Library
William Appleton Collection of Theatrical Correspondence and Ephemera, 1697–1930. Billy Rose Theatre Collection, Box 4, Folder 14.

Victoria and Albert Museum
Charles Macklin Biographical File Notebook on Charles Macklin, THM/368/1/6/5.
Autograph Letter from Macklin to Garrick, 28 April 1763, David Garrick's Correspondence and Papers, 1717–79, Collection, F. 48. F. 22 (items #52–60).

Newspapers

Bell's Weekly Messenger
Daily Advertiser
E. Johnson's British Gazette and Sunday Monitor
Gazetteer and New Daily Advertiser
General Advertiser
Lloyd's Evening Post
London Daily Advertiser
London Daily Post and General Advertiser
London Evening Post
London Gazette

Middlesex Journal
Morning Chronicle
Morning Post
Parker's General Advertiser and Morning Intelligencer
Public Advertiser
Public Ledger
St. James's Chronicle
Theatrical Monitor
True Briton
Whitehall Evening Post or London Intelligencer

Online sources

Bently L., and M. Kretschmer (eds), *Primary Sources on Copyright (1450–1900)* (2008). www.copyrighthistory.org.
Buekers, Martinus, Bas Nugteren, and Katrien Maes, LERU Briefing Paper: 'Creative Arts and Research-Intensive Universities: A Crucial Partnership' (Leuven: LERU, 2012). www.leru.org/files/Creative-Arts-and-Research-Intensive-Universities-A-Crucial-Partnership-Full-paper.pdf.
A Catalogue of the Library of the Late Mr Charles Macklin, Comedian, Deceased (London, 1797). www.librarything.com/profile/CharlesMacklin.
The Censorship of British Theatre, 1737–1843. https://tobeomitted.tcd.ie.
Felicity Digital Residency. www.livecollision.com/special-edition-2016/digital-residency-felicity-present-pseudaria.
The Irish and the London Stage Conference website. https://londonirishtheatreblog.wordpress.com.
John Larpent Plays from the Huntington Library Manuscript Collections, San Marino, California, Also available from Adam Matthew Digital, *Eighteenth Century Drama* database. www.eighteenthcenturydrama.amdigital.co.uk.
'London Electoral History 1700–1850'. http://leh.ncl.ac.uk.
Love à la Mode. After Charles Macklin. Programme Notes. https://cordis.europa.eu/docs/results/333/333592/final1-love-a-la-mode-programme.pdf.
McPherson, Heather. 'Garrickomania: Garrick's Image', on *Folgerpedia* (2015). https://folgerpedia.folger.edu/Garrickomania:_Garrick%27s_Image.
Old Bailey Online. www.oldbaileyonline.org.
Oxford Dictionary of National Biography (online). www.oxforddnb.com.
Sainty, J. C., 'Commissioners of Bankrupts *c.*1720–1831: A Provisional List'. https://web.archive.org/web/20180929194740/https://www.history.ac.uk/publications/office/comms-bankrupts.
'Shatner Pause (punctuation)'. *Urban Dictionary.* www.urbandictionary.com/define.php?term=Shatner%20Pause.
Sheppard, F. H. W. (ed.), *Survey of London*, vol. 36, *Covent Garden* (London, 1970); *British History Online.* www.british-history.ac.uk/survey-london/vol36.

Reviews of *Love à la Mode After Charles Macklin* (2017) and *Love à la Mode* (2018)

Brunström, Conrad, 'Sheridans and Macklin at Smock Alley in Dublin …'. https://conradbrunstrom.wordpress.com/2018/06/14.
Burdett, Sarah, 'Love a la Mode After Macklin'. www.bsecs.org.uk/criticks-reviews/love-la-mode-macklin.
Doherty, Michael, 'The Farce and The Furious', *RTE Guide*, 5 June 2018.
Hayes, Katy, 'A Journey Back in Time with *Love à la Mode*, Smock Alley Theatre', *Irish Independent*, 17 June 2018.
Jones, Richard, '*Love à la Mode* by Charles Macklin (review)', *Theatre Journal* 71.2 (2019), 225–27.
Lynch, Andrew, '*Love à la Mode*: Larger-than-Life Farce Takes Plenty of Stylistic Liberties', *Sunday Business Post*, 10 June 2018.
O'Kelly, Emer, 'Here's a Kite that Plods Rather than Runs', *Sunday Independent*, 10 June 2018.

Pre-1850 sources

Ambler, Charles, *Reports of Cases Argued and Determined in the High Court of Chancery, with some few in other Courts* (London, 1790).
Beattie, James, 'An Essay on Laughter and Ludicrous Composition, written in the Year 1764', in *Essays on Poetry and Music, as they Affect the Mind, on Laughter and Ludicrous Composition; on the Usefulness of Classical Composition* (Edinburgh, 1776).
Bernard, John, *Retrospections of the Stage*, 2 vols (London, 1830).
Bibliotheca Beauclerkiana: A Catalogue of the Large and Valuable Library of the late Honourable Topham Beauclerk (London, 1781).
A Catalogue of the Library of the Late Mr Charles Macklin, Comedian, Deceased (London, 1797).
Charke, Charlotte, *The Art of Management; Or, Tragedy Expell'd* (London, 1735).
[Chudleigh, Elizabeth], *Britannia in tears: An elegiac pastoral on the death of Frederick, prince of Wales. By a Maid of Honour* (London, 1751).
Cibber, Colley, *A Letter from Mr Cibber to Mr Pope* (Dublin, 1742).
[Colman, George and Thornton Bonnell], *The Connoisseur by Mr Town, Critic and Censor-General*, 2 vols (London, 1754–56).
Congreve, Francis Aspry, *Authentic Memoirs of the Late Charles Macklin, Comedian* (London: 1798).
Cooke, George W., *The History of Party; From the Rise of the Whig and Tory Factions, in the Reign of Charles II, to the Passing of the Reform Bill*, 3 vols (London, 1836–1837).
Cooke, William, *Memoirs of Charles Macklin, Comedian* (London, 1804).
—— *Memoirs of Samuel Foote, Esq.: with a collection of his genuine bon-mots, anecdotes, opinions, &c. mostly original: And three of his dramatic pieces, not published in his works*, 3 vols (London, 1805).
The Country Journal or, the Craftsman, by Caleb Danvers (London, 1726–52).

[Fielding, Henry], *Covent-Garden Journal* (London, 1752).
Finn's Leinster Journal (Kilkenny, 1767–1801).
Foot, Jesse, *The life of Arthur Murphy, esq.* (London, 1811).
Genest, John, *Some Account of the English Stage From the Restoration in 1660 to 1830*, 10 vols (Bath, 1832).
Gentleman, Francis, *The Dramatic Censor; or, Critical Companion*, 2 vols (London, 1770).
The Gentleman's Magazine, by Sylvanus Urban, Gent. (London, 1731–1818).
George's Coffee House. A poem (London, 1761).
Hazlitt, William, *Characters of Shakespear's Plays* (London, 1817).
Hibernian Magazine, Or Compendium of Entertaining Knowledge, Containing the Greatest Variety of the most Curious and Useful Subjects in Every Branch of Polite Literature (Dublin, 1771–1812).
Hiffernan, Paul, *The Tuner* (London, 1753–54).
Hill, Aaron, *The Art of Acting* (London, 1746).
Holcroft, Thomas, *Alwyn: or the Gentleman Comedian* (London, 1780).
Hutcheson, Francis, 'Reflections upon Laughter', in James Arbuckle (ed.), *Hibernicus Letters*, 2 vols (Dublin, 1729).
Inchbald, Elizabeth (ed.), *The British Theatre; or, A Collection of Plays*, 25 vols (London, 1808).
The Irish Musical Repository: A Choice Selection of Esteemed Irish Songs Adapted for the Voice, Violin, and German Flute (London, 1808).
Johnson, Samuel, *A Dictionary of the English Language in which the words are deduced from their Originals*, 2 vols (London, 1755–56).
Kenrick, W.B., *The Pasquinade. With Notes Variorum* (London, 1753).
Kimber, Edward, *The juvenile adventures of David Ranger, Esq; from an original manuscript found in the collections of a late noble Lord. In two volumes*, 2nd edn (London, 1757).
Kirkman, James Thomas, *Memoirs of the life of Charles Macklin, Esq. principally compiled from his own papers and memorandums*, 2 vols (London, 1799).
Lennox, Charlotte, *The Female Quixote*, 2 vols (London, 1752).
[Lewis, Richard], *The robin-Hood Society: a satire. With notes variorum. By Peter Pounce, Esq;* (London, 1756).
The Life and Memoirs of Elizabeth Chudleigh, Afterwards Mrs Hervey and Countess of Bristol (London, [1788]).
The London Magazine, Or Gentleman's Monthly Intelligencer (London, 1732–85).
Macklin, Charles, *The Case of Charles Macklin, Comedian* (London, 1743).
—— *Mr Macklin's Reply to Mr Garrick's Answer* (London, 1743).
—— *The genuine arguments of the council, with the opinion of the Court of King's Bench, on cause shewn, why an information should not be exhibited against John Stephen James ... By a citizen of the world* (London, 1774).
—— *Case, Mr. Macklin late of Covent-Garden Theatre, against Mess. Clarke, Aldys, Lee, James, and Miles* (Edinburgh, [1775]).
—— *The True Born Irishman; or, Irish Fine Lady, A Comedy of Two Acts* (Dublin, 1783).
—— *Love à la Mode, a Farce* (London, 1793).

——— *The Man of The World, A Comedy* (London, 1793).
M-ckl-n's Answer to Tully (London, 1755).
Misson de Valbourg, Henri, *Memoirs and Observations in his Travels over England*, trans. Ozell (London, 1719).
The Monthly Mirror; Reflecting Men and Manners (London, 1795–1811).
[Murphy, Arthur], *The Gray's Inn Journal, By Charles Ranger* (London, [1753–54]).
Murphy, Arthur, et al., *Case of the Appellants: Alexander Donaldson, and John Donaldson, Booksellers (1774) to be heard at house of Lords 4th Feb 1774* (London, 1774).
Pasquin, Anthony, pseud. of John Williams, *The Children of Thespis. A Poem. Part the Second* (London, 1767).
The Poetical Review, A Poem (London, n.d.).
Scriblerus, Stephanus, *The Censor. Numb. I. To be continued occasionally* (London, 1755).
Sheridan, Thomas, *An Humble Appeal to the Publick* (Dublin, 1758).
Stevens, George Alexander, 'XXIII. Humorous speech at Macklin's', *Gentleman's Magazine*, 24.12 (1754).
[Stevens, George Alexander], *The Birth-Day of Folly, an Heroic-comical poem, by Peter: with notes variorum, for the illustration of historical passages relating to the hero of the poem, and other remarkable personages* (London, 1755).
Thomson, George (ed.), A *Select Collection of Original Scottish Airs for the Voice with Introductory and Concluding Symphonies & Accompaniments for the Piano Forte, Violin & Violoncello*, 4 vols (Edinburgh, 1793–1802).
[Thornton, Bonnell], *Have at You All; or, the Drury-Lane Journal, By Madam Roxana Termagant* (London, 1752).
The Trial (At Large) of Joseph Stacpoole, Esq, William Gapper, Attorney at Law, and James Lagier; for Wilfully and Maliciously Shooting at John Parker Esq ... Thursday, March 20, 1777 (London, 1777).
Vanbrugh, Sir John and Colley Cibber, *The Provok'd Husband; or a journey to London* (London, 1728).
Victor, Benjamin *The history of the theatres of London and Dublin, from the year 1730 to the present time. To which is added, an annual register of all the plays, &c. performed ... in London, from the year 1712. ... by Mr. Victor, ... In two volumes* (London, 1761).
Wendell, Cornelius, *The Young Clerk's Magazine: or English Law-Repository, Fourth Edition* (London, 1763).
Whatley, Robert, *The Dernier Resort: Or, An Appeal to the King, in the Cause Between the Right Honourable Sir Robert Walpole and Mr Whatley* (London, 1741).
Wilkinson, Tate, *Memoirs of His Own Life*, 4 vols (York, 1790).

Post-1850 sources

Addison, Joseph, and Richard Steele, *The Spectator*, ed. Donald F. Bond, 5 vols (Oxford: Clarendon Press, 1965).
Altick, Richard Daniel, *The Shows of London* (Cambridge, MA: Belknap Press of Harvard University Press, 1978).

Anderson, Emily Hodgson, 'Autobiographical Interpolations in Maria Edgeworth's *Harrington*', *ELH* 76.1 (2009), 1–18.
—— 'Celebrity Shylock', *PMLA* 126.4 (2011), 935–49.
—— *Shakespeare and the Legacy of Loss* (Ann Arbor: University of Michigan Press, 2018).
Appleton, William W., *Charles Macklin: An Actor's Life* (Cambridge, MA: Harvard University Press, 1960).
Aristotle, *Politics*, trans. H. Rackham (Cambridge, MA: Harvard University Press, 1932).
Armstrong, Nancy, *Desire and Domestic Fiction: A Political History of the Novel* (Oxford: Oxford University Press, 1987).
Avery, Emmett L., Charles Beecher Hogan, William van Lennep, Arthur Hawley Scouten, and George Winchester Stone (eds), *The London Stage, 1660–1800: A Calendar of Plays, Entertainments & Afterpieces together with Casts, Box-Receipts and Contemporary Comment, Compiled from the Playbills, Newspapers and Theatrical Diaries of the Period*, 5 parts, 11 vols (Carbondale: Southern Illinois University Press, 1960–1968).
Aycock, Roy, 'Arthur Murphy, the *Gray's-Inn Journal*, and the *Craftsman*: Some Publication Mysteries', *Papers of the Bibliographical Society of America* 67.3 (1973), 255–62.
Bailey, Craig, 'From Innovation to Emulation: London's Benevolent Society of St Patrick, 1783–1800', *Eighteenth-Century Ireland* 27 (2012), 162–84.
—— *Irish London: Middle-Class Migration in the Global Eighteenth Century* (Liverpool: Liverpool University Press, 2013).
Bannerman, G.E., 'The "Nabob of the North": Sir Lawrence Dundas as Government Contractor', *Historical Research* 83 (2010), 102–23.
Barnard, Toby, 'The Irish in London and the "London Irish", ca.1680–1780', *Eighteenth-Century Life* 39.1 (2015), 15–40.
Barnett, David, *Brecht in Practice: Theatre, Theory and Performance* (London: Bloomsbury/Methuen, 2015).
Bataille, Robert, *The Writing Life of Hugh Kelly: Politics, Journalism and Theater in Late Eighteenth-Century London* (Carbondale: Southern Illinois University Press, 2000).
Benedetti, Jean, *Stanislavski: An Introduction* (New York: Routledge, 2005).
Berman, David, 'David Hume on the 1641 Rebellion in Ireland', *Studies: An Irish Quarterly Review* 65.258 (1976), 101–12.
Bertelsen, Lance, '*Have at You All*: Bonnell Thornton's Journalism', *Huntington Library Quarterly* 44.4 (1981), 263–82.
Bharucha, Rustom, *The Politics of Cultural Practice: Thinking Through Theatre in an Age of Globalization* (Middletown, CT: Wesleyan University Press, 2000).
Black, Scott, 'Social and Literary Form in the *Spectator*', *Eighteenth-Century Studies* 33.1 (1999), 21–42.
Blumenau, Colin, 'Restoring a Georgian Playhouse: An Interview with Colin Blumenau', in Julia Swindells and David Francis Taylor (eds), *The Oxford Handbook of the Georgian Theatre, 1737–1832* (Oxford: Oxford University Press, 2014), 333–43.

Bolter, Jay, and Richard Grusin, *Remediation: Understanding New Media* (Cambridge, MA: MIT Press, 2000).
Bolton, Betsy, 'Theorizing Audience and Spectatorial Agency', in Julia Swindells and David Francis Taylor (eds), *The Oxford Handbook of the Georgian Theatre, 1737–1832* (Oxford: Oxford University Press, 2014), 31–52.
Bourke, Algernon, *The History of White's* ([London, Waterlow and Sons for Algernon Bourke, 1892]).
Boyd, Amanda Weldy, *Staging Memory and Materiality in Eighteenth-Century Theatrical Biography* (London: Anthem Press, 2017).
Bricker, Andrew Benjamin, 'Libel and Satire: The Problem with Naming', *ELH* 81.3 (2014), 889–921.
Brown, Beatrice Curtis, *Elizabeth Chudleigh, Duchess of Kingston* (London: Gerald Howe, 1927).
Brown, Michael, *The Irish Enlightenment* (Cambridge, MA: Harvard University Press, 2016).
Brown, Wendy, *Walled States, Waning Sovereignty* (Cambridge, MA: MIT Press, 2010).
Burke, Helen, *Riotous Performances: The Struggle for Hegemony in the Irish Theater, 1712–1785* (Notre Dame, IN: University of Notre Dame Press, 2003).
Burney, Frances, *Evelina, or a Young Lady's Entrance into the World* (1778), ed. Susan Kubica Howard (Peterborough, ON: Broadview Press, 2000).
Burns, Robert, *The Letters of Robert Burns*, ed. J. De Lancey Ferguson and G. Ross Roy, 2nd edn, 2 vols (Oxford: Oxford University Press, 1985).
—— *The Oxford Edition of the Works of Robert Burns*, vol. 4, *Robert Burns's Songs for George Thomson*, ed. Kirsteen McCue (Oxford: Oxford University Press, 2021).
Calhoun, Craig, 'The Public Sphere in the Field of Power', *Social Science History* 34.3 (2010), 301–35.
Chartier, Roger, 'Texts, Symbols and Frenchness', *Journal of Modern History* 57.4 (1985), 682–95.
Cholij, Irena, 'Music in Eighteenth-Century London Shakespeare Productions', unpublished PhD thesis, King's College London (1995).
Cibber, Colley, *An Apology for the Life of Colley Cibber: With an Historical View of the Stage during his Own Time*, ed. B.R.S. Fone (Ann Arbor: University of Michigan Press, 1968).
Clark, Peter, *British Clubs and Societies, 1580–1800: The Origins of an Associational World* (Oxford: Oxford University Press, 2000).
Clarke, Norma, *Brothers of the Quill: Oliver Goldsmith in Grub Street* (Cambridge, MA: Harvard University Press, 2016).
Coke, David, and Alan Borg, *Vauxhall Gardens: A History* (New Haven, CT: Yale University Press, 2011).
Colson, Percy, *White's, 1693–1950* (London, Heinemann, [1951]).
Conolly, L.W., *The Censorship of English Drama, 1737–1824* (San Marino, CA: Huntington Library Press, 1976).
Conquergood, Dwight, 'Of Caravans and Carnivals: Performance Studies in Motion', *Drama Review* 39.4 (1995), 137–41.

—— 'Performance Studies: Interventions and Radical Research', *Drama Review* 46.2 (2002), 145–56.
Cowan, Brian, 'Mr Spectator and the Coffeehouse Public Sphere', *Eighteenth-Century Studies* 37.3 (2004), 245–366.
—— 'Public Spaces, Knowledge, and Sociability', in Frank Trentmann (ed.), *The Oxford Handbook of the History of Consumption* (Oxford: Oxford University Press, 2015).
Cox Jensen, Oskar, 'The Diminution of "Irish" Johnstone', in David O'Shaughnessy (ed.), *Ireland, Enlightenment and the English Stage, 1740–1820* (Cambridge: Cambridge University Press, 2019), 79–97.
Craft-Fairchild, Catherine, 'The "Jewish Question" on Both Sides of the Atlantic: *Harrington* and the Correspondence between Maria Edgeworth and Rachel Mordecai Lazarus', *Eighteenth-Century Life* 38.3 (2014), 30–63.
Critchley, Simon, *On Humour* (London; Routledge, 2002).
Cross, W.L., *The History of Henry Fielding*, 3 vols (New Haven, CT: Yale University Press, 1918).
Cunningham, John, 'The Reception and Re-Use of Thomas Arne's Shakespeare Songs of 1740–1', in Bill Barclay and David Lindley (eds), *Shakespeare, Music and Performance* (Cambridge: Cambridge University Press, 2017), 131–44.
Darnton, Robert, 'Workers Revolt: The Great Cat Massacre of the Rue Saint Séverin', in *The Great Cat Massacre and Other Episodes in French Cultural History* (New York: Basic Books, 1984).
Dean, Ann C., *The Talk of the Town: Figurative Publics in Eighteenth-Century Britain* (Lewisburg, PA: Bucknell University Press, 2007).
Dickie, Simon, 'Tobias Smollett and the Ramble Novel', in Peter Garside and Karen O'Brien (eds), *The Oxford History of the Novel in English*, vol. 2, *English and British Fiction, 1750–1820*, (Oxford: Oxford University Press, 2015), 92–108.
Dobson, Michael, *The Making of the National Poet: Shakespeare, Adaptation and Authorship, 1660–1769* (Oxford: Clarendon Press, 1992).
Donohue Jr., Joseph W. (ed.), *The Theatrical Manager in England and America: Player of a Perilous Game* (Princeton, NJ: Princeton University Press, 1971).
Dundes, Alan (ed.), *Cracking Jokes: Studies of Sick Humor Cycles and Stereotypes* (Berkeley, CA: Ten Speed Press, 1987).
Edgeworth, Maria, *Harrington*, in Marilyn Butler, et al. (eds), *The Novels and Selected Works of Maria Edgeworth* (London: Pickering & Chatto, 1999).
—— *Harrington* (Peterborough, ON: Broadview Press, 2004).
Ellis, Markman, 'The Coffee-Women, *The Spectator* and the Public Sphere in the Early Eighteenth Century', in Elizabeth Eger and Charlotte Grant (eds), *Women and the Public Sphere* (Cambridge: Cambridge University Press, 2001), 27–52.
—— 'Coffee-House Libraries in Mid-Eighteenth-Century London', *The Library: Transactions of the Bibliographical Society* 10.1 (2009), 3–40.
—— 'Poetry and Civic Urbanism in the Coffee-House Library in the Mid-Eighteenth- Century', in Kyle Roberts and Mark Towsey (eds), *Before the Public Library: Reading, Community, and Identity in the Atlantic World, 1650–1850* (Leiden: Brill, 2017), 52–72.

Emery, John Pike, *Arthur Murphy: An Eminent English Dramatist of the Eighteenth Century* (Philadelphia: University of Philadelphia Press, 1946).
Eze, Emmanuel Chukwudi (ed.), *Race and the Enlightenment: A Reader* (Cambridge, MA: Blackwell, 1997).
Farmer, Lindsay, 'Of Treatises and Textbooks: The Literature of Criminal Law in Nineteenth-Century Britain', in Angela Fernandez and Markus D. Dubber (eds), *Law Books in Action: Essays on the Anglo-American Legal Treatise* (Oxford: Hart Publishing, 2012), 145–64.
Fawcett, Julia H., 'The Canon of Print: Laurence Sterne and the Overexpression of Character', *Spectacular Disappearances: Celebrity and Privacy, 1696–1801* (Ann Arbor: University of Michigan Press, 2016), 98–135.
Felsenstein, Frank, *Anti-Semitic Stereotypes: A Paradigm of Otherness in English Popular Culture, 1660–1830* (Baltimore, MD: Johns Hopkins University Press, 1999).
Fielding, Henry, *Joseph Andrews*, ed. Martin C. Battestin, *The Wesleyan Edition of the Works of Henry Fielding* (Oxford: Oxford University Press/Wesleyan University Press, 1966).
—— *The Covent-Garden Journal*, ed. Bertrand A. Goldgar (Middletown, CT: Wesleyan University Press, 1988).
—— *The Wedding-Day*, in Bertrand A. Goldgar and Hugh Amory (eds), *Miscellanies by Henry Fielding, Esq.*, *The Wesleyan Edition of the Works of Henry Fielding*, vol. 2 (Oxford: Oxford University Press/Wesleyan University Press, 1993).
—— *The Journal of a Voyage to Lisbon, Shamela, and Occasional Writings*, ed. Martin C. Battestin (Oxford: Oxford University Press, 2008).
Freeman, Lisa A., *Character's Theater: Genre and Identity on the Eighteenth-Century English Stage* (Philadelphia: University of Pennsylvania Press, 2001).
Frow, John, *Character and Person* (Oxford: Oxford University Press, 2014).
Garrick, David, *Harlequin's Invasion*, in Harry William Pedicord and Fredrick Louis Bergmann (eds), *The Plays of David Garrick*, vol. 1, *Garrick's Own Plays, 1740–1766* (Carbondale: Southern Illinois University Press, 1980), 201–25.
Gatrell, Vic, *The First Bohemians: Life and Art in London's Golden Age* (London: Allen Lane, 2013).
Geertz, Clifford, *The Interpretation of Cultures* (London: Fontana, 2010).
Gerland, Oliver, 'The Haymarket Theatre and Literary Property: Constructing the Common Law Playwright, 1770–1833', *Theatre Notebook* 69.2 (2015), 78–81.
Goldsmith, Oliver, *The Collected Works of Oliver Goldsmith*, ed. Arthur Friedman, 5 vols (Oxford: Clarendon Press, 1966).
Gordon, Thomas, and John Trenchard, *Cato's Letters: Or, Essays on Liberty, Civil and Religious, and Other Important Subjects*, ed. Ronald Hamowy, 4 vols (Indianapolis, IN: Liberty Fund, 1995).
Goring, Paul, '"John Bull, pit, box, and gallery, said No!": Charles Macklin and the Limits of Ethnic Resistance on the Eighteenth-Century London Stage', *Representations* 79.1 (2002), 61–81.

—— (ed.), 'Volume 2: Charles Macklin', in Michael Caines, et al. (eds), *Lives of Shakespearian Actors I: David Garrick, Charles Macklin and Margaret Woffington by their Contemporaries* (London: Pickering, 2008).
—— 'Theatrical Riots and Conspiracies in London and Edinburgh: Charles Macklin, James Fennell and the Rights of Actors and Audiences', *Review of English Studies* 67.278 (2016), 122–45.
—— 'The Sinking of Charles Macklin's Scholarship', *Notes & Queries* 66.4 (2019), 577–81.
—— 'John Opie's Portrait of Charles Macklin and the Shakespeare Gallery', *Source: Notes in the History of Art* 39.3 (2020), 184–93.
Greene, John C., *Theatre in Dublin, 1745–1820: A History*, 2 vols (Bethlehem, PA: Lehigh University Press, 2011).
Gross, John, *Shylock: A Legend and its Legacy* (London: Simon & Schuster, 1992).
Habermas, Jürgen, *The Structural Transformation of the Public Sphere*, trans. Thomas Burger with Frederick Lawrence (Cambridge, MA: MIT Press, 1991).
Harris, Susan Canon, 'Mixed Marriage: Sheridan, Macklin, and the Hybrid Audience', in Michael Cordner and Peter Holland (eds), *Players, Playwrights, Playhouses: Investigating Performance, 1660–1800* (Basingstoke: Palgrave Macmillan, 2007), 189–212.
Heron, Jonathan, and Nicholas Johnson, 'Critical Pedagogies and the Theatre Laboratory', *Research in Drama Education: The Journal of Applied Theatre and Performance* 22.2 (2017), 282–87.
Herzog, Don, *Poisoning the Minds of the Lower Orders* (Princeton, NJ: Princeton University Press, 1998).
Highfill, Philip H., Kalman A. Burnim, and Edward A. Langhans, *A Biographical Dictionary of Actors, Actresses, Musicians, Dancers, Managers & Other Stage Personnel in London, 1660–1800*, 16 vols (Carbondale: Southern Illinois University Press, 1973–1993).
Hoad, Neville, 'Maria Edgeworth's *Harrington*: The Price of Sympathetic Representation', in Shelia A. Spector (ed.), *British Romanticism and the Jews: History, Culture, Literature* (New York: Palgrave Macmillan, 2002), 133–34.
Hobbes, Thomas, *The Elements of Law Natural and Politic* (Oxford: Oxford University Press, 1994).
Holland, Peter, 'Hearing the Dead: The Sound of David Garrick', in Michael Cordner and Peter Holland (eds), *Players, Playwrights, Playhouses: Investigating Performance, 1660–1800* (Basingstoke: Palgrave Macmillan, 2007), 248–70.
Hopkinson, Cecil, and C.B. Oldman, 'Thomson's Collection of National Song, with Special Reference to the Contributions of Haydn and Beethoven', *Edinburgh Bibliographical Society Transactions* 2.1 (1938–1945), 1–64.
Horkheimer, Max, and Theodor W. Adorno, *Dialectic of Enlightenment: Philosophical Fragments*, ed. Gunzelin Schmid Noerr, trans. Edmund Jephcott (Stanford, CA: Stanford University Press, 2002).
Hughes, Leo, *The Drama's Patrons: A Study of the Eighteenth-Century London Audience* (Austin: University of Texas Press, 1971).

Hume, Robert D., 'The Value of Money in Eighteenth-Century England: Incomes, Prices, Buying Power—and Some Problems in Cultural Economics', *Huntington Quarterly* 77.4 (2014), 373–416.

Ihalainen, Ossi, 'The Dialects of England since 1776', in Robert Burchfield (ed.), *Cambridge History of the English Language*, 6 vols (Cambridge: Cambridge University Press, 1994).

Jakobson, Roman, 'On Linguistic Aspects of Translation', in Reuben Brower (ed.), *On Translation* (Cambridge, MA: Harvard University Press, 1959).

Johnson, Nicholas E., and David Shepherd, '*The David Fragments* in Performance', *Brecht Yearbook/Brecht Jahrbuch* 44 (2019), 61–80.

Johnson, Nicholas E., and Colm Summers, '*Enemy of the Stars* in Performance', in Philip Coleman, Kathryn Milligan, and Nathan O'Donnell (eds), *BLAST at 100: A Modernist Magazine Reconsidered* (Leiden: Brill, 2017), 147–67.

Kant, Immanuel, 'An Answer to the Question: What is Enlightenment?' in *Practical Philosophy*, trans. and ed. Mary J. Gregor (Cambridge: Cambridge University Press, 1996).

Kerrigan, John, *Archipelagic English: Literature, History and Politics, 1603–1707* (Oxford: Oxford University Press, 2008).

Kinservik, Matthew J., 'A Sinister *Macbeth*: The Macklin Production of 1773', *Harvard Library Bulletin* 6.1 (1995), 51–76.

—— '*Love à la Mode* and Macklin's Return to the London Stage in 1759', *Theatre Survey* 37.2 (1996), 1–21.

—— 'New Light on the Censorship of Macklin's *The Man of the World*', *Huntington Library Quarterly* 62.1–2 (1999), 43–66.

—— *Disciplining Satire: The Censorship of Satiric Comedy on the Eighteenth-Century Stage* (Lewisburg, PA: Bucknell University Press, 2002).

Klein, Lawrence E., 'Gender, Conversation and the Public Sphere in Early Eighteenth-Century England', in Judith Still and Michael Worton (eds), *Textuality and Sexuality: Reading Theories and Practices* (Manchester: Manchester University Press, 1993), 100–15.

—— 'Coffeehouse Civility, 1660–1714: An Aspect of Post-Courtly Culture in England', *Huntington Library Quarterly* 59.1 (1996), 30–51.

LaCapra, Dominick, 'Darnton, Chartier and the Great Symbol Massacre', *Journal of Modern History* 60.1 (1988), 95–112.

Leerssen, Joep, *Mere Irish and Fíor-Ghael* (Cork: Cork University Press, 1997).

Lejeune, Anthony, *White's: The First Three Hundred Years* (London: A & C Black, 1993).

Leslie, Charles, and Tom Taylor, *The Life and Times of Sir Joshua Reynolds, with Some Notices of His Contemporaries*, 2 vols (London: John Murray, 1865).

Liesenfeld, Vincent J., *The Licensing Act of 1737* (Madison: University of Wisconsin Press, 1984).

Lindley, David, *Shakespeare and Music* (London: Thomson Learning, 2006).

Lobban, Michael, 'Preparing for Fusion: Reforming the Nineteenth-Century Court of Chancery, Part I', *Law and History Review* 22.2 (2004), 389–427.

Loveman, Kate, 'The Introduction of Chocolate into England: Retailers, Researchers, and Consumers, 1640–1730', *Journal of Social History* 47.1 (2013), 27–46.

Lupton, Christina, *Reading and the Making of Time in the Eighteenth Century* (Baltimore, MD: Johns Hopkins University Press, 2018).
Mcbride, Ian, 'The Edge of Enlightenment: Ireland and Scotland in the Eighteenth Century', *Modern Intellectual History* 10.1 (2013), 135–51.
McDonald, Paul, *The Philosophy of Humour* (Penrith: Humanities-Ebooks, 2012).
McDowell, Paula, *The Invention of the Oral: Print Commerce and Fugitive Voices in Eighteenth-Century Britain* (Chicago: University of Chicago Press, 2017).
McGirr, Elaine, *Heroic Mode and Political Crisis, 1660–1745* (Newark: University of Delaware Press, 2009).
McKenzie, Jon, *Perform or Else: From Discipline to Performance* (London: Routledge, 2001).
Macklin, Charles, *The Covent Garden Theatre; or, Pasquin Turn'd Drawcansir* (1752), Augustan Reprint Society, no. 116, ed. Jean B. Kern (Los Angeles: William Andrew Clark Memorial Library, University of California, 1965).
—— *Four Comedies by Charles Macklin* ed. J.O. Bartley (London: Sidgwick & Jackson, 1968).
—— 'Prologue', to *The Wedding-Day*, in Bertrand A. Goldgar and Hugh Amory (ed.), *Miscellanies by Henry Fielding, Esq.*, *The Wesleyan Edition of the Works of Henry Fielding*, vol. 2 (Oxford: Oxford University Press/Wesleyan University Press, 1993).
MacMillan, Dougald, 'The Censorship in the Case of Macklin's *The Man of the World*', *Huntington Library Bulletin* 10 (1936), 79–101.
McPherson, Heather, 'Theatrical Riots and Cultural Politics in Eighteenth-Century London', *The Eighteenth Century: Theory and Interpretation* 43.3 (2002), 236–52.
—— *Art and Celebrity in the Age of Reynolds and Siddons* (University Park: Pennsylvania State University Press, 2017).
Magyar, John J., 'Millar v Taylor as a Precedent for Statutory Interpretation', *Common Law World Review* 47.3 (2018), 217–21.
Mah, Harold, 'Suppressing the Text: The Metaphysics of Ethnographic History in Darnton's Great Cat Massacre', *History Workshop* 31.1 (1991), 1–20.
Matthews, W., 'The Piracies of Macklin's *Love à-la-Mode*', *Review of English Studies* 10.39 (1934), 311–18.
Mee, Jon, *Conversable Worlds: Literature, Contention, and Community, 1762–1830* (Oxford: Oxford University Press, 2011).
Midgley, Graham, *The Life of Orator Henley* (Oxford: Clarendon Press, 1973).
Milhous, Judith, 'Company Management', in Robert D. Hume (ed.), *The London Theatre World, 1660–1800* (Carbondale: Southern Illinois University Press, 1980).
Milhous, Judith, and Robert D. Hume, 'The Drury Lane Actors' Rebellion of 1743', *Theatre Survey* 42.1 (1990), 57–80.
—— *The Publication of Plays in London, 1660–1800: Playwrights, Publishers, and the Market* (London: The British Library, 2015).
Miller, Fred D., *Nature, Justice, and Rights in Aristotle's Politics* (Oxford: Clarendon Press, 1997).
Moore, Judith, *The Appearance of Truth: The Story of Elizabeth Canning and Eighteenth-Century Narrative* (Newark: University of Delaware Press, 1994).

Moritz, Karl Philipp, *Journeys of a German in England in 1782*, trans. Reginald Nettel (London: Jonathan Cape, 1965).
Mugglestone, Lynda, *Talking Proper: The Rise of Accent as a Social Symbol* (Oxford: Oxford University Press, 2003).
Newman, Ian, 'Edmund Burke in the Tavern', *European Romantic Review* 24.2 (2013), 125–48.
—— *The Romantic Tavern: Literature and Conviviality in the Age of Revolution* (Cambridge: Cambridge University Press, 2019).
Newman, Ian, and Gillian Russell, 'Metropolitan Songs and Songsters: Ephemerality in the World City', *Studies in Romanticism* 58.4 (2019), 436–38.
Nussbaum, Felicity, *Rival Queens: Actresses, Performance at the Eighteenth-Century British Theater* (Philadelphia: University of Pennsylvania Press 2010).
—— 'Straddling: London-Irish Actresses in Performance', in David O'Shaughnessy (ed.), *Ireland, Enlightenment and the English Stage, 1740–1820* (Cambridge: Cambridge University Press, 2019), 31–56.
Oldman, C.B., 'Beethoven's Variations on National Themes: Their Composition and First Publication', *Music Review* 12 (1951), 45–51.
Orihel, Michelle, '"Treacherous Memories" of Regicide: The Calves-Head Club in the Age of Anne', *Historian* 73.3 (2011), 435–62.
Oring, Elliott, *Jokes and their Relations* (Lexington: University Press of Kentucky, 1992).
—— *Engaging Humor* (Urbana: University of Illinois Press, 2003).
O'Quinn, Daniel, *Staging Governance: Theatrical Imperialism in London, 1770–1800* (Baltimore, MD: Johns Hopkins University Press, 2005).
—— *Entertaining Crisis in the Atlantic Imperium, 1770–1790* (Baltimore, MD: Johns Hopkins University Press, 2011).
O'Shaughnessy, David, 'Introduction: "Tolerably Numerous": Recovering the London Irish of the Eighteenth Century', *Eighteenth-Century Life* 39.1 (2015), 1–13.
—— (ed.), 'Networks of Aspiration: The London Irish of the Eighteenth Century', *Eighteenth-Century Life* 39.1 (2015), 1–240.
—— '"Rip'ning buds in Freedom's field": Staging Irish Improvement in the 1780s', *Journal for Eighteenth-Century Studies* 38.4 (2015), 541–54.
—— '"Bit, by some mad whig": Charles Macklin and the Theater of Irish Enlightenment', *Huntington Library Quarterly* 80.4 (2017), 559–84.
—— (ed.), *Ireland, Enlightenment and the English Stage, 1740–1820* (Cambridge: Cambridge University Press, 2019).
Parry, Edward Abbott, *Charles Macklin* (London: Kegan Paul, Trench, Trübner & Co., 1891).
Pascoe, Judith, *The Sarah Siddons Audio Files: Romanticism and the Lost Voice* (Ann Arbor: University of Michigan Press, 2011).
Pearce, Charles E., *The Amazing Duchess Being the Romantic History of Elizabeth Chudleigh*, 2 vols (London: Stanley Paul & Co., 1911).
Pentland, Gordon, '"We Speak for the Ready": Images of Scots in Political Prints, 1707–1832', *Scottish Historical Review* 90.1 (2011), 64–95.

Phillips, Hugh, *Mid-Georgian London: A Topographical and Social Survey of Central and Western London about 1750* (London: Collins, 1964).
Piercy, Marge, *To Be of Use* (Garden City, NY: Doubleday, 1973).
Pisani, Michael, 'Music for the Theatre: Style and Function in Incidental Music', in Kerry Powell (ed.), *The Cambridge Companion to Victorian and Edwardian Theatre* (Cambridge: Cambridge University Press, 2004).
—— *Music for the Melodramatic Theatre in Nineteenth-Century London and New York* (Iowa City: University of Iowa Press, 2014).
Pope, Alexander, *The Dunciad in Four Books*, in John Butt (ed.), *The Poems of Alexander Pope* (New Haven, CT: Yale University Press, 1963).
Powell, Manushag N., *Performing Authorship in Eighteenth-Century English Periodicals* (Lewisburg, PA: Bucknell University Press, 2012).
Powell, Martyn J., 'Scottophobia versus Jacobitism: Political Radicalism and the Press in Late Eighteenth-Century Ireland', in John Kirk, Michael Brown, and Andrew Noble (eds), *Cultures of Radicalism in Britain and Ireland* (London: Routledge, 2016), 49–62.
Ragussis, Michael, *Figures of Conversion: 'The Jewish Question' and English National Identity* (Durham, NC: Duke University Press, 1995).
—— 'Jews and Other "Outlandish Englishmen": Ethnic Performance and the Invention of British Identity under the Georges', *Critical Inquiry* 26.4 (2000), 773–97.
—— *Theatrical Nation: Jews and Other Outlandish Englishmen in Georgian Britain* (Philadelphia: University of Pennsylvania Press, 2010).
Raushenbush, Esther M., 'Charles Macklin's Lost Play about Henry Fielding', *Modern Language Notes* 51.8 (1936), 505–14.
Richards, Thomas, *At Work with Grotowski on Physical Actions* (London: Routledge, 1995).
Richardson, Samuel, *Pamela, or, Virtue Rewarded*, ed. Albert Rivero (Cambridge: Cambridge University Press, 2011).
Ritchie, Leslie, *David Garrick and the Mediation of Celebrity* (Cambridge: Cambridge University Press, 2019).
Rizzo, Betty, 'Male Oratory and Female Prate: "Then Hush and Be an Angel Quite"', *Eighteenth-Century Life* 29.1 (2005), 23–49.
Roach, Joseph R., 'The Inscription of Morality as Style', in Thomas Postlewait and Bruce A. McConachie (eds), *Interpreting the Theatrical Past: Essays in the Historiography of Performance* (Iowa City: University of Iowa Press, 1989), 99–118.
—— *Cities of the Dead: Circum-Atlantic Performance* (New York: Columbia University Press, 1996).
Robinson, Nicholas K., *Edmund Burke: A Life in Caricature* (New Haven, CT: Yale University Press, 1996).
Rudolph, Julia, *Common Law and Enlightenment in England, 1689–1750* (Woodbridge: Boydell & Brewer, 2013).
Russell, Gillian, *Women, Sociability and Theatre in Georgian London* (Cambridge: Cambridge University Press, 2007).

—— 'The Novel and the Stage', in Peter Garside and Karen O'Brien (eds), *The Oxford History of the Novel in English*, vol. 2, *English and British Fiction, 1750–1820* (Oxford: Oxford University Press, 2015), 513–28.

Salisbury, Joyce E., *Encyclopedia of Women in the Ancient World* (Santa Barbara, CA: ABC-CLIO, Inc., 2001).

Sarlós, Robert K., 'Performance Reconstruction: The Vital Link between Past and Future', in Thomas Postlewait and Bruce A. McConachie (eds), *Interpreting the Theatrical Past: Essays in the Historiography of Performance* (Iowa City: University of Iowa Press, 1989), 198–229.

Schoch, Richard W., '"A Supplement to Public Laws": Arthur Murphy, David Garrick, and *Hamlet, with Alterations*', *Theatre Journal* 57.1 (2005), 21–32.

Scott, Walter, *Waverley; or, 'Tis Sixty Years Since*, ed. Claire Lamont (Oxford: Clarendon Press, 1981).

Sechelski, Denise S., 'Garrick's Body and the Labor of Art in Eighteenth-Century Theater', *Eighteenth-Century Studies* 29.4 (1996), 369–89.

Shakespeare, William, *The Complete Works*, ed. Stanley Wells and Gary Taylor (Oxford: Clarendon Press, 1988).

Sharp, William, *The Life and Letters of Joseph Severn* (London: Sampson, Low, Marston & Co., 1892).

Shenstone, William, *The Letters of William Shenstone*, ed. Marjorie Williams (Oxford: Basil Blackwell, 1939).

Shepherd, David J., and Nicholas E. Johnson, *Bertolt Brecht and the David Fragments (1919–1921): An Interdisciplinary Study* (London: Bloomsbury, 2020).

Sherman, Stuart, 'Garrick among Media: The *"Now"* Performer Navigates the News', *PMLA* 126.4 (2011), 966–82.

—— '"The General Entertainment of My Life": The *Tatler*, the *Spectator*, and the Quidnunc's Cure', *Eighteenth-Century Fiction* 27.3–4 (2015), 343–71.

Simmel, Georg, 'The Sociology of Sociability', trans. Everett C. Hughes, *The American Journal of Sociology* 55.3 (1949), 254–61.

Siskin, Clifford, and William Warner (eds), *This is Enlightenment* (Chicago: Chicago University Press, 2010).

Smith, Gay, *Lady Macbeth in America: From the Stage to the White House* (New York: Palgrave Macmillan, 2010).

Smith, Nicholas D., *An Actor's Library: David Garrick, Book Collecting and Literary Friendships* (New Castle, DE: Oak Knoll Press, 2017).

Smithers, Peter, *The Life of Joseph Addison*, 2nd edn (Oxford: Clarendon Press, 1968).

Smyth, Adam (ed.), *A Pleasing Sinne: Drink and Conviviality in Seventeenth-Century England* (Cambridge: D.S. Brewer, 2004).

Stanislavski, Constantin, *Stanislavski's Legacy*, ed. and trans. Elizabeth Reynolds Hapgood (New York: Routledge, 2015 [1968]).

Stern, Tiffany, *Rehearsal from Shakespeare to Sheridan* (Oxford: Oxford University Press, 2000).

Sterne, Laurence, *Letters of Laurence Sterne*, ed. Lewis Perry Curtis (Oxford: Oxford University Press, 1935), 88–91.

Straub, Kristina, 'The Newspaper "Trial" of Charles Macklin's *Macbeth* and the Theatre as Juridical Public Sphere', *Eighteenth-Century Fiction* 27.3–4 (2015), 395–418.

Swain, Warren, *The Law of Contract, 1670–1870* (Cambridge: Cambridge University Press, 2015).

Swindells, Julia, and David Francis Taylor (eds), *The Oxford Handbook of the Georgian Theatre, 1737–1832* (Oxford: Oxford University Press, 2014).

Taylor, David Francis, 'Discoveries and Recoveries in the Laboratory of Georgian Theatre', *New Theatre Quarterly* 27.3 (2011), 229–43.

—— 'Theatre Managers and the Managing of Theatre History', in Julia Swindells and David Francis Taylor (eds), *The Oxford Handbook of Georgian Theatre, 1737–1832* (Oxford: Oxford University Press, 2014).

Taylor, Diana, *The Archive and Performance: Performing Cultural Memory in the Americas* (Durham, NC: Duke University Press, 2003).

Thackeray, William Makepeace, 'Jerome Paturot', in *Miscellaneous Essays, Sketches and Reviews* (London: Smith, Elder, 1885).

Thale, Mary, 'The Robin Hood Society: Debating in Eighteenth-Century London', *London Journal* 22.1 (1997), 33–50.

—— 'The Case of the British Inquisition: Money and Women in Mid-Eighteenth-Century London Debating Societies', *Albion: A Quarterly Journal Concerned with British Studies* 31.1 (1999), 31–48.

Turner, Victor, *Dramas, Fields, and Metaphors: Symbolic Action in Human Society* (Ithaca, NY: Cornell University Press, 1974).

—— *From Ritual to Theatre* (New York: PAJ Publications, 1982).

Van Hulle, Dirk, 'Modern Manuscripts and Textual Epigenetics: Samuel Beckett's Works between Completion and Incompletion', *Modernism/modernity* 18.4 (2011), 801–12.

Wagoner, Michael M., 'The "Merry Tragedy" of *Henry VII* as written by "Charles Macklin, Comedian"', *New Theatre Quarterly* 31.4 (2015), 372–80.

Wahrman, Dror, *The Making of the Modern Self: Identity and Culture in Eighteenth-Century England* (New Haven, CT: Yale University Press, 2006).

Walpole, Horace, *The Yale Edition of Horace Walpole's Correspondence*, 48 vols (New Haven, CT: Yale University Press, 1937–1983).

Warner, Michael, *Publics and Counterpublics* (New York: Zone Books, 2005).

Weissbort, Daniel, and Astradur Eysteinsson (eds), *Translation: Theory and Practice* (New York: Oxford University Press, 2006).

Wessel, Jane, 'Possessing Parts and Owning Plays: Charles Macklin and the Prehistory of Dramatic Literary Property', *Theatre Survey* 56.3 (2015), 268–90.

West, Shearer, *The Image of Actor: Verbal and Visual Representation in the Age of Garrick and Kemble* (London: Pinter, 1991).

Wheeler, Roxann, *The Complexion of Race: Categories of Difference in Eighteenth-Century British Culture* (Philadelphia: University of Pennsylvania Press, 2000).

Williams, Abigail, *The Social Life of Books: Reading Together in the Eighteenth-Century Home* (New Haven, CT: Yale University Press, 2017).

Wood, James Robert, *Anecdotes of Enlightenment: Human Nature from Locke to Wordsworth* (Charlottesville: University of Virginia Press, 2020).
Woodruff, Paul, *The Necessity of Theatre: The Art of Watching and Being Watched* (New York: Oxford University Press, 2008).
Worrall, David, 'Quiet Theatres, the Rise of Celebrity and the *Case [of] Mr Macklin, Late of Covent-Garden Theatre* (1775)', *Arrêt sur scene/Scene Focus* 3 (2014), 207–17.
—— 'Charles Macklin and Arthur Murphy: Theatre, Law and an Eighteenth-Century London Irish Diaspora', *Law and Humanities* 14.1 (2020), 113–30.
Worthen, William B., *The Idea of the Actor* (Princeton. NJ: Princeton University Press, 1984).
Wrigley, E.A., et al., *English Population History from Family Reconstitution, 1580–1837* (Cambridge: Cambridge University Press, 1989).
Yeo, Richard, 'Notebooks as Memory Aids: Precepts and Practices in Early Modern England', *Memory Studies* 1.1 (2008), 115–36.
—— *Notebooks, English Virtuosi, and Early Modern Science* (Chicago: University of Chicago Press, 2014).

Index

adaptation 17, 25, 162, 168, 270–75, 283
Addington, William, *An Abridgment of Penal Statutes* 93
Addison, Joseph 78, 87, 253
  Cato 236
  The Spectator 78, 156, 236, 253, 255
Adorno, Theodor 15–16
Aldus, Ralph 103, 104
Almack's Assembly Rooms 220
Altick, Richard 221
Anderson, Emily Hodgson 24, 36, 73–74, 89, 117, 175
anti-Semitism 12–13, 18, 19, 45, 117, 175, 180, 268n7, 282
Appleton, William W. 102, 133–34, 141, 147, 149, 151, 153, 175, 215, 237
Aristotle 275
Armstrong, Nancy 13–14
Arne, Thomas 94, 150, 154n19, 155–61, 162
Aston, Sir Richard 107
Aungier Street Theatre (Dublin) 143

Bacon, Francis 70
Bailey, Craig 10, 16, 59, 109
  Irish London 91, 101
Bannerman, G.E. 210
Barlow, Inigo 43
Barry, Spranger 133, 139–40, 141–43, 219
Basset, Francis, 'Thoughts on equal representation' 67
Beattie, James 187–88, 191
Beauclerk, Topham 55, 68
Beaumont, Francis 66
Beckett, Samuel 272, 282
Benevolent Society of St Patrick 10, 11, 16, 68
Bernard, John 6, 30, 31
  Retrospections of the Stage 12, 55, 65, 69–71
Betterton, Thomas 133
Bhabha, Homi 271
Bingley, William 86
Birch, Thomas 222
Black, Scott 255–56
Blackstone, William, *Commentaries on the Laws of England* 64, 93

Blount, Thomas, *Nomo-Lexikon: A Law Dictionary* 64
Blumenau, Colin 277–78
Bolingbroke, Henry St John 251
Bolton, Betsy 77
Boswell, James 176
Boyd, Amanda Weldy 75
Boyne, Viscount Gustavus Hamilton 105–6
Boyne, John 47–52
Brecht, Bertolt 271, 276–77
  The David Fragments 282, 288
  The Threepenny Opera 276
Brexit 270, 283, 293
Bristol 152
Brook, Peter 289
Brooke, Henry, *Gustavus Vasa* 193
Brown, Michael 12–13, 14
  The Irish Enlightenment 7–8, 56
Bunyan, John, *Holy War* 63
Burgoyne, John
  The Heiress 66
  The Maid of the Oaks 66
Burke, Edmund 3, 7, 8, 219, 237, 261
Burke, Helen 4–5, 12, 77, 92, 100, 141, 163, 202, 215
Burnet, Thomas, *Sacred Theory of the Earth* 23
Burney, Francis, *Evelina* 113
Burns, Robert 8, 165–66, 169
Burrow, Sir James 64
Bury St Edmunds, Theatre Royal 265, 273, 278

Canning, Elizabeth 3, 141, 243–44
Capell, Edward 203, 205
Centlivre, Susanna, *The Busy Body* 4, 78
Charke, Charlotte, *The Art of Management* 135–38
Chateauneuf, Marie 104, 105
Chatterton, Thomas, *Miscellanies in Prose and Verse* 59

Chester 34
Cholij, Irena 156
Chudleigh, Elizabeth 196, 205–7, 208–9
  Brittania in tears 207, 208–9
Churchill, Charles, *Gotham* 207
Cibber, Colley 4, 114, 133, 134, 135
  Apology 114, 137–38
  Love Makes a Man 4
  The Non-Juror 194
  The Provok'd Husband 114, 202, 245–46
  The Refusal 4, 222
Cibber, Theophilus 4, 59–60, 133
Clark, Peter 228
Clarke, Joseph 103
Clive, Catherine 'Kitty' 104, 137, 160–61
Clive, George 101
coffeehouses 11, 74, 77, 188, 208, 224, 226–27, 229, 237, 241, 248, 254, 256
  Antigallican 221
  Bedford Arms Coffeehouse 3, 131, 220, 223
  Button's 220
  George's 229–31
  Macklin's 4–5 11, 16, 141, 143, 163, 208, 215–28, 237, 252–54, 256
  Moll King's 220
  Tom's 220
  White's 230
Colman, George 10, 85, 95–96, 106–8, 115, 131–32, 144, 145–46, 225, 247–48
  Connoisseur 225
  Polly Honeycombe 114
  The Oxonian in Town 87n44
Congreve, Francis Aspry 27, 47, 87, 115, 136, 152
  The Mourning Bride 223
Congreve, William
  Love for Love 149
  The Old Bachelor 4

Conolly, L.W. 195
Conquergood, Dwight 270–71, 286n3
Cook, Henry 29
Cooke, William 12, 25–26, 27, 63, 115, 117, 118n21, 120, 136, 139, 141, 143–44, 152–53
Covent Garden (London) 215–20, 228, 246, 252–53
  coffeehouses 11, 188, 216, 220–22, 230, 238–39, 241
  Covent Garden Theatre 4, 12, 13, 39, 84n36, 86n42, 92, 96, 105, 115, 131, 138, 195
  Macklin's coffeehouse 4–5 11, 16, 141, 143, 163, 208, 215–28, 237, 252–54, 256
  Macklin's home 56–57, 151, 163
  taverns 11, 188, 216, 220, 228–30, 241
  theatre riots 100–4, 108–9
Critchley, Simon 185
Crow Street Theatre (Dublin) 5, 12n23, 60, 133, 141–43
Cunningham, John 154n19, 155, 171–72
Cunningham, Timothy, *A New and Complete Law-dictionary* 93

Dagge, Henry, *Considerations of Criminal Law* 64n26
Dalton, John, *Comus* 162
Darnton, Robert 173, 190
Davenant, Thomas 82
Day, Thomas, *Reflections upon the present state of England* 67
Delaval, Sir Francis 4, 138–39
Denoyer, Philip 104, 105
D'Hannetaire, Jean Nicolas Servandoni, *Observations sur l'art du Comedien* 65
Diderot, Denis 65
Dobson, Michael 37
Doggett, Thomas 25
Donegal 3, 30

Donohue, Joseph 134, 135
Drury Lane Theatre 2, 4, 5, 25, 81, 82, 84, 86n42, 87, 94, 96n14, 99, 100, 104, 107, 112, 113, 114, 122, 133, 133–39, 143, 154, 160, 193, 223, 253
Dryden, John, *Oedipus* 4, 152
Dublin 4, 5, 62, 80, 238, 258, 262, 266, 270
Dublin theatres *see* Aungier Street; Crow Street; Smock Alley
Dundas, Lawrence 196, 209–11
Dundas, Thomas 210
Dundes, Alan 191

Edgeworth, Maria, *Harrington* 28–29, 115, 116–20
Ellis, Markman 4–5, 11, 92, 141, 163, 208n42, 253, 257
Enlightenment 7–15, 18–19, 52–53, 69–72, 80, 91, 109, 208–11, 217–19, 236–37, 247–48, 261–62, 271–74
  figures of 6–10, 13, 19, 69–72
  Irish 7–8, 56, 218

Fabian, Robert, *Trick for Trick* 94
Farce 12, 17, 92, 94–95, 98, 112, 127, 135, 144, 168, 194, 202–3, 209, 248, 256, 268, 270, 282, 293
Felicity (theatre company) 168, 170, 268, 273, 274, 281–82, 283, 289–90
Felsenstein, Frank 34, 42n35
Fielding, Henry 3, 77, 122, 123, 127, 232, 244, 250, 255
  Authors of the Town 126
  Enquiry into the Causes of the Late Increase in Robbers 202
  Joseph Andrews 124
  Pasquin 202, 248
  The Author's Farce 247
  The Wedding-Day 123–24, 247
Fielding, Sarah 123
Fitzwilliam, Lady Charlotte 210

Fleetwood, Charles 3–4, 6, 86n42, 88, 94, 133–34, 193–94
Fletcher, John 66
Folger Shakespeare Library 57, 134, 234
Fontenelle, Bernard Le Bovier de 65
Foot, Jesse 99, 100, 101, 108
Foote, Samuel 10, 133, 138–39, 141, 207, 230, 233, 234, 237, 258
   The Diversions of the Morning 139–40
   Trip to Calais 207
Ford, John, *Perkin Warbeck* 194
Fortescue, Sir John, *In Praise of the Laws of England* 64
Fox, Charles James 45–52, 68
France 258
Freeman, Lisa 74–75, 155

Gainsborough, Thomas 37
Garrick, David 2–3, 4, 6, 10, 36–53, 82n29, 86n42–88, 91, 99, 122, 127, 133, 137, 147, 151, 222
   book collection 56
   disputes with Macklin 94–95, 96, 107, 108
   Harlequin's Invasion 42
   public identity 37–53, 75
   Richard III 2, 37, 75, 114, 139
   The Jubilee 147
Garton, Jonathan 107
Gascoyne, Sir Crisp 243–44
Gay, John, *The Beggar's Opera* 149, 153
Geertz, Clifford 173
Genest, John 153
Gentleman, Francis 28, 156, 219
Gleeson, Colm 291
Globe Theatre (London) 273
Goldsmith, Oliver 8, 76, 114–15, 122, 237
   She Stoops to Conquer 114–15
   The Vicar of Wakefield 115
Goodman's Fields Theatre 4, 36, 114
Gordon, Thomas, *Cato's Letters* 197

Goring, Paul 6, 7, 16, 30, 39, 73–74, 79, 93, 115–16, 122, 123
Granville, George, *The Jew of Venice* 2, 25
Greene, John C. 142
   Theatre in Dublin 147
Gross, John 174–75
Grotowski, Jerzy 289, 291

Habermas, Jürgen 11, 229
Hallam, Thomas 11, 34–36, 63, 85, 94
Hampton 37
Harding, George 231
Harris, Susan Canon 80, 168
Harris, Thomas 131–32
Hart Street (Covent Garden) 220, 243, 253
Hastings, Warren 46
Haydn, Joseph 168–69
Haymarket Theatre 138, 139, 141, 147, 231, 233, 249, 258, 259, 261
Hazlitt, William 28
Henley, John 246–48
Hervey, Augustus John 205
Herzog, Don 45–46
Hiffernan, Paul 258–59
Hill, Aaron 23, 52
Hill, John 'The Inspector' 3, 77, 138–39, 244, 249
Hoadley, Benjamin, *The Suspicious Husband* 113, 121, 122, 124–26, 198
Hobbes, Thomas 185, 191
   The Elements of Law 180–81
Holcroft, Thomas 10, 113–14
Holland, Peter 151
Hook, James, *The Trial* 46–48
Horkheimer, Max 15–16
Howard, Sir Robert, *The Committee* 4
Hume, David 8, 217
   History of England 34
Hunter, Maria 123
Hutcheson, Francis 185–86, 191, 217

Inchbald, Elizabeth 31, 127
Ireland
   Enlightenment 7–8, 56, 218
   Macklin's racial stereotypes 8–9, 19, 53n46, 180, 260–61
   theatres *see* Aungier Street; Crow Street; Smock Alley
Irish Sea 59

Jacobites, Jacobitism 80, 105–6, 119, 194–95
Jakobson, Roman 274–75
James, John Stephen 103
Jensen, Oskar Cox 53n46, 152n12
Jephson, Robert, *Julia, Or, The Italian Lover* 66
Johnson, Nicholas 17, 18
Johnson, Samuel 1–2, 3, 7, 15, 23, 55, 66, 70–71, 162, 273–74
Johnstone, John 53n46, 152n12
Jones, Richard 272n14
Jonson, Ben
   The Alchemist 139
   Volpone 198

Kant, Immanuel 9, 10, 15, 17–18
Keach, Benjamin, *Scripture Metaphors* 63
Kelly, Hugh 86
Kelly, John, *The Levee* 194
Kemble, John Philip 154
Kenrick, William, *The Pasquinade* 250
Kerrigan, John 190
Kimber, Edward, *Juvenile adventures* 115, 121–22
King Street (London) 56–57n5
King, Thomas 56–57
Kinservik, Matthew 4, 12, 16, 80–81, 187, 196, 207–8
Kirkman, James Thomas 27, 31, 59–61, 100, 111, 115, 151–53
Kitchingham, John 31, 33
Klein, Lawrence 216, 254

Larpent Collection 194n6
Lavater, Johann Kaspar 28

Law, Edward 46
Lawrence, Thomas 237
Lee, Nathaniel
   Oedipus 4, 152
Lee, Thomas 103
Leerssen, Joep 176, 182n38
legal cases
   Donaldson v. Beckett 100
   Macklin v. Richardson 92–93, 95–100, 102, 109
   Millar v. Taylor 92–93, 96–100, 109
Lennox, Charlotte 71
Lessing, Gotthold Ephraim 271
Lewis, Wyndham 277
   Enemy of the Stars 274–75, 277, 282, 283, 288
Lichtenberg, George 36, 175
Lincoln's Inn Fields Theatre 3–4, 152
Little Theatre Haymarket *see* Haymarket Theatre
Littlewood, Joan 289
Lodge, John 26
London *see* Covent Garden; Drury Lane; Globe Theatre; Goodman's Field; Haymarket; Lincoln's Field; Tavistock Row
   George's Club 229–31
   Hart Street 220, 243
   Pantheon 227
   Ranelagh 221
   Tyburn 244
   Vauxhall 227
   Westminster Abbey 42
   White's Club 229–31
Lori-Parks, Suzan 272n15
Lowe, Thomas 154n19, 155
Lucas, Charles 258
Lupton, Christina 55, 72

Macaulay, John, *The Genius of Ireland: A Masque* 66
McBride, Ian 7–8, 13
McDowell, Paula 247
McGirr, Elaine 76–77
Mackenzie, Henry 123

Macklin, Ann (née Grace) 4, 5, 196, 198, 199
Macklin, Charles
  A Will and No Will 61, 196–201, 207, 217
  acting coach 138–41
  An Infallible Recipe 34, 35–36, 45, 52
  anti-Semitism 12–13, 18, 180, 282
  appearance and physicality 23–24, 27–36, 73–74, 118
  'British Inquisition' debates/lectures 3, 69, 92, 133, 141, 153, 210, 215, 219, 233–38, 243–62
  censorship 12–13, 193–211
  coffeehouse 4–5, 11, 16, 141, 143, 163, 208, 215–28, 237, 252–54, 256
  'Commonplace Book 1778–1790' 7, 25, 104–6, 111, 134, 217–18
  concept of celebrity 24–26, 52–53, 73–76
  encounter with Dr Johnson 1–2, 6, 14–15, 70–71
  Enlightenment credentials 69–72, 80n19
  ethnic jokes and racial stereotypes 79–81, 161–62, 167, 173–92, 250, 260–61, 270
  intellectual ambitions 6–8, 13, 14, 55–56, 69–72
  Irishness 1–2, 8–11, 18–19, 53n46, 78–79, 151–52, 260–61
  legal acumen 91–109
  library 1, 6, 55–72, 93, 122
  Love à la Mode 5, 12, 17, 56, 63, 80–81, 91–92, 95–97, 99–100, 112–13, 144–45, 163–65, 176–83
    restaging 265–79, 281–93
  Macbeth riots (1773) 5, 10, 24, 37–39, 64, 69, 76–77, 82–84, 100–4, 108, 146–47, 163, 262
  Macklin v. Richardson 95–97, 99
  modern restaging of plays 265–79
  pigeonholed as comedic actor 11–12
  professional longevity 3–4
  public association with acted characters 24–26, 37–53
  repertoire of songs 149–72
  Scotophobia 12–13, 14, 19, 80–81, 175–76, 180, 186–87
  as Shylock 5–6, 16, 18–19, 24–36, 42, 75, 77–78, 89, 153, 154–61, 174–75
  subject of periodicals 74–89
  The Covent Garden Theatre 12, 115, 126–27, 161, 196, 198, 202–9, 248–52
  The Irish Fine Lady 183
  King Henry VII; or, The Popish Impostor 195, 210
  The Man of the World 5, 80–81n23, 161–63, 176, 186–90, 195n10, 196–97, 208, 209, 217
  The Merchant of Venice 2, 18, 24–36, 42, 75, 77–78, 89, 116, 133, 136–37, 153, 154–61, 174–75
  The New Play Criticiz'd 115, 127–28, 198
  The School for Husbands 13, 197n15
  The True Born Irishman 161–62, 176, 182n39, 183–86, 197
  theatre management 86–89, 131–47
  theatre riots (1740) 104–8
  trial for murder 4, 11, 34–36, 63, 75, 94
  understanding of literary 'character' 111–28
Macklin, Elizabeth (née Jones) 5, 56, 84
Macklin, Maria 4, 5, 30, 60–61, 107–8, 139, 142–43, 223
Macnally, Leonard 98
McPherson, Heather 25, 37
Magee, John, *An Irishman's reception in London* 68

Manchester 5
Mandeville, Bernard 251
Mansfield, Lord William Murray 67, 85, 92, 97–98, 99, 103–4, 106, 109
Massinger, Philip 66
Mee, Jon 14
Miles, William Augustus 103
Milhous, Judith 136, 137–38
Millar, Andrew 96–97
Miller, James, *The Coffee-House* 74
Milton, John, *Comus* 162
Misson, Henri 226
Montesquieu, Charles-Louis de Secondat, Baron de La Brède et de 65
Moore, Thomas 169
Morton, Thomas, *Zorinski* 66
Mossop, Henry 143
Mugglestone, Lynda 177, 183, 190
Murphy, Arthur 76, 84, 91, 95, 98–100, 106, 108, 219, 223–25, 237, 254
   Gray's Inn Journal 223
   The Grecian Daughter 99, 108–9
   The Orphan of China 99
   The Way to Keep Him 99
Murray, William 64

New York Public Library 57
Newman, Ian 13–14, 16, 208, 228–29
Newton, James 31, 33
Newton, Richard, *Cries of London* 46

Opie, John 11, 16
O'Quinn, Daniel 46–47, 247
Oring, Elliott 186, 187, 188
O'Shaughnessy, David 7, 12, 13, 69, 72, 163, 218, 261, 266, 269
Otway, Thomas, *Venice Preserv'd* 149
Owen, Henry 144

Parker, John 101
Parry, Edward Abbott 70
Pascoe, Judith 151
Paterson, William, *Arminius* 194

periodicals culture 73–89
Phillips, Ambrose 156
Piercy, Marge, *To Be of Use* 286
Pisani, Michael 154
Pope, Alexander 25, 27, 246
Powell, Manushag 18, 249, 253
Powell, Martyn 182
practice-as-research (PaR) projects 282–93
Pufendorf, Samuel von 217
Priestley, Joseph 67

Quin, James 4, 9, 27–28, 88n46, 104, 118n21

Ragussis, Michael 42, 176, 183
Reddish, Samuel 84n36
Reed, Isaac 98
Reeve, Clara 123
Regnard, Jean-François, *Le Légataire universel* 198
rehearsals 120, 146, 269, 277–78, 281, 289–91
Restoration comedy 265
Reynolds, Joshua 14, 42
Rich, Christopher 137–38
Rich, John 3–4, 6, 131, 152, 193–94, 203, 205
Richardson, Samuel 81, 97–98, 123
   Pamela 114
Ritchie, Leslie 2, 52–53
Roach, Joseph 28, 45, 74–75
Robin Hood Society 3, 10–11, 234–37, 247–48, 251–52, 257
Roubiliac, Louis-François 37
Rousseau, Jean-Jacques 65, 123
Rowe, Nicholas, *Jane Shore* 4
Russell, Gillian 113, 208, 216, 239–41
Russell Street (Covent Garden) 220
Rutherford, James 131–32

Salway, Thomas 94
Sarlós, Robert K. 273
Savage, Richard 74
Schiller, Friedrich 271

Schoch, Richard W. 99
Scott, Walter, *Waverley* 118–19, 120
Servandoni, Jean Nicolas (D'Hannetaire) 65
Severn, Joseph 151
Shakespeare, William 25–27, 36–49, 133, 273
　As You Like It 4, 160
　Hamlet 75, 104, 291–92
　King Lear 260
　Love's Labour's Lost 160
　Macbeth 5, 10, 37, 64, 69, 76, 82–83
　Othello 4, 139
　Richard III 2, 37, 75, 114
　The Merchant of Venice 2, 4, 5–6, 18, 24–36, 42, 45, 75, 77–78, 89, 114, 116, 133, 136, 150, 153, 154–61, 174–75
　Twelfth Night 4, 160
Shenstone, William 231
Sheridan, Richard Brinsley 8, 79, 122
　The Rivals 114
Sheridan, Thomas 4, 6, 143, 168
Sherman, Stuart 247
Shirley, James, *The Triumph of Peace* 273
Shirley, William, *Electra* 194, 195
Shuter, Edward 96
Siddons, Sarah 99, 151
Simmel, Georg, *Geselligkeit* 216–17
Siskin, Clifford 17, 52
Smart, Christopher 247, 249–50
Smith, Adam 253
Smith, Nicholas D. 56
Smith, Sir Thomas, *De Republica Anglorum* 64
Smith, William 'Gentleman' 96n14, 147
Smock Alley Theatre (Dublin) 143, 266–67, 277
Smollett, Tobias 8
Sparks, James 84, 103
Sparks, Luke 84
Stacpoole, Joseph 101

Stanislavski, Konstantin 265
Steele, Richard 78, 87, 253, 255
　The Spectator 78, 156, 236, 253, 255
Stern, Tiffany 134, 139–40
Sterne, Laurence, *Tristram Shandy* 114
Stevens, George Alexander 236, 250–51, 258, 261
　The Birth-Day of Folly 232–33, 250–51, 258
Stratford-upon-Avon 37
Straub, Kristina 39, 73–74, 76, 81
Stuart, Charles Edward 118, 119
Summers, Colm 13, 17, 168, 268, 269, 277
Swift, Jonathan 8

taverns 11, 121, 222, 226–30, 238–40
　Bedford Arms *see* coffeehouses, Bedford Arms
　London Tavern 228
　Shakespeare (aka Shakespeare Head) 220, 228
　Turk's Head 228
Tavistock Row (Covent Garden) 56–57, 69
Taylor, David 16, 135, 149, 265–66n2, 273
Taylor, Diana 150, 163–64, 167
Taylor, Robert 96–97, 99
Temple, Sir John, *History of the Irish Rebellion* 34
Thale, Mary 215, 236, 238–39, 257, 258
The Bourbon League (anon) 194–95
The Fortune Tellers (pantomime) 104–5
Theobald, Lewis 255
Thomson, George 166, 168–69
Thomson, James
　Edward and Eleonora 194
　The Seasons 96–97, 100
Thornton, Bonnell 202, 225, 250–51
　Connoisseur 225

Drury-Lane Journal 202, 207, 225, 250, 251
Tinkler, John 219–21, 238, 241
Toland, John 251
translation 122, 267, 272–74
Trenchard, John, *Cato's Letters* 197
Turner, Victor 271

Vanbrugh, John, *The Provok'd Husband* 114, 202, 245–46
Van Hulle, Dirk 267–68
Vickery, Amanda 216
Victor, Benjamin 143
Villiers, George, *The Rehearsal* 202
Vispi, Annachiara 286
Vollan, Rebecca 122
Voltaire (François-Marie Arouet) 65
Voyage to the Island of Cytherea, A (dance) 105

Wahrman, Dror 190
  The Making of the Modern Self 177
Walpole, Horace 123, 197, 233
Walpole, Robert 31–32, 193, 194
Warner, Michael 243–44
Warner, William 17, 52
Weeler, Frances 144

Wenman, Joseph 31, 32
Wessel, Jane 96, 144
Wheeler, Roxann 177–78
Whitley, James 98, 100, 144
Wilkes, John 188, 196, 210, 258
  North Briton 187
Wilkinson, Tate 6, 96, 98
Williams, Abigail, *The Social Life of Books* 59
Williams, John ('Anthony Pasquin') 37
Williams, William Peere 93
Wilson, George 64
Woffington, Margaret 'Peg' 6, 124
Wood, James Robert 2
Woodruff, Paul, *The Necessity of Theatre* 291–92
Woodward, Henry 104
Worrall, David 5, 7, 10, 24, 76, 254
Worthen, William 155
Wycherley, William 87

Yates, Mary Ann 96n14, 99
Yorke, Philip 222

Zoffany, Johan 30–31, 47